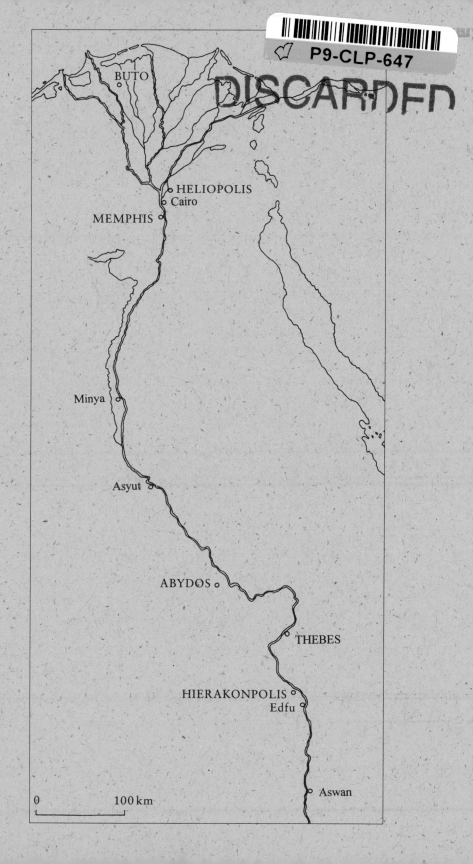

BUTO

HELIOPOLIS
Cairo
MEMPHIS

Minya

Asyut

ABYDOS

THEBES

HIERAKONPOLIS
Edfu

Aswan

0   100 km

THE PYRAMIDS

Miroslav Verner

THE PYRAMIDS

The Mystery, Culture, and Science
of Egypt's Great Monuments

Translated from the German by Steven Rendall

Grove Press
New York

Copyright © 1997 by Miroslav Verner
Copyright © 1998 by Rowohlt Verlag GmbH
Translation copyright © 2001 by Steven Rendall
Illustrations copyright © 1997 by Jolana Malátková
Color photos copyright © 1997 by Milan Zemina

Originally published in Czech in 1997 under the title *Pyramidy, tajemstvi minulosti* by Academia, Prague.
Basis for this translation is the German edition as published by Rowohlt Verlag GmbH, Reinbek bei Hamburg, which has been completely revised and extended by the author.
Published by permission of Rowohlt Verlag GmbH, Reinbek bei Hamburg

Published simultaneously in Canada
Printed in the United States of America

FIRST EDITION

Library of Congress Cataloging-in-Publication Data
Verner, Miroslav.
   The pyramids : the mystery, culture, and science of egypt's great monuments / Miroslav Verner.
      p. cm.
   Includes bibliographical references and index.
   ISBN 0-8021-1703-1
   1. Pyramids—Egypt.   2. Egypt—Antiquities.   I. Title.
DT63.V469 2001
932—dc21   2001035084

Grove Press
841 Broadway
New York, NY 10003

01 02 03 04   10 9 8 7 6 5 4 3 2 1

CONTENTS

CONTENTS

*Pyramids have been built in various places on earth,
at various times, and for various purposes.
But only a few have been considered wonders of the world
ever since antiquity—the Egyptian pyramids.
This book is dedicated to them and to their creators.*

A NOTE ON USAGE

The following notations have been used to augment the text throughout:

(?)—Indicates that the accuracy of the preceding statement is in doubt.

(after ___)—Indicates that the preceding information corresponds to the opinion of the cited scientist (see "Select Bibliography" for relevant works by the scientist).

()—Parentheses around a ruler's or monument's title indicate that the title was given during a tradition later than the ruler's or monument's own. The style follows that of *The Oxford Encyclopedia of Ancient Egypt* (D. B. Redford, ed.), 4 vols., Oxford University Press 2000.

Both English and metric measures are given in "Appendix 1: Basic Dimensions of the Pyramids," but elsewhere only metric measures have been used. A conversion chart is provided below:

METRIC SYSTEM

LENGTH

unit	abbreviation	number of meters	approximate U.S. equivalent
kilometer	km	1,000	0.62 mile
hectometer	hm	100	109.36 yards
dekameter	dam	10	32.81 feet
meter	m	1	39.37 inches
decimeter	dm	0.1	3.94 inches
centimeter	cm	0.01	0.39 inch
millimeter	mm	0.001	0.039 inch

AREA

unit	abbreviation	number of square meters	approximate U S. equivalent
square kilometer	sq km *or* km^2	1,000,000	0.3861 square mile
hectare	ha	10,000	2.47 acres
are	a	100	119.60 square yards
square centimeter	sq cm *or* cm^2	0.0001	0.155 square inch

VOLUME

unit	abbreviation	number of cubic meters	approximate U.S. equivalent
cubic centimeter	cu cm *or* cm^3 *also* cc	0.000001	0.061 cubic inch
cubic decimeter	dm^3	0.001	61.023 cubic inches
cubic meter	m^3	1	1.307 cubic yards

CAPACITY

unit	abbreviation	number of liters	approximate U.S. equivalent		
			cubic	*dry*	*liquid*
kiloliter	kl	1,000	1.31 cubic yards		
hectoliter	hl	100	3.53 cubic feet	2.84 bushels	
dekaliter	dal	10	0.35 cubic foot	1.14 pecks	2.64 gallons
liter	l	1	61 .02 cubic inches	0.908 quart	1.057 quarts
cubic decimeter	dm^3	1	61.02 cubic inches	0.908 quart	1.057 quarts
deciliter	dl	0.10	6.1 cubic inches	0.18 pint	0.21 pint
centiliter	cl	0.01	0.61 cubic inch		0.338 fluidounce
milliliter	ml	0.001	0.061 cubic inch		0.27 fluidram

MASS AND WEIGHT

unit	abbreviation	number of grams	approximate U.S. equivalent
metric ton	t	1,000,000	1.102 short tons
kilogram	kg	1,000	2.2046 pounds
hectogram	hg	100	3.527 ounces
dekagram	dag	10	0.353 ounce
gram	g	1	0.035 ounce
decigram	dg	0.10	1.543 grains
centigram	cg	0.01	0.154 grain
milligram	mg	0.001	0.015 grain

FOREWORD

It is both surprising and unfortunate that in recent decades professional researchers of the pyramids have seldom made their fascinating work accessible to the general public. There are a few short guides to specific excavation sites and specialized works that discuss questions relating to the construction of the pyramids and the fantastic theories associated with them in particular historical periods, yet only three significant general presentations of the subject addressed to a wider audience are currently available. *The Pyramids of Egypt* (1st ed., London, 1947), by the late Eiddon Edwards, a British Egyptologist and celebrated connoisseur of the Egyptian pyramids, has gone through several reprintings and has been translated into several languages. In addition, there is *Die ägyptischen Pyramiden: vom Ziegelbau zum Weltwunder* (1st ed., Mainz, 1985), by the no less celebrated German expert Rainer Stadelmann; its success with readers led the author to publish an expanded version of this work. There is also *The Complete Pyramids* (London and Cairo, 1997), a richly illustrated overview of the subject by the American archaeologist Mark Lehner.

Archaeologists continue to deepen our knowledge of the pyramids and to produce new theories about them. As a result, many earlier views concerning these monumental edifices, their creators, and their epoch have had to be partly corrected or wholly revised. Even today, it is possible to find previously undiscovered or completely unknown pyramids. Thus even if Egyptologists were able to provide satisfactory answers to many questions still outstanding today, research on the pyramids would continue. This work has recently been complicated by the fact that excavators are now responsible for the preservation of archaeological monuments and have even less time for research. This book presents the general state of research on the pyramids in the late 1990s, and is based primarily on the results of excavations undertaken by the University of Prague's Czech Institute of Egyptology over the last twenty years.

The complexity of the subject makes it particularly difficult to present it to nonspecialists. The construction of the Egyptian pyramids can be adequately explained only in relation to the social relationships, religious conceptions, administrative and organizational capabilities, technical knowledge, and modes of labor that existed at the time of construction. Just describing the pyramids and explaining their individual parts is harder than it might at first seem, because there is considerable disagreement as to their exact dimensions as well as to how each of these monumental building complexes is to be explained. I have tried to avoid oversimplification and to offer a complete presentation of this very complex subject, even though doing so requires that certain standard situations and fundamental facts be repeatedly described. I have also sought to respond to the broadest possible spectrum of interests, ranging from those of a reader looking for a fascinating account of research, to those of the critical expert on the pyramids.

To that end, I have chosen to present a wealth of illustrations that help the reader form an image of the pyramids while at the same time offering a survey of objects dating from the age when the pyramids were being constructed. These illustrations will allow the reader to become familiar with ancient Egyptian art's specific mode of expression and with the most notable individuals who have devoted their lives to research on the pyramids. Appendices offer biographical information on these researchers, basic dimensions of the pyramids, a list of the pharaohs and dynasties, and a glossary of important technical terms. A selected bibliography gives suggestions for further reading.

I would like to express my gratitude to all those who made important contributions to the publication of this book. Special thanks are due to Milan Zemina for his outstanding photographs of the Egyptian pyramids, to Jolana Malátková for her drawings and general editing of the Czech manuscript, to Dirk Moldenhauer for his careful supervision of the German edition of this book and many useful comments on it, to Kathrin Liedtke, who translated the book into German, and to Steven Rendall for his translation of the book into English.

Miroslav Verner

INTRODUCTION: THE REDISCOVERY
OF THE PYRAMIDS

The temple of the goddess Isis, known as the Pearl of Egypt, stands on the little island of Philae near the first cataract of the Nile, not far from Aswan. Although it was built long after the last Egyptian pyramids, it is nonetheless a curious milestone in the history of the land of the pyramids and the hieroglyphs.

Far removed from cultural and political centers on the southernmost border of Egypt, this temple remained, at the end of the fourth century C.E., one of the last bastions of paganism. Here were still practiced the age-old Egyptian religious cults whose traditions had been adopted by the tribes of Nubia. And it was here, on 24 August 394, that the last known hieroglyph was inscribed.*

The ancient Egyptian hieroglyphic script was subsequently forgotten. In its Coptic form, which used the capital letters of the Greek alphabet along with a few symbols based on demotic models, the spoken language survived a few centuries longer. The fall of the Egyptian Babylon (in what is now the Misr al-Qadima quarter of modern Cairo) and the ultimate victory of the Arabs in 642 ended the epilogue of ancient Egyptian culture in late antiquity and inaugurated an entirely new era in Egyptian history. Pyramids and temples, along with much of ancient wisdom, were inexorably lost in the depths of time—forever, it seemed. These grandiose, mysterious structures inscribed with incomprehensible symbols gradually fell into ruins. Increasingly, they became the subject of legends and superstitions and

---

* The most recent known Egyptian inscription is not in hieroglyphs, but rather in a simplified alphabet, the so-called demotic script, and is dated 2 December 452.

the prey of thieves looking for plunder and adventurers hungry for knowledge. But above all they became a source of easily accessible stone useful for other purposes.

In the Middle Ages, Arab scholars seldom showed any interest in ancient Egyptian structures, but when they did—as in the cases of Abd al-Latif Shelebi, Ja'ut ar-Rumi, Shams ad-Din al-Jashari ad-Dimashqi, and Taki ad-Din al-Maqrizi—they generally approached the subject in a serious way. At the same time, Arab culture developed myths and legends about the pyramids, some of which endure to this day. According to one of these legends, three hundred years before the biblical flood King Saurid had a dream in which the (flat) earth turned over and the stars began to fall on it. This so frightened him that, fearing that the end of the world was near, he decided to erect the pyramids and to enclose within them all the knowledge of his age.

Christian Europe in the Middle Ages based its idea of Egypt mainly on the Bible, assuming that the pyramids were Joseph's grain storehouses (Genesis 41–42). In addition, hermetism exercised a significant influence that was not limited to intellectuals. (The doctrine of hermetism traced its ancestry back to Hermes Trismegistus, a Greek version of Thoth, the ancient Egyptian god of wisdom and writing; it combined ancient Egyptian religious ideas with abstract Greek philosophical conceptions and emphasized the occult aspect of the Egyptian heritage.) In fifteenth- and sixteenth-century Europe the mysterious image of ancient Egypt gradually assumed more rational features. Renaissance humanists, who returned to the works of ancient authors and rediscovered the roots of European culture, made an important contribution to this development. Travelers and conquerors also played an important role by exploring the lands along the Nile. The knowledge and documents they collected and brought back with them laid the foundations for further research.

In the first half of the seventeenth century, John Greaves (1602–1652), a leading English astronomer, mathematician, and orientalist, went to Egypt to study the pyramids. His *Pyramidographia, or a Discourse of the Pyramids in Egypt,* the first study to report relatively precise measurements of the Great Pyramid, ranks among the most significant forerunners of the future scientific discipline of Egyptology. Travelers from

In medieval Europe, the pyramids were long regarded as having originally been Joseph's grain storehouses. The mosaic on the ceiling of the portico of St. Mark's in Venice reflects this view.

Central Europe also visited Egypt, for example, men such as Christof Harant von Polžice und Bezdružice (1564–1621), the author of *Die Reise nach Ägypten* (1598). But the person who clearly dominated research on ancient Egypt in the seventeenth century was the German Jesuit Athanasius Kircher (1602–1680). A multifaceted expert on mathematics, philosophy, and oriental languages, Kircher invented the "magic lantern" and constructed the first calculating machine. His greatest achievement, however, was in linguistics. Kircher believed that the ancient Egyptian language that had been written in hieroglyphics was concealed within Coptic. Yet, because he regarded this ancient writing as being purely symbolic, he was not able to decipher it.

Further light was shed on the subject in the eighteenth century. Captain Frederik Ludwig Norden (1708–1742), a Dane who assembled a remarkable collection of drawings and descriptions of edifices, traveled through Egypt, as did the English clergyman Richard Pococke (1704–1765). Scholars working in the tranquil atmosphere of their European libraries also devoted increasing attention to ancient Egypt, and particularly to deciphering the apparently incomprehensible hieroglyphics. In 1761, the French abbé Jean-Jacques Barthélemy (1716–1795) published a study in which he arrived at the conclusion that symbols enclosed in an oval—known as a *cartouche*—represented royal names. The German scholar Carsten Niebuhr (1733–1815) started out from the correct assumption that some of the hieroglyphs were alphabetic signs and that with the help of Coptic it might be possible to read them.

The Bohemian aristocrat, traveler, and humanist Christof Harant von Polžice und Bezdružice.

These steps toward understanding marked the end of a long phase of discovery in which ancient Egypt was still a mysterious world wreathed in myths and legends. The next period, which was to end with the deciphering of the hieroglyphs, the lost key to genuine research on ancient Egypt, was already on the horizon. It began at the end of the eighteenth century, as a result of Napoleon's Egyptian expedition.

"Egypt was a province of the Roman republic; it must become a province of the French republic! Roman government led to the decline of this land, French government will bring it prosperity," announced the Directorate's foreign minister, Charles Maurice de Talleyrand-Périgord, in a famous speech delivered in February 1798. Three months later some four hundred ships carrying some 36,000 men left for Egypt under Napoleon's command. His effort to gain mastery of the world ultimately ended in the defeat and capitulation of the French forces in 1802, but the expedition's cultural and scientific consequences laid the foundations of a new discipline: Egyptology.

The French had planned an expedition of considerable scope and made their military preparations with great care. Thus the expedition included a "scientific and artistic commission" comprising 167 specialists in the most diverse areas—mathematicians, Arabists, astronomers, surveyors, physicians, mining engineers, draftsmen, and printers. This commission was to investigate, measure, and make sketches and maps in order to provide a solid basis for the administration of the future "French province."

The ancient Egyptian monuments were central to French concerns. Toward the end of September 1798, accompanied by his whole staff, Napoleon visited for the first time the Great Pyramid and the Sphinx at Giza. The artist and draftsman Dominique Vivant Denon (1747–1825) went along. While the French army pursued the vanquished Mamluks through the Nile Valley, Denon continually sketched new sights. Like other members of the commission, and like the officers and ordinary soldiers, he was fascinated and deeply impressed by the monuments. When the expedition reached the ruins of the enormous Temple of Amon in Karnak, they all stared in astonishment and, enchanted by the fabulous scene that lay before them, began to clap their

"Soldiers, forty centuries are looking down on you!" Historical illustration of Napoleon's famous cry.

hands. Denon set down his impressions in masterly fashion in the pictures illustrating his book *Voyage dans la Basse et la Haute Égypte* (1802), which was translated into English and German. More than any other work of its time, Denon's book ignited the Egyptomania that swept through European culture and influenced the plastic arts, fashion, and design.

Denon's *Voyage* was the first of several books bearing witness to this great expedition. At the urging of one of the leaders of the expedition, General Jean-Baptiste Kléber, the members of the French "commission" began to write down a systematic list of all their discoveries, which later became the famous *Description de l'Égypte*. By 1798, at Napoleon's command, scientists and artists at the Institut d'Égypte founded in Cairo were already working on this study, which remains unparalleled. Set forth in four large-format volumes—*Antiquités, État moderne, Histoire naturelle,* and *Carte topographique*—it became a

Self-portrait of Dominique Vivant Denon, a member of Napoleon's expedition and an artist whose pictures first gave the world a comprehensive idea of the ancient Egyptian monuments.

source of national cultural pride among the French. The first volume appeared in 1809, the last in 1828. The foundations of Egyptology had been laid.

In the development of this discipline, as is so often the case in the history of science, chance played a great part. In July 1799, while extending the fortifications of Rosetta (Arabic El-Rashid), a town that guarded the western branch of the Nile where it flows into the Mediterranean, the French discovered a fragment of a dark stone slab, or *stela,* on which were inscribed hieroglyphics as well as demotic and Greek writing. The French scholars immediately recognized the value of the "Rosetta stone": it was the key to deciphering the hieroglyphs. This was also recognized by the English, which is why the French, after being defeated by them in 1801, were required by the terms of the surrender to hand over the Rosetta stone along with all the scientific documentation they had assembled up to that point.

The discovery of the Rosetta stone and the rapid dissemination of copies of the inscriptions on it lent fresh impetus to efforts to decipher the hieroglyphs. In 1802, the Swedish scholar and diplomat Johan David Åkerblad (1763–1819) was able, by comparing the texts, to identify the personal names, and he also succeeded in determining the cardinal numbers. Scholars' efforts were nearing their goal. One of the main figures in this process was the English physician and physicist Thomas Young (1773–1829), a prodigy who had learned to read fluently at the age of two and by the age of fourteen had mastered half a dozen languages, including oriental languages. Chiefly as a hobby, he procured a copy of the inscriptions and quickly arrived at astounding conclusions. Starting out from the demotic, he was able to draw up a list of 204 words and thirteen hieroglyphs, and he correctly interpreted more than a fourth of them before abandoning his analysis in 1818.

Like Young, Jean-François Champollion (1790–1832) was considered a prodigy; as a youth, he too had mastered a series of foreign languages, including six ancient oriental languages. It is said that as a boy he had seen a copy of the Rosetta stone at the home of Baron Fourier, who had taken part in Napoleon's expedition, and decided he was going to decipher the hieroglyphics. The traditional view, which was then still dominant, held that the hieroglyphics were secret symbols that represented the "highest truths" and were intended to conceal those truths from ordinary people.

Champollion made his first great discovery on 23 December 1821, his thirty-first birthday, when he suddenly realized that the theory that the hieroglyphics were purely ideographic (each symbol signifying a specific referent) was untenable. He decided to count all the Greek words and all the hieroglyphs in the corresponding versions on the stela, and noted that 1,419 hieroglyphs were required to express 486 Greek words.

On 14 September 1822, he made another breakthrough. On that day, Champollion received copies of reliefs found at Abu Simbel in which a cartouche was associated with a royal name. He knew the last two symbols, which were the same, and read them as *ss*. The preceding symbols he did not recognize, but on looking at the first sign in the group, a small image of the sun, it occurred to him to interpret it as *re*, on the basis of the Coptic. The name *re——ss:* it was the royal name Ramses! His assumption was immediately confirmed by a similar name in the cartouche, in which the first character was

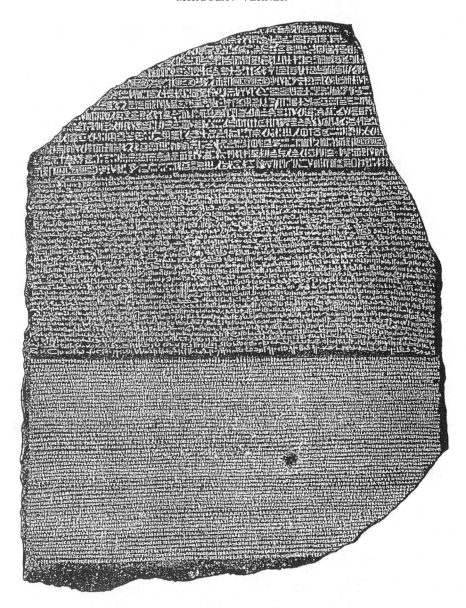

The Rosetta stone (today in the British Museum, London), a document written in Egyptian (hieroglyphic and demotic) and Greek characters, was the cradle of Egyptology. The text on the stone was a decree issued on 27 March 196 B.C.E. by the synod of Egyptian priests that had assembled in Memphis to honor the young ruler Ptolemy V Epiphanes (204–180 B.C.E.).

an ibis symbol instead of the sun image. The ibis was a bird sacred to the god Thoth. He was thus also looking at the name Tuthmosis. A symbol he did not know, but which he found in both inscriptions, had to be read as *mes,* Coptic *mise, mose,* which meant "to give birth." He summoned his brother Jacques-Joseph, threw a handful of papers with the copies of the hieroglyphs on the table before him, and shouted, "Je tiens l'affaire!" (I've got it!), whereupon he fell in a faint on the floor, overcome by excitement and exhaustion. The path to research on ancient Egypt, which had been blocked for a millennium and a half, was now open.

However, a great deal of work remained to be done. Inscriptions on the walls of temples and tombs and on papyrus scrolls began to

The famed French savant Jean-François Champollion, the decipherer of the hieroglyphics and the founder of Egyptology.

speak. For a time, scholarly activity focused on the Egyptian texts, but soon it began to include archaeological work as well. Early archaeological investigation is probably best characterized by the peculiar figure of Giovanni Battista Belzoni, a former circus performer and prodigious adventurer, who was considered by his contemporaries to be a phenomenal archaeologist because he had made a great deal of money by dealing in antiquities. The work of John Perring (1813–1869), together with that of an expedition of Prussian scholars led by Richard Lepsius (1810–1884) that explored Egyptian antiquities from 1842 to 1845, first provided archaeological research with a genuinely scientific orientation.

The true age of systematic archaeological excavations, however, began in 1850, with the famed French Egyptologist Auguste Mariette (1821–1881). Near Saqqara, he discovered and opened up the Serapeum, the famous underground catacomb with the tombs of the sacred Apis bulls. This discovery won him scientific fame as well as the favor of the Egyptian viceroy, Said Pasha. Mariette was not originally an archaeologist; he had been sent to Egypt to collect samples of Egyptian, Coptic, Ethiopian, and Syrian handwriting for the Louvre in Paris. After his return, he decided to devote his life to excavations. In Bulaq, he established the first museum of ancient Egyptian culture and also laid the foundations for the Egyptian Antiquities Service. Strangely, Mariette was never very interested in the pyramids. He was drawn instead to the great private tombs that still had inscriptions and pictures on their walls. The pyramids first attracted the attention of researchers in the early 1880s, when Gaston Maspero (1846–1916), William Petrie (1853–1942), and others started to explain them. This marked the beginning of archaeological research on the pyramids.

PART ONE

THE BIRTH OF THE PYRAMIDS

CHAPTER ONE

BEFORE THE PYRAMIDS

The Early Dynastic Period
(From the Zero Dynasty to the Second Dynasty)

THE BIRTH OF EGYPT

Among the oldest and most important extant Egyptian historical documents ranks a palette commemorating King Narmer's victory over a rebellious principality in the Nile Delta (c.3000 B.C.E.). Until recently, most Egyptologists saw this palette as providing evidence that by finally subjugating the last independent princes in the delta, Narmer created the first united Egyptian kingdom that included both Upper and Lower Egypt.

Recent archaeological research suggests, however, that Narmer was not the first king to unify Upper and Lower Egypt. In particular, the German excavations in the cemetery at Umm el-Qaab, near Abydos, have shown that the fourteen predecessors of Narmer buried there, who constituted the so-called Zero Dynasty, must have reigned over all Egypt at least part of the time, so that the true era of unification had already begun some two centuries earlier.

The arrangement of the tombs at Umm el-Qaab allows us to discern a clear continuity with the subsequent First Dynasty, and this tends to confirm the assumption that the first king of this dynasty, King Aha (fl. c.2925 B.C.E.?), was one of Narmer's sons.* Construc-

---

* It remains uncertain whether the princely name Meni, which appears on an ebony tablet from Naqada, can also be associated with Aha and thus provide the

Narmer's palette, made of dark gray slate, was found by British archaeologists at the beginning of the twentieth century, near Hierakonpolis in Upper Egypt. It is an important document for understanding the origins of Egyptian writing. Originally, palettes were rectangular or oval stone slabs on which pigments were rubbed, but the Narmer palette is already a work of art both memorial and celebratory in character. It is thought to symbolize the ruler's success in putting down a rebellion in the delta.

On the front side of the stela is a delicate bas-relief divided into three registers. In the center of the upper register, between two cow's heads usually interpreted as "Hathor-heads," is a stylized image of the palace facade, with the Horus name of the last ruler of the Zero Dynasty, Narmer. This name should probably be translated as "Pungent catfish." The middle register is dominated by the figure of Narmer, wearing the crown of Upper Egypt, about to strike with a stone club an enemy who has fallen to his knees and may be a chieftain from the east delta. The servant standing behind Narmer is wearing the pharaoh's sandals. In front of the king the Horus-falcon holds an enemy's head on a rope. The latter is connected with a flat oval representing a piece of land on which a papyrus plant with six blooms is growing. The papyrus symbolized Lower Egypt and also transcribes the numeral one thousand. The whole scene can thus be interpreted as follows: "The pharaoh overcame six thousand enemies from Lower Egypt and took them prisoner." The scene rounds out the image of the triumphant Narmer and, according to the British Egyptologist Alan Gardiner, the author of the celebrated *Egyptian Grammar,* is a classical example of ancient Egyptian thinking in the earliest times. In the lower register two other vanquished enemies are represented.

tion of the White Walls, the fortified residence of the Egyptian kings, began in the age of unification, and was located on the boundary between the Nile Valley and the delta. The city that gradually grew up around the fortification was later known as Mennefer (Greek Memphis) and ultimately extended over several square miles. Archaeologists have still not succeeded in determining the site of the fortress, the oldest part of the city.

historical basis for Meni (in Greek, Menes), the unifier of the kingdom represented in later drawings. Some researchers consider Menes a purely legendary figure.

On the back side of the stela the decoration is divided into four registers. The first from the top is identical with the corresponding one on the front side. The second shows Narmer, this time with the crown of Lower Egypt on his head and in a cortege of men bearing standards with the symbols of the provinces of the victorious Upper Egyptian coalition, viewing executed enemies. The third pictorial field takes up a decorative motif that may be of Elamite origin: two fabulous creatures with intertwined necks. It is considered evidence of Near Eastern cultural influence in the Nile Valley at the beginning of the Early Dynastic Period. In the lowest register field, a bull, which like the falcon is a symbol of the ruler, smashes a fortified city and tramples down the enemies living in it.

Until well into the First Dynasty Egyptian rulers had no permanent residence. In the biennial "Horus-procession" they crossed the whole country with their retinue, in order to collect taxes, administer justice, and show themselves to the people.* The north-south dualism, which subsided only gradually, was still clearly reflected in the peculiar names of the first governmental institutions in the era of unification. Thus, e.g. the "White House," the royal treasury, became the "Red House" after being moved to the Memphis area; the change in its name is related to the fact that the "red crown" was the symbol of Lower Egypt and the "white crown" the symbol of Upper Egypt.

As a result of increasing centralization, the administrative apparatus grew significantly larger during the First Dynasty. Members of the royal family still stood at the apex of its hierarchy. Officials were chiefly responsible for regional administration, the registration of inhabitants, controlling floods on the Nile, the construction of irrigation canals, the cultivation of fields and gardens, workshop production, and the tax system.

* European rulers did the same thing in the early Middle Ages, thus creating the system of palatinates.

The consolidation of governmental administration went hand in hand with the development of writing, which ancient Egyptians considered to be divine in origin. The oldest literary traditions commemorate episodes in the battle to unify the kingdom, rites connected with the introduction of agricultural labor, and religious festivals. In addition, more practical contents are found in inscriptions on vessels, funerary stelae, annals tablets, and sealings. The oldest papyrus scroll currently known, though it bears no writing, was found in Saqqara, in the tomb of the official Hemaka. It shows that under the fifth king of the First Dynasty, Den (fl. 2850 B.C.E.), Egyptians already knew how to produce the writing materials that later became so widespread.

The ruler was at the center of the Egyptian world. He was seen as the connecting link between human beings and the gods. It was around him that the administrative apparatus of the newly developed state began to form. Royal estates were established, and undeveloped regions, particularly in the south and in the marshes of the Nile Delta, were settled and made productive by means of "internal colonization." Despite the organization of Egypt into provinces (Greek *nomoi*)—ultimately twenty-two in Upper Egypt and twenty in Lower Egypt—the political unity and stability of the country remained fragile. At the end of the First Dynasty the latent oppositions between north and south resurfaced.

The first ruler of the Second Dynasty, Hetepsekhemwy (twenty-eighth century B.C.E.), whose name means "the two powers [Upper and Lower Egypt] are reconciled," succeeded in reestablishing Egyptian unity, but not for long. Two generations later the two parts of the country were being ruled separately again. Upper Egypt was ruled from Thinis, the old center of power and administration close to Abydos, while the rest of the country was ruled from the White Walls. This internal political instability was reflected in royal titles: unlike his predecessors, the ruler Peribsen was not identified in any way with the god Horus, but rather was identified with the latter's ideal opponent Seth, the god of evil and war. The unsettled conditions under the Second Dynasty are also manifested in the deliberate destruction of the preceding dynasty's royal monuments in Abydos, Naqada, and Saqqara, which was motivated by the desire to obliterate not only the

The upper border of the palace facade with Khasekhemwy's name is unusual in depicting together the two enemy divinities Horus and Seth.

tombs and worship of the dead, but also and especially all memory of the dynastic opponent. The last ruler of this dynasty finally succeeded in subjugating Lower Egypt. He was originally named Khasekhem, "power shines" (or "appears in brilliance"), but changed his name to Khasekhemwy, "the two powers shine," in order to express the unity of the gods Horus and Seth, the latter representing not only the opposing principles of good and evil, but also the formerly opposed parts of Egypt, the north and the south.

In ancient Egypt's relationships with the ancient world surrounding it, we can already discern a few principles that were to characterize the country's whole history. The ancient Egyptians' religion led them to see their neighbors as enemies. Egyptians waged many wars of conquest against their neighbors, whether they lived in the east, west, or south. The most common target was Nubia, perhaps because it was more easily accessible through the corridor of the Nile Valley. In the reign of Djer, the third king of the First Dynasty, the Egyptians were already seeking to extend their influence as far as the border of present-day Sudan (see illustration p. 20).

Yet Egypt's relationships with neighboring countries were not exclusively hostile. The people of the Nile Valley also traded with their African and Near Eastern neighbors. For instance, they exported agricultural products to Palestine, evidenced by Egyptian pottery from Rafah and Arad, as well as by imprints of Egyptian seals from Tell Erama near Jerusalem. In return, they imported primarily metal prod-

The stone relief from Gebel Sheikh Suleiman is considered by many Egyptologists to reflect the pharaoh Djer's policy of conquering the region lying to the south of Egypt.

ucts, even after the copper mines in the Sinai came under Egyptian control in the course of the First Dynasty. By way of Palestine, the ancient Egyptians also had long-standing contacts with more remote regions, as is shown by some Sumerian or Elamite motifs—a winged griffin, interlaced serpents, a man tying up animals, and zoomorphic urns and ships with towering sterns—that appeared in the Nile Valley during the First Dynasty. Some researchers found these foreign elements so striking and surprising that they arrived at the view—today outdated—that people belonging to a so-called dynastic race from Mesopotamia had ruled and "civilized" Egypt toward the end of the prehistoric era. Scholars found themselves unable to explain in any other way the rapid rise of Egypt at the beginning of the historical period. Only after new discoveries were made and evaluated did they realize that the notion of a "civilizing phase" had been based not on a sudden developmental rupture but on gaps in their own knowledge.

KINGSHIP AND STATE DOGMA

During the early or Thinite period (as the reign of the first two dynasties is also known), the prolonged, complicated, and often conflictual process of shaping the ancient Egyptian state that had begun toward the end of the prehistoric era, around the middle of the fourth millennium B.C.E., was finally brought to a conclusion. The fusion of the fun-

The figures incised on the ebony handle of a knife from Gebel el-Arak (Louvre E. 11517) used to be considered evidence of Near Eastern influence in Egypt at the end of the prehistoric era. On one side are hunting scenes representing a hero between two lions facing each other. The other side is decorated with scenes of battle on land and on water.

damentally different cultural groups of the delta and the Nile Valley played a major role in this process.

In the southern part of the country, which was inhabited primarily by nomadic shepherds, economically prosperous centers began to emerge and gain political power; among these were Hierakonpolis, Naqada, and Abydos. The rise of these new centers was aided by nearby sources of raw materials in the eastern desert and the development of foreign trade in gold and other materials.

Before the age of unification, northern Egypt, where a rather sedentary population lived and practiced agriculture, developed differently from southern Egypt. Major economic centers may have emerged there even earlier than they did in southern Egypt, especially along the banks of the navigable branches of the Nile. Closer contacts were probably established with Near Eastern urban cultures, both by land and by sea. Buto and Sais became important cities. However, archaeological sources in this part of the country remain inadequate because the complicated environmental situation makes excavation very difficult.

In contrast to the predynastic monarchs from Hierakonpolis, the princes of the great cities in the delta were probably not able to extend their rule beyond the local level. Consequently, they could not avoid military subjection to the king. Initially, the violently created bond between Upper and Lower Egypt was not very stable, being threatened by various political, economic, and religious interests.

As a result, during the Early Period the inhabitants of Lower Egypt made great efforts to win independence that culminated in the rebellions that finally led King Khasekhem to take energetic punitive action against them. This time, it seems he was successful. The subsequent long period of internal stability and relative shelter from outside influences was the crucial precondition that allowed the Old Kingdom (from the Third Dynasty to the Sixth Dynasty) to flourish.

In addition, the ideology of the ancient Egyptian state developed through the process of culturally assimilating Lower Egypt. According to the Egyptian worldview, a divine principle called *maat* was the foundation of everyday life. At its center stood law and order, and it was typically represented in the figure of the goddess of justice. Only if an individual obeyed the rules of maat could he achieve happiness and fulfillment, and only then could his life have any meaning in the framework of creation. This world order had to be constantly defended against the hostile powers of chaos. The ancient Egyptians believed that was why the gods set up the monarchy, which had to be supported and honored. Only the ruler, as the sole divinity living among men, could guarantee the survival of the divinely established order. In the context of the eternal myth, during his reign the ruler was obligated to overcome evil, either actually or symbolically, and evil was embodied in enemy countries and peoples. For this reason the ruler was usually represented as triumphing over Nubians, Libyans, and Asians, even when no historical facts justified such a representation.

The whole system of the ancient Egyptian state was based on these ideas, which have often been described, not very precisely, as theocratic. During the Early Dynastic Period in particular, the state and the monarchy were virtually identical. The increasing importance of the state is shown by additions to the royal nomenclature. At first, the latter consisted simply of the name Horus, written in a rectangle called a *serekh* that was a stylized representation of the royal palace's facade. Within this rectangle was symbolized the falcon god Horus, the ruler over heaven and earth, embodied on earth by the ancient Egyptian kings. During the reign of King Den, the king's titulary was extended to include the so-called throne name "King of Upper and Lower Egypt." Up to the Fourth Dynasty, further names were added. The name "the two ladies" connected him with the vulture goddess Nekhbet and the cobra goddess Wadjet, the tutelary divinities of Upper and Lower Egypt respectively. "Golden Horus" and "Son of Re" completed the list of five royal names.

The word *pharaoh* itself is of Egyptian origin and is derived from *per aa,* "Great House," the name of the royal residence. Starting in the New Kingdom, the rulers themselves were designated metonymically by this term. Finally, from the Twenty-Second Dynasty onward, this word became an essential component of the royal nomenclature and was written in front of the cartouche with the king's name.

The conception of the king's role in the historical and state-building myth expanded with the country's boundaries. In theory, Egypt included every place where Egyptians and their gods existed, where the pharaoh exercised power, and where there was thus divine order. In practice, however, Egyptians identified themselves and their country only with the area of the Nile Valley, from the delta to the first cataract, and later on, as far as Nubia.

State dogma emphasized not only the ruler's military role, but also his creative role. The mythical conception of the king required him to "extend the borders," both by defeating Egypt's enemies on the battlefield and by erecting new edifices whose size and importance were expected to surpass those built by his predecessors. In accord with this conception, the construction of the ancient Egyptian temple, in contrast to the Greek temple, was never completed; it was always possible to add new rooms, gateways, courtyards, chapels, and obelisks, or at least statues or stelae. In the "Instruction for Merikare," a famous literary work from the First Intermediate Period, the ruler Khety called on his successors to "enlarge what he made." Both myth and history urged every pharaoh to "go beyond everything that was accomplished in the time of his predecessors."

THE TOMBS OF THE EARLY DYNASTIC PERIOD

In the Early Dynastic Period tombs in Abydos and North Saqqara, the most important elements of later pyramid construction appeared in simple form. However, the oldest royal tombs in Abydos differ from the later ones in North Saqqara in both their underlying religious conception and their ideal significance. It is clear that the tombs in Abydos and Saqqara represent different traditions and ideas about life after death, and reflect two different cultural milieus. The tombs in Saqqara are based on a conception of the deceased as living on after death in a building resembling an earthly dwelling, which is embodied in a stylized form by the so-called *mastaba*. In Abydos, the primary conception is that of a funeral mound symbolizing the primeval mound of sand, the site of the creation and the resurrection.

From predynastic times onward, the royal tombs in Abydos were linked to the religious traditions of Upper Egypt. These tombs already consisted of entire complexes of rooms and were located in the desert. In the late Zero Dynasty, a tomb's underground portion consisted of a burial chamber and one or more storerooms for accessories to be used by the dead pharaoh in the beyond. The aboveground portion consisted of a low mound of sand about 2.5 meters high and surrounded by a stone wall. Two stone stelae stood in front of the facade of the tomb. From the time of King Aha onward, the royal tombs were surrounded by so-called secondary tombs, the number of which came to 338 under King Djer. The royal cemetery in Abydos was later plundered and burned, and its original form is now virtually impossible to reconstruct. However, the rulers' servants and wives seem to have been buried in the secondary tombs. We do not yet know whether they were killed during the burial ceremony and immediately interred with the ruler.

The tomb area at Abydos is known as Umm el-Qaab, "Mother of Potsherds," because of the great number of remnants of sacrificial ves-

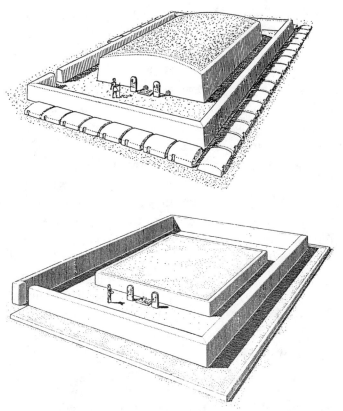

Reconstruction of
the tomb of Queen
Meretneith, the
mother of King
Den, in Abydos
(after Lauer and
Ricke).

sels found there. The valley where the Early Period tomb complexes
are located lies on the edge of the Nile Valley, some two kilometers
to the northeast. Nearby, in modern-day Kom es-Sultan, Khontamenti,
and later Osiris, was worshiped at a religious center for the local god
of the dead. The edifices there date from the time of King Djer and
are surrounded by huge brick walls (archaeologists call these structures "great enclosures" or "fortresses"). These walls were whitewashed and decorated with niches. For a long time, researchers
thought that almost nothing was inside these structures. However, a
meticulous investigation of Khasekhemwy's enclosure carried out by
a team of American Egyptologists has recently made highly interesting discoveries. In a courtyard within the structure, a low mound of
sand covered with mudbricks was discovered. It is a stylized prime-

val mound, the symbolic site of the creation of the world and of the resurrection. In addition, a dozen thirty-meter-long boat-pits were discovered in front of the east wall; hence, the great enclosures should probably be seen as centers for the worship of the dead kings.

At the same time they were constructing a new capital, known as "the White Walls," Egyptian rulers also built a new tomb site, which is known today as the Early Dynastic Period necropolis in North Saqqara. At first, probably only members of the royal family and the highest state officials who lived in the royal residence were interred there. The rulers of the First Dynasty continued to have themselves entombed in the traditional royal cemetery in Abydos in Upper Egypt. Thus neither the real nor the symbolic tombs of the early rulers of the united Egypt were in Saqqara.

The tombs in North Saqqara had a rectangular ground plan and were built of mudbricks; their facades, which were sometimes several meters high, were originally rendered in white plaster and decorated with colorful mat-like patterns, as well as with numerous niches. In the underground portion they consisted of a burial chamber and storerooms for burial equipment. A large boat was often included in the tomb; it was supposed to allow the spirit of the deceased to travel into the beyond in order to join the sun god Re's entourage. In form, the tombs in Saqqara resembled the low clay benches found in front of country houses in modern Egypt, and which are called mastaba in Arabic. Therefore, workers employed in the first archaeological excavations in the middle of the nineteenth century used this word to designate these tombs.

With a few exceptions, most of the royal tombs of the Second Dynasty have not yet been precisely located. In contrast to the First Dynasty, only a few kings of the Second Dynasty—for example, Peribsen and Khasekhemwy—were buried in Abydos. The tombs of a few other kings appear to have been located not in the northern but rather in the middle part of the Saqqara cemetery, near Djoser's later "Step Pyramid." Their substructures probably consisted of large, interconnected underground catacombs. East of the pyramid of the last ruler of the Fifth Dynasty, Unas, archaeologists have discovered two tombs attributed to King Raneb and King Ninetjer. The super-

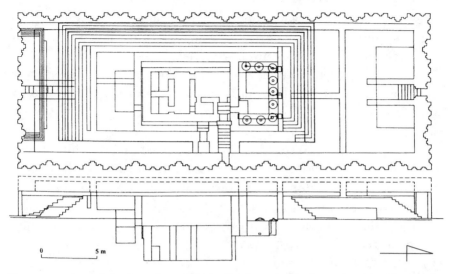

Reconstruction of the "royal tomb" no. 3038, probably from the time of Adjib, a First Dynasty king, in Saqqara (ground plan and north-south vertical section, after Emery). All four tomb facades are decorated with a system of niches, so-called recesses. Most of the inner area is filled with storage rooms. The vertical section (below) shows the stepped superstructure.

structure (the aboveground portion) of these tombs was completely destroyed during the construction of Unas's pyramid. This fact, along with the lack of dates for the other royal tombs of the Second Dynasty, makes it difficult to provide a precise explanation for the transition to building pyramids.

We have already described the ancient Egyptian conception of the state as an expression of the divine will and the center of the harmonious and ordered world created by the gods. Even after his death, the ruler had to fight for the welfare of his country in the eternal battle against chaos. Because of the ruler's extraordinary role as both a god among men and the mediator between humans and the world of the gods, it was necessary to preserve his presence in the world of the living. This was the goal of mummifying the ruler's body and worshiping him after his death. Only in this way could the dead pharaoh remain forever among his people to ensure their happiness. Hence the mummified body of the pharaoh had to be protected from various external dangers, and it was necessary to erect for him an indestructible tomb-residence, a structure that could be damaged neither by the ravages of time nor by human hands in times of unrest.

Religiously, the pharaoh's last resting place was a representation of the primeval mound that emerged from the waters at the creation of the world, and on which life first appeared. That is, it was a symbol of resurrection and eternal life. The external appearance of the royal tomb, inspired by the idea of the primeval mound, went through a complicated development at the beginning of Egyptian history, finally culminating, during the Third Dynasty, in the pyramids.

The pyramid was supposed to be the death residence of the pharaoh—unshakable, indestructible, eternal. Other temple buildings nearby were dedicated to the worship of the deceased, which was also supposed to go on forever, for it was in the highest interest of the ancient Egyptian state and of every inhabitant of the lands along the Nile that the good god should remain forever in his country and among his people. The building of the pyramids and the enduring worship of the dead pharaoh thus became the top priority of the ancient Egyptian state.*

It is precisely from this point of view, and in their historical context, that the gigantic structures known as the Egyptian pyramids must be considered. The architectural and religious development that ultimately led to the royal tomb in the form of a pyramid was an inseparable part of the process of shaping and strengthening the oldest

---

* It has also been maintained that the main goal of building the pyramids was to found the ancient Egyptian state, whose bases and chief functions were systematically defined and generated by this gigantic project, which required unprecedented organizational structures and technical expertise. Thus the building of the pyramids is said to be a source of the dynamic development of Egyptian society. It is incontestable that the gigantic edifices of the pyramids required of their time enormous organizational efforts and willingness to work, and that they lent a powerful impetus to the development of administration, crafts, astronomy, mathematics, and systems of construction. However, it is surely an exaggeration to see behind all this the "higher" goal of programmatically establishing a state, and such a claim is in accord with neither the historical facts nor simple logic: the creators of this kind of sophisticated conception would certainly have chosen more practical and more profitable projects than tombs or pyramids.

strongly centralized Egyptian state. In this context the pyramid becomes more than just a royal tomb; it becomes a symbol of the ruler's
historical and state-building role, the symbol of the state and of the
order the Egyptian gods established when they created the world.

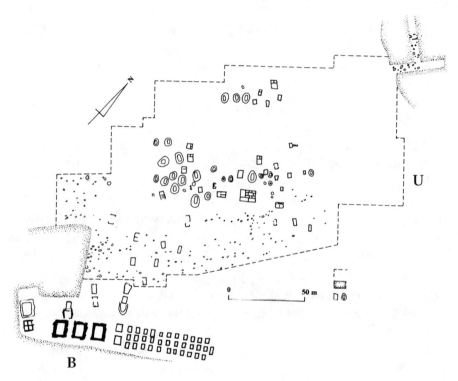

Abydos, Umm el-Qaab. Cemetery B (below) and U (after Dreyer).

CHAPTER TWO

THE WAY TO ETERNITY: RITUAL AND CULT

The Burial Ritual

The green, fertile Nile Valley was the "beloved land" of the ancient Egyptians, the world in which they lived and wanted to die. Its polar opposite was the boundless, inhospitable desert that stretched out to the west. This was the place where the sun died every evening, the realm from which no one returned, and which was ruled by the god Osiris. The dividing line between life and death was as distinct as that between the flourishing valley and the endless desert. The gods created man and gave him life. Depending on his conduct while he was on earth, after death he experienced either eternal bliss or eternal damnation. Earthly life was merely an episode on the way to eternity.

In predynastic times cemeteries were already being established, particularly on the edge of the desert west of the Nile. There went the funeral processions, and from them the family members, associates, and priests came back to make sacrifices and practice the worship of the deceased. All were equal before the god Osiris and his divine tribunal in the beyond, but kings took a different path into the beyond. The pharaoh was the god who lived among humans on the earth, and after his death he returned to the gods.

Every important individual's death was accompanied by ceremonies of mourning whose course can be reconstructed from the images and inscriptions on the walls of the tombs. In essence, they were the same for everyone, but how humble or pompous they were depended on the social standing of the deceased and the survivors' means, and

In front of the tomb entrance, a lector priest carries out the ritual of the opening of the mouth on the mummy. In the shaft of the tomb, the *ba*-soul is already hovering in the form of a bird. In the burial chamber lies the mummiform coffin. After all the revival rites are completed, the resurrection follows, and the deceased emerges from the tomb into the sunlight.—After a vignette on the Nebqed papyrus from the Eighteenth Dynasty (Louvre AE-N 3068).

in the case of the pharaoh, there were certain peculiarities. The ceremonies were carried out in several places and over an extended period. As a result, local customs and religious conceptions regarding the beyond were introduced into these ceremonies. Some elements of the ritual were performed only symbolically.

After death, the body of the deceased was laid in a coffin and carried out of his residence, followed by the wailing wives. The funeral procession, which included the bearers, relatives, and friends as well as the embalmers and the lector priest, then moved toward the banks of the Nile, accompanied by continuous lamentations.

The coffin was loaded onto a boat and ferried over to the left bank of the Nile, where the purification tent stood. There certain purification rituals were performed on the deceased, in the presence of the embalmer, while a lector priest read from a papyrus scroll. Various vessels and religious objects kept in the tent were also used.

From the purification tent the body of the deceased was taken to the embalming area in the "Hall of the God Anubis." The embalmers laid the body on a wooden or stone table, cut open the abdomen, and removed all the entrails, including the liver and the lungs. The heart was, as a rule, left in the body. Then they broke the nasal septum and removed the brain by that route. They placed the liver, lungs, stomach, and intestines in four canopic vessels, special stone jars under the protection of the divine sons of Horus. After removing the en-

A boat carrying the coffin of the Sixth Dynasty ruler Snefruinishtef to the necropolis (after Junker). The lector priest, who is standing in a chapel and reading the funerary formulas from a papyrus scroll (right), escorts the boat with the coffin to the final resting place. At the entombment site on the opposite bank, two priests receive the boat; one has offerings in his hands and the other is a second lector priest. Two butchers are cutting up a sacrificial bull.

Reconstruction of a "purification tent," a lightweight wooden structure hung with mats, in which the ritual of the purification of the deceased was carried out during the burial ceremonies (after Badawi).

trails, they sprinkled a thick layer of natron on the body and left it for four to five weeks. During the following purification, they filled the abdomen and breast with balls of cloth or straw and applied various oils and resins. Then they sewed up the incision and sometimes painted the corpse—usually red for men and yellow for women. Finally, they wrapped the body, which might in some cases be richly decorated with jewels, in linen, laying amulets and small ornaments between the layers of the windings. It has been shown that in one case

some 375 square meters of linen were used for the filling and winding of a single mummy. The mummies, sometimes provided with a face mask, were then put into a wooden coffin for further rituals.

In the case of a dead king, after the embalming and the sacrificial rituals, the mummy set out on a symbolic path toward Sais, the ancient religious and cult center in the west delta. It is assumed that in the case of a royal entombment, Sais was symbolically represented by a part of the valley temple, or perhaps even the whole temple.

Rituals and sacrifices were then performed, and afterward the procession with the coffin, which lay under a canopy on a funerary boat or wooden sledge, moved symbolically from Sais to other religious sites. First it went to Buto, a very old religious center in the delta whose "palm grove" was considered the national cemetery of ancient Egypt. In the burial ritual this place was represented by the entombment site, from which the *muu* came down to receive the body of the deceased. The muu were mythical creatures represented wearing wreathes and tall headdresses woven from plant material; they were believed to carry the deceased from this world into the beyond.

Then came the symbolic visit to the town of Iunu (Greek Heliopolis), which ancient Egyptians regarded as the site of the cult of the sun god and of *benben,* the primeval mound. This probably took place inside the royal pyramid complex, in rooms in the mortuary temple.

Further stages in the ritual included the lamentation, the smoking of the coffin containing the mummy, the transportation of the coffin, and the "opening of the mouth," an ancient ceremony in which the deceased's son or a priest, using various tools (such as the *peseshkaf,* a stone knife in the form of a swallow's tail), touched the mummy in order to put its members in movement and revive the deceased's senses.

The cortege of the *tekenu,* a figure sitting or lying on a bier or wooden sledge and wearing a mantle or an animal (bull?) skin, was an important element of the burial ritual. Egyptologists' views of this cortege have changed over time. At first, it was assumed that the tekenu was originally a living person to be sacrificed as part of the burial ritual. This now seems to have been disproven, but there is no broad consensus regarding an alternate view. Some Egyptologists think the tekenu was a case for the body parts that were removed during the process of mummification but not placed in canopic vessels; for example, pieces of skin and blood. Others believe the tekenu represented the mystical sun bull.

After the coffin was placed in the tomb, a statue was buried to represent the mummy of the deceased making its way along the ritual "journey to Abydos" (Abydos was not only the cemetery of the oldest Egyptian kings, but also the center for worship of Osiris, the god of the dead). Finally, priests performed apotropaic rituals intended

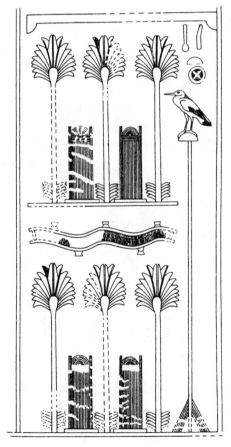

The sacred cemetery in Buto, with repeated representations of the Lower Egyptian shrine in the palm grove. Detail from a decorated gateway of the Twelfth Dynasty ruler Senusret II's in Memphis.

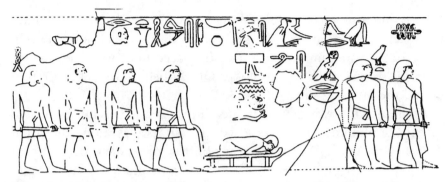

Transport of the enigmatic *tekenu,* which is represented in the form of a cowering man being carried on a sled by several other men. Detail from the tomb of Mentuherkhepeshef from the Eighteenth Dynasty in Dra Abu el-Naga.

to ensure the security of the deceased's tomb and his peace in the beyond.

The whole burial ritual, including the mummification, was generally expected to last seven days, but it sometimes took the better part of a year to complete. In the case of a royal burial, after the mummy had been laid to rest in the pyramid and the last prescribed rituals were completed, all the components of the security system were put in place. The entrance was hidden by a stone slab and was indistinguishable from both the pyramid wall and the pavement of the open courtyard in front of it. The pharaoh in the coffin had been symbolically united with the sky goddess Nut, in order to be born again from her as the sun god. At this point, worship of the deceased began.

A lector priest reads from a papyrus scroll while mythological figures, *muu,* wearing their characteristic tall headdress woven of plant material, perform a ritual dance. Detail from the decoration on the Sixth Dynasty tomb of Nebkauhor (after Hassan).

The Worship of the Dead

Every Egyptian wanted to die in Egypt, to be buried there, and to be worshiped after death as an eternal memory. For ancient Egyptians, the belief in a life after death was inseparably bound up with the preservation of the whole person of the deceased, both body and spirit. To separate a person's body from his "double" (*ka*) and "soul" (*ba*) would have amounted to destroying him forever. Embalming and mummifying were intended to prevent this separation.

However, there was a fundamental difference between ordinary mortals and the pharaoh. In exceptional cases even gods could die physically, but their life went on eternally. In contrast, human beings could only hope that their memory would not be extinguished. In the person of the pharaoh the world of the gods and the world of men intersected. The king and "great god" was immortal, but he was unable to escape the transitory nature of his physical being or to achieve immortality on his own.

After his death, the pharaoh returned to be with the other gods. This event had to be constantly reenacted, and the survival of the pharaoh's earthly achievements thus repeatedly ensured. This was the purpose of the worship of the dead, which, since it concerned the pharaoh, was also a state religious cult. In this context, the gigantic structures of the pyramids take on their true meaning. The official

In the form of a bird, a dead man and his soul (ba) leave the tomb (detail from the Nineteenth Dynasty Ani papyrus in the British Museum).

cult was extended to other gods only later on; in the Fifth Dynasty it was widened to include the god Re (this also had to do with the erection of sun temples by certain rulers of this dynasty) and, in the Middle Kingdom, to Amon. In addition, other social strata gradually began to adopt for themselves many religious ideas and practices that were originally reserved exclusively for the pharaoh.

Central to the worship of the dead pharaoh was the preparation of a symbolic funerary repast. The deceased was offered everything he needed in the form of offerings and gifts. This was not a unique event, but rather a ritual regularly repeated throughout the year, especially on important feasts. To the pharaoh's altar flowed the products of his lands and workshops. In this way during his own lifetime the ruler was able to furnish the materials for his worship in times to come. To guarantee that these supplies would be regularly provided in perpetuity, "eternal" scenes of the delivery of sacrifices and long lists of the victims were carved in stone at the cult sites.

The continuity of the family and of power, through succession to the throne, further guaranteed the continued worship of dead monarchs. Therefore, the relationship between father and son, and in a

The Last Judgment: Before the god Osiris stands a dead man whose heart is being weighed on a scale in the presence of Thoth, the god of wisdom (in the form of a baboon), and Maat, the goddess of truth. Detail from the Nineteenth Dynasty Nebseni papyrus (after Budge).

figurative sense between the deceased and the priest, assumed exceptional importance, and also found its expression in myth. Here we may recall that Egyptian myth recounts the pious relationship between Horus, as heir to the throne, and his murdered father, Osiris.

The tomb was thus not merely a final resting place, but also the site of eternal life, of the encounter between the living and the dead. It was the scene of mythical events and rituals that were supposed never to end.

The Pyramid Texts

In the late 1870s, Auguste Mariette still controlled the Egyptian monuments with an iron hand. He was an energetic and experienced man who not only made great discoveries and initiated systematic archaeological excavation in Egypt, but also laid the foundations for the preservation of monuments and established the first museum of Egyptian antiquities. In the second half of the nineteenth century, Egyptologists worked in a context very different from the one in which they work today: the spirit of scientific pioneering and romantic adventuring went hand in hand, and the longing to discover treasures was very great. Mariette Pasha, whom the viceroy Said appointed "director of the excavations," received all the men he needed for his work—they were commandeered as forced labor. In order to accelerate the excavations, the overseers did not hesitate to make use of all the means at their disposal, from leather whips to explosives. Such methods have long since been abandoned.

When the French archaeologist Gaston Maspero, Mariette's presumptive successor and director of the French Institute for Oriental Archaeology in Cairo, came to Egypt in 1880, he went to South Saqqara, where he chose for his first excavation a hill that had been mapped decades earlier by the Lepsius expedition. Maspero found there the ruins of a large structure he thought was a pyramid. To his surprise he discovered that the walls of the underground rooms were covered with hieroglyphs. Mariette, who was already suffering from severe diabetes, was immediately informed, but he rejected

Auguste Mariette
Pasha

Maspero's conjecture, since in none of the previously studied pyramids were the walls of the underground rooms decorated with reliefs, paintings, or any other ornamentation. In Mariette's view, the structure must therefore have been a large mastaba.

However, Maspero did not abandon his conviction that this structure must be the pyramid of a Sixth Dynasty ruler, Pepi I. About a kilometer to the southwest, there were more ruins of what looked like an edifice of some kind. When Maspero began to investigate them, he saw to his great joy that he had stumbled upon the pyramid of Merenre I, Pepi I's successor, and that its underground rooms were also decorated with hieroglyphs. He immediately went with this news to see Mariette, who was on his deathbed and confined himself to remarking skeptically: "In thirty years of Egyptian excavations I have never seen a pyramid whose underground rooms had hieroglyphs written on their walls."

In 1880 and 1881 Maspero investigated other pyramids and in those of Unas, Teti, and Pepi II he found underground rooms with hieroglyphs that he called "pyramid texts." Archaeological excavations gradually led to the discovery that these texts had appeared in the pyramids only during a limited period, from the reign of the last ruler of the Fifth Dynasty, Unas, to that of Ibi in the Eighth Dynasty. Further pyramid texts were found in the tombs of some of the queens.

The investigations and discoveries in the pyramids greatly contributed to Maspero's fame around the world, although they also aroused criticism. Petrie thought some of Maspero's procedures were reckless, considering the poor condition of the structures being excavated. This did not, however, diminish Maspero's achievement or his popularity. He gradually became the greatest archaeological authority of his time and wrote some thirty scientific monographs and countless articles and shorter studies. Maspero himself never counted up all his writings and publications. This little man with pink cheeks and a round face simply had so much work to do that he had no time to look backward. In his knitted, slightly soiled, yellow linen trousers and close-fitting coat, he sat at a desk that was in danger of collapsing under the weight of papers, books, letters, ancient Egyptian objects, and scraps of mummy windings. Books even lay on the chairs surrounding the desk.

Maspero first published the pyramid texts in 1894, under the title *Les inscriptions des pyramides de Saqqarah.* A new, updated translation of this corpus of inscriptions was published between 1908 and 1910 by the outstanding German Egyptologist and philologist Kurt Sethe (1869–1934), under the title *Die altägyptischen Pyramidentexte.* After more than half a century, this was followed in 1969 by a third presentation of the texts in *The Ancient Egyptian Pyramid Texts,* by the British Egyptologist Raymond Faulkner (1894–1982).

The pyramid texts are the oldest collection of ancient Egyptian religious inscriptions. Their central subject is the ruler and his life in the beyond. However, they do not constitute a coherent, self-enclosed body of thought about the ruler's movement into the beyond, the conditions of his new existence, and his relationships with specific places or gods. Instead, they compile various conceptions of the beyond, drawn from different origins and periods. In them we encounter elements of the dog, star, sun, and Osiris cults. After his death, the ruler becomes one of the eternal stars near the North Star, and at the same time he is on a boat with the sun god, crossing the celestial ocean of day and night, and he may experience the mythical, pathetic fate of Osiris before finally coalescing with this god of death and ruler of the underworld. The dead ruler's beyond is thus located both in the heavens and in the underworld.

From a formal point of view, the pyramid texts are composed mainly of maxim-like formulas, but they also include recitations, divine utterances, litanies, hymns, dramatic passages, and so on. We encounter elements of various ceremonies, such as the burial, sacrificial, and mouth-opening rituals. Here we may cite as representative Unas's so-called cannibal hymn. This is not evidence of ritual cannibalism in the ancient Egypt of Unas's time; rather, it is a religious text whose meaning operates on a strictly symbolic and magical level:

> The King is the Bull of the Sky,
> Who conquers (?) at will,
> Who lives on the being of every god,
> Who eats their entrails (?),
> Even of those who come with their bodies full of magic
> From the Island of Fire
> . . .
> The King is one who eats men and lives on the gods,
> A possessor of porters who dispatches messages,
> . . .
> It is king who eats their magic
> And gulps down their spirits,
> The big ones are for his morning meal,
> The medium-sized ones for his evening meal,
> The little ones are for his night meal,
> Their old men and their old women are for his incense-burning,
> . . .
> (R. O. Faulkner, *The Ancient Egyptian Pyramid Texts,*
> Oxford 1969 [passages from §§397–404])

The belief in the magical effects produced by the symbols included in the pyramid texts was so deep that artists who chiseled hieroglyphic signs in the form of dangerous beasts of prey and serpents in the underground chambers of the pyramids intentionally damaged them to prevent them from doing harm. A serpent or lion that had been chopped in two could no longer be resurrected and threaten the pharaoh in his burial chamber.

In the early 1950s the German Egyptologist Siegfried Schott published a study on the pyramid cult that revived the debate about the meaning of the pyramid texts. Schott maintained that the texts were an inseparable part of the burial ritual; he tried to connect the development of a given segment of the text with a sequence of cult practices, and given expressions with specific places in the pyramid complex.

Although Schott's views are no longer considered generally valid today, they did significantly influence later research. Some recent investigations show that there is a certain order in the sequence of individual segments of the text. The path taken by the pharaoh on leaving this world, in moving from death to new life, resembles the path taken by the sun from its setting on the horizon to its rise toward the zenith the next morning. In the ritual resurrection of the king as Osiris, the coffin was equated with the goddess Nut, from whose lap the sun was born daily and eternally, in order to be swallowed by her again every evening. Thus the burial chamber, on whose western wall the coffin stood, represented the underworld out of which the pharaoh moved through the antechamber, understood as the "horizon," and began his ascent toward the exit from the pyramid and up to heaven.

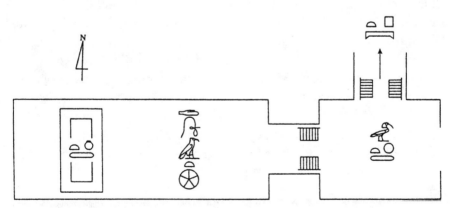

Schematic arrangement of the pyramid texts in accord with the idea of the resurrection of the pharaoh in the coffin and his way out of the burial chamber—through the underworld toward the zenith (after Allen).

The pharaoh's ultimate goal was to rise as high as the sun that "shone over the horizon." This idea, understood as the "emergence [of the deceased's spirit] into the daylight," is central to the various "books of the dead," later collections of religious burial texts.

In the unsettled conditions of the First Intermediate Period, and especially during the Middle Kingdom, broader levels of society arrogated royal privileges to themselves.* In this way many formulas and some other elements from the pyramid texts made their way into a new body of religious texts called, after the place where they are usually found, coffin texts. In the New Kingdom and in the Late Period, these were incorporated—very freely and only partially—into the books of the dead. They were usually written on papyrus scrolls and laid alongside the coffin in order to ensure that they would accompany the deceased on his way into eternity.

The oldest collection of ancient Egyptian religious texts was discovered and first evaluated by Gaston Maspero, and France continues to play a leading role in the area of research on the pyramid texts. In the early 1950s, French archaeologists in Saqqara began a far-reaching research project on the pyramids. Along with Jean-Philippe Lauer, who was in charge of the architectural aspect, the young Egyptologist and gifted philologist Jean Sainte Fare Garnot (1908–1963) took part in this project. Unfortunately, the latter's premature death and the diplomatic disputes connected with the 1956 Suez conflict complicated the French scientists' archaeological activities. However, the situation soon improved. Another important French Egyptologist, Jean Leclant, joined Lauer and ultimately assumed leadership of the project. Today a team of French Egyptologists—epigraphists, archaeologists, and architects—is using the latest computer technology to reconstruct, out of hundreds of fragments, the ruined walls bearing pyramid texts in the underground part of Pepi I's pyramid in South Saqqara. The result will be a high point of Egyptological research in our time.

---

* Egyptologists do not agree regarding the precise chronological limits of the Middle Kingdom. However, the prevailing opinion is that it begins with Mentuhotep II's reign and ends with the outgoing Twelfth Dynasty. The Thirteenth Dynasty is assigned to the Second Intermediate Period.

The Pyramid Complex—The Dead Pharaoh's Residence

To suppose that the pyramid's only function in ancient Egypt was as a royal tomb would be an oversimplification. The pyramid complex consisted of a group of buildings, of which the pyramid was only one element, even if it was the most important one. The pyramid complex was the site of the dead pharaoh's mystical transfiguration, rebirth, and ascent to heaven, as well as his residence in the beyond, from which he ruled over all the people of his time. The arrangement of the complex mirrored the ancient Egyptians' worldview: the beginning of the world was associated with the primeval mound the pyramid symbolized.

The essential appearance of the pyramids did not change over time, if we set aside differences in size and the shift from the step pyramids of the Third Dynasty to the classical form of the pyramid that emerged at the beginning of the Fourth Dynasty. However, in response to developing religious ideas and cultural practice, the structures *surrounding* the pyramid underwent striking changes in both their architectonic outline and their orientation and arrangement.

The oldest pyramid, that of King Djoser of the Third Dynasty, was surrounded by structures whose meaning is still debated. Egyptologists nevertheless generally agree that they were supposed to represent the ruler's death residence, which might have been inspired to some extent by parts of his earthly residence. In this complex, the mortuary temple was placed—as it was in all the other known step pyramids of the Third Dynasty—in front of the north side of the pyramid. Here was located the entrance to the underground rooms, which also served as the exit from the inner part of the pyramid and the burial chamber, through which the dead pharaoh went north to become one of the eternal stars around the North Star that never set.

At the beginning of the Fourth Dynasty, the sun religion gained prominence. The pharaoh was then believed to be born in the light of dawn, like the sun, to rise in splendor toward the zenith and die in the west, in order to be born anew in the eternal cycle of life, death, and resurrection. Under the influence of this significant religious transformation, the layout of the pyramid complex also underwent certain changes. The earlier north-south orientation was abandoned in favor of an east-west orientation. A valley temple was added to the complex, and from it a causeway climbing west toward the mortuary temple, which stood at the foot of the pyramid. The entrance to the underground rooms, that is, to the inside of the pyramid, continued to be located on the north side.

This new conception quickly became dominant, but its optimal architectonic realization in the pyramid complex crystallized only in the course of the Fourth Dynasty. Sahure's pyramid complex, built at the beginning of the Fifth Dynasty, was a milestone in the development of royal tombs, a masterwork not only in its fully achieved architectonic balance as a whole and in its individual parts, but also in its decoration and in the construction materials used. With a few modifications, Sahure's complex became the model for the royal tombs that followed during the Fifth and Sixth Dynasties, and to a large extent for later periods as well.

During the Middle Kingdom, pyramid complexes continued to be constructed, but they were already conceived differently in many ways. The entrance into the underground part of the pyramid was no longer necessarily placed on the north side, but might be in other, not precisely prescribed, locations. Above all, it was now important to conceal the entrance so that it would be invisible to thieves. In addition, the substructure of the pyramid—that is, the descending corridor, the barriers, and the burial chamber, which in some cases was accompanied by an antechamber—no longer had a fixed, unified layout. The

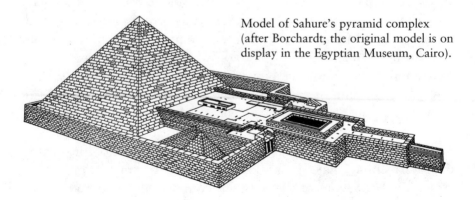

Model of Sahure's pyramid complex (after Borchardt; the original model is on display in the Egyptian Museum, Cairo).

influence of the Osiris cult favored the increasingly dominant conception of pharaoh's last resting place as the tomb of Osiris, surrounded by a labyrinth of passages, some of which led to dead ends or to hidden chambers. The king's grave was now accompanied by those of queens and princesses, and important changes were made in the decoration and the construction materials used for the other components of the complex.

In the New Kingdom, the royal tomb no longer took the form of a pyramid complex. The pyramid memorial nonetheless lived on in the architecture of private tombs and outside the borders of Egypt, in the royal tombs of the kingdoms of Napata and Meroe.

Let us return, however, to Egypt in the time of the Old Kingdom and to Sahure's complex in Abusir, and by examining its individual components try to understand something of its meaning and function. This will also shed light on the complex as a whole.

The entrance to Sahure's pyramid complex began where the Nile Valley and the desert met, metaphorically on the boundary between life and death. The lower or valley temple was both a monumental gateway and a landing ramp for the artificially constructed canal that connected the royal burial site with the Nile. It consisted of limestone blocks and, because of its high, only slightly inclined walls and flat roof terrace, it looked like a monolith.

From the main landing ramp on the east side of the temple—there was another landing ramp on the south side—a ramp led to a portico with black basalt pavement and pink granite columns in the form of stylized date palms. In the reigning conceptions of the beyond, the palm tree was a symbolic plant, connected with the Palm Grove in Buto, the ancient Egyptians' sacred cemetery. The ceiling of the portico was composed of enormous blocks of limestone decorated with yellow stars on a blue background, which looked very much like the night sky. He who entered there was entering the underworld, the world of the beyond.

Inside the temple was only a small room with two columns. Its walls were decorated with colorful scenes and inscriptions in bas-relief that had a ceremonial religious and mythical character. They included a representation of Sahure in the form of a lion tearing a captured enemy

to pieces with his claws, as well as a scene showing the tutelary goddess of Upper Egypt, Nekhbet, suckling the ruler and thus ensuring
his eternal life among the gods. The reliefs in this temple and in the
other parts of Sahure's pyramid field cover an amazing amount of
ground—nearly ten thousand square meters. Many early Egyptologists
believed that the embalming and mummifying rituals took place in the
valley temples, yet in the valley temples discovered thus far no reliefs
or other evidence support this view. While from the architectonic
standpoint the valley temple was also the monumental gateway to the
royal residence in the realm of death, its overall religious and cultic
meaning remains in many respects obscure.

From the valley temple, the way into the interior of the tomb complex led through a long, covered, stone corridor that gradually ascended toward the west and was built on a ramp that compensated
for the uneven terrain and the difference in elevation between the valley
temple and the mortuary temple, which lay on the desert plateau.

Relief with the warlike
lion-goddess Sekhmet,
who is suckling the
pharaoh Niuserre and
thus ensuring the latter's
power and eternal life;
the king's pyramid
temple in Abusir (after
Borchardt).

Egyptologists call this corridor the causeway. It was also constructed of limestone blocks, and the indirect light that fell through the narrow openings in its flat ceiling slabs dimly illuminated the polychrome bas-reliefs. In the lower part of the causeway, mythical themes of an apotropaic character—the dismemberment of the leaders of enemy tribes, the incarnation of the powers of Evil and Chaos by the ruler in the form of a sphinx—were predominant. The reliefs in the causeway have been largely destroyed, as in other parts of the complex, but more secular subjects seem to have been depicted in its upper half: the completion of the work on the pyramid and an associated celebration including dance and sport performances, scenes of bringing offerings, and so on.

The mortuary temple (sometimes also called the pyramid temple or upper temple) was a spacious structure more or less rectangular in shape, its longer sides aligned with the east-west axis along which the pyramid complex as a whole was oriented. In spite of the structure's size, we can tell that it consisted of five basic elements: an entry hall, an open courtyard for sacrifices, a room with five niches for statues, an offering hall, and storerooms. A concern for symmetry is evident both in the arrangement of the parts and in the whole. Here as well, the dominant construction material was limestone blocks, but considerable quantities of other more valuable materials were also used: red and black granite, alabaster, and basalt.

The transition between the causeway and the temple was represented by the entry hall, a long and dimly lit room. Apparently, it was modeled on the contemporary royal palace and on court etiquette. Egyptologists used to associate it with the Sed festival, the symbolic celebrations held on the occasion of the thirty-year jubilee of the king's ascent to the throne. Today, basing their opinions on the original Egyptian description of the entry hall as "the house of the great," Egyptologists generally maintain that high dignitaries kept a vigil there during Sahure's entombment, in order to be able to greet the dead ruler. The entry hall led to a granite doorway that opened out onto a spacious courtyard.

Around this courtyard ran an ambulatory supported by pink granite columns in the form of palm trees. On the courtyard side of each column was carved a hieroglyphic inscription with the ruler's name, his titles, and symbols of the tutelary goddesses—on the north side of the courtyard Wadjet, and on the south side, Nekhbet. The pavement of black basalt slabs contrasted with the white limestone walls, richly ornamented with polychrome bas-reliefs. The ambulatory's ceiling was also colored blue with yellow stars to represent the night sky or the sky of the underworld. The subjects of the reliefs in the courtyard included the royal family, hunting, sea voyages, and enemies being ripped apart. It is even possible that additional statues stood there, representing kneeling, bound Asians, Nubians, and Libyans, in order to stress the idea of the pharaoh's mythical triumph. In the north-west corner of the courtyard stood the alabaster monolith of the altar, whose sides were decorated with scenes of sacrifice. Today it is still unclear why the altar was in this particular corner of the court-yard; we know only that the famous "royal offerings of the broad courtyard" were regularly sacrificed there.

A longer corridor that ran straight across the main axis of the temple and was richly decorated with reliefs divided the eastern, outer part from the western, inner area, to which only a few priests had access. This inner area represented the main crossing point for the passageways both inside the mortuary temple and in its imme-diate environment.

A smaller but very important room with five niches was located west of this transverse corridor. It was reached by a short, steep ala-baster stairway. The statues in the niches have not been preserved in Sahure's pyramid complex or in any other, and thus it is not sur-prising that only hypotheses exist regarding the appearance and meaning of the whole room. It was long supposed that these five statues symbolized five names, that is, five figures or functions of the Egyptian pharaoh. However, this assumption was shaken by the discovery of papyri in the archives of the nearby pyramid temple of Sahure's successor Neferirkare in the late nineteenth century. Writ-ing on one of the papyrus fragments suggests that one of the statues represented the king as ruler of Upper Egypt, a second as ruler of Lower Egypt, and a third as ruler over the realm of the dead, as Osiris. The identification of the two remaining statues does not appear on the papyrus.

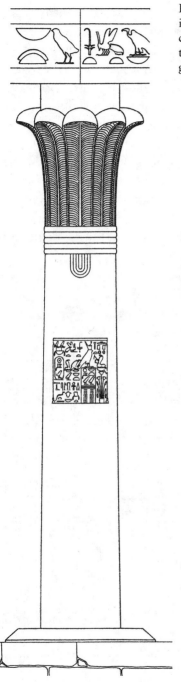

Palm-shaped column; Sahure's pyramid temple in Abusir (after Borchardt). On the shaft of the column is an inscription with the name and titles of the pharaoh Sahure and of the tutelary goddess of Lower Egypt, the cobra Wadjet.

Relief with Asiatic and Libyan prisoners, enemies of Egypt. Sahure's pyramid temple in Abusir (after Borchardt).

   In the farthest, westernmost part of the temple, near the east wall of the pyramid, was located the most significant place with regard to the worship of the dead—the offering hall. Its vaulted ceiling was illuminated by a flickering light only when ceremonies of sacrifice were being performed. It was entered through a black granite door, and the materials that were used to construct it produced striking color effects: the floor was of alabaster and the dado on the lower part of the wall was of black granite, while the upper part of the wall was of white limestone decorated with colorful scenes in bas-relief. On the west wall of the room, the one closest to the king's mummy inside the pyramid, was a "false door" made of granite, which may have been covered with copper or gold. Through it the spirit of the dead ruler was supposed to enter the room to eat his meal for the dead and

Prince Iunu's (Fourth Dynasty) funerary repast. Clad in a leopard skin, he sits at the offering table. His name and titles are recorded in the horizontal row of hieroglyphs on the upper border. Another component of the scene is a representation and a list of sacrificial offerings, which includes incense, fragrant balm, a basket of figs, and storehouses with various kinds of grain. (after Junker)

then return to his tomb. In this room stood a statue of the ruler carved in black granite, which embodied the spirit during the ceremonies of sacrifice.

On either side of this room, in the northwest and southwest parts of the mortuary temple, were two larger systems of storerooms of considerable capacity, built on two levels. Neither reliefs nor inscriptions appeared on the walls of the storerooms, so today it is difficult to determine with precision the function of the individual rooms. The smaller, northwestern storeroom apparently served as the temple's treasure chamber, in which, for example, cult vessels made of precious materials were kept.

In contrast, the larger, southwestern storeroom served to accommodate temporarily the sacrificial offerings, vessels with food and drink, sacks of grain, chests of linen, and the like. A smaller side entrance from the southwest, framed by two black granite columns, provided convenient access.

The mortuary temple included other spaces, such as the temple archive, in which papyrus scrolls and documents relating to religious activities were kept, and a room for the temple guard. There was also a small stairway that led to the roof terrace known as the "the temple's head," from which the priests observed the heavens day and night and made various astronomical measurements.

Near the mortuary temple's south wall, at the southeast corner of the pyramid, stood a miniature copy of its great neighbor. In the underground part of this tiny pyramid lay another burial chamber, but no one was buried in it. The meaning of this somewhat bizarre structure within the pyramid complex has long been debated by experts. It seems to have been purely symbolic and was perhaps meant to provide lodging for the ruler's spirit. Egyptologists call it the satellite or cult pyramid.

Sahure's true tomb was the great pyramid, which concluded the whole complex in the west. A corridor that began at the foot of the north wall led into the underground burial chamber. After the burial rites were completed and the king's mummy had been laid in a basalt sarcophagus, the entrance was sealed with huge stone blocks. The place in the north wall where the corridor came out was covered with a limestone slab in such a way that it could not be differentiated from the rest of the outside of the pyramid. Henceforth, nothing was to disturb the pharaoh's eternal rest. The enormous stone wall that surrounded the pyramid and the mortuary temple increased the seclusion and inaccessibility of the place where the god on earth rose into heaven.

The pyramid complex included auxiliary administrative and commercial buildings that had no direct ceremonial function but were nonetheless necessary to the worship of the dead. These were concentrated in immediate proximity to the valley temple, in the area where there was still vegetation and water. They provided lodging for the priests, as well as space for laundries, bakeries, slaughterhouses, offices, and markets. Sometimes they constituted whole "pyramid towns," large settlements with streets and many splendid buildings. It is assumed that the royal palace was also part of this complex.

Excavations have shown that the pyramid complex was in no sense a dead city in the scorching hot desert, but they have not yet produced much concrete information regarding its administrative background, the means by which it was financed, or the worship of the dead king. Surprisingly, not archaeologists but grave robbers have contributed most to the unraveling of this enigma.

The Testimony of the Temple Archives

At the end of the nineteenth century, grave robbers discovered scraps of papyrus in the ruins of Neferirkare's mortuary temple in Abusir, in close proximity to the royal pyramid. Shortly afterward, these fragments, after passing through several intermediaries, fell into the hands of Egyptologists, causing great excitement among scholars. Examination showed that these papyri came from the archive of Neferirkare's pyramid temple and were by far the oldest written documents of their kind. Most of them were bought by museums in Cairo, London, Berlin, and Paris—and the matter rested there for the moment. The ancient cursive (i.e., hieratic) writing proved difficult to decipher and, far from providing sensational new information, seemed at first to consist only of administrative records with no historical interest. The papyri once again fell into oblivion for a long time.

More than half a century later, another event attracted the attention of Egyptologists, this time in Paris. A librarian at the Sorbonne happened to open a folio of Maspero's papers, which had been brought back from Cairo after his death, and found in them a papyrus fragment. Subsequent analysis by the leading French papyrus expert, Georges Posener (1906–1988), showed that the fragment came from Neferirkare's temple archive. Posener's wife, the Egyptologist Paule Posener-Kriéger, took care of the fragment and gradually examined all the associated documents, which were scattered in museums all over the world. In 1976, after twenty years of arduous labor, she published an edition of the papyri from Neferirkare's temple archive and thereby offered Egyptologists an unexpected, completely novel, and sometimes astonishingly detailed view of the necropolis in Abusir and of "life" in the realm of the dead. The Czech archaeological expedition has recently made two further papyrus archives available. The smaller was found in the pyramid temple of the queen mother Khentkaues II, and the larger, which is comparable in scope to Neferirkare's, in Neferefre's pyramid complex.

The bureaucratic expertise and pedantic care with which the scribes prepared and archived their official and financial documents are today of incalculable assistance to Egyptologists. The documents' value is increased by the fact that the information recorded is factual, authentic, immediately and absolutely objective. It concerns the temple's accounts, duty rosters for priests, supervision of the temple's inventory, repair and improvement of damaged parts of the temple, preparations for ceremonies, correspondence with various offices, and much more. There is also no lack of royal decrees. What defect can we find in an archive in which a scribe notes that a chest in the storehouse contains a single pellet of natron, which was commonly used in the daily ceremonies? Probably only that no more than a small portion of the entire body of documents has been preserved.

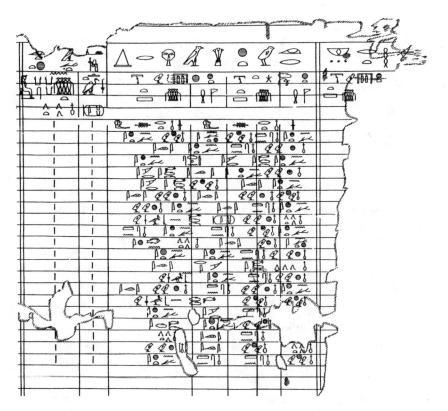

Hieroglyphic transcription of a segment of a text on a papyrus fragment from Neferirkare's mortuary temple. The text mentions the performance of ceremonies in the open courtyard around Neferirkare's pyramid and in the mortuary temple of the queen mother Khentkaues II (after Posener-Kriéger).

These papyri show that the activity in the mortuary temple was focused on the religious service. Rituals regularly enlivened the dark hall, and the spirit of the dead ruler came to his death table to feast. Every morning and evening a procession of priests passed, in flickering lamplight, into the five-niche room. They opened one small niche door after another and ritually cleaned the ruler's statue and rubbed it with fragrant oil before setting the magnificent table of sacrifices before the spirit who entered the statue. The lector priest rolled out the papyrus scroll and recited the formulas written on it. When the ritual was completed, the priests sprinkled the room with water and wiped away the traces of their presence as they went out, so that they could not be exploited by evil spirits. Then they went into the offering hall, in which they performed a similar ritual.

Every morning and every evening, the priests also went around the pyramid, sprinkling it with water and ritually cleaning it. When they had finished this and other prescribed ceremonies, they put the cult equipment in a chest and sealed it. The consumable part of the offerings was divided between the priests and the secular temple servants. The latter were numerous; dozens or even hundreds of people performed a range of auxiliary activities, from transporting offerings to guarding the complex, the number of servants depending on how well the temple was funded and its material needs met.

The meal provided for the spirit of the dead pharaoh was not the only ritual performed every day. Many other rituals relating to the festivals of the gods and important events in the life of the whole country also took place. The most common of these was the monthly lunar festival, which included the worship of the ruler's statue.

The famous Sokar festival occurred only once a year, on the twenty-sixth day of the fourth month of flood season.* On this occasion the god Sokar (the ruler of tombs and the dead, from whose name that of Saqqara was probably derived) visited the dead king. The large, very colorful procession, which could not enter the interior of the pyramid complex, stopped at the mooring point, and the ritual was carried out in the valley temple.

The festival of Re fell on the twenty-first day of the fourth month of the harvest season. All the priests stayed up during the preceding night and offered, under the direction of the lector priest, a sacrifice to the sun god, which ended before dawn with a ceremonial procession to the nearby temple of the sun.

The festival of the annual, life-giving Nile flood was evidently the feast day of the fertility goddess Hathor. Her return from the realm

---

* There were three seasons in the ancient Egyptian calendar: inundation season, sowing (literally "coming out") season, and harvest (literally "heat") season. Each consisted of four months of thirty days apiece. The remaining days were dedicated to the gods.

of the gods to the Nile Valley was associated with the return of the moon and the beginning of the floods.

The sed festival, as mentioned previously, was simply a memory of the thirty-year jubilee of the pharaoh's ascent to the throne, and it later took place at shorter intervals.

One of the most important festivals was that of the divine symbols— the griffin, the cobra goddess Wadjet, the scorpion goddess Selket, and others. This involved a large ceremonial gathering, in which not only all the priests and servants of the pyramid complex, but also the local population took part. Because of the great number of participants, the ceremonies, in which fetishes were worshiped, had to take place outside the pyramid complex.

The magnitude of some of these festivals is shown by one of the papyrus fragments from the temple archive of Neferirkare's successor, Neferefre, that was recently discovered by the Czech archaeological expedition in Abusir. It is an account indicating that on the occasion of a ten-day festival (about which we have no details), thirteen oxen were sacrificed to the pharaoh every day. Afterward, the priests divided all these sacrifices among themselves and the other participants. It is estimated that one ox was divided among as many as two thousand people. However, there are many indications that the meat was not used all at once; part of it was dried and stored.

It is clear that a large number of people and a considerable amount of financial support were required to keep the pyramid complex functioning with its daily sacrificial ceremonies and its religious festivals. For this reason the pharaoh, almost from the moment he ascended the throne, set about constructing his pyramid and chose land, villages, and workshops whose production was to ensure his eternal life. These so-called mortuary temple estates constituted only one of the pyramid complex's sources of income; other sources included the sun temple, which had its own resources and income, the royal residence, the palace, and temples of some gods. The size of the royal tomb complex, the large number of private tombs, and the scope of the worship of the dead would gradually but steadily exhaust the material resources and workforce. Indeed, the longing to be guaranteed eternal life in the beyond contributed in no small measure to the ex-

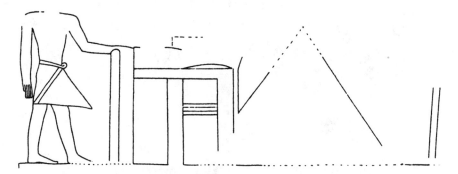

Fragmentary, somewhat enigmatic, but unique representation of a "priest opening the door to the temple at the foot of the pyramid" (?). Detail from the decoration of the tomb of Inti, called Shedu, in Deshasha (after Petrie).

haustion of the economic resources of the state and to doubts about the meaning of life in this world.

The basic echelon of the priests employed at the pyramid complex was "god's servants" and those who bore the ambiguous title of *khentiu-she*. The latter were responsible for various kinds of agricultural and technical work, the transportation of goods into the temple, and guard duty; they also took part in the ceremonies. Together with god's servants, they regularly spelled each other in their duties. A relatively small proportion of the temple personnel consisted of the priests who were known as "the pure." The lector priests constituted a very small and in many respects exclusive group that was not expected to perform any economic or guardian function but was responsible solely for the conduct of the ritual; they organized the ceremonies in accord with the principles of the temple cult.

In addition to the priests involved in the worship of the dead ruler, many other people worked at secular tasks connected with the daily life of the temple complex, and today it is still difficult to determine their precise function in relation to the king's tomb, despite the valuable information discovered in temple archives. This second group included high state officials—the vizier, judges, scribes, directors of royal affairs in the various areas of Upper and Lower Egypt, military commanders, storeroom supervisors, heads of the weaving shops, and so on. However, there were also butchers, hairdressers, manicurists,

Women personifying the funerary estates that provided the sacrifices for the worship of the dead. Ti's mastaba, Saqqara (Fifth Dynasty; after Wild).

physicians, and singers. Even the "flute-player of the White Crown," who played a role in the veneration of this symbol of dominion over Upper Egypt, must have been there.

The pyramid complex was thus in no way a secluded and abandoned world of eternal silence, a realm of death. It lived, and with it the whole cemetery around it lived its daily life and its festivals. No sharp dividing line was drawn between the world of the living and the world of the dead; the boundary was barely discernible. Life was preparation for eternity and death only an episode on the way toward it.

The discovery of the papyrus archives in Neferirkare's mortuary temple in Abusir made it possible to situate archaeological excavations in the pyramid necropolises in a much broader context. They helped answer many questions but also raised, as usual, new problems. For the first time, research on the pyramids entered a completely new, sensational dimension: archaeological discoveries could be directly checked against written descriptions, insofar as the latter were informative and well preserved. Conversely, archaeological discoveries helped to determine the meaning and wider context of unclear passages in the descriptions.

The papyri also refer to temples and palaces that once existed in the necropolis near Abusir but have not yet been discovered. Up to now, not a single royal palace from the Old Kingdom has been discovered and archaeologically explored. The papyrus archives can therefore necessitate more intensive excavations, particularly since discoveries of similar documents from that period are unlikely.

CHAPTER THREE

THE CONSTRUCTION OF THE PYRAMIDS

The White Stone

An accessible abundance of many kinds of building stone so strongly marked ancient Egyptian civilization that the latter was sometimes called the state of stone. Limestone was especially plentiful because during the Cretaceous period Egypt was covered with seawater.

The ancient Egyptians called limestone white stone and made full use of its advantages, especially in construction and statuary. For a long time limestone was the fundamental construction material, and its characteristics had a profound effect on the works of the age of the pyramids. Only in the middle of the second millennium B.C.E., at the beginning of the New Kingdom, did architects begin to make increasing use of sandstone, especially in the southern part of the country.

The Egyptians first became acquainted with quarrying and shaping limestone during the construction of the oldest tombs in Saqqara. Here, not far from the White Walls, the capital city of united Egypt, the oldest monumental stone architecture in the world was born.

Several favorable circumstances led to the use of limestone for construction in Saqqara. The stone there is not of very high quality, but it is sedimented in regular, strong layers as much as half a meter thick, some of which differ in color and are separated from each other by thin layers of clay. This made quarrying easy, and it could even be carried on near the construction site. All workers had to do was measure the length and breadth of the building blocks and mark them out on the stone; their thickness was determined by that of the layer. Between the marks corresponding to the length of the future blocks, small passageways were left that were just wide enough for a worker to dig out a deep ditch. In this way it was possible to rapidly break out blocks of a standard size.

The workers used copper pickaxes and chisels, as well as hammers made of granite, dolerite, and other kinds of hard stone. The work of any given laborer was controlled by means of a stick wielded from the top of the shaft. The remains of such quarries have been found not only in Saqqara but also in Giza, Dahshur, and elsewhere. The limestone from those quarries was of lesser quality, however—coarse grained and with yellow to greenish gray shadowing; therefore, it was used for the inner parts of the wall and for the inner core of the pyramid. For the outer casing, fine-grained white limestone was used, but it was not available on the west bank of the Nile in the area of the capital city.

The nearest source of such finer stone to the capital was in the Muqattam hills west of the Nile, not far from modern Tura and Maasara. The stone lay far from the surface there and had to be mined by digging tunnels, which created enormous caverns that were sometimes ten meters high and descended as much as fifty meters below the surface. Some of the rock debris has remained, but not many written documents—instructions, marks on the stone, and the like—could be preserved, since shortly after being incised on the rock walls, they were usually knocked off along with the stone blocks. The ancient Egyptians broke the large chunks of stone into smaller blocks and then listed them in their registers with bureaucratic precision, in the interest both of monitoring performance and of determining whether the blocks met the demands of the construction project that was planned or already being carried out.

The blocks were dragged down to the mooring on the banks of the Nile by men and animals working together, as demonstrated by one of the images preserved on a rock wall near Tura. It shows a large block of limestone lying on a wooden sledge, hitched to three brace of oxen. The path to the bank had to be well prepared, leveled out and sprinkled with water mixed with mud from the Nile, in order to reduce the friction. The work in the quarries did not continue uninterrupted with a set group of laborers but was instead carried out

The map of the quarry in Wadi Hammamat is preserved on a papyrus from the Twentieth Dynasty (Egyptian Museum in Turin, nos. 1879, 1899, 1969).

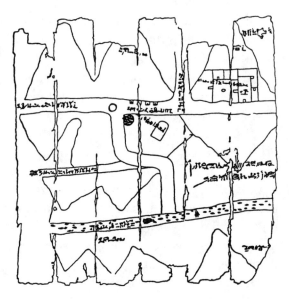

periodically, depending on the size of the edifice under construction. The state organized workforces, placed them under paramilitary command, and sent them into the quarries. As the sole proprietor of the country's natural resources and labor, the ruler had ultimate control over the entire process.

Expeditions to the Quarries

For construction, especially royal construction, other kinds of stone were needed as well. These generally lay far from the capital city, around which the greatest construction activity was concentrated. Pink granite was quarried far in the south, at the first cataract of the Nile, near modern Aswan; alabaster around Hatnub in Central Egypt; diorite in the eastern desert or in Nubia, near modern Abu Simbel; and slate and many other kinds of stone in Wadi Hammamat, in the "valley of baths," and in other places in the eastern desert. While unskilled labor, which was sufficient for the quarrying and transportation of large volumes of stone, constituted most of the workforces sent to quarries near the capital city, more qualified workers were sent to the distant places where precious materials were found, accompanied by a considerable number of soldiers who protected them in regions populated by dangerous Bedouins.

Many extant sources, including inscriptions on rock walls along the way or in the quarries themselves, yield information about these expeditions. Some of them suggest that the expeditions were carried out under the ruler's command. Often we encounter references to dates, the expedition's goal, the number of participants, and expressions of gratitude to the tutelary divinities. The organizational structure and leadership of the expeditions are significantly reflected in the titles of their leaders and other participants. Expedition leaders were commonly called "troop commanders," "fleet commanders," "chiefs of the royal works," and "bearers of the god's seal" (the ruler's seal). Scribes and priests aided the expedition's leadership. There were specialists such as prospectors and stonemasons. The inscriptions at the alabaster quarries in Hatnub indicate that an overall number of workers ranged from three hundred to sixteen hundred, and alabaster was one of the more valuable stones used to a limited extent, so there would have been fewer workers in the alabaster quarries than in the limestone quarries.

Transporting the quarried building stones presented an exceptionally difficult task from a technical and organizational standpoint. The size and weight of the blocks varied considerably. Some of the blocks from nearby quarries used in the construction of Menkaure's pyramid in Giza reached the gigantic proportions of 8.5 by 5.3 by 3 meters, and a weight of some 220 tons. When the stone was not available close to the building site, it sometimes had to be brought down the Nile as far as several hundred kilometers. This was the fastest and least difficult mode of transportation, and written and pictorial evidence proves that it was quite often used, taking advantage of a network of artificial canals, and especially the annual floods, which caused the Nile's level to rise several meters so that its water flowed far out over the land, right up to the foot of the desert plateau chosen as a construction site. In that way, overland transport could be reduced to a minimum, and in the higher locations it offered a natural means of moving heavy stone blocks onto the construction site.

Transportation of
a huge statue.
Scene from the
tomb decoration of
the nomarch
Djehutihotep in
Bersha.

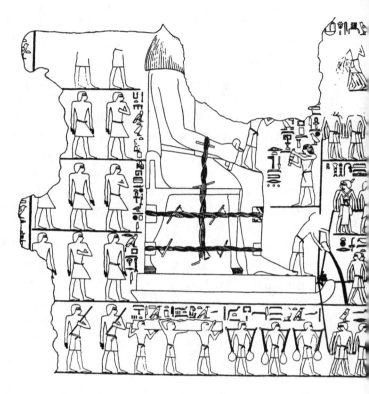

Not all researchers agree that the main transportation work was done during the period of flooding on the Nile. They point out, for example, that the heavily laden boats would not have been able to navigate the overflowing Nile without peril, and the flooded banks would have made unloading more difficult. The French scholar Georges Goyon assumes that the transportation of materials for the construction of the pyramids went on over the whole year, and that for this purpose the ancient Egyptians used an artificial waterway, which they called the Great Canal. This canal, which may have been laid out during the First Dynasty and is now called in Arabic Bahr el-Jussef (Joseph's River), branches off from the Nile in Upper Egypt and runs parallel to it for some two hundred and twenty kilometers; then it turns west into the Fayyum oasis. From there it runs northward, under the name of Bahr el-Libeini (the Libyan Canal), past the

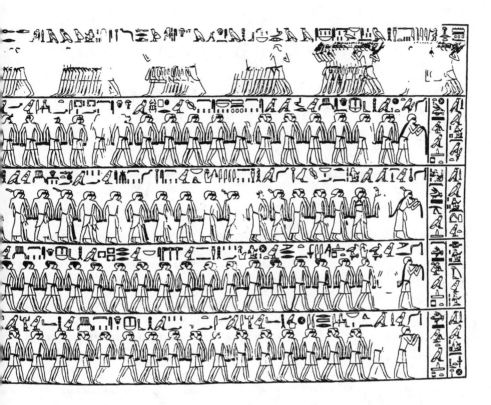

foot of the rock plateaus with the pyramids, and finally flows, near Alexandria, into Lake Maryut and the Mediterranean. Goyon found archaeological remnants of a port on the canal that was established for the construction of Khafre's and Menkaure's pyramid complexes in Giza, as well as those of Unas and Pepi II in Saqqara.

However, water did not provide transportation for the greater part of the materials necessary for the construction of the pyramids. As previously mentioned, most of the stone came from quarries near the construction sites. Indeed, the proximity of a sufficient supply of easily accessible limestone was one of the chief criteria determining the choice of the site for a pyramid. On the basis of archaeological evidence, we can reconstruct the local production of limestone and its transport to the building site. For example, south and southwest of the Red Pyramid in Dahshur, limestone quarries were discovered from

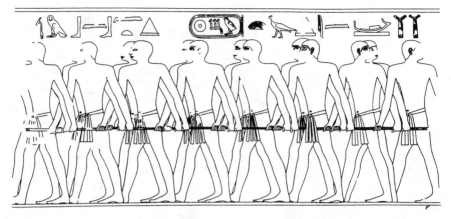

The transportation of a pyramidion to Sahure's pyramid construction site in Abusir. The representation of the pyramidion itself was on a subsequent block, which has not yet been found. This can be inferred from the inscription, which even implies that the pyramidion was covered with gold. Detail of the decoration of the causeway leading to the king's pyramid.

which three access roads (ca. one kilometer long and fifteen meters wide) led to the pyramid. On the ruins of the core of this structure are three mason's inscriptions that make it possible to estimate the scope of the works. According to them, workers transported three hundred to six hundred blocks daily.

Sun and Stars, Poles and Ropes

Building a pyramid involved more than supplying and transporting the necessary materials; it was a multifaceted enterprise involving a

Late Period rock drawing from the Tura limestone quarries depicting the transport of a limestone block on a wooden sledge drawn by three brace of oxen.

number of specialists led by the "royal master builder." The vizier, in his capacity as "head of all royal works," was ultimately responsible for the success of this enterprise and had at his disposal all the necessary means, including a list of all the residents capable of working, which was kept in the "bookhouse" or archive of the royal residence.

The first step in the process was taken in the "project office," where specialists drew up plans on papyrus; while building was under way, they drew sketches of construction details on papyri or flat slabs of limestone. It can even be assumed that planners made models of whole projects. Evidence of this appears in some archaeological discoveries, such as the limestone model of the substructure of an unknown pyramid (probably from the Thirteenth Dynasty) that was found in Amenemhet III's valley temple in Dahshur.

The extent of ancient Egyptian mathematical knowledge is evident in many extant written documents. The Rhind papyrus and the Moscow papyrus, for example, contain various mathematical procedures and problems that show that although ancient Egyptians were not able to formulate mathematical laws with precision, they possessed sound practical knowledge and knew how to make the fullest use of it. They worked with a decimal system and were able to use fractions. They could calculate the area of a triangle, a rectangle, a circle, and even the surface area of a hemisphere; they could determine angles and the volumes of geometrical shapes, including pyramids, cylinders, and cones. They also knew the relationship between the sides of a right triangle—Pythagoras's theorem—constructing the right angle using a triangle whose sides were in a ratio of 3 : 4 : 5.

Schematic plan of the stone tomb of Ramesses IV, sketched on papyrus (Twentieth Dynasty; Egyptian Museum in Turin, no. 1885).

The ancient Egyptians' constructions are the best evidence of their mathematical capacities. Let us take, for instance, the Great Pyramid in Giza. If we imagine a circle whose radius is the height of the pyramid, then the circumference is identical with the base of the pyramid. This could be achieved only if the wall had the correct angle, and everything had to be calculated in advance. We can conclude that although the ancient Egyptians could not precisely define the value of *pi,* in practice they used it.

The subsequent stages were no less demanding than the preparations. The selection of the site of the future pyramid was very important, and Egyptologists are still trying to decide what actually influenced it. At this point, we do not always know exactly why one ruler had his pyramid built in Giza, while another from the same dynasty had his built in Dahshur. Different considerations probably played a role in the decision.

The importance of easy availability of limestone has already been mentioned. According to another view, expressed many years ago by the famed German Egyptologist Adolf Erman, the sites chosen for the construction of pyramids varied with the placement of the royal residences. The latter were in the Nile Valley, amid gardens and fields near the capital city, Memphis.* According to this view, the pyramid's construction was directed from the royal residence, imposing an enormously expensive burden and a complicated task on the state's administrative apparatus.

In a few cases, the selection of a site was also influenced by the insufficient amount of space remaining in the previous tomb area. Additional motives might be religious-political (for instance, having one's pyramid erected near the oldest step pyramid in Saqqara) and might also, of course, have to do with family relationships (for example, Neferirkare's family members had their own enclosed family cemetery set up near Abusir).

---

* Since no royal residence from the Old Kingdom has yet been found, the question arises whether it might be the other way around, that is, whether the construction of a pyramid was not a reason for constructing a royal residence nearby. We shall return to this problem later on, when we deal with the manner in which the pyramids were built.

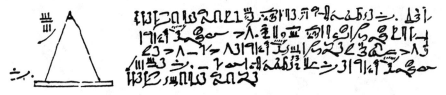

Mathematical problems on the Rhind papyrus (Second Intermediate Period) concerning the calculation of the height of a pyramid (after Peet).

The chosen site was prepared and important foundation ceremonies were carried out before construction began. In the course of the foundation rituals a special role was played by Seshat, the goddess of writing and the protectress of scribes and master builders. In the extant depictions—which are not directly connected with the pyramids—Seshat and the ruler hold in their hands a pole and a loop of rope, both of which were important tools for measuring the foundation of the future pyramid. During the ceremonies, animal sacrifices were offered to the gods and then laid, along with other objects—such as vessels symbolizing additional offerings, small tablets with the names of the owner of the future structure, and models of the construction tools—in the foundations, usually in the corners of the structure, atop a layer of pure sand.

Determining the precise orientation of the pyramid was a very important and demanding operation. The axes of its sides were aligned with the four cardinal directions (a few small step pyramids built at the end of the Third Dynasty and the beginning of the Fourth Dynasty are exceptions to this rule, but they were not tombs). Egyptologists used to believe that the builders determined the pyramid's north-south axis by reference either to the Pole Star (then the star Alpha Draconis) or to other circumpolar stars. According to this view, a man stood in the middle of a simple circular structure made of mudbricks and observed the rise and setting of a given star in relation to this artificial horizon. The observations were carried out using a simple, fork-shaped sight called a *bay*. Then a second man, following the directions of the observer, used a plumb line, a *merkhet*, to mark on the top and bottom of the wall the precise points over which the star had risen and

During the "stretching the cord" ceremony, the goddess Seshat and Queen Hatshepsut, represented as a male pharaoh, found the shrine by driving in the baseline stakes, to which a cord is tied. Egyptologists disagree regarding the precise technical meaning of this ceremony. Some think it had to do with the determination of the axis or corners of the planned structure, while others see it as a way of keeping the baseline stakes in a vertical position without using a plumb bob. Detail from the decoration of the so-called Red Chapel in Karnak (Eighteenth Dynasty).

set. The line connecting the midpoint between the two marks and the observer's standpoint thus determined the north-south axis. The measurement could be made more precise through observation of other stars.

Quite recently, a new theory was published by the British scholar K. Spence. According to Spence, the ancient Egyptians aligned the pyramids by using the simultaneous transit of two circumpolar stars (Delta Ursae Majoris and Beta Ursae Minoris or Epsilon Ursae Majoris and Gamma Ursae Minoris) in order to establish true north. On the basis of this hypothesis, Spence calculated the accession dates of some ancient Egyptian kings. This theory will certainly incite further scholarly debate.

However, it is just as possible that the orientation of the foundation was determined by observing not the stars, but the sun. As demonstrated, for example, by a Slovak Egyptologist, D. Magdolen, the east-west axis could be determined with the help of wooden stakes and ropes such as those the goddess Seshat and the ruler hold in their hands in the depictions of the foundation ceremonies. At the equinox, a stake driven vertically into the earth threw a shadow that pointed exactly to the west at the moment of sunrise, and at the moment of sunset pointed exactly to the east. This determination could

Offerings were made when important construction projects such as temples and pyramids were begun. A few symbolic objects, including certain sacrifices—so-called foundation deposits—were usually laid in a hole in the building's foundation. In a fragment of a scene from Niuserre's sun temple in Abu Ghurab, the ruler is shown kneeling while performing this rite.

Merkhet and *bay*, tools used by ancient Egyptian astronomers and architects (after Borchardt).

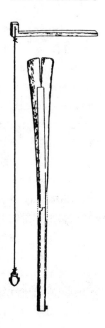

be made not only at the equinox but at any time of the day or year; one had only to make additional measurements.

The pyramid's foundation had to be precisely level, and the architects made use of a simple method for determining it. They built a trough out of mudbricks and filled it with water. Marking the water level on the walls of the trough enabled them to obtain a precisely horizontal line. The remains of these clay structures, used to determine and inscribe a horizontal line on the east wall of the foundation platform, have been found in Neferefre's unfinished pyramid in Abusir. Our knowledge of this process helps explain a slight error made in determining the foundation level of the Great Pyramid in Giza, where the southeast corner is about two centimeters higher than the northwest corner. The prevailing wind from the north probably raised the water level by two centimeters at the south end of the trough on that side of the pyramid.

The angle of the pyramid's walls was not calculated but rather constructed with the help of a right triangle. The hypotenuse was always one ell long, whereas the adjoining legs of the triangle varied

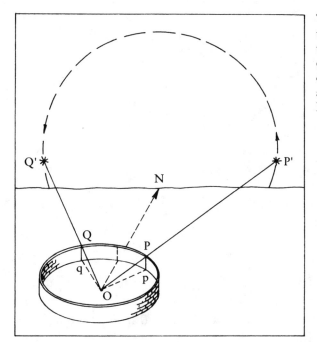

The determination of the north-south axis on the basis of observations of the rising and setting of a selected star on the artificial horizon (after Edwards).

in length. The relationship between the two sides was called *seked*. Using the angles determined in this way, the architects set up a simple wooden frame for the construction itself. Today Egyptian architects employ a similar tool in reconstructing monuments.

The completion of a pyramid was accompanied by celebrations and ceremonies such as those depicted in bas-reliefs on stone blocks from Sahure's causeway in Abusir; in them, workers pull a sledge bearing a gilded pyramidion (as the inscription over the scene allows us to infer, see fig. on p. 68), foremen and work teams render homage to the ruler, harem women perform ceremonial dances, and so on.

The Secret Lies in the Organization of the Work

The size of the pyramids and of stone blocks used to build them led the ancients to make fantastic estimates of the number of workers that had been involved. To a certain extent this is understandable. At the

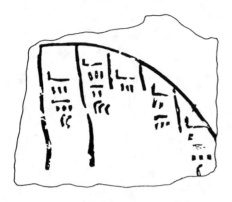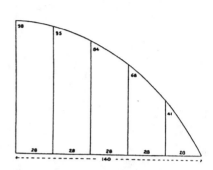

Limestone shard from the Djoser pyramid field with information on the construction of a vault (after Lauer).

beginning of the Fourth Dynasty, for example, King Snefru, in the course of his more than three-decade rule (cf. p. 179), constructed three pyramid (and, in addition, a small pyramid in Seila) complexes with a combined volume of about 3.7 cubic meters of stone. The volume of the masonry of all the royal structures built during the century and a half reign of the Fourth Dynasty is estimated to be about nine million cubic meters. These figures are all the more astounding when one considers that no more than one and a half million people lived in all Egypt at that time.

The Greek historian Herodotus wrote that during the construction of the Great Pyramid in Giza, 100,000 men worked for twenty years, three months at a time. (These work periods clearly correspond to the three seasons of the ancient Egyptian calendar.) Herodotus's view was considered plausible by even so experienced an archaeologist as Petrie. In his opinion, the main work was done during flood season, when the rural population could not work in the fields.

Other scholars have based their estimates on the construction work to be done. Ludwig Borchardt and Louis Croon assumed that the work could have gone on throughout the year. On the basis of research on the pyramid at Meidum, they came to the conclusion that about 10,000 men took part in its construction, including the transportation of materials. Extrapolating from this figure, they estimated that

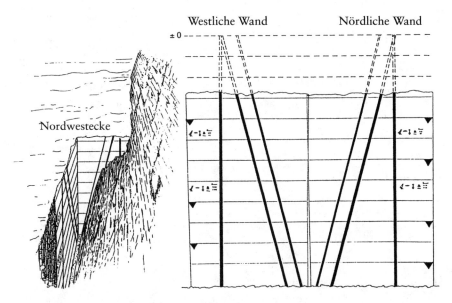

During excavations in Meidum, Petrie discovered next to mastaba no. 17 (beginning of the Fourth Dynasty) an important measuring device that provides clear evidence of the procedure used by the ancient Egyptian architects to determine the gradient of the outer tomb walls and to check it during construction. On the northwest corner of the mastaba, where the structure was below the level of the surrounding terrain, a network of lines was inscribed on the side walls of the stone foundation—horizontal lines one cubit apart as well as vertical lines and sloping lines showing the gradient of the mastaba walls. These lines were accompanied by short, explanatory inscriptions with information concerning the distance from the side of the foundation.

for the Great Pyramid in Giza approximately 36,000 men would have sufficed. Yet even this figure ultimately seemed too high to them, given the limited area of the construction site and the difficulties connected with lodging and supply.

By calculating the work that must have been involved in transporting an object of a given mass over a given distance, Kurt Mendelssohn, an American mathematician and physicist of German descent, arrived at a figure of 50,000 workers and at most 70,000 helpers. The calculations of the Polish architect Wieslaw Koziński, who believes that it must have taken an average of 25 men to transport a block weighing one and one-half tons, led in an entirely different direction. Since he

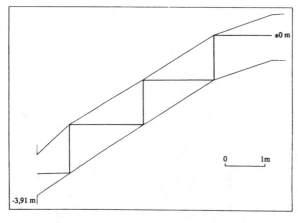

The mason's drawing inscribed on the ceiling of the descending and bending corridor leading to the burial chamber of Ptahshepses's mastaba in Abusir shows a system of lines enclosing a right angle. By means of this simple procedure the precise alignment with the cardinal directions was also transferred to the burial chamber, which lay almost four meters under the foundation level of the mastaba.

estimates that there were 60,000 men outside the construction site and 300,000 inside it, he arrives at the same figure as Diodorus did in antiquity. However, Koziński based his calculations on the erroneous assumption that Egypt's population was between 5 and 10 million people at that time.

Recent discoveries suggest a new way of approaching this problem. In the mid-1980s a French and Egyptian team researching the Great Pyramid began to use ultrasound technology. Their measurements showed that in the core of the Great Pyramid large cavities had been filled with pure sand. During construction the "chamber method"* was probably used, which significantly accelerated the work and made it easier and less expensive. In the light of these discoveries, all the complicated calculations and estimates concerning how many million stone blocks make up the Great Pyramid, and the speculations based on them, are thus built on sand.

Another valuable source of information is provided by the signs, simple inscriptions, and sketches marked in red, black, and sometimes

---

* In this method, the perimeter walls were first built, and then the space within the structure was filled with sand or chunks of limestone held together here and there by mortar.

yellow on the pyramid's stone blocks and walls. In comparison with the monumental and artistically achieved hieroglyphic inscriptions, these are humble inscriptions, and for a long time they were considered historically insignificant—perhaps in part because they are often scraped away, difficult to access, and hard to read. Together with other inscriptions that have been discovered, and that generally have to do with state administration, they now allow us to reconstruct the mode of organization and direction of the work on the largest construction sites of ancient Egypt. In particular, they tell us what procedural systems existed at the time of the construction of the pyramids.

Part of the labor force was organized in accord with the ancient organizational principle originally used to direct a boat crew. The basic unit of the "team" included about two hundred men and was composed of five "phyloi" (from the Greek *phylē*: tribe, group, brotherhood), named after the different parts of the boat—bow–right side, bow–left side, stern–right side, stern–left side. The name given to the fifth and last group has not yet been satisfactorily explained; perhaps it was related to the helmsman's position. Each "phylē" was then divided into four (at a later time, two) groups. These also had names, which were sometimes related to the workers' geographical origin and sometimes to the required skills or virtues, such as endurance, strength, and a sense of teamwork. Apparently, no more than three teams, comprising six hundred men, worked on the project at any given time. Each unit—team, phylē, or group—had a leader. The question remains

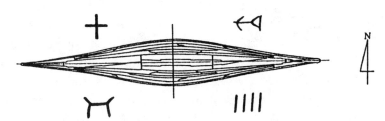

The distribution of the labor force on the model of the organization of a boat crew is illustrated by the schema of Khufu's (Cheops's) death boat, with signs indicating the four different parts of the boat. The latter have been marked out by the master builders in order to organize the workers simply and quickly (after Abu Bakr and Ahmad Yousef).

what the workers directed in this way actually did. The origin of the system suggests that they were probably involved with transportation, since this work required that the strength of smaller groups of men be coordinated to ensure the smooth, rapid delivery of construction materials by both water and land.

In addition to the "team" system, another system was used in construction, which involved dividing up workers according to the cardinal compass points, north, south, and west. An eastern group is nowhere documented, and another term was used in its place, perhaps because in Egyptian *eastern,* like *left,* meant "bad." The four sides together made up a larger unit called a troop. Much evidence suggests that the craftsmen and specialized workers on the pyramid construction sites were organized in accord with this model. However, there is no indication in the extant documents of how many workers made up a side or a whole troop.

Workers divided into teams or troops represented only a minority on the construction site. These two categories of workers, although specialized and no doubt productive, could not have erected a pyramid by themselves. From the layout and volume of the masonry we can conclude that it constituted the largest part of the work required, but it is nonetheless certain that a significant number of helpers must also have been involved in the construction, although no extant written sources from the period give us any precise information about them. We can only infer their existence from the magnitude and complexity of the construction and from a few documents.

In Pepi II's decrees granting privileges to the Min Temple in Coptos, we find, in connection with the exemption of temple servants from the duty to work for the ruler, the expression "assignment to every task for the King." The text goes on to explain that this work duty includes "carrying" and "transport using wood." Other inscriptions inform us about additional kinds of heavy labor—for example, working in the fields or digging trenches for irrigation canals. These tasks were imposed in particular on the largest population group in ancient Egypt, the agricultural workers, who could not work in the fields during the annual flood season. During that season they were the only available source of unskilled labor large enough for the construction of pyramids.

It is not known how many rural people were involved in the construction. We also do not know how these seasonal workers were commanded, and it is possible that their work could not even be registered, among other reasons because doing so would have involved too great an administrative expenditure. Concerning the magnitude of the anonymous mass of people who worked on the pyramids, we have merely a few estimates. In the case of the Great Pyramid at Giza, the current consensus among Egyptologists sets the figure at a little more than 30,000.

Ancient Egyptian documents and depictions tell us nothing about the conditions under which the construction workers lived and how they were compensated for their labor. Herodotus asserts that "on the pyramids, the quantities of radishes, onions, and garlic consumed by the workers are written in Egyptian writing," but this assertion is not reliable. Against it speaks not only the fact that no such inscription has ever been found, but also and especially the ancient Egyptians' belief that such banal evidence of calculation would profane the pharaoh's tomb. However, it is fairly certain that the ancient Egyptian scribes did keep such records, and with their usual bureaucratic precision preserved them in the corresponding archives, which either have been destroyed or remain undiscovered.

Among the few extant documents relating to construction work in the era of the pyramids, a Sixth Dynasty papyrus text found in Saqqara is of particular interest. This is a letter from the foreman of a work party in the limestone quarry near Tura to the official entrusted with directing the construction work or with receiving deliveries of construction materials. In his letter, the foreman complains that clothes for his workers have not been received on time and that time has been lost waiting for them; thus he indirectly draws attention to the resulting delays in the planned work schedule. This text also suggests that the work party was staying near the royal residence. It can therefore be assumed that the state not only provided clothing for the workers, but also fed and lodged them. Naturally, this holds true only for large royal construction projects, whereas quite different conditions obtained in the case of smaller private projects, which became increasingly common, particularly in the later Old Kingdom.

Lifting Devices or Ramps?

Questions regarding the number of people involved in the construction of the pyramids and the conditions under which they worked constitute only one of the pyramids' riddles. No less important and interesting is the question of how heavy materials, sometimes stone blocks weighing several dozen tons, were lifted so high.

Two ancient historians attempted to answer this question. Herodotus (*Histories,* Book 2, chapter 125) provides the older of the two accounts: "At first, it [the pyramid] was built with steps, like a staircase. . . . The stones intended for use in constructing the pyramid were lifted by means of a short wooden scaffold. In this way they were raised from the earth to the first step of the staircase; there they were laid on another scaffold, by means of which they were raised to the second step. Lifting devices were provided for each step, in case these devices were not light enough to be easily moved upward from step to step once the stone had been removed from them. I have been told that both methods were used, and so I mention them both here. The finishing-off was begun at the top, and continued downward to the lowest level."

In his *Bibliotheca,* Diodorus Siculus offers another explanation: "It is said that the stone was brought over a great distance, from Arabia, and that the construction was undertaken with the help of ramps, since at that time cranes had not yet been invented."

These very different accounts provide the basis for modern approaches to the problem. Some researchers, relying on Herodotus, assume that the stone blocks were raised with the help of simple wooden structures, while others, following Diodorus, maintain that massive, elaborate ramps were used. There are other theories as well, ranging from the technically plausible to the highly fantastic, but they are contradicted by archaeological information concerning the ancient Egyptians' technical capacities.

When miniature models of simple wooden "cradles" constructed of arched elements bound together with short poles were found during nineteenth-century excavations, it was suggested that they might be the "lifting devices" mentioned by Herodotus. (It should be noted that these discoveries were not made in the area around the pyramids, but rather in Upper Egypt.) These devices consisted of slings and wooden wedges and could be used to lift small stone blocks. In no case, however, would they have been able to lift huge monoliths weighing several dozen tons, and so they do not provide an answer to the fundamental question.

Herodotus's account also prompted other reflections. At the beginning of the twentieth century, Louis Croon imagined a simple water-scoop crane consisting of horizontal and vertical beams that worked like a lever. When a block had been raised to a higher level, the wooden structure was also moved to the next level. Croon's conception had one drawback, however: once again, such a device could have been used to raise only small blocks. Also, up to this point, no remains of such devices have been found in the course of excavations. Moreover, although the ancient Egyptians were acquainted with this kind of device, which they used to scoop up water and which is now known in Egypt as a *shadoof,* the first evidence of its existence dates from the New Kingdom, more than a thousand years after the pyramids were constructed.

Egyptologists have made further suggestions based on a similar principle. One of these assumed that a counterweight was used to lift heavy burdens. Others posited the existence and use of a winch, block and tackle, or pulley, but all these technical devices were unknown at the time of the construction of the pyramids. A discovery made in the 1930s by the Egyptian archaeologist Selim Hassan near the valley temple of the pyramid field in Giza reopened the debate. He found a large stone object that looked like a nail in whose hammered head three parallel notches had been cut. This object was probably once firmly anchored in some sort of structure, with a rope running through the notches. Therefore, it could have been a pseudo-pulley.

The use of a pseudo-pulley, or merely a simple round beam, is central to the theory proposed by the French architect Guerrière. His solution is based on the assumption that the central part of the core of the pyramid was first built up to a certain height and then broadened by means of "accretion layers" of stonemasonry constructed in separate stages. In his view, two groups of workers raised the blocks, using ropes thrown over the top of the central part of the core and

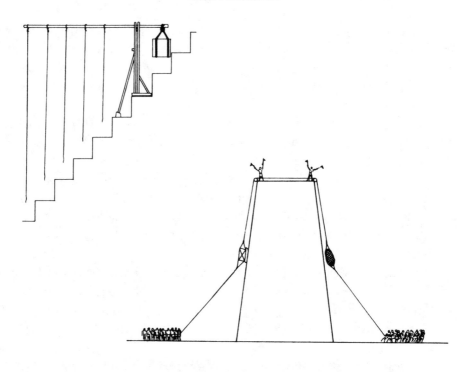

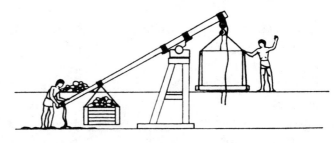

Modern concep-
tions of simple
devices that,
according to some
researchers, might
have been used in
the construction of
the pyramids. After
Croon (upper left),
Guerrière (middle),
Adam (lower
right), and Isler
(following page).

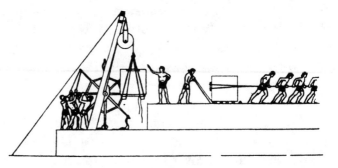

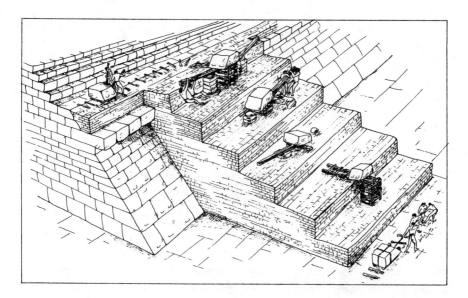

running either over a round, greased beam or through the notches in a pseudo-pulley. A counterweight may have been used to make the task easier. The work was directed by means of flag signals given from the apex of the structure. However, grave objections have been raised against this theory. It remains unclear just how the tall central portion of the structure is supposed to have been constructed, and in any case even very strong ropes made of papyrus, grasses, or palm fronds could not have held the enormous stone blocks. Finally, archaeological investigations of pyramid cores that lie open in ruins have not provided any evidence to support Guerrière's suggestion.

Today, most conceptions of pyramid construction are based on Diodorus's account, which describes the use of inclined planes or

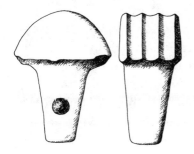

Stone pseudo-pulleys discovered in Giza by Selim Hassan.

\ 85 \

ramps. His account has been lent some support by archaeologists' discovery of the remains of ramps, which have been found in Meidum, Dahshur, Abu Ghurab, and Abusir. However, it might be more appropriate to see these ramps as having been used for delivering construction materials.

The ramp theory is also based on certain ancient Egyptian written documents, such as papyruses featuring mathematical problems connected with construction projects. The Anastasi I papyrus mentions an inclined plane that was 730 cubits long (1 cubit = 18 inches) and 55 cubits wide, and as high as 60 cubits. The outside walls and the framework of the ramp were made of bricks, while the inside was filled with sand. However, those who adhere to this theory disagree as to what such a ramp looked like. The German architect and archaeologist Uvo Hölscher (1878–1963), who conducted excavations at Khafre's pyramid complex in Giza, assumed that a ramp was constructed on each of the four sides of the pyramid, zigzagging upward from one corner to the other as building moved upward. However, this kind of ramp would not have provided an adequate means of delivering materials for the construction of the lower- and middle-level parts of the pyramid, since at those levels the amount needed was enormous.

The American researchers Dows Dunham and W. Vose assumed that a single ramp about three meters wide, which wound in a spiral around the whole structure, was used. But the previously mentioned objection is pertinent here as well: on such a small ramp—which would have grown narrower as the structure rose and grew narrower itself—the required materials could not have been delivered as quickly as written sources indicate they were.

Goyon's theory overcomes some of these objections. In his view, there was a single ramp, but it did not go around the whole structure, and it was so wide that several ox teams could have been used simultaneously to drag the stone blocks upward. In addition, Goyon's theory posits a ramp structure that left all four corners of the pyramid free so that ongoing measurements could be made. However, in this case as well, the ramps would necessarily have grown narrower as they rose, and they would also have had to be extremely long. In

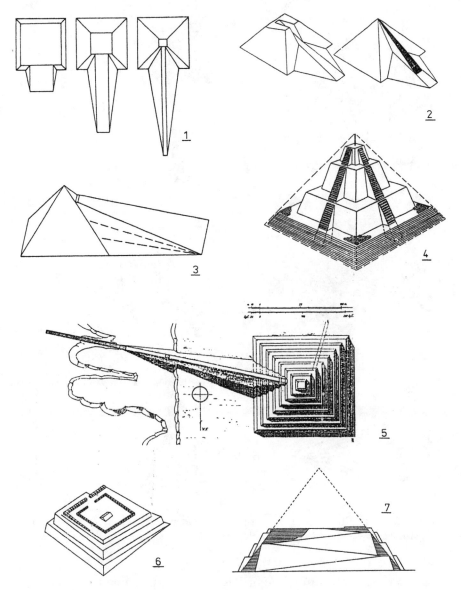

Some types of ramps that are supposed to have been used on the pyramid construction sites (1 and 2 after Arnold; 3 after Petrie; 4 after Isler; 5 after Borchardt; 6 after Goyon; 7 after Hölscher)

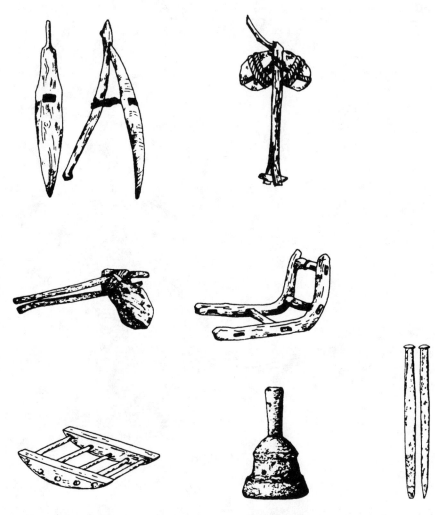

Tools used by the builders of the pyramids: wooden pickaxes, stone-mason's flint drill, stone ax, wooden sledge, "cradle," wooden mallet, copper chisels.

other words, such ramps might have made it possible to build small pyramids, but not large ones.

The English archaeologist Petrie, who devoted a great deal of time to research on the pyramids, imagined that a single, vertical ramp was built on only one side of a pyramid and extended as the structure grew. According to Petrie, the ramp was built with bricks, clay, and sand, as well as with round wooden beams, and its overall volume would have been at least as great as that of the pyramid itself. A basic defect in this theory is the fact that the construction of such a ramp would itself have required an enormous amount of material. We are again forced to ask when and by whom the ramp would have been removed, and especially where it would have been placed. So far, no such huge mass of material has been found near the pyramids.

Dieter Arnold agrees with Petrie that there was a single, vertical ramp going up one side of the pyramid. However, he supposes that the ramp was considerably smaller and ended inside the pyramid. Construction material could thus have been used twice as effectively, being employed both for the ramp and for the pyramid itself. Although Arnold's theory seems fairly plausible, it also has a weakness: it does not explain how the upper part of the pyramid was finished off, including the installation of a monolithic pyramidion as the apex. Arnold surmises that this was managed by means of a steep staircase built directly in the center of the pyramid, but in practice that would have been difficult to achieve.

What can we conclude from all this? When we consider everything that has been written on this subject, and all that is known to archaeologists, a combination of the two basic methods seems the most promising explanation. To the question of whether lifting devices or ramps were used, we may reply simply: both. In addition, we should also recognize the importance of the highly effective organization and coordination of individual workers on the construction site, as well as the complete use made of the main source of energy: the workers' muscle power.

Jean-Philippe Lauer, the best-known expert on the Egyptian pyramids, has provided the most carefully thought out solution to the problem. He suggests that during construction a whole system of cleverly combined ramps of various sizes and gradients was built. At the same time, of course, additional tools and lifting devices were used— wooden levers, round beams, poles, and ropes. To illustrate his theory, Lauer chose the largest and most complex of the Egyptian pyramids, the Great Pyramid in Giza.

For the construction of the lowest part of the pyramid, four large frontal ramps were used, one running vertically up each side. There

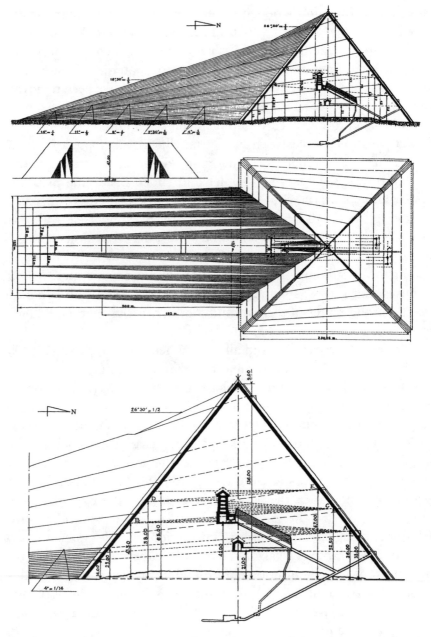

Reconstruction of a ramp used for the construction of the Great Pyramid in Giza (after Lauer).

was one further ramp, which ran southeast directly to the stone quarries in the area. The ramp was initially short; it ran into the pyramid and had a very slight gradient of about four degrees. Gradually, it was extended toward the south to a length of about three hundred meters, and at the same time toward the north, into the interior of the pyramid. When it reached that length, the ramp was about thirty-five meters high on the north side, and thus made it possible to erect the Great Gallery, the somewhat higher King's Chamber, and even the so-called relieve chambers built above that. To construct them, and to transport stone blocks weighing forty to sixty tons, a system of smaller ramps was built directly in the interior of the pyramid core.

According to Lauer, these enormous blocks of stone were set in place by means of a system of counterweights made of sacks of sand. The remaining upper part of the pyramid was finished off using the base ramp, whose gradient was gradually increased while its width was decreased. With an angle of about fourteen degrees, the ramp allowed blocks weighing as much as a ton to be raised to a height of 112 meters; and with an angle of eighteen degrees, blocks weighing around 700 kilograms could be raised to about 136 meters.

A special and particularly difficult task was finishing off the structure by placing at its apex the pyramidion, which weighed about five or six tons. Lauer assumes that large wooden trestles, heavy greased beams, thick ropes, and counterweights were used.

The overall volume of the base ramp, which was composed of unfired bricks, stone rubble, and sand, Lauer calculates to have been 1,560,000 cubic meters. If his views and estimates are correct, the volume of the ramp combined with that of the pyramid itself was 4,160,000 cubic meters—4,160,000 cubic meters of construction material that had to be found, transported, and raised to a height of as much as 146.6 meters! This would be an extraordinary achievement even with modern technical means. Moreover, Lauer's theory does not explain how the bulk of the ramp was removed. The American archaeologist Mark Lehner, who also has spent long years studying the pyramids in Giza, proposes, against Lauer's view, that the ramp was not linear but spiral in form, and began in the local stone quarries southeast of the Great Pyramid.

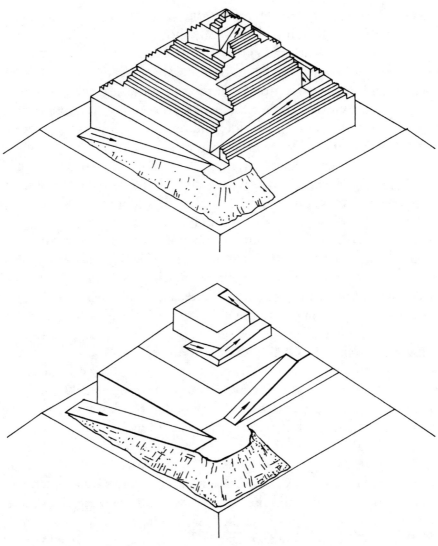

Two suggestions by N. Hampikian for how the pyramidion could have been laid in its position.

So much for the largest Egyptian pyramid. The question as to how the pyramids were built has still another dimension. Archaeological investigations clearly show that the ancient Egyptian pyramids differed not only in size, location, and period, but also in their basic construction plans, materials, and methods. The following section is devoted primarily to this subject, which is based on the results of Czech research.

Craftsmen's Guilds in Abusir

As a typical example of how the same or very similar construction methods were used in a given place at a given time, let us consider the case of King Neferirkare's family cemetery in Abusir. The group of trained master builders, artists, and workmen who labored there can to some extent be compared with craftsmen's guilds in the European Middle Ages.

During the excavations carried out in Abusir since 1960 by the University of Prague's Czech Egyptological Institute, a number of pyramids—many of them long known, and others discovered during the research work—were investigated. The results of this work offer a new, interesting view of the inner structure and mode of construction of the pyramids in Abusir.

NEFERIRKARE'S PYRAMID

In the ruins of Neferirkare's pyramid we can discern two clearly distinct types of layers in the pyramid core, which differ both in the material used and in the method of construction. The inner layers consist of larger, qualitatively more valuable, well-aligned blocks that are carefully set in the corners, whereas the outer levels are constructed in a relatively careless way out of small and sometimes crudely dressed fragments of stone.

Lepsius, and later on Borchardt as well, thought that the core of Neferirkare's pyramid was composed of stone accretion layers set at an angle of about seventy-seven degrees and supported by the massive, dense "spindle" of the core stone masonry. This mode of construction, the use of which has been proven in the case of the Third Dynasty step pyramids, is sometimes compared with the layers of an onion. Lepsius and Borchardt claimed that the cores of all the other pyramids in Abusir, and also to some extent in other places such as Meidum, were constructed in the same way. Closer examination of Neferirkare's pyramid shows that they were mistaken.

The Czech team's archaeological investigation of the pyramid's construction has shown that its core is composed of horizontal strata and is built in layers. Originally, there were six of these layers, constructed with high-quality stone blocks laid in regular rows. The pyramid was conceived as a step pyramid. When the inner core was completed, work began on the casing, which was to be made of white limestone. However, the outer shell had reached only the first level when the construction plan was changed to increase the size of the structure and to transform it from a step pyramid into a genuine pyramid. To this end, the core was broadened and its height increased by two layers, using small and roughly dressed stone fragments. Finally, work on the casing began again, though after the lowest level was finished off, it was made of pink granite—no doubt because in the interim the ruler had died. The structure was never completed.

It is hardly conceivable that at every stage in the construction a large ramp was built to deliver materials, but the size of the blocks that were used for the original six-layered step pyramid makes it clear that without them, or without a whole system of smaller ramps, the work could not have been completed. During the subsequent work—the casing of the six-level step pyramid and the broadening of the core—the casing slabs as well as the small stone fragments were probably lifted or dragged up the already completed wall by means of a simple wooden device resembling a block and tackle. To make it easier to drag these materials, slabs or small, round beams smeared with grease may have been used. Similar tools were probably used in building the casing of the true pyramid, and at the lowest levels a ramp may also have been used. The extant documents show that the size of the blocks diminished at successive levels of the pyramid.

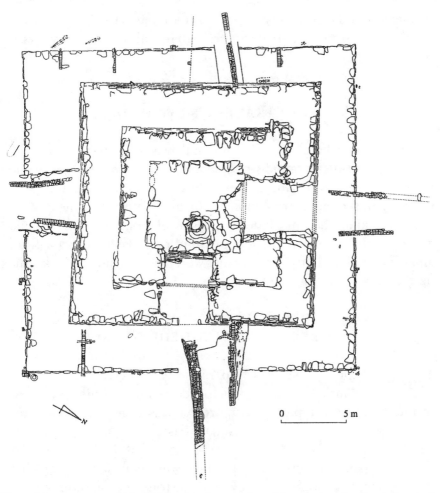

Plan of the step pyramid in Sinki, with the remains of four ramps for the delivery of construction materials (after Dreyer and Swelim). This number and arrangement of the ramps allowed the lower half of the pyramid, which represented more than 80 percent of the overall volume of its masonry, to be quickly and efficiently built.

The Czech archaeological team has in fact recently discovered, while completing excavations in the nearby unfinished pyramid of Neferefre, the ruins of a construction ramp that was probably built for broadening Neferirkare's pyramid into an eight-layered pyramid. This ramp, which is about twenty meters wide, rises slowly from south to north. It consists of sand, and its surface was strengthened

\ 95 \

by means of a layer of clay about ten centimeters thick. This discovery is an important contribution to debates about the construction of the pyramids.

KHENTKAUES II'S PYRAMID

The casing of Khentkaues II's pyramid was also installed after the completion of the pyramid's step-shaped core, or at least of its four-meter high first level. This is clearly shown by the stratification of the masonry in the mortuary temple that stands in front of the east side of the pyramid. The white limestone casing blocks were relatively small and became even smaller as the pyramid rose. Their superior fitting and the overall stability of the casing were strengthened by lock seams on the upper and lower sides.

NEFEREFRE'S (UNFINISHED) PYRAMID

The construction of Neferefre's pyramid was interrupted as a result of the king's untimely death, which occurred before the lowest level of the core was completed. The project was hastily converted to a stylized primeval mound with a square base, whose outer appearance was more like that of a mastaba. After the end of the New Kingdom, thieves dug into the substructure, which was about seven meters high high. There, in the open air, they set up a stone-cutting shop that specialized in removing the fine white limestone of the tomb's substructure. Today we have direct access to this area, and the knowledge gained from it is striking and certain.

Although it has been seriously damaged, the plan of the substructure of Neferefre's pyramid can now be reconstructed with relative precision. It consisted of a descending corridor, slightly curving from the north toward the southeast, which ended in the antechamber of the burial chamber. Both rooms were aligned with the east-west axis of the tomb and had gabled ceilings made of blocks of fine white limestone. Thieves destroyed and removed the ceilings of both chambers as well as that of the access corridor, so that only a few blocks remain. Thus, the inner structure of the masonry of the core is revealed on the side walls of the enormous crater that now yawns over the ruins of the substructure. This makes it possible to reconstruct with precision the work methods used by the builders of the tomb.

Once again, the core consists not of embankments but of horizontal layers, each of which has a "frame" of regularly set, roughly dressed limestone blocks. The outer blocks are as large as 5 m. × 5.5 m. × 1 m., and are well fitted into the corners, whereas those laid around the pit for the burial chamber and the access corridor are much smaller. The space between two frames was filled with crude chunks of limestone, clay, pottery shards, and sand. The huge blocks were probably moved into place with the help of ramps. Distinct traces of broad paths are found in the desert south of the unfinished pyramid. About a kilometer to the south is also a rock ledge of yellow to greenish gray limestone where quarrying was done, and which Borchardt believed to be the site of the main stone quarry for the construction of the pyramid cores in Abusir.

To close up the gigantic, empty space that remained after the completion of the substructure, builders used stone rubble. As a foundation, a layer of smaller pieces of the same stone was laid over the gabled ceiling, bound together here and there with mortar and filled in with gravel. The upper, more or less horizontal, surface of this layer was made of large, flat limestone fragments, which often bore the cursive, semi-hieratic inscription *Hut Neferefre,* which can be roughly translated as "[burial] area of Neferefre." The remaining open space above this layer was filled with diagonally oriented walls made of stone rubble that intersected approximately in the middle of the structure. Here as well, gravel, sand, and mudbricks were used as filler. Finally, the flat roof terrace of the tomb was covered with a layer of clay a few centimeters thick and with rough gravel from the surface of the surrounding desert. The outside of the structure was covered with fine white limestone blocks. Neferefre's tomb, a stylized primeval mound, was completed.

THE PYRAMID "LEPSIUS NO. 24"

The extensive damage wrought during the Ramesside period (thirteenth century B.C.E.)—and especially during the Saite period (624–525 B.C.E.), in connection with the construction of shaft tombs—laid open this pyramid both inside and outside. The extant remains allow an instructive view of the work of the stonemasons who built not only this pyramid but apparently also other pyramids in Abusir during the time of Niuserre.

Thus we can follow the individual phases of construction almost step by step. First, the site had to be leveled, since the pyramid stood near the sloping edge of the western desert plateau. Then a cavity for the substructure was dug out and walled in, and around this cavity a square foundation made of limestone blocks was built for the pyramid.

The construction of the first step of the core, about five meters high, began with the erection of a perimeter wall, in which a gap was left on the north side. A regular opening as high as the wall was left for the delivery of materials for the construction of the burial chamber and the corridor leading to it, which began on the north wall some twenty centimeters above the base of the pyramid. Another opening, irregular and about three meters wide, was located in the south wall near the southeast corner. Through it a passageway probably led down into the inside of the pyramid, perhaps a ramp for transporting fill into the space, which was surrounded by a perimeter wall of the first layer of the core. The lower part of the fill, up to about two meters, was composed of a layer of pieces of limestone, over which builders apparently put sand, rubble, and construction waste. The second level of the core consisted of a system of diagonally aligned walls built of irregular stone fragments. The different construction methods used for the first and second levels significantly increased the stability of the pyramid core. The core of the whole pyramid probably had three levels.

The temple on the east side of the pyramid stood, just as in the case of Khentkaues II's pyramid, immediately on the wall of the core. The casing, which has been partly preserved on the north side, was installed after the completion of the first step, at the earliest. Given the small size of the blocks used, it might have been constructed in a way similar to that already described in connection with Neferirkare's pyramid.

Recent research on the pyramids in Abusir has broadened our knowledge and made it more precise. It has confirmed the view that some construction methods were employed in ancient Egypt throughout the whole period of pyramid construction. For example, the stronger masonry of the core was first built of qualitatively inferior stone blocks and then sheathed with more valuable and well-dressed stones. The ancient Egyptians produced most of the compact masonry by building a perimeter wall and then filling the space inside it with construction waste and other less valuable materials. Unfortunately, these discoveries still do not provide conclusive answers to all questions concerning the construction of the pyramids in Abusir and elsewhere.

Outlook

A reader who has sought in the preceding pages a simple, satisfying, and exhaustive explanation of how the Egyptian pyramids were built will probably be somewhat disappointed. Egyptology at the end of the twentieth century, after existing for nearly two hundred years, is still not really capable of providing such an explanation. This is the result of neither inadequacies in the approach to the problem nor prejudices against other untraditional or even unscientific views. The problem is far more complicated than it may at first seem.

The Egyptian pyramids were built over a period of more than a thousand years, in various places, from different materials, and in differing sizes. Thus we can scarcely expect to discover a single method that was always and everywhere used to construct them.

The evolution undergone by the Egyptian pyramids is characterized by their builders' efforts to learn from earlier mistakes and deficiencies, in order to find the optimal relationship between the materials used and the pyramid form, methods of construction, and other factors. Obviously, it also reflects the desire to surpass preceding works in size, richness of ornamentation, and the balance of the whole system of structures represented by the pyramid complex. And this desire was pursued to a certain critical limit, beyond which serious conceptual changes had to be made, which in turn influenced work methods. The role of economics, religion, and aesthetics in this development must be emphasized, too.

To arrive at a genuinely fundamental and precise reconstruction of the methods used to build the pyramids, we would have to take them apart and put them back together again. Let us hope that archaeological research does not go to this extreme. Above all, further revisionary research must be undertaken on most of the pyramids, which up to now have unfortunately been inadequately investigated. This will involve using the increasingly powerful procedures borrowed from the exact sciences, and we can expect interesting discoveries to be made, but the goal of revealing all the secrets of the Egyptian pyramids will not be reached for a long time.

According to the views of earlier Egyptologists, the diagonal orientation of the brick walls became commonplace from the Twelfth Dynasty on, but in 1995 that method, which increased the cohesion of the core masonry, was also shown to have been used in the pyramid Lepsius no. 24, built in Abusir in the Fifth Dynasty.

PART TWO

THE PYRAMIDS

Everything fears Time,
only the pyramids laugh at it.
—Arab proverb

CHAPTER FOUR

THE OLD KINGDOM
(THIRD TO SIXTH DYNASTY)*

The Third Dynasty—Steps Toward Eternity

The culminating phase of Egypt's economic, political, and cultural ascent, known to modern historians as the Old Kingdom, began with the Third Dynasty. The transition from the Second Dynasty took place under conditions that have not been entirely explained. Egyptologists agree that the key figure in the murky dynastic situation of this time was Queen Nimaathap I, but it is unclear exactly what role she played. Some scholars believe that Nimaathap was Khasekhemwy's daughter, Sanakht's consort, and the mother of Netjerikhet. Other researchers see her as a secondary wife of Khasekhemwy who gained power after the main queen failed to produce a son and heir. They identify Nimaathap's son Nebka with Sanakht and see him as the founder of the Third Dynasty. However, although Nebka appears as the first ruler of the Third Dynasty in the Abydos king list and in the Turin papyrus, we know little more about him, and most Egyptologists now think Sanakht ruled in the second half of the Third Dynasty.

Discoveries made by the German archaeological team during excavations in Abydos shed new light on the beginnings of the Third Dynasty. They make it clear that King Netjerikhet arranged Queen Nimaathap I's funeral, and that he may also have been the founder of the Third Dynasty. In any case, Netjerikhet, more commonly known

---

* According to some scholars, the Old Kingdom lasted until the end of the Sixth Dynasty, while others say it lasted until the end of the Eighth Dynasty. The first view seems predominant and has been adopted in this book.

Geb (?), an earth god. Fragment of a bas-relief from a temple of Djoser in Heliopolis.

under his later name, Djoser,** was the most impressive figure in the early years of this dynasty. Researchers have found the ruins of temples Djoser built in Heliopolis in Lower Egypt and in Gebelein in Upper Egypt. Djoser's most significant work, however, is his tomb, the famed Step Pyramid in Saqqara, the first example of this kind of tomb and an architectural milestone.

Egyptologists used to attribute to Djoser, in addition to the pyramid in Saqqara, the enormous brick mastaba near Beit Khallaf, which was considered to be his symbolic grave. Today that tomb is thought to be that of a high official to whom the king had entrusted, during his relatively long rule, the administration of that part of the country.

Djoser's monumental edifices testify to a powerful upswing in the Egyptian economy at the beginning of the Third Dynasty and to a rise in the productivity of agriculture, crafts, and building. At the same time, writing was developing, along with astronomy, mathematics, land measurement, and—of course—governmental administration. Later generations also considered this to be an important epoch in Egypt's history. In the Ptolemaic period (305–30 B.C.E.), priests of

** This name is first documented in texts from the Middle Kingdom, while Netjerikhet was the contemporary Horus name.

the god Khnum from Elephantine carved the so-called famine stela on Sehel, a nearby island on the Nile. It mentioned a seven-year period of hardship with low flood levels, poor harvests, and famine, which ended only by the intercession of the god Khnum, the lord of the sources of the Nile. Khnum's priests back-dated the inscription to the time of Djoser, thus lending importance and antiquity to their cult and substantiating their claims to ownership.

Djoser's successor, Sekhemkhet, decided to have an equally splendid tomb erected near that of his predecessor. The construction plan of his tomb complex resembled Djoser's, but the pyramid was projected to have seven steps, and when finished it was supposed to be higher than its model. A graffito on the complex's perimeter wall indicates that the brilliant architect Imhotep built this pyramid as well as Djoser's. (Were Sekhemkhet and Imhotep both Djoser's sons and thus brothers? See pp. 114 and 142.) Sekhemkhet ruled only a short time, however, and his tomb remained unfinished.

The subsequent period is fairly murky. Several kings followed in quick succession, suggesting a weakening of the royal family and the central power. One of these rulers was Khaba, whose name is known from seal impressions on clay tablets found at Hierakonpolis as well as from stone vessels found in Dahshur and Zawiyet el-Aryan, where archaeologists discovered an unfinished step pyramid—the so-called Layer Pyramid—which was probably built by Khaba.

Toward the end of the Third Dynasty, another king, Huni, was probably the first to write his throne name in a cartouche (with the exception of the somewhat unclear fragment of a cartouche from Beit Khallaf)—an oval that symbolized the eternity and universality of sovereign power. During his rule the construction of a palace on Elephantine, an island on the Nile near Aswan, was begun. Some scholars maintain that it was also Huni who began building the pyramid near Meidum, but no direct evidence supports that view. Today the prevailing opinion is that Snefru, whose original residence, Djedsnefru, was also in Meidum, had this pyramid built from the outset. Because of its intermediate position between step pyramids and true pyramids, this edifice is of particular significance.

Pyramids were not the only things that changed during this transitional period, which was also marked by profound economic and social transformations. This is shown by an inscription from the tomb of the great magnate Metjen. It contains information about Metjen's career as an official and his social standing, and also about his property holdings—fields, gardens, vineyards, and fig groves. He inherited part of his property from his father and purchased another part; ultimately, he owned some sixty hectares of land. At the beginning of the Egyptian state, the pharaoh was still the sole legal owner of everything—land, stone quarries, water, livestock, and, when he needed it, human labor. The inscription from Metjen's tomb shows that as early as the end of the Third Dynasty, even a man who was not descended from the royal family could own property, including agricultural land.

DJOSER'S STEP PYRAMID

Few monuments hold a place in human history as significant as that of the Step Pyramid in Saqqara. Together with the structures that surround it, the pyramid composes Djoser's tomb complex. It can be said without exaggeration that his pyramid complex constitutes a mile-

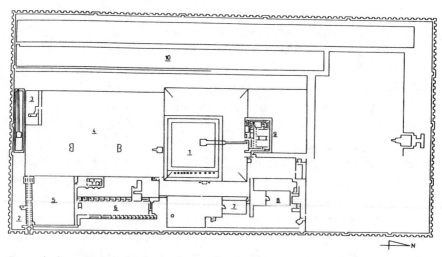

Ground plan of Djoser's pyramid complex (after Lauer). 1. pyramid; 2. entry colonnade; 3. south tomb; 4. south courtyard; 5. "T" temple; 6. *Sed* festival complex; 7. south pavilion; 8. north pavilion; 9. mortuary temple; 10. west mounds.

stone in the evolution of monumental stone architecture in Egypt and in the world as a whole. Here limestone was first used on a large scale as a construction material, and here the idea of a monumental royal tomb in the form of a pyramid was first realized. In a Nineteenth Dynasty inscription found in South Saqqara, the ancient Egyptians were already describing Djoser as the "opener of stone," which we can interpret as meaning the inventor of stone architecture.

At first, the architectonic forms did not precisely correspond to the new material; the latter required different work procedures and methods, which the builders of that time had to find and then try out. They were—how could it be otherwise?—strongly influenced by the architecture of the Early Dynastic Period, which had used light, natural materials such as mudbricks, wood, reeds, straw, and matting. The result of their efforts was an original, monumental, and therefore in many respects bizarre work, which united, in a matchless harmony, the mentality of earlier architecture and the new "stone order."

The contradiction between the traditional lightweight architecture and the characteristics of the new construction material, for which builders had been seeking a suitable artistic expression, was resolved by literally copying the earlier architectonic elements in stone. Limestone walls with niches imitate structures made of wooden planks, along with ropes and poles hung with mats, while stone pillars represent enormous papyrus stalks or rushes, and in the stone portal, there were wide-flung stone doors. The French Egyptologist Jacques Vandier (1904–1973) described the effect the Djoser complex produced on visitors: "In the Djoser pyramid complex, it often feels as if we were in Sleeping Beauty's palace. Everything is dead, and everything is made for death."

It was not only the architectonics of the Step Pyramid complex that were new. In comparison with the Predynastic and Early Dynastic Periods, this complex reflects in many ways a different mentality. In the course of the struggle to establish a unified realm, a stronger central government had been established, and for this reason Djoser's pyramid complex is usually seen as the expression of Egyptian political stability at the beginning of the Old Kingdom.

According to written reports, seventeenth-century European travelers attempted to enter the Step Pyramid, but archaeological research on the Djoser complex, as well as on many other important Egyptian monuments, did not begin until Napoleon's Egyptian campaign at the turn of the nineteenth century. Somewhat later, in 1821, the Prussian general Johann Heinrich Freiherr von Minutoli discovered the access tunnel that leads under the pyramid from the north. But not until 1837 did the English pyramid researcher John Perring find the underground galleries beneath the pyramid, along with some thirty mummies from the later period. Shortly afterward, the Prussian expedition led by Lepsius also worked there.

However, truly systematic archaeological research on the Djoser complex was first conducted in the 1920s by the English archaeologist Cecil Firth. He was soon joined by the young French architect Jean-Philippe Lauer, for whom these excavations ultimately became a lifelong mission. Although a series of other professional archaeologists have worked on this site, Egyptology owes primarily to Lauer its current knowledge of the complicated archaeological-structural and historical problematics connected with the Step Pyramid.

The Great Trench

Djoser's pyramid complex was not only bounded by a monumental perimeter wall of limestone, it was completely surrounded by an enormous trench that lay farther out. The trench was originally dug in the underlying rock, and although it has long since been filled up with sand and rubble, it is still clearly recognizable in aerial photographs and photogrammetric maps of Saqqara. In its main outlines, it resembles the hieroglyphic sign for *h,* "ground plan for a house."

The trench, 750 meters long and about 40 meters wide, is the largest structure of its kind in the Memphis necropolis. It is rectangular in form and oriented north and south; the southern segment is shorter, but in some parts it is doubled into two trenches with offset openings, making access to the true perimeter wall of the Djoser complex more difficult (*en chicane*). Thus, a single entrance to the whole area from the south was probably created near the southeast corner.

The southern part of the trench was explored by Egyptian archaeologists, in particular Selim Hassan, Zaki Saad, and Ahmad Musa. Archaeological investigation has shown that the walls were origi-

nally decorated with niches. According to another Egyptian archaeologist, Nabil Swelim, in the builders' conceptual world these niches
were the place where the spirits of the courtiers and magnates came
out of the trench, in order to serve the pharaoh after their deaths.
This view is obviously based on the secondary tombs near the early
royal tombs in Abydos, in which, according to some Egyptologists,
ritually killed servants were buried after the ruler's death. Nothing
like this has been found, however, in the neighborhood of Djoser's
complex.

As we have said, the trenches seem to have been intended to make
entry into the complex more difficult. When the architects were drawing their plans, they may have been influenced by a water canal that
surrounded the royal palace in Memphis. We must also take into
consideration the enormous volume of underlying stone that had to
be removed during the digging of the trenches, and which has not been
found anywhere in the neighborhood. Was this stone used in the construction of the Step Pyramid itself? If so, were the protective and
religious functions of the Great Trench only secondary?

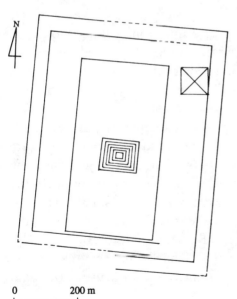

Reconstruction of the Great Trench
around the Step Pyramid, based on a
photogrammetric plan. Userkaf's
pyramid stands near the northeast
corner of the trench (after Swelim).

0   200 m

The Perimeter Wall

The outer surface of the perimeter wall, modeled on woven mats, is decorated with niches and fifteen not quite equally distributed doors, of which fourteen are false; only one, in the east facade, is a true entrance. According to some Egyptologists, the decorative motif imitates a wooden-framed structure covered with mats, while other Egyptologists maintain that it is a Mesopotamian motif. In Egyptian worship of the dead, niches often marked the places where sacrifices were brought to the spirit of the deceased.

Lauer believes that the perimeter wall was modeled on the earthly royal residence, the White Walls. This view is contradicted, however, by the large number of doors. According to Hermann Kees (1886–1964), the fifteen doors were connected with the sed festival and referred to half the lunar month as the period for the ceremonies. This motif is found on other monuments, probably directly inspired by Djoser's complex—for example, on the perimeter wall of Senusret III's pyramid complex in Dahshur and on the sides of his sarcophagus.

The Entrance Colonnade

It took ten years—from 1946 to 1956—to reconstruct the single entry to Djoser's complex along with the adjoining parts of the perimeter wall. It consisted of a corridor whose limestone ceiling looked as though it were made from whole tree trunks. At its end, within an enormous portal, stands a stone imitation of two open doors. Beyond them is the way into the interior of the complex, which passes through a long hall with twenty pairs of limestone columns.

The columns reached a height of almost six meters and were composed of drum-shaped segments. They were not freestanding, but were rather connected with the side walls by masonry projections. The architects obviously did not yet trust them as supports. Between the columns, on both sides of the hall, were twenty-four small chambers, which some Egyptologists think represented chapels for each of the provinces of Upper and Lower Egypt. Remains of decoration or sculptures that might have shown that the main divinities of these provinces were worshiped in them, or anything of the kind, were not found in any of them, however.

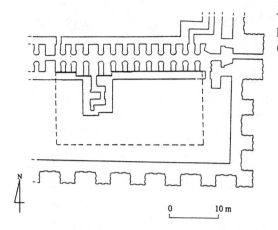

The Djoser complex: entrance hall and "oblique building" (after Ricke).

0   10 m

The form of the columns is modeled on a bundle of plant stems. In Lauer's opinion, a bundle of reeds might in fact have been used to support a light roof. On the other hand, Herbert Ricke (1901–1976), a respected German expert on ancient Egyptian architecture, believed that the columns imitated the ribs of palm fronds, which were used in early building to protect the fragile and exposed ends of walls made of mudbricks. He also suggested that the columns were originally painted green. The ceiling of the columned hall was made of limestone slabs and is again supposed to have imitated whole tree trunks. At the west end stood the so-called transverse vestibule, which was decorated with four similar pillars about one meter shorter.

A thorough investigation of the columned hall has shown that it was not built all at once, but in stages, and is characterized by certain structural peculiarities: its longer axis is not oriented precisely east-west but is angled slightly to the southwest, and the outside walls are slightly inclined. The entry corridor was evidently built along the old, "oblique" building that had at some time in the past stood in the southeast corner of the grounds. The oblique building owes its name to the fact that in contrast to the other buildings in the complex, it is not aligned precisely with the four cardinal directions.*

* Similar oblique buildings were discovered in the valley structures ("great enclosures") of the early dynastic tomb complexes in Abydos.

According to Wolfgang Helck, this was the so-called statue palace, in which the ruler's statue was originally housed. This statue is supposed to have been erected during the ruler's lifetime, although it represented the deceased pharaoh in the guise of the Great White, a kind of baboon. The task of erecting the statue and conducting the resurrection ritual was assigned to the first prince, who was thus supposed to play the role of the future king. Helck based his view in part on fragments of stone statues Firth had found. In addition to lions' heads and two busts of captive enemies of Egypt, the torso of a statue of a king and especially the base of Djoser's statue (Egyptian Museum, Cairo, JE 49889) were found in the entrance hall. On them, alongside religious symbols, were the remains of an inscription that, besides the ruler's Horus name and his titles, gave the name of Imhotep, which suggests that this high priest of the temple of the sun in Heliopolis and leading royal architect was also Djoser's son and the builder of the Step Pyramid.

On the other hand, according to Hans Goedicke, the structural arrangement of the hall reflects a symbolic conception of the court of judgment: the side chambers between the columns would be reserved for two enneads as judges, presided over by the ruler.

The Pyramid

The Step Pyramid, which dominates the entire complex, has been thoroughly studied in recent decades. It is only a slight exaggeration to say that the knowledge thus gained has produced as many questions as answers. Investigations have shown that the original construction plan was changed several times, and that the pyramid's current form is the result of a long process of development that includes both experimental and improvised elements. At the outset, the structure had the form of a rectangular mastaba (stage M1), which was gradually enlarged, first equally on all four sides (stage M2), and then only on the east side (stage M3). The mastaba, which was erected using the chamber method described above, already had a step shape in the M3 stage.

The step-shaped mastaba was finally rebuilt in two stages, first as a four-step (P1) and then as a six-step (P2) pyramid, which no longer

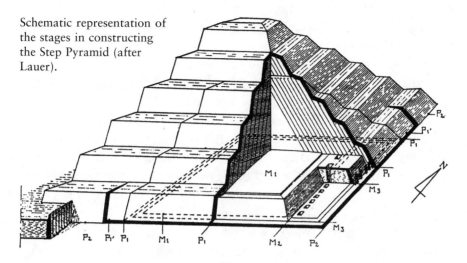

Schematic representation of the stages in constructing the Step Pyramid (after Lauer).

had—and this is the noteworthy point—a square base; it now had a rectangular base, oriented east-west.

A simple but effective construction method was used. The masonry was laid not vertically but in courses inclined toward the middle of the pyramid, thus significantly increasing its structural stability. The basic material used was limestone blocks, whose form resembled that

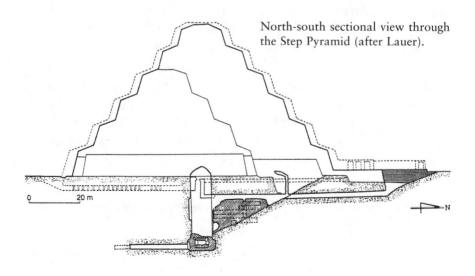

North-south sectional view through the Step Pyramid (after Lauer).

of large bricks of dried clay. In this respect as well, the builders of the pyramid were indebted to earlier tradition and experience.

The motives that led to the fundamental decision to transform the structure from a mastaba into a pyramid are still a subject of debate among professionals in the field. Lauer suggests that the intention was to make the royal tomb visible from the Nile Delta. In addition, he maintains that the oldest stage in the pyramid's construction, the mastaba M1, was not Djoser's tomb, but instead belonged to his predecessor, Sanakht. However, there is no solid evidence for this view. On the contrary, most experts now believe that Sanakht was one of the later kings of the Third Dynasty.

Hartwig Altenmüller also rejected Lauer's hypothesis regarding the reconstruction. In his view, the decision to change the outward appearance of the tomb was motivated by religious or ritual concerns. Was the pyramid supposed to recall the gigantic staircase, mentioned later in some of the pyramid texts, that the spirit of the deceased ruler was to climb on his way into the heavens? Or was it instead an imitation of the primeval mound that appeared from the original flood when the world was created?

The Czech astronomer Ladislav Křivský has also reflected on the reasons behind the choice of a step-pyramid form. He believes that the builders of Djoser's tomb were inspired by the form of the rising and setting sun. From time to time, under specific physical conditions connected with the varying temperatures of different atmospheric layers over the earth, an optical illusion is produced that gives the sun's disk the form of a step pyramid. The structure would thus have expressed the idea, connected with the worship of the sun, that the ruler in his step-shaped grave is as immortal as the sun, awakening every morning on the eastern horizon and dying every evening on the western horizon.

Thus a whole range of theories regard the reconstruction of the original mastaba M1, and others may still appear. But the reason for the transformation of the mastaba into a pyramid may be more complicated than it seems, and none of the structural-archaeological and geodetic studies that have so far been carried out may be adequate.

Characteristically, it was the architect Lauer who noted many years ago that the original mastaba (M1) did not have the usual rectangular, north-south–oriented ground plan, but rather a square one! This discovery was connected with a clash between the novice Lauer and Borchardt, who was then a generally respected authority in the area of Egyptian archaeology and architecture. During one of Borchardt's visits to Saqqara, Lauer excitedly reported on his discovery, only to be curtly warned, "Young man, don't try to teach me archaeology— a mastaba is never square!"

The question therefore arises as to whether the original stage of Djoser's tomb really was a mastaba. Rainer Stadelmann is probably correct in doubting that it was, and he suggests that from the outset, the tomb was planned as a square-based pyramid. Why should the Step Pyramid be the only royal mastaba of the Old Kingdom with a rectangular ground plan, and ultimately turn out to be the only pyramid with a square, east-west–oriented ground plan? Today there is much evidence to suggest that Borchardt was right after all. New research conducted by the American expedition in the "great enclosures" in Abydos has shown, for example, that approximately in the middle of the grounds, which were surrounded by a large perimeter wall, a small mound of sand was covered with mudbricks. It symbolized the site of the creation, the resurrection, and eternal life. Drawing on this symbolism, the original phase of the construction of the Step Pyramid probably represented a stylized primeval mound, which for the first time was directly connected in this form architecturally with the royal tomb.

The original entrance into the Step Pyramid's substructure was a tunnel running along the north-south axis of M1. It emerged in the floor of the mortuary temple north of the pyramid. At the beginning of the tunnel was a staircase, and at its end, a diagonal shaft, whose upper part originally ran through the whole aboveground structure of M1 as far as the roof terrace. The tomb was located on the floor of this shaft, at a depth of about twenty-eight meters, in the so-called granite chamber. Over its ceiling was a room that Lauer called the maneuvering chamber, because it was there that the pharaoh's mummy was prepared for interment in the burial chamber. The mummy was taken down through a round opening in the floor, which was afterward closed with a granite block weighing about three tons.

Jean-Philippe Lauer.

Shortly after it was built, the burial chamber of pink granite blocks may have undergone a complete reconstruction, which Lauer attributes to the legendary Imhotep. In Lauer's opinion, the chamber was originally built only of limestone blocks, and its ceiling was decorated with stars. During the reconstruction, the limestone blocks with stars were removed, and fragments of them were discovered in the surrounding area. Stadelmann disagrees with Lauer on technical grounds, however, since a ceiling built of those small, limestone blocks (0.52 m long) over the 4 m-x-2.56 m chamber would have collapsed as soon as it was completed. In his view, the limestone blocks were used to close up the door and the opening in the floor of the so-called maneuvering chamber. Stadelmann thereby also contradicts Werner Kaiser, who is not willing to exclude the possibility that the limestone blocks may have been used in connection with the reconstruction of earlier arrangements in the underground part of the pyramid.

Only minor bone fragments were found in the tomb, and it is not clear whether they really came from Djoser's mummy. Minutoli, who visited the burial chamber in 1821, found fragments of a gilded sandal and a skull. In 1926, Lauer found splinters of bone from a left foot and an upper arm, as well as a few bits of skin. Northwest of the burial chamber, in a small corridor that thieves later destroyed down to its stone floor, a wooden chest was found that bore Djoser's Horus name, Netjerikhet (Egyptian Museum, Cairo, JE 69498–501).

The complicated system of rooms and corridors around the burial chamber, a genuine labyrinth, was investigated by Lauer at the beginning of the 1930s, though not in every detail. It is very difficult to determine what is part of the original, unfinished construction project and what is the later work of thieves. In immediate proximity to all four sides of the burial chamber are four galleries, which are connected with each other by corridors. Some of them were never finished. The walls are supposed to have been originally decorated with blue-green ceramic tiles imitating woven reed mats, and for this reason the rooms are known as the blue chambers. For the ancient Egyptians, turquoise was the color of rebirth, life, and prosperity. Perhaps even the surface of the heavenly and underworld oceans was embodied in the blue chambers ceramic tiles, as the American Egyptologist Florence Friedman believes.

In the east gallery three false doors made of limestone were found, on which the ruler is twice depicted walking, wearing a red or white crown, and once standing, wearing the white crown; the latter image is accompanied by the royal names and the emblems of the gods Anubis and Horus of Behdet. Lepsius took one of these, plus a few tiles, to the Berlin Museum in 1843. It is thought that the furnishing and decoration of the underground rooms were inspired by the real royal palace in Memphis. The bas-reliefs on the false doors are supposed to refer to the ceremonies of the sed festival, one of whose components was the king's ritual circumambulation of the palace.

At about the same time that the royal burial chamber was completed in stage two of the construction (M2), eleven shafts approximately thirty meters deep were built along the east facade of the tomb, and from them interconnected galleries ran west. The openings of the shafts, which were probably intended for the burial of the ruler's wives and children, were covered over by the masonry of the widened tomb during the subsequent stage (M3). In the gallery that ran out of the fifth shaft (numbering them from north to south), an empty alabaster sarcophagus was found, and at the end of the shaft, a smaller

Ground plan of the mortuary temple and the underground galleries of the Step Pyramid (after Lauer).

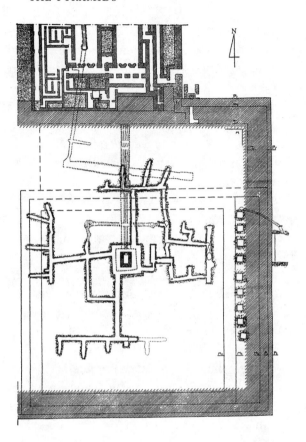

wooden coffin with the body of a boy between eight and ten years old. Next to it lay two vessels decorated with gold leaf and carnelian coral. Other fragments of alabaster sarcophagi were discovered in the first and second shafts, while in the third a seal imprint bearing the name Netjerikhet was found.

The greatest surprise for archaeologists was waiting in the other shafts, especially in the sixth and seventh, where they discovered some forty thousand stone vessels of the most varied forms and materials, many of alabaster, diorite, limestone, and slate. Some vessels were polished, faceted, or fluted, while others bore inscriptions, engraved or painted in colors, with both royal and non-royal names. Among the royal names are those of the rulers of the First and Second Dynas-

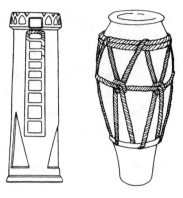

Stone vessels found in the underground gallery beneath the Step Pyramid. The oval vessel on the right imitates a clay container bound with rope. The vessel on the left, which looks like the tower of a fortress, might also have been used as a base.

ties—Nar(mer), Djer, Den, Adjib, Semerkhet, Kaa, Hetepsekhemwy, Ninetjer, Sekhemib, and Khasekhemwy.

The discovery of such a large number of stone vessels bearing the names of rulers of the Early Dynastic Period in the substructure of the Step Pyramid immediately launched a debate among Egyptologists that continues to this day. Lauer believes that the vessels originally belonged to the furnishings of royal tombs in the Early Dynastic Period, which are supposed to have been destroyed by the penultimate ruler of the Second Dynasty, Peribsen. His successor, Khasekhemwy, would then have had the vessels, including the damaged ones, put in sacks and kept in the royal storehouse, whereupon Djoser decided to give them a reverent final resting place in the substructure of his pyramid. Helck was convinced that the vessels came from the temple storehouses and supply centers, and that it was simply unknown why Djoser had them piled up. According to Stadelmann's theory, which resembles Lauer's, Djoser had the damaged tombs of the Early Dynastic Period kings near his tomb restored and the broken vessels dumped in the substructure of his own pyramid. In contrast, Donald B. Redford maintains that in making preparations for the construction of his tomb, Djoser must have had to remove a whole series of tombs built by his predecessors. However, he kept their furnishings—the vessels— and reverently had them buried in his own tomb in order to show his respect for the past and also the continuity of power.

This latter theory seems somewhat paradoxical. The destruction of a whole series of tombs belonging to his royal ancestors would have shown neither reverence nor the continuity of power. Moreover, there is no evidence of intentional destruction or usurpation of royal tombs from the Old Kingdom, though no doubt there were sometimes savage battles among opposing branches of the royal family.

Much also remains unexplained in the other theories mentioned. Why, for example, did Djoser have only the stone vessels reburied among many elements in the burial equipment? Why didn't he have the religious objects, weapons, games, and many other things buried as well? It is impossible to maintain that everything in these tombs except the stone vessels was stolen or destroyed. If we assume (with Peter Munro, a German Egyptologist) that the construction of the Djoser complex involved removing the superstructures of the Second Dynasty royal tombs of Raneb and Ninetjer, which lay just south of the site of Djoser's tomb, why among the vessels found in the latter's substructure are there so many that demonstrably belonged to First Dynasty kings who were not buried in Saqqara? Why were thirteen vessels belonging to Djer found here alongside thirteen belonging to Ninetjer? Moreover, how can we maintain that construction required the removal of the superstructures of royal tombs from the Second Dynasty, when we know nothing further about any of them in Saqqara? We don't know what these superstructures looked like, whether they were simple or complicated, large or small. We would have to examine once again—so far as possible after so many years—the archaeological circumstances under which the vessels were found, reflect on the fact that some of the sacks bore the seal of Djoser's predecessor Khasekhemwy, and also decide why the vessels were deposited during the M2 phase of construction and immediately afterward permanently sealed up by the M3 extension. At the same time we would need to take into account not only the previously unexamined parts of the pyramid complex itself, but also its immediate surroundings, in which the remains of the Second Dynasty royal tombs of Ninetjer and Raneb have been found.

The South Courtyard

The entry corridor ends with its columned vestibule, which opens onto a large courtyard, some 180 meters by 100 meters, that lies between the Step Pyramid and the south wing of the perimeter wall. The court-yard was open, and originally contained only a few buildings. In the northeast corner stood a small temple with three niches and a low limestone altar, which was attached to the south side of the pyramid. The altar was reached by a small ramp, in front of which a bull's head was found in a cavity lined with limestone.

Approximately in the middle of the courtyard were two low lime-stone buildings, whose ground plan resembled the capital letter *B*. Their purpose is still being debated. Because of their form, which reminds us of the half moon–shaped objects on Narmer's stone mace, they have been associated with the king's symbolic royal circumam-bulation of his palace during the sed festival.

During archaeological excavation, forty stone slabs were found, one of which bore the names of Djoser's consort Hetephernebti and his daughter Inetkaus. They probably once marked the boundary of the area of the royal tomb, before they were removed and reused as con-struction material during the extension of the complex.

Among the interesting archaeological discoveries made in the south courtyard was that of a limestone block with the remains of

During the ceremony of the sed festival, Narmer, shrouded in a tight-fitting mantle, wearing the crown of Lower Egypt, and holding a scepter in his hand, sits on the throne in an open pavilion. Over the pavilion hovers the vulture Nekhbet, the tutelary goddess of Upper Egypt. On the right, half moon–shaped objects can be seen. Detail from the decoration of a limestone mace belonging to the ruler, which was found during excavations in Hierakonpolis.

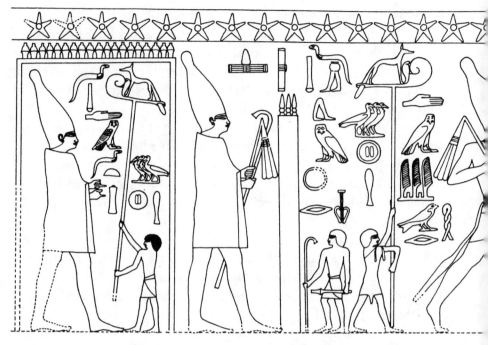

A scene of the sed festival, preserved on a fragment of a bas-relief from Nieuserre's sun temple in Abu Ghurab. It shows the ruler, wearing the crown of Upper Egypt, in various episodes of the festival (after von Bissing). On the extreme left, wearing a tight-fitting mantle, he visits a chapel, accompanied by a "servant of Nekhen's souls" carrying the standard of the wolf god Upuaut, "the opener of the way." On the right, wearing a short skirt (*shendjet*) and carrying a scourge in his hand, he completes the ritual walk, once again accompanied by the bearer of Upuaut's standard.

Khaemuase's so-called restoration text. Khaemuase, a son of Ramesses II and high priest of the temple of Ptah in Memphis, was known for his interest in the monuments of his royal ancestors in the Memphis necropolis. On many of these monuments inscriptions prove that the prince ordered damaged monuments to be repaired. Khaemuase had his own monument erected near the Step Pyramid, which a Japanese expedition discovered a few years ago on a rocky rise west of the Serapeum. Except for the apexes of the pyramids, which were then still inaccessible, this was the only place from which the prince could look out over the whole splendid panorama of the Memphis necropolis.

THE SOUTH TOMB

The low building in the southwest corner of the south courtyard is one of the most enigmatic in the whole Djoser complex. Its underground part consists of a massive block of limestone masonry, whose north and east niche-facades are magically "protected" by a frieze representing a series of erect cobras. An entrance leads from the north into a small room. According to Lauer, a statue of the king once stood here, but Ricke believes that this was where the royal crowns of Upper and Lower Egypt were kept.

The substructure of the south tomb is entered through an ascending, tunnel-like corridor with a staircase. After about thirty meters—approximately at the point where, if we prolonged the line of the Step Pyramid's north-south axis, the corridor would cross it—an inclined shaft opens, at whose end is a burial chamber of pink granite. This chamber is a slightly smaller, almost exact copy of the tomb under the Step Pyramid. Even the maneuvering chamber is included. The descending corridor with the staircase continues west and leads to a gallery that imitates the subterranean blue chambers under the Step Pyramid. Here as well are bluish green faience tiles and three false doors made of limestone. On these doors, however, the king was represented only once walking with the White Crown on his head, and twice in a relaxed pose, wearing the Red Crown (the episodes of the sed festival). In sum, this decoration is a more perfect and more detailed elaboration than that of the underground chambers of the Step Pyramid, and this supports the assumption that it was completed earlier. Many researchers have considered this to be Djoser's real tomb. However, on religious grounds it is difficult to understand why the ruler would have had a pyramid built and then not have had himself buried beneath it.

The entrance to the south tomb was discovered by Firth and Lauer together. Because he was slim, Lauer was the first to force himself through the opening in the maneuvering chamber and into the underground part of the tomb. A few seconds later he called out in great excitement to Firth, who was waiting at the opening: "Stelae! There are stelae in here!" The following days were full of grueling work and great joy at the discoveries made. Lauer recounts the following anecdote: The bluish green faience tiles had fallen from the walls and were covered with dust, and so one day he and Firth's wife, Winifred, decided to gather them up and clean them. They took them into the Firths' little house, and Lauer left to do other work. He had gone only a few steps when he heard a loud hissing sound. Terrified, he hurried back to Mrs. Firth, who explained that she had decided to soak the tiles in pails of water. When the faience, which had been drying out for thousands of years, came into contact with the water, a powerful reaction resulted—thus the hissing, which frightened Lauer more than all the dangers lurking in the ruins of Djoser's pyramid complex.

The function of the south tomb remains unclear. In many ways, the substructure replicates that of the north tomb under the Step Pyramid, but there are significant differences. The floor plan of the north tomb is oriented along a north-south axis, and so is the access corridor leading to it; in the case of the south tomb, the same elements are

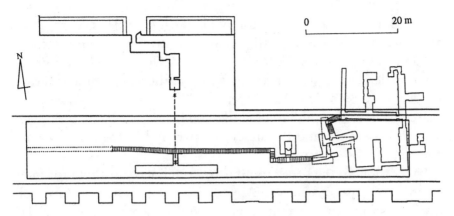

The Djoser complex: diagram of the south tomb (after Ricke).

oriented along an east-west axis. During the whole of the Old Kingdom only the Bent Pyramid in Dahshur had a west entry. The north-
south orientation can be explained by the influence of the then
dominant astral religion, according to which the ruler's spirit was
supposed to become one of the northern circumpolar stars. The east-
west orientation, in contrast, would be an expression of the solar
religion that was gradually establishing itself in Djoser's time.

The existence of two almost identical tombs aligned along the same
north-south axis in Djoser's pyramid field remains an enigma and the
subject of conflicting theories.

The British Egyptologist James Quibell suggested that after Djoser's
birth the royal placenta were ritually buried in the south tomb; there
is, however, no written or archaeological evidence to support this view.

Firth initially maintained that it functioned as a symbolic tomb in
the context of the sed festival but ultimately decided that it was a
provisional tomb, prepared in the event that the death of the ruler
occurred unexpectedly during the construction of his tomb complex.

To the celebrated British pyramid scholar Eiddon Edwards, who
was inspired by Firth, the bas-reliefs on the structures prove that Djoser
intended to use the south tomb. He sees the Bent Pyramid and the
Red Pyramid in Dahshur as confirming this theory.

According to Ricke, the south tomb was a characteristic Lower
Egyptian tomb type in Buto, in contrast to the Upper Egyptian Step

Pyramid. He saw in it the ka tomb, in which the ruler's spirit rested, and suggested, as we have already mentioned, that its aboveground portion was a religious site for the crowns of Upper and Lower Egypt. Altenmüller's analysis of texts on the royal burial ritual lent further support to Ricke's view. The Swiss Egyptologist Gustave Jéquier, who also considered the south tomb the ka tomb, was the first to seek a connection between it and the small cult pyramid in the later pyramid complex.

Lauer thought the south tomb was a symbolic substitute for interment in the royal cemetery in Abydos. The best solution to this problem seems to lie in a combination of Jéquier's view and Lauer's: The south tomb was the burial place of the king's ka and at the same time a symbolic substitute for the ruler's tomb in southern Egypt.

THE "T" TEMPLE

North of the entry colonnade lies a rectangular building that owes its somewhat peculiar name to Lauer's working identification of it as "T." As in many other buildings in the Djoser complex, the old, Early Dynastic Period construction method for mudbrick architecture was here carried over to stone block construction. The temple could also be entered from the south and the east; it consisted of an entry colonnade, an antechamber, three inner courtyards, and a square room. Here, the columns were already functional, supporting the heavy limestone slabs in the ceiling without additional reinforcement. On the north wall of the square room were niches framed by pilasters and topped by a frieze with the hieroglyphic symbols for *djed* ("endure," "be strong"). There may also have been a statue of the king in the room.

The meaning of the "T" temple is also a subject of debate among professionals in the field. Ricke maintained that it was a "royal pavilion" and, like Firth, believed that it served as a symbolic resting place for the ruler and as a place for changing clothes during the ritual of the sed festival. Stadelmann saw it as a prototype of the later so-called temple palaces in the mortuary temples of the New Kingdom.

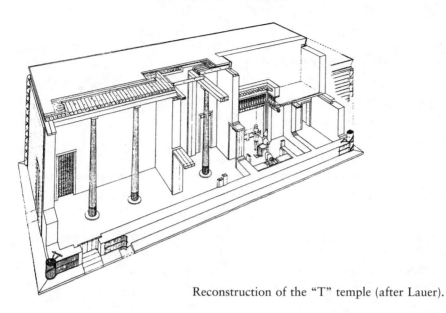

Reconstruction of the "T" temple (after Lauer).

THE SED FESTIVAL COMPLEX

The space between the "T" temple and the southeast corner of the Step Pyramid was filled with a complex of symbolic buildings to which a narrow passageway led, turning north right after the beginning of the entry colonnade. This complex has come to be called the sed festival complex or the sed festival courtyard.

The precise meaning of the word *sed* is not known, and not much is known about the meaning of the festival, which is generally seen as a celebration of the king's accession to the throne and a ceremony of renewal intended to strengthen the ruler's power. This festival was supposed to take place after the king had reigned for thirty years, but since kings involved seldom lived that long, in practice the length of time was abridged and the ceremony only symbolically performed—but we will come back to that. For the moment, let us limit ourselves to pointing out that the ruler did not actually move around the palace from one sacred place to another, as is shown in the images on the temple walls. The burial of the aged ruler in the form of a statue was also symbolic. The whole festival may have been a distant echo of a harsh prehistoric ritual in which the ruler had to prove his physical strength or be ritually killed and replaced by a younger successor.

The core of the sed festival complex is an open courtyard whose east and west sides were originally flanked by rows of chapels. There were twelve of these chapels on the east side, and their smooth facades, framed by half-round molding, were topped by arched vaults. In each chapel was a niche for a statue. The model for this architectonic element was the Lower Egyptian chapel type (*per nu*), which was originally built of mudbricks, wood, reeds, and straw. Today three unfinished limestone Osiris-statues of the king still stand on the east side of the courtyard.

On the west side stand thirteen chapels with two kinds of facades. The "Hall of the God" type (*seh netjer*) has a facade surrounded along the sides by half-round moldings. The "Great House" type (*per uer*) represented the Upper Egyptian shrine, which originally consisted of a light, wood-frame structure over which matting was attached. The facade was decorated by a group of three fluted half-columns, which imitated the plant *Herculaneum giganteum,* including its dried flower petals. It represented a small chapel with an opening into which a symbol of the god was inserted at some time. The upper edge of the facade took the form of an arched vault. As on the east side, each chapel had a niche for the statue, which was accessible by a low ramp. On the north end of the western row of chapels a group of four statues originally stood, of which only the pedestals, two large pairs on

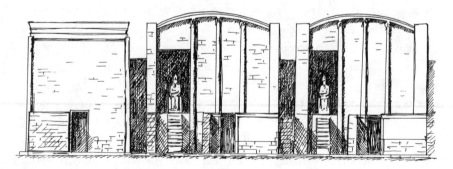

Djoser complex: reconstruction of three chapel facades on the west side of the sed festival courtyard (after Lauer).

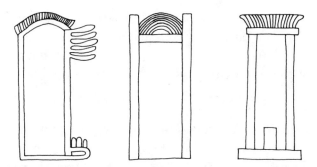

Facades of Early Dynastic Period chapels, *per uer, per nu,* and *seh netjer*. The first two were the "national shrines" of Upper and Lower Egypt, respectively. The third was closely connected with the death god Anubis in the form of a jackal. Originally, they were structures made of light plant material—wood, reeds, and mats.

the right and two smaller ones on the left, have been preserved. Usually, they are said to have represented Djoser, his possible mother Nimaathap, and his wife and daughter, Hetephernebti and Inetkaus.

At the south end of the courtyard was an elevated platform, on which the king's throne stood under a baldachin during the ceremonies. Here the ruler was symbolically crowned.

In the southwest part of the sed festival complex stood a smaller building, aligned north-south. Since we still do not know its function, it is generally called the Small Temple, and it also has slender, fluted half-columns. A corridor, whose arched shape repeats that of the southwest corner, provided access to this building from the coronation platform. No doubt here as well the architect was influenced by

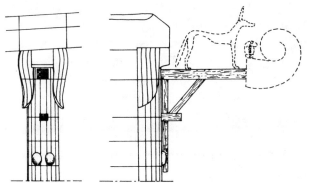

Detail of the capital of a fluted half-column imitating the plant *Herculaneum giganteum,* and a reconstruction of its original decoration (after Lauer).

the construction methods of Early Dynastic Period buildings. The curve is modeled on either woven mats or mudbrick masonry, whose strength would have been reduced by using a right angle.

According to Lauer, the subject of the sed festival later ceased to be expressed by the architecture, and was represented instead by bas-reliefs in the mortuary temple and the sun temple. Arnold follows Ricke in viewing the complex as the prototype of a special room with images of the sed festival, which has been shown to have existed in the pyramid temples from the end of the Fifth Dynasty on, and which has come to be called the *antichambre carrée* (square antechamber). Stadelmann, elaborating on Werner Kaiser's archaeological analysis of the construction of the complex, maintains that this room is not merely a structure symbolizing the sed festival, but is rather part of a more comprehensive scene of burial rituals; seen from a functional point of view, the sed festival complex is close to the open statue courtyards of the later pyramid temples from the Fourth to the Sixth Dynasties.

SOUTH PAVILION AND NORTH PAVILION

The ruins of the south pavilion were so imposing that the Lepsius expedition erroneously took them for a pyramid and gave them the number 34. Part of the structure consists of an extensive courtyard accessible from the sed festival complex as well as from the courtyard along the pyramid's east side. In the southwest corner of the courtyard the remains of an altar were found whose base is in the form of the capital letter *D*. The east and south sides of the courtyard were decorated with niches, and in its northeast part is the opening of a shaft some twenty-five meters deep. Firth found many charred papyri in the courtyard, which suggests that in later times the administration of the whole Saqqara necropolis was located here.

The north side of the courtyard is bounded by the south pavilion, which imitates the characteristic facade of the previously mentioned per uer. The reconstruction and identification of this symbolic structure we owe to Lauer. The south pavilion was constructed using the

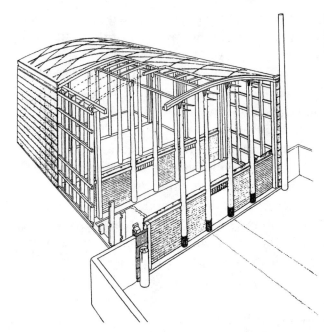

Reconstruction of the south pavilion (after Lauer).

wood-frame and matting method, with a slightly arched roof supported by four fluted half-columns. The latter were probably painted red, with black bases, and were supposed to represent cedar tree trunks. Over the entrance to the chapel ran a continuous frieze with hieroglyphic symbols for *kheker* ("decorate," "ornament"). Their model can be seen on the upper border, a colorful mat that in the Early Dynastic Period decorated the building's facade. The small chapel is shaped like a letter *L,* and at its end is a niche with a cruciform floor plan. On the walls, many so-called visitors' graffiti from the Eighteenth and Nineteenth Dynasties have been preserved, including those of the treasury scribe Hednakht and the vizier's scribe Panakht. The graffiti are of considerable historical importance, because for the first time they refer to Djoser as the possessor of the complex and also show that the structures were still in relatively good condition at that time.

The plan of the north pavilion resembles in many respects that of the south pavilion. The courtyard is smaller, has no niches, and no altar was found there. In its floor, however, there is a shaft about twenty meters deep, which leads into an underground gallery. In contradistinction to the south pavilion, in the east wall of the courtyard stand three papyrus half-columns, the oldest known examples of this kind. Neither the facade of the north pavilion nor the little chapel in it differ significantly from their counterparts in the south pavilion.

The theories regarding the significance of both pavilions vary considerably. Lepsius thought they were pyramids (nos. 33 and 34). Firth saw in them the tombs of the princesses Hetephernebti and Inetkaus, whereas Ricke saw them as the symbolic royal administrative residences of Upper and Lower Egypt. Lauer's similar view is the one that is currently most widely accepted. In his opinion, the pavilions symbolize the northern and southern parts of united Egypt. After the ceremonies connected with the king's symbolic ascent to the throne, his ka was supposed to go there, in order to receive his subordinates from Upper and Lower Egypt.

THE MORTUARY TEMPLE

The mortuary temple was the center of the cult of the ruler. It lay at the foot of the north wall of the Step Pyramid, and its longer axis is oriented east-west. The temple floor is slightly elevated in comparison to the surrounding buildings. The main entrance was in the southeastern part. The "secluded," inner part of the temple, which was adjacent to the pyramid, was entered through two double-columned porticos. Inside there were false doors and the cult statue of the king. The northern part of the temple consisted essentially of a courtyard. It is difficult to reconstruct the layout and meaning of the individual parts, because this confusing complex of rooms, corridors, and courtyards differs significantly from other similar structures built in the preceding and following eras. It is even possible that the temple was originally intended to be much larger and for as yet undiscovered reasons—for example, the ruler's premature death—was reduced in size.

Among the noteworthy archaeological discoveries made in the mortuary temple grounds are clay sealings belonging to a priest of the goddess Neith, which bear the name of King Sanakht.

THE SERDAB AND THE NORTHERN PART
OF THE DJOSER COMPLEX

The extensive grounds lying between the mortuary temple and the north pavilion are called the serdab courtyard, after the small structure that stands near the entrance to the mortuary temple. The *serdab* (Arabic *cellar*) consists of a small, enclosed chamber in whose north wall are a pair of round observation holes. Through them the statue of the sitting Djoser gazed out on the forecourt of the whole tomb complex and on the rituals performed there. The partly damaged, life-sized statue of Djoser in limestone is now in the Egyptian Museum in Cairo (JE 49158). It represents the ruler sitting on the throne. He is wearing a close-fitting mantle and a long, tripartite wig, as well as the crown known as *nemes*. The statue radiates a feeling of great royal grandeur.

A few other fragments resembling the statue were found in the mortuary temple grounds. Was there another serdab there? In the courtyard many fragments of so-called boundary stelae were discovered that resemble those in the south courtyard. They probably marked the initial boundary of the royal tomb and were removed when it was extended and reconstructed.

The north courtyard, which lies north of the mortuary temple and the serdab courtyard, almost a third of the Djoser complex, has not yet been carefully investigated. In the northeastern part of the grounds symbolic storehouses were found with round openings in their roofs through which grain was poured. There was also a group of chapels reminiscent of the buildings in the sed festival courtyard. On the northern edge of the complex, along its north-south axis, from the inner wall of the northern wing of the perimeter wall is a raised platform, reached by a stairway ramp. Above, on the platform, there is a depression eight meters square and a few centimeters deep. This enigmatic structure led to an interesting and still unconcluded debate among Egyptologists.

Stadelmann thought it was a sun temple, supporting his view by reference to the short cursive inscription *seket re* ("decline of Re") on an ostracon found not far away. In contrast, Altenmüller believes that the square depression indicates the spot where an obelisk originally stood, the symbol of the revered stone fetish in Heliopolis known as benben. His suggestion is supposed to be indirectly confirmed by the fact that the high priest there, Imhotep, also was in charge of the construction of the pyramid complex. However, it must be pointed out against both theories that neither the obelisk nor its fragments were found on the grounds of the Djoser complex. A subsequent analysis of the inscription showed that it bore not the name of a sun temple, but that of a pavilion connected with the sed festival.

For an explanation of the raised platform we will have to wait until the systematic archaeological investigation of the northern part of the complex is completed. That investigation will surely produce a broad range of interesting and possibly unexpected discoveries. Various soundings have already shown that in this area are so-called stairway tombs that are older than the complex itself. It is also interesting that Mariette discovered, near the previously mentioned platform, the so-called Lion Altar, which Borchardt dated to the Second Dynasty. Moreover, Djoser's and Khasekhemwy's sealings were found in the subterranean corridors in the northwest corner of the complex. These discoveries seem to be connected with the archaeological issues raised by the enigmatic "west mounds."

THE WEST MOUNDS

West of the south courtyard and the Step Pyramid, three low mounds run north and south. The westernmost and largest of them is about 400 meters long, 25 meters wide, and 5 meters high. In its northern segment, remains of a brick structure were found; Lauer thinks it was the lodging of the master builder of the Djoser complex. The easternmost and lowest mound is immediately adjacent to the Step Pyramid.

The still incomplete investigation of the west mounds has shown that their superstructures contain no chambers and were constructed using stone fragments. The mounds differ slightly from each other in appearance. For example, according to Lauer, the easternmost had a flat roof, whereas the middle one had a gently arched roof. The slightly inclined side walls were decorated with niches. Five shafts and staircases provided access to the substructure, which is composed of long, partly destroyed corridors and projecting side chambers. In the previously unexplored parts, a large number of fragments of stone vessels were found, along with grains (barley and wheat) and dried fruits.

As long as a careful archaeological investigation of the whole structure has not been concluded, the meaning of the west mounds will remain unknown to us. According to Lauer, Djoser's servants are buried in it. On the other hand, Stadelmann thinks it is composed of older structures from the Second Dynasty that were later included in Djoser's complex.

Even though remains of older structures are found both inside and outside the complex, quite a few facts conflict with Stadelmann's view. For one thing, the superstructure's masonry probably consists of waste material from the pyramid complex construction site, and for another, the way the west mounds lean on the Step Pyramid suggests that they were built at a later date. The ground plan of the subterranean part of the west mounds that has been so far investigated resembles that of a storeroom more than anything else. In addition, there is no reason to assume that any Old Kingdom ruler usurped or destroyed the tomb of one of his predecessors in order to use its materials in constructing his own.

IN CONCLUSION

Because of its originality, the group of buildings constituting Djoser's tomb is very difficult to interpret. It is sure to remain a subject of debate among Egyptologists for a long time and to give rise to various, often conflicting theories. In general, researchers agree that the complex manifests the consolidation of the political and economic situation in Egypt after the turbulent and often strife-ridden period of the Second Dynasty.

Ricke sees the complex as the ruler's symbolic residence in the beyond, and thus rejects the view that it is a faithful copy of the ruler's earthly residence. In his view, the complex represents an ideal combination of the religious ideas of Upper and Lower Egypt expressed by architectural means and forms and at the same time the symbolic unity of the main parts of the royal residence—the residential palace, the administrative buildings, the coronation palace, and the festival courtyards.

Approaching the problem from the point of view of chronology and archaeology, Kaiser asks whether the complex was built at one time according to a single plan, or in differing stages. He sees the second possibility as the more likely, even if it is difficult to reconstruct the stages of development. It is clear that it was not until the final stage (P2) that an attempt was made to weld the individual buildings into a harmonious unity, a complex that would be coherent in both function and meaning. Even then the construction did not fully realize the projected goal, since in the course of that final phase the ruler prob-

Imhotep holds an unrolled papyrus scroll on his knees. His name is on both the papyrus and the base of the sedentary statue. Bronze, Late Period. Egyptian Museum, Cairo.

ably died, which led to the mortuary temple's being simplified and significantly reduced in size.

Lauer, the most competent expert on this subject, is of the opinion that the builder of the Djoser complex did not follow a plan laid out in advance, but rather relied on his experience with two very different kinds of buildings. The first were symbolic buildings, so-called simulacra, which were connected with the sed festival and were intended to house the ruler's ka in the beyond (for example, the sed festival complex, the "T" temple, and the south and north pavilions). The second were functional buildings for the interment and mortuary rituals (the columned vestibule on the western edge of the entrance colonnade, the "oblique" building south of the entrance colonnade, and the mortuary temple).

Lauer's views have found the greatest acceptance thus far. Precisely because he is such a celebrated authority in the field, we must mention here fundamental and still unresolved problems that in his opinion must be given more attention in further research. In an interview with the journalist Philippe Flandrin, Lauer formulated these problems in the form of questions he would have liked to ask Imhotep, whose role as architect he has never for a moment doubted:

- Was the initial structure (M1) planned for Djoser or for his predecessor Sanakht? (As we have already indicated, an answer to this question is gradually emerging.)
- Was Imhotep the architect not only of the Step Pyramid in Saqqara but also of the Djoser temple discovered in Heliopolis, on whose ruins the names of the ruler's wife Hetephernebti and his daughter Inetkaus were found?
- How were the architraves of the entrance corridor aligned?
- In the initial phase, the stone perimeter wall of the tomb complex must have enclosed a much smaller area than it does today. Is there any convincing evidence regarding the original extent of the grounds?
- Why was the original square ground plan (in M1) retained during the gradual enlargement of Djoser's tomb, and then changed to a rectangular plan in the final phase?
- Was the south tomb built at the same time as the Step Pyramid?

- What was the south tomb's meaning? Was it a symbolic substitute for the royal tomb in Abydos? Or did it play an important role in the sed festival rituals, during which the ruler's statue was buried in it to symbolize his seeming death?
- The rock under the Step Pyramid is partly friable, but in places is so hard that during the excavation of the subterranean corridors and chambers explosives sometimes had to be used. What means and methods did the ancient Egyptians use, when it seems they had only copper chisels?
- During the M2 phase eleven shaft tombs for members of the royal family were dug in front of the mastaba's east side. Why were some of these (nos. 6, 7, and 8) used for the burial of stone vessels from the First and Second Dynasties, even before the tomb was enlarged (M3) and the entrances to the shafts covered up?
- Why were the entrances to the south and north pavilions not in the middle, but rather somewhat outside the axis of the facades?
- At the time that Djoser ascended the throne, was the astral religion still dominant, or was the sun religion already prevalent? (Lauer believes that it was precisely in Djoser's time, through the influence of Imhotep, that sun worship became widespread at the royal court.)
- Were Djoser's servants buried in the west mound?

To Lauer's questions we might add others, one of which Lauer would certainly have liked to ask: Where was Imhotep himself buried? This question has fascinated several generations of Egyptologists. Walter Emery, Firth's and Quibell's successor, who had been involved in the British excavations in Saqqara since 1936, was almost obsessed by it, for example. A highly successful British archaeologist who was regarded by some of his contemporaries as authoritarian and cocky, Emery looked for Imhotep's grave in North Saqqara, perhaps because when Imhotep was deified in the Late Period, he was worshiped in the vicinity of the Serapeum. Although he sometimes felt he was on the verge of discovering it, Emery ultimately failed to find the grave.

Sekhemkhet's Step Pyramid

Like ancient tragedy, Egyptian archaeology has heroes who rapidly rise to eminence and then, just when they have achieved well-deserved success, suffer an abrupt fall. Before the Second World War, the young Egyptian archaeologist Zakaria Goneim was already working in Saqqara, where he supervised the excavations in the pyramid temple of the last ruler of the Fifth Dynasty, Unas. He spent the war years in Luxor and afterward returned to Saqqara, where he had long been fascinated by a huge, rectangular structure whose outlines could be vaguely discerned under a dune, and which was oriented more or less north and south. It was near the site where Goneim had worked before the war, only about a hundred meters southwest of Unas's pyramid temple.

On the advice of Lauer, who was at that time pursuing excavations not far away in Djoser's pyramid complex, Goneim concentrated on uncovering the four corners of the enigmatic structure, in order to determine its surface area. He was ultimately able to do so, and to the great surprise of both archaeologists, it turned out that the corners were those of a limestone perimeter wall that surrounded a previously unknown pyramid complex. Its facade, ornamented with deep niches, was strikingly similar to that of the boundary of the Djoser pyramid complex. There was hardly any doubt that the newly discovered structure had also been built in the Third Dynasty.

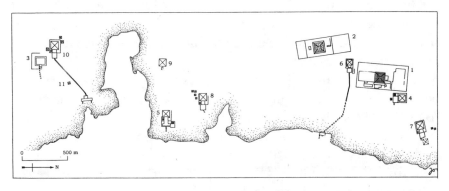

The pyramid field at Saqqara. 1. Djoser, 2. Sekhemkhet, 3. Shepseskaf, 4. Userkaf, 5. Djedkare, 6. Unas, 7. Teti, 8. Pepi I, 9. Merenre, 10. Pepi II, 11. Ibi.

Goneim intensified his excavations, continuing them throughout the first half of the 1950s. Additional archaeological knowledge was acquired, and it seemed as though the veil of mystery that hung over the pyramid complex was gradually lifting. The complex was constructed on an uneven rock surface, forcing the builders to level the terrain and build large terraces, some of them more than ten meters high. Why did they choose this place as a construction site, when it required such laborious preparations and was so remote that the pyramid would be almost invisible from the Nile Valley? The presence of older royal tombs from the Second Dynasty in the immediate surroundings may have played a role in that choice. A few such tombs have been found there already, and others probably lie hidden under the sand dunes. Yet to answer this question, another, not insignificant aspect must be taken into consideration. Before the beginning of the Third Dynasty, royal tomb builders did not seek to draw attention to the tombs by making them very large or by choosing a site that would be clearly visible from the Nile Valley. That changed in Djoser's time, with the conversion of the mastaba into the Step Pyramid.

The boundary of the complex was built in two stages. A significant extension to the south and especially to the north brought it closer to the dimensions of the Djoser pyramid complex, which it strikingly resembled: rows of niches alternated in a regular rhythm with false doors, and it seems that there was only a single genuine door, through which one entered the ruler's death residence. Unfortunately, as we will later see, the excavations inside this pyramid complex were never completed, and the true entrance has not yet been found. The casing on the perimeter wall is of brilliant white blocks of fine limestone, which came from the quarries in Tura on the opposite bank of the Nile. After it was completed, the wall must have been as high as ten meters, with a walkway on its upper surface leading to the sentry posts, just as in the Djoser complex. The striking similarity between the two complexes may be explained by a mason's inscription on the perimeter wall, which includes Imhotep's name. If Imhotep was also the builder of this complex, then its possessor must have been Djoser's immediate successor.

Goneim's excavations quickly revealed that the pyramid had been built only to a height of some twenty-six feet. Egyptologists are still in disagreement as to whether six or seven steps were originally planned. The structure had a square ground plan, with sides 230 ancient Egyptian cubits long (1 cubit = approximately 0.52 meters), and its core was built using the method of accretion layers. It is estimated that given these parameters, the pyramid would have reached a height of about seventy meters, and thus would have been higher than Djoser's.

On Lauer's recommendation, Goneim began to focus special attention on the area in front of the north wall. Here, after a short time, he discovered, more or less along the pyramid's north-south axis, a tunnel some eighty meters that led under the pyramid and ended in a burial chamber. As in the case of the contemporary mastabas in Upper Egypt's Beit Khallaf, this tunnel was interrupted by a vertical shaft passing not only through the substructure but also through the masonry of the aboveground part of the pyramid. The shaft was part of a security system intended to protect the entrance to the ruler's burial chamber.

There Goneim found archaeological objects of various kinds and ages. Farthest up were bones and horns, which probably came from animals that had been sacrificed—cattle, rams, and gazelles. Farther down he discovered sixty-two demotic papyri from the Twenty-Sixth

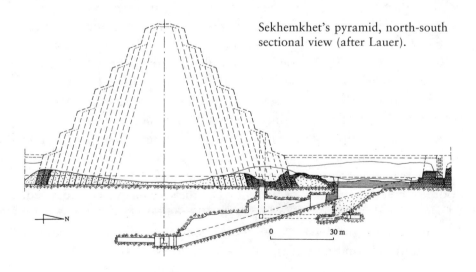

Sekhemkhet's pyramid, north-south sectional view (after Lauer).

Dynasty, or more precisely from the reign of Ahmose II. Finally, he came upon about seven hundred stone vessels and a gold treasure trove from the Third Dynasty, which included twenty-one bracelets, small mussel shells, and faience corals covered with gold leaf. This is the oldest collection of ancient Egyptian gold ornaments yet found, and it remains unclear how the treasure came to be in this place and how it escaped the greed of grave robbers, having doubtless been taken already from the ruler's burial equipment.

Under the vertical shaft, some forty-seven meters before the burial chamber, a U-shaped corridor opens in the east wall of the descending access tunnel. In it is the entrance to a series of narrow, long storerooms lined up along one side.

The burial chamber is at the lower end of the descending tunnel, about a hundred feet under the pyramid's ground level, precisely on its vertical axis. In the corridor leading to the chamber, seal impressions with Sekhemkhet's name were found on the clay stoppers of vessels. Therefore, he is considered the possessor of the pyramid complex.

In the north-south–oriented chamber stands an alabaster box-sarcophagus with a highly polished surface. Alabaster was rarely used for a royal sarcophagus; the only other known examples are the coffins of Queen Hetepheres I (Fourth Dynasty) and Seti I (Nineteenth Dynasty). It was also unusual in having no cover; instead, there was a sliding partition with two openings through which the maneuvering ropes could be inserted. When he saw the sarcophagus, Goneim gasped: the partition was sealed. A wooden lever and the remains of a bunch of dried flowers that lay on the sarcophagus strengthened Goneim's impression that he had discovered an intact royal grave. Lauer dampened his enthusiasm, however, telling him not to expect too much, because when he had examined the burial chamber, it had seemed to him that it had already been looted by grave robbers. But his warning did no good; Goneim would not give up his conviction that he had made a sensational discovery. He invited high state officials, journalists, reporters, and film teams to be present when the sarcophagus was opened. Then came the shock: the sarcophagus was empty.

After a time, the wave of disappointment on Goneim's part and of schadenfreude on that of some of his colleagues subsided. Even without an intact royal grave, Goneim's discovery of Sekhemkhet's pyramid complex was a sensation, exciting great interest among professionals, particularly abroad. Goneim was invited to go on a lecture tour in the United States, and he wrote a book about his discovery, *The Buried Pyramid,* which had great success and was later translated into other languages. However, he was not to be able to complete his research in the Sekhemkhet complex.

After his return from the United States, Goneim was accused of stealing and smuggling antiquities, an accusation that put an end to his excavations in Saqqara. It was alleged that he had carried off a large, valuable vessel that Quibell and Lauer had found two years earlier in Djoser's pyramid field. The authorities had no hard evidence, only slanders and suppositions. Goneim was subjected to repeated interrogations by the police and was devastated by the accusation, which also dismayed his friends, especially Lauer, who never doubted Goneim's innocence. When the whole affair had already gone on for some time, Lauer decided to act. Convinced that a tragic misunderstanding must be involved, he went to the Egyptian Museum in Cairo to have a look at the documentation. The allegedly stolen vessel might accidentally have been taken there.

After making a patient search in 1957, Lauer found the vessel he was looking for in the corner of the Egyptian Museum's depository. Overjoyed, he hurried off to an appointment in Saqqara, intending to inform Goneim of his discovery the next morning. But he was too

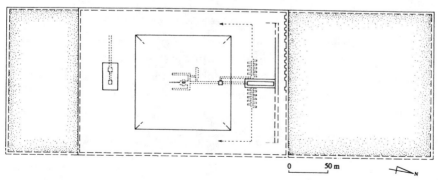

Plan of Sekhemkhet's pyramid complex (after Lauer).

late. Goneim committed suicide by jumping into the Nile before Lauer got in touch with him.

Afterward, work on this excavation site came to a standstill for a while. Only in 1963, thirteen years after Goneim's first discovery, were pickaxes and work songs heard there again. It was Lauer who resumed the investigation and continued it, with a few interruptions, until 1976. He was motivated not only by his friendship for Goneim, but also by his passion for archaeological research and his sense of responsibility. The excavation had to be concluded at least in its main outlines, because it was likely to yield valuable information concerning the development of the step pyramids and the still inadequately researched and largely unknown history of the Third Dynasty.

Lauer wanted to resolve a number of issues, ranging from the possibility that for unknown reasons Sekhemkhet's mummy had been removed to a place other than the burial chamber, to certain technical data necessary to reconstruct the plan of the pyramid complex. After a few weeks he made his first discovery when he came across the foundations of the south wing of the perimeter wall. From there it was only a short step to determine more precisely the probable location of the south tomb, and yet it took Lauer four more years to find it, in 1967. The aboveground part consisted of a mastaba built of limestone blocks. The entrance was on the west side, as in the Djoser complex. A longer corridor, descending toward the east and interrupted by a vertical shaft, leveled out at its lower end and led to a small burial chamber. In the corridor, near the burial chamber, Lauer found fragments of a small wooden coffin with the remains of a child about two years old, perhaps Sekhemkhet's son. Though the burial chamber bore clear traces of having been looted by grave robbers, he found fragments of thin gold leaf impressed with a pattern imitating reed matting, along with animal bones and stone vessels.

Goneim's and Lauer's research showed that with the exception of the pyramid itself, Sekhemkhet's complex was initially planned to be smaller than Djoser's, but changes and extensions were made to the original plans. Precise reconstruction of the plans and the construction phases is almost impossible, however, as long as the archaeological investigation has not been concluded. Yet even the incomplete information acquired so far has produced the most varied theories concerning the fate of the complex and its possessor.

Hanns Stock, an important German archaeologist who was the director of the German Archaeological Institute in Cairo at the time Goneim was pursuing his excavations in Saqqara, expressed the view that the Sekhemkhet complex was originally intended to be a copy of the Djoser complex. As a result of unforeseeable and unknown circumstances, instead of being completed it was filled in and transformed into an enormous mastaba whose outside wall consisted of the original perimeter wall. The Italian researchers Vito Maragioglio and Celeste Rinaldi complemented this view by noting that Sekhemkhet probably always intended to erect not a pyramid, but rather a large mastaba like the one that Lauer discovered underneath the Step Pyramid, and that he considered to be the original or initial phase of the construction of Djoser's tomb.

But what happened to Sekhemkhet's mummy? Lauer, who is second only to Goneim as the most competent expert on Sekhemkhet's pyramid, was of the opinion that Sekhemkhet's mummy and the precious burial equipment were removed during the First Intermediate Period, when a large number of Old Kingdom pyramids were broken into and plundered. Edwards held a similar view. In his opinion, it might even have been during the burial ritual that the ruler's mummy was destroyed and the royal treasure plundered—assuming that Sekhemkhet's tomb was not conceived from the outset as a simple cenotaph.

Maragioglio and Rinaldi rejected Lauer's theory, basing their demurral on two discoveries. One was the wall blocking the entrance into the substructure, which according to Goneim was undamaged at the time he made his discovery. The other stemmed from the Fourth Dynasty: a sealed but empty sarcophagus of Queen Hetepheres I found in a shaft near Khufu's pyramid and that of an unknown pharaoh in the so-called Great Pit in Zawiyet el-Aryan. However, Maragioglio and Rinaldi were also unable to provide a satisfactory answer to the riddle.

Another archaeological investigation might help unveil this structure's secret. The grounds in front of the pyramid's north side, where the remains of the mortuary temple are assumed to lie, have not yet been investigated. Should archaeological excavations show that it was there that the dead pharaoh was worshiped, it would be almost certain that Sekhemkhet was also buried there.

Similarly, the various theories about Sekhemkhet's pyramid pay remarkably little attention to the body of the two-year-old child found there. The archaeological circumstances of this discovery and its possible historical contexts are very interesting. Was it really Sekhemkhet's son? If he died before his father, why was the south tomb, which was supposed to perform a different, quite special function in the whole tomb complex, used for his burial? Or did the child die after his father? Is there any convincing archaeological evidence that would allow us to date precisely the child's burial?

The knowledge acquired thus far clearly indicates that the structure was enlarged shortly after work on it began, but construction was interrupted soon thereafter. Why? Was it quickly terminated in order to transform the unfinished pyramid into a large mastaba, as was done in Abusir two centuries later in the case of the tomb of a Fifth Dynasty pharaoh, Neferefre? Or was the unfinished pyramid complex filled in—as Stock thinks—and the work thus ritually ended? The absence of the royal mummy in the sealed alabaster sarcophagus speaks in favor of the latter. However, the question then arises of whether the reason for stopping construction and for the empty sarcophagus was not the pharaoh's sudden death under circumstances that made it impossible to arrange an orderly burial, including the mummification of the body and its interment in the sarcophagus. However, to suggest further that Sekhemkhet might have died during an expedition into the remote areas of the Sinai or Nubia or drowned in the Nile, or been violently removed, would be pure speculation without any ground in Egyptological knowledge.

Khaba's (?) Layer Pyramid

Zawiyet el-Aryan is a village that lies on the bank of the Nile, about halfway between Giza and Abusir. To the west, a necropolis spreads across the slightly elevated, rolling edge of the desert. It is unique in the region around Memphis, in that it contains two uncompleted pyramids and nothing else. Egyptologists call the older of these two pyramids, whose construction is more advanced, the Layer Pyramid, and the local people call it in Arabic *Haram el-Meduwara*, the Round Pyramid.

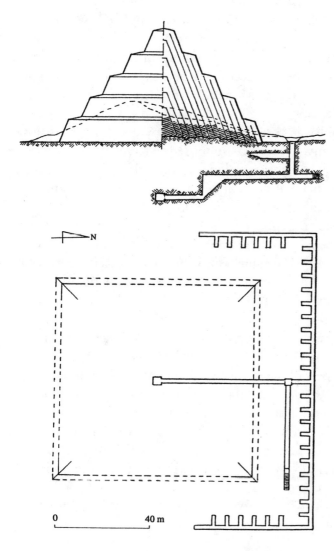

The Layer Pyramid in Zawiyet el-Aryan. North-south sectional view and ground plan (after Lauer).

0   40 m

This pyramid was first investigated and summarily described by Perring in 1839. It is also mentioned in the Lepsius expedition's report. Genuine archaeological investigation did not begin until around 1900, with the Italian artist, restorer, and archaeologist Alexandre Barsanti, who had earlier carried out excavations in the neighborhood of Unas's pyramid in the nearby necropolis in Saqqara. Shortly afterward, and still before the First World War, the American expedition, led by George Reisner, renewed the excavations. Unfortunately, neither of these archaeological investigations was completed. Worse yet, fundamental parts of the technical documentation, such as certain measurements and the plans made from them, contradict each other. The necropolis has long been inaccessible because it now lies within a military reservation, and this has made it impossible to complement or correct earlier findings.

The Layer Pyramid was conceived as a step pyramid, but it is not entirely clear how many steps it was supposed to have; estimates vary from five to seven. Even a cursory glance at the ruins shows that the core was built with internal accretion layers—hence the pyramid's name. However, the casing of fine white limestone has not yet been found, and this tends to support the view that the whole structure was never completed. Extensive remains of brick masonry were discovered alongside the pyramid, however, and that led Reisner to formulate the very unusual thesis that the casing consisted not of limestone blocks but of mudbricks. This theory has not yet found much support. It is generally thought that those remains are the ruins of temporary ramps that were not removed after construction was prematurely terminated.

The underground part of the Layer Pyramid in many ways resembles that of Sekhemkhet's, though its plan is somewhat simpler and more advanced. The entrance to the substructure is located inside the site, near the northeast corner. It begins as a steep staircase and continues westward as an open trench until it reaches the northwest axis of the pyramid, where it is interrupted by a vertical shaft. From the floor of the shaft a horizontal corridor turns off; the corridor is U-shaped, and one of its sides is lined with thirty-two storerooms intended for the royal burial equipment.

A second corridor leads directly to a burial chamber that lies precisely under the pyramid's vertical axis. Nothing was found here that might indicate a sarcophagus or interment. Moreover, the corridor is so narrow that one wonders how it would be possible to get a large stone sarcophagus into the burial chamber at all.

Like the pyramids themselves, the immediate surroundings have never been carefully investigated. The remains of brick walls built vertically at the pyramid's east wall might be all that is left of a cult place where stone stelae probably originally stood. Still farther to the east, at the edge of the desert, lie the ruins of an enigmatic, not yet investigated structure that the local people call *el-gamal el-barek,* the "Recumbent Camel." Nabil Swelim believes that this might have been the ruins of a valley temple. If he is right, the Layer Pyramid in Zawiyet el-Aryan would be the first pyramid complex to have an east–west–oriented valley temple.

North of the pyramid the American expedition discovered a large mastaba, identified as Z-500 on the map of the necropolis. In this mastaba were found, among other things, eight alabaster vessels with the name of a Third Dynasty ruler named Khaba. These vessels are so far the only indirect proof that Khaba might have been the possessor of the Layer Pyramid. However, not all Egyptologists accept this view. Swelim, for instance, attributes the pyramid to Neferka, another Third Dynasty ruler.

All this can be cleared up only by making a thorough archaeological investigation of the whole Layer Pyramid complex. One thing is certain, however: typologically, this structure is intermediate between Sekhemkhet's pyramid in Saqqara and Snefru's pyramid in Meidum and was, therefore, surely built in the middle or the second half of the Third Dynasty.

Lepsius Pyramid (?) No. 1

In Abu Rawash, only a few kilometers north of Giza, there is not only the pyramid of a Fourth Dynasty king, Djedefre (sometimes spelled Radjedef), but also the ruins of a very puzzling monument that the

Lepsius expedition had discovered and identified as a pyramid. Because it was the northernmost pyramid on the expedition's archaeological map, it was given the number 1.

Both Vyse and Perring had visited this site before Lepsius, yet they had not carefully examined the monument. Its lamentable state kept other Egyptologists—such as Fernand Bisson de la Roque, a Frenchman who became the first to study the Abu Rawash site intensively in the 1920s—from systematically investigating it.

Already in the time of Vyse, Perring, and Lepsius the ruins resembled an enormous, shapeless mass of brick masonry, which then reached a height of almost twenty meters. When Swelim began to work on them in the mid-1980s, they had already fallen down almost completely.

Swelim's conclusions are interesting but controversial. In his view, these are the remains of an enormous step pyramid, about one quarter of whose core consisted of a rock outcropping. This made the structure enormously strong, as well as quick and cheap to build. Swelim dates it to the end of the Third Dynasty and thinks it probably belonged to Huni.

There are several objections to this theory. First of all, the choice of the pyramid's site, on the farthest edge of the Nile flood zone—that is, not in an elevated, dominant place, as was usual for Old Kingdom pyramids—is strange. In addition, the rock outcropping on which the core is supposed to have been built is honeycombed with more than thirty rock-cut tombs built in the Fifth and Sixth Dynasties. It is hard to imagine that the structure was so fully destroyed in the course of the Fourth Dynasty alone that a whole necropolis of rock-cut tombs could be built. Further objections may also be raised. The investigation and explanation of the puzzling brick structure that Lepsius considered to be the northernmost Egyptian pyramid thus remains one of the many unresolved issues in Egyptian archaeology.

CHAPTER FIVE

THE FOURTH DYNASTY—
THE GREATEST OF THE GREAT

Snefru was Huni's immediate successor (although the family relationship between them is not entirely clear), and yet the Ptolemaic historian Manetho sees him as beginning a new dynasty, the Fourth. Under
his reign the strongly centralized Egyptian state reached the apex of
its power, and indirect but eloquent testimony to this fact is provided
by the greatest Egyptian pyramids, in Giza.

According to later tradition, Snefru was a great, benevolent ruler.
Written documents—especially the annals inscribed on the famous
Palermo stone—suggest that he built great ships and a palace of cedar
wood, opened the diorite quarries near Abu Simbel, and conducted
military campaigns in Nubia and Libya. However, his most spectacular
feat in the course of his long reign was the construction of four pyramids. Two of these stand close to his new residence near Dahshur,

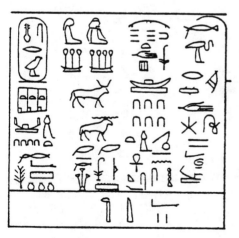

The annals on the Palermo stone
show that Snefru brought seven
thousand prisoners and twenty
thousand head of livestock back from
Nubia, as well as forty shiploads of
conifer wood from Lebanon (after
Schäfer).

one in Meidum, and one in Seila. How much construction material and human effort must have been mobilized in order to raise up, at the ruler's command, artificial mountains of stone with a combined volume of about 3.7 million cubic meters. This achievement makes Snefru, and not Khufu, as is usually supposed, the greatest pyramid builder of all time.

Khufu (in Greek, Cheops), the builder of the Great Pyramid, was the son of Snefru and Queen Hetepheres I; his full name was Khnemkhufu. While Memphis remained the capital, he probably moved his residence to modern-day Giza, on the western edge of Cairo. Khufu consolidated his power by concentrating the key offices in the hands of his closest family members.

Snefru had this inscription celebrating the victory over the Bedouins chiseled into the rock cliff at Wadi Maghara in the Sinai, in order to frighten away the savage nomadic tribes that threatened Egyptian turquoise- and copper-mining operations.

Khufu also took over the turquoise and copper resources in the Sinai, sent ships to bring cedar wood from Byblos on the coast of modern-day Lebanon, exploited the diorite mines near Abu Simbel, and undertook campaigns against Nubia and Libya, where he won rich spoils. During his reign the earliest known dam in the world was built in Wadi Gerawi, in the mountains west of modern Helwan. However, in history Khufu is known above all as the builder of the largest Egyptian pyramid, one of the seven ancient wonders of the world. The uniqueness of this structure consists not only in its size but also in the very complicated system of its inner chambers.

Around the pyramid was built a necropolis with smaller pyramids for the queens and mastabas for other members of the royal family and high state officials. It was an expression of the longing even after death to lie near the "good god"—that is, the pharaoh—and at the same time it reflected the hierarchical social order of ancient Egypt, which resembled a pyramid in form.

To guarantee the worship of the dead king, which was to continue forever, the rulers' mortuary temples received rich contributions from the fields and workshops of the funerary estates. If we consider the gigantic material resources and human labor required for the construction of the tombs, the growing economic difficulties and the resulting social tension in ancient Egypt seem inevitable, even at this time when

The relief with the fragment of an inscription containing Khufu's name and title may come from the ruler's pyramid complex in Giza; at the beginning of the Twelfth Dynasty it was used in building Amenemhet I's pyramid in Lisht (after Goedicke).

its civilization was flourishing. Nonetheless, there were other, subtler reasons for this decline, such as the supposition that Khufu's eldest son, prince Kauab, predeceased him. This unanticipated event could have led to a deep split within the royal family and hastened the decline of the Fourth Dynasty.

After Khufu's death, Djedefre first came to the throne, possibly outside the legitimate line of succession; he seems to have been the husband of the queens Khentetenka and Hetepheres II. The latter, to whom Egyptologists formerly attributed a Libyan heritage, had a rather eventful life. She may have been married to prince Kauab before she married Djedefre, and after the latter's death she married his successor, Khafre. The allegedly intentional destruction of Djedefre's pyramid complex in Abu Rawash used to be seen as evidence of the conflicts within the royal family, which were supposed to have resulted in the coronation of Khufu's younger son Khafre. Djedefre was apparently an adherent of the sun cult that was then becoming prevalent, and he was the first ruler to assume the title of "son of Re." The most recent archaeological research allows us to conclude that intensive devastation began in Roman times, when the monument degenerated into a stone quarry.

Before he ascended the throne, Khafre was probably called Khafkhufu, and a mastaba in the first row of tombs in the so-called East Cem-

Reconstruction of part of the west cemetery in Giza, near the mastabas of Nisutnefer and Kaninisut (after Junker).

etery of the Great Pyramid was apparently prepared. We can assume that with him the main branch of the royal family once again became dominant. Along with the growing importance of sun worship, the Re priesthood's power further increased during Khafre's reign. As a result, the Sphinx, which was worshiped as an image of the sun god Harmakhet (Greek Harmachis, "Horus in the horizon"), might have been incorporated into Khafre's pyramid complex. The ruler retained strict control over the central state power and, through his family, over all the important offices of the land as well. Khafre's pyramid complex is only slightly inferior to that of his father. The surrounding cemeteries were not as heavily used, however, and were not built according to a unified plan. A diorite statue found in the valley temple of the Khafre complex in Giza is considered a complete artistic expression of the authority of the divine pharaoh. The pharaoh's head is sheltered from behind by the outspread wings of the falcon god Horus. The statue, which is now in the Egyptian Museum in Cairo, expresses the ideal connection between earthly and divine power.

After Khafre's death, the situation within the royal family apparently came to a head. For a short time Djedefre's son Baka probably came to power, before Khafre's son Menkaure (Greek Mykerinos) succeeded him, presumably as the last legitimate representative of Snefru's line. Menkaure had the third and smallest royal pyramid in Giza built for himself. In conception and elaboration, his tomb complex reveals a certain relaxation of the forceful style that characterized his father's complex. The strikingly smaller dimensions probably reflect the decreasing possibilities and material resources available to Menkaure. Although he may have reigned as many as three decades, and therefore perhaps even longer than his father, he was unable to complete his pyramid complex. The premature death of Khuenre, his son and the legitimate heir to the throne, probably led to a serious crisis in the Fourth Dynasty that foreshadowed its decline.

After Menkaure, Shepseskaf ascended the throne for a short time; he may have been Menkaure's son by one of the secondary queens. To him fell the task of completing Menkaure's complex in Giza. The fact that he no longer used stone but rather mudbricks testifies to the great haste and apparently reduced means with which he fulfilled that duty. Afterward, Shepseskaf chose as the site of his own tomb a place that was then very remote, in South Saqqara. There no pyramid was built, however, only a large mastaba. The fact that Shepseskaf had his tomb built outside the royal cemetery in Giza and did not have a pyramidal tomb erected for himself is interpreted by some Egyptologists as evidence that he rejected the sun religion, whose influence was steadily increasing.

During the transition from the Fourth to the Fifth Dynasty, which is still not well understood, a woman, the queen mother Khentkaues I, came into the foreground. As a probable daughter of Menkaure, she became, in a situation that obviously cast into doubt the legitimacy of the succession to the throne, a connecting link between the old Snefru lineage and the "sun kings" of the Fifth Dynasty. She bore a title unique in ancient Egypt, which many scholars translate as "Mother of Two Kings of Upper and Lower Egypt," and others as "King of Upper and Lower Egypt and Mother of the King of Upper and Lower Egypt."* Her tomb, the so-called Fourth Pyramid in Giza, is a unique combination of a rock-cut grave and a mastaba, which was later transformed into a step-shaped structure.

In the late 1970s a small pyramid complex was discovered in Abusir that belonged to another queen, also called Khentkaues, whose titles corresponded to those of the elder Khentkaues buried in Giza. They were, however, two different individuals. The Queen Khentkaues interred in Abusir was more than a generation younger, and she was the consort of the third ruler of the Fifth Dynasty, Neferirkare. The pyramid complex in Abusir, and especially written documents discovered in it, finally provided a new and unexpected basis for solving this complicated historical and genealogical problem, which probably centered on a conflict between two competing branches of the royal family. This conflict broke out in Giza in the time of Khentkaues I and culminated in Abusir in the time of Khentkaues II.

---

* The oddity of this title has been the source of considerable debate among Egyptologists. See pp. 262–264.

Snefru's Pyramid in Meidum

Traveling south from Cairo, after about a hundred kilometers one sees, on the edge of the western desert above the lush green of the fields and gardens in the Nile Valley, the silhouette of a huge, three-stepped structure. From a distance one might think a mirage had brought a ziggurat from the banks of the Tigris and the Euphrates. The bizarre, tower-shaped image conceals only for a moment, and only from the uninitiated visitor, the true meaning of the structure, which was once a pyramid and is today called, after the nearby village, the Meidum Pyramid. As the earlier local designation of it as *el-haram el-kaddab* (False Pyramid) shows, the native population, which doubtless drew its knowledge from the tradition of grave robbing, knew what it was.

Because of its form, the pyramid attracted attention in the Middle Ages. At the beginning of the fifteenth century, the famed Arab historian Taqi ad-Din al-Maqrizi thought it looked like a huge, five-stepped mountain. During the subsequent six centuries it eroded so much that in the travel notes taken by Frederik Ludwig Norden in the eighteenth century the pyramid seemed to have only three levels. Archaeological findings indicate that human beings played the greatest role in eroding the monument.

In 1799, Napoleon's expedition passed by Meidum, but the famous draftsman Denon was able to make only a few sketches and prepare a short description of the pyramid. It was investigated and measured much more carefully by Perring in 1837 and especially by the Lepsius expedition in 1843. However, the inside of the structure remained inaccessible. Maspero was the first to open the pyramid and some of the mastabas in the area, in the framework of a wide-ranging archaeological project whose goal was to discover and document the pyramid texts.

Archaeological investigations of the Meidum Pyramid began precisely ten years later. These were led by no less a figure than Petrie, the founder of modern Egyptian archaeology, in collaboration with his compatriots, the architect George Fraser and the Egyptologist Percy Newberry. They investigated the inside of the pyramid and discovered the pyramid temple, an approach causeway, and a series of private tombs in the area around the pyramid.

After a long interruption, Petrie returned to Meidum, this time with two other Egyptologists, Ernest MacKay and Gerald Wainwright. They conducted excavations at the northeast corner of the pyramid, in the so-called South Pyramid, and in other places. The tunnel they dug into the pyramid showed that its core consisted of five accretion layers whose outer surfaces were built of carefully dressed limestone blocks.

Petrie's research provided an answer to only one of the many Egyptological questions relating to the Meidum Pyramid, and raised many new questions. In the mid-1920s Borchardt arrived in Meidum, and after a few days accumulated so much knowledge that it filled a whole book, still highly regarded today: *Die Entstehung der Pyramide an der Baugeschichte der Pyramide bei Mejdum nachgewiesen.* He even reconstructed, on the basis of the ruins, a corridor leading toward the pyramid from the southeast, which Petrie had discovered in 1910, and which in his opinion had been used to transport construction materials. The ramp had a gradient of ten degrees and made it possible to construct the lower half of the pyramid, which composes 88.5 percent of the total volume of the masonry. The builders increased the gradient of the upper half of the ramp. On these assumptions, everything about the construction strategy seemed to be explained.

A few years later, in the late 1920s, an American expedition under the leadership of the British archaeologist Alan Rowe came to Meidum. After investigations had been interrupted for half a century, an Egyptian archaeological expedition began to work here; it was led by Ali el-Kholi and concentrated on the enormous gravel mound at the foot of the pyramid. Shortly before, Kurt Mendelssohn, who was visiting Meidum as a tourist, had been intrigued by this wall and by the unique form of the remains of the pyramid. It seemed to him that a catastrophe might have occurred during the construction of the pyramid, and he published his theory in the book *The Riddle of the Pyramid,* which immediately became a best-seller. Mendelssohn's interesting argument based on physics has not, however, convinced Egyptologists. We shall return to this argument later.

The bizarre, truncated pyramid is today about sixty-five meters high, and its summit offers a panorama of the extensive and strategically important entry corridor to the Fayyum oasis. It is no accident that this pyramid was chosen as the initial reference point for the "Land Survey of Egypt." The explanation of the current strange form of the monument and the many riddles that surround it lies in the complicated transition from the previous step pyramids to true pyramids.

The tunnel that Petrie's collaborator Wainwright dug into the inside of the pyramid showed that the pyramid core was constructed of accretion layers of limestone blocks, inclined at an angle of about seventy-five degrees and standing on a square base about thirty-eight meters on a side. Some scholars therefore ask whether this square

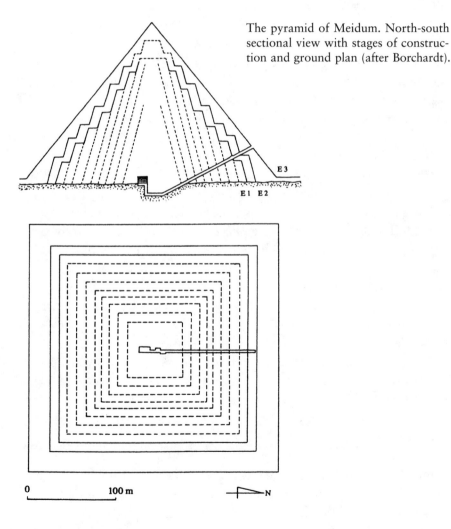

The pyramid of Meidum. North-south sectional view with stages of construction and ground plan (after Borchardt).

0   100 m

N

structure might be analogous to the initial mastaba (M1) that Lauer discovered in Djoser's pyramid.

The fact that the core was built using accretion layers did not particularly surprise archaeologists, since that was a fairly widespread construction method. What did surprise them was the smooth outside surface of each level, which seemed illogical and must have considerably decreased the cohesion of the layers and that of the structure as a whole. The explanation was provided largely by Borchardt. He showed that the Meidum Pyramid was built in three stages, during which its outward appearance changed significantly.

Originally, a seven-step pyramid was built on the rock foundation. This was enlarged to eight steps, perhaps even before it was finished. Each of the two stages, which Borchardt designated E1 and E2, was intended to be the final structure. This makes it all the harder to explain why they were ultimately rebuilt (E3) in order to transform them into a genuine pyramid. In contrast to E1 and E2, the extension E3 rested not on a solid rock foundation, but on three layers of limestone blocks laid on sand.

The construction method also differed. During stages E1 and E2 the blocks were angled toward the middle of the pyramid, as in the case of Djoser's pyramid, and that significantly increased the structure's strength. In contrast, during stage E3 they were laid horizontally. This fact had already been noticed by Borchardt, and Mendelssohn thought it supported his own theory, according to which stage E3 destroyed the cohesion with the preceding stages, with the result that during the final phase of construction a massive slippage buried the workers under rubble.

Mendelssohn's theory contradicted the archaeological discoveries Petrie had described and that are still obvious today, even upon a superficial examination of the pyramid's ruins. The truncated pyramid is surrounded on all four sides by gravel mounds that are striking in their magnitude, yet their stratification shows that the erosion of the pyramid took place gradually over a long period of time, and that there can therefore have been no sudden slippage of the masonry. At the same time, it must be emphasized that the change in the methods of laying the blocks of stone made the work of stone thieves considerably easier. Borchardt had pointed this out, and explained that the rings of rough masonry bound the individual layers of the core more strongly and were simply laid bare when those layers were destroyed.

Not long ago an American, George Johnson, sought an explanation of the large gravel mound around the pyramid. In his opinion, the wall concealed the remains of a construction ramp that ran around the pyramid and was built in connection with the transformation from E2 to E3. In support of this assumption he pointed to the unused limestone blocks that had not been part of the masonry and that el-Kholi had found during his investigation of the gravel mound on the northwest corner of the pyramid.

The entry into the pyramid is on the north-south axis, in the north wall, about fifteen meters above ground level. The placing of the entry corridor so high in the superstructure's masonry is unique among the step pyramids. A few meters below the base of the pyramid, the corridor breaks off, turning into a horizontal passageway and finally coming out in the burial chamber. There are niches on both the east and west sides of the horizontal part of the corridor. Their purpose is not entirely clear; they may have been intended to make it easier to

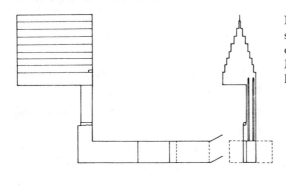

North-south and east-west sectional views and diagram of the substructure of the Meidum Pyramid (after Borchardt).

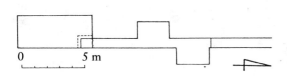

0   5 m

maneuver the blocks used to seal the corridor after interring the pharaoh's mummy in the burial chamber.

The burial chamber was entered through a vertical shaft that led upward from the south end of the corridor and came out in the northeast corner of the floor of the burial chamber. Maspero, the first archaeologist to enter the pyramid, discovered ropes and beams there. He thought the shaft was what remained of a structure built by grave robbers to facilitate their work and therefore dated from the period when the burial chamber was plundered. Some Egyptologists believe it was part of the original structure, to be used in raising the ruler's sarcophagus into the burial chamber; however, there was never a sarcophagus in the burial chamber, and apparently no one was ever interred there, either. And why should workers have undertaken the complicated task of using ropes to move a heavy stone sarcophagus through the corridor when it could have been put in place during construction? In fact, in the entry corridor Petrie found the remains of a wooden coffin he considered to be very old, possibly dating from the Old Kingdom, although he does not provide any direct evidence for this (his comments on this discovery are few and somewhat confused). Recently discovered rooms to the north of the burial chamber and above the horizontal section of the corridor probably resulted from the alteration of the pyramid's construction plan.

Following the tradition of the step pyramids of the Third Dynasty, the burial chamber is aligned with the pyramid's north-south axis. The so-called false vault constructed of large limestone blocks is worth noting. The idea behind it is very ancient and draws on the brick architecture of the Early Dynastic Period. It was intended to prevent the enormous weight of the pyramid from shattering the ceiling of the burial chamber. Given the new situation in Meidum, the builders apparently chose it over the granite ceiling slabs with which they were also familiar, and the vault withstood the pressure.

At the east side of the pyramid, Petrie discovered a mortuary temple built of limestone blocks. It is unique in a number of ways. Above all, it was the first mortuary temple to be built on the east and not the north side of the pyramid. At the same time, it is almost intact and is therefore the best preserved temple from the Old Kingdom (even the limestone ceiling slabs have remained in place); it is also very simple. The mortuary temple is no doubt connected with the whole conceptual transformation of the pyramid complex in Meidum during the E3 stage of construction.

The temple has an almost square ground plan and consists of three parts: an entry corridor with a double bend in the southeast corner, an open courtyard, and a room with two stelae. The latter, which stand close to the foot of the pyramid, consist of pieces of smooth-sided limestone rounded at the top. They bear neither inscriptions nor images, and between them stands an offering table. The lack of any kind of ornamentation emphasizes the temple's simplicity, but at the same time shows that it was not used for any cult purposes.

The temple may have had a profound effect on visitors in antiquity, as later graffiti show. Graffiti date chiefly from the Eighteenth Dynasty, and some of the writers are fulsome in their praise, as for example Ankhkheperreseneb, who came, in the forty-first year of the rule of Thutmose III, "to see the marvelous temple of Horus Snefru. He saw it, as if heaven were in it and in it the sun rose." And he exclaimed: "May cool myrrh rain down from the heavens and fragrant incense drip onto the temple roof of Horus Snefru!" It must be added that in the time of Ankhkheperreseneb's visit part of the temple was already in poor condition and full of garbage. Sometime during the First and Second Intermediate Periods herdsmen actually lived in it.

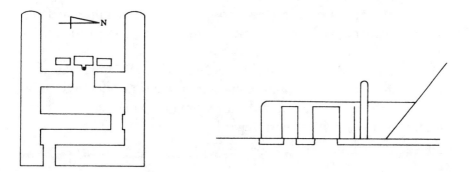

Mortuary temple of the Meidum Pyramid. Plan and east-west sectional view (after Petrie).

Archaeological investigations have also shown that the pyramid was destroyed at the end of the New Kingdom, since in the piles of rubble at its foot secondary graves from the Twenty-Second Dynasty were found at a height of between seven and ten meters above the temple floor. It is assumed that the removal of the casing blocks had already begun during the reign of Ramesses II.

The pyramid and the temple were surrounded by a high perimeter wall made of limestone blocks. The large, open courtyard it enclosed had a floor made of dried clay. On the east, a huge mastaba lay adjacent to the wall; it may have been built for the crown prince, but it has not been possible to identify its possessor, so it has simply been given the name Mastaba no. 17 on the map of the necropolis. From a structural and architectural point of view it is remarkable that stone rubble from the pyramid was used to construct it and that its mudbrick mantle was originally plastered and whitewashed.

In the courtyard, near the southwest corner of the pyramid, was a small pyramid—probably built originally as a step pyramid. It is the oldest known example of a cult pyramid. Its substructure was accessible from the north through a descending corridor. In its ruins was found a fragment of a limestone stela bearing the image of the falcon god Horus. On the opposite side of the courtyard lie the remains of a mastaba that was probably intended for the royal consort.

A causeway more than two hundred meters long probably connected the pyramid with the valley temple on the edge of the Nile Valley. However, because of the marshy terrain and the high water level, it has not yet been possible to discover this temple. Snefru's residential city of Djedsnefru (which translates to "Snefru endures") was probably located east of it.

If we set aside Mendelssohn's theory, we have to acknowledge that archaeological investigations have thus far provided no answer to some fundamental questions connected with the pyramid in Meidum. Above all, there is no agreement with regard to its possessor. The Egyptian archaeologist Ahmad Fakhry, like some other Egyptologists, believed that Huni, the last ruler of the Third Dynasty and Snefru's predecessor, was the builder of both the first two phases (E1 and E2). According to that view, only the final phase E3 is Snefru's work.

However, up to this point there is little evidence for Fakhry's assumption. Huni's name was not found at the pyramid in Meidum; on the contrary, since the Middle Kingdom many written documents have emerged that suggest that both the Meidum pyramid and the nearby residential city were once called Djedsnefru, and therefore that Snefru was then considered to be their builder. Tombs belonging to members of Snefru's family were also found alongside the pyramid.

The builders' marks on some of the blocks from which the pyramid was built are very interesting. Among them are stylized images of two-, three-, and four-level pyramids that led some scholars to assume that they show the original, gradually altered form of the pyramid. Today, this question seems to be resolved: the images determined the placement of the blocks on the corresponding levels. No less interesting are the inscriptions that include dates and designations of the work groups. They come from the years of the seventh through eighteenth cattle counts of a ruler whose name was not recorded. Given the current chronology for the end of the Third Dynasty and the beginning of the Fourth Dynasty, it is unlikely that these dates concern a ruler other than Snefru. As we shall see later, similar information is contained in a mason's inscription from Snefru's pyramid in Dahshur.

In addition, the significant alteration of the structure in stage E3 has not been fully explained. The monument's step-shaped form was abandoned in favor of a pyramid form, and the north-south orientation in favor of an east-west orientation. This apparently reflects an important shift in religious ideas that occurred during the transition from the Third to the Fourth Dynasty. According to Ricke, it was at this time that the Osiris myth was incorporated into the worship of the dead king. The king was identified with Osiris, the ruler of the realm of the dead, and his death became a mythical event. According to another interpretation, the change in the tomb's form and orientation was connected with the decline of the astral religion and the rise of the solar religion. Similarly, the German Egyptologist Dietrich Wildung argued that the pyramid complex in Meidum was a predecessor of the later sun temples of the Fifth Dynasty pharaohs.

An equally important and still unresolved question is why Snefru abandoned his pyramid complex, the royal cemetery, and his residential city of Djedsnefru and established a new residence and a new pyramid necropolis near Dahshur. Did he want to be nearer the fortress of the White Walls? Or did he want to found a new, more strategically located residential city, from which he could more effectively direct the colonization of the vast area of the Nile Delta and military expeditions toward Libya and the Sinai? Or were dynastic problems within the royal family the main reason? Stadelmann believes that the pyramid in Meidum was built for Snefru from the outset, and that the surrounding tombs belonged to the queen mother and the princes of the so-called first generation. According to him, only a later generation of Snefru's family was buried in Dahshur.

Another riddle arose from a recent discovery in Seila, on the edge of the Fayyum oasis some ten kilometers west of the Meidum pyramid. There stand the remains of a small pyramid that has long been known to Egyptologists, but whose date and builder were unknown. In the course of the excavations conducted during the second half of the 1980s, the Egyptian archaeologist Swelim, working with an American expedition from Brigham Young University, discovered written evidence that supported the view that Snefru had also built this pyramid. In contrast to the three other, much larger pyramids, this one had no underground chambers and could therefore not have been used as a tomb. What was its true meaning? The pyramid is one of a group of seven small but, in many respects, enigmatic step pyramids that are scattered all over Egypt. The northernmost of them is in Seila, while the southernmost is near the first cataract of the Nile, on the small island of Elephantine.

Small Step Pyramids—End of the Third Dynasty and Beginning of the Fourth Dynasty

SEILA

Today, the ruins of the small step pyramid in Seila are barely seven meters high. The first investigation of the monument was carried out by Borchardt, immediately after the turn of the twentieth century. The pyramid, whose four-stepped core was built of smaller blocks of local limestone held together by mortar made of clay and sand, was aligned along a north-south axis angled twelve degrees to the west. On some of the blocks the remains of builders' marks and inscriptions were found. During the most recent excavations the remains of an offering table and a limestone stela were discovered that made it possible to identify Snefru as the possessor of the pyramid.

It is surprising that the pyramid has no chambers either inside it or in its substructure and that, with the exception of the previously mentioned stela and offering table, no evidence of a funerary cult has been found near it. Its meaning thus remains unclear, as does that of the structures associated with it.

ZAWIYET EL-MEIYITIN

This small pyramid, about seven kilometers south of the modern administrative center of Central Egypt, Minya, is the only one that is located on the east bank of the Nile. Its location may have been connected with the remains of the city of Hebenu buried in the nearby hill.

The pyramid, whose ruins today reach a height of scarcely five meters, was built of limestone bound with mortar made of mud, sand, and lime. The structure is not precisely aligned; the west side runs parallel to what was then the course of the Nile near Zawiyet el-Meiyitin and is angled about twenty degrees to the northwest. In 1911 the pyramid was investigated by the French Egyptologist Raymond Weill, and Lauer later added further information.

SINKI

The remains of the pyramid in Sinki, near the modern village of Naga el-Khalifa, about five miles south of Abydos, were discovered in 1883 by Charles Wilbour and Gaston Maspero. Only a century later it was carefully investigated by Swelim and Günther Dreyer.

The east side of the pyramid, whose construction material also consists of limestone and mortar made of clay and sand, runs parallel to the Nile. Its remains now reach a height of about four meters. Also worth mentioning is that the remains of ramps built of mudbricks, mud, rubble, and sand have been preserved (see p. 95). The ramps originally led to the level of the upper edge of the second layer.

There are many indications that the removal of stones from the pyramid began during the Old Kingdom and that nomadic shepherds with goats and sheep settled near it. Fourteen secondary graves from the Old and New Kingdoms were also discovered nearby.

NAQADA

Near Naqada, about three hundred kilometers north of the ruins of the ancient city of Ombos, stand the remains of a pyramid about fourteen meters high. Its core, like that of the pyramid in Sinki, was built of rough pieces of limestone mortared with clay and sand. The east side of this pyramid also ran parallel to the course of the Nile.

In 1895, Petrie and Quibell conducted an investigation here. Under the southwest corner of the pyramid they discovered a pit not in any way connected with the substructure. Its meaning and why the pyramid was erected right over it have not yet been discovered.

KULA

The small pyramid at Kula, not far from the village of Naga el-Mamariya and about six kilometers north of the ancient Egyptian city of Hierakonpolis, is the best preserved of this whole group. It stands on the west bank of the Nile, and like the others it is built of rough pieces of limestone held together with mortar made of clay, mud, sand, and small bits of limestone. However, it differs from the others in that its corners and not its sides are oriented toward the four cardinal directions. The west side of the pyramid thus again lies parallel to the Nile.

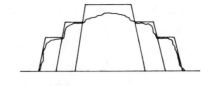

The pyramid in Kula. Sectional view through the axis, reconstruction, and ground plan (after Stiénon).

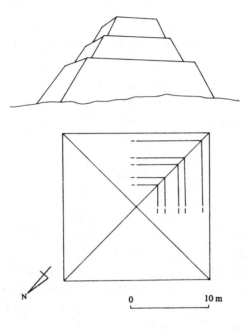

Perring and Vyse were the first to investigate and describe the pyramid, in 1837, when it was still about twelve meters high. Toward the end of the nineteenth century Henri Édouard Naville (1844–1926) made a sounding on its northwest corner. Finally, it was examined in 1929 by a Belgian team led by Jean Capart. Since the Mesopotamian ziggurats were oriented in the same way, the pyramid in Kula and the nearby predynastic fortress in Hierakonpolis have been seen as further proof of Mesopotamian influence in Egypt—and as a place that was then playing an important role in the initial formation of the ancient Egyptian state. Hierakonpolis was at that time the capital of Upper Egypt and the center of the cult of the falcon god Horus. It has been proven that there were contacts between the Nile Valley and the Near East before the end of the Early Period, but this does not allow us to draw any conclusions regarding the relationship between the pyramid in Kula and the ziggurats. This pyramid cannot simply be dated as the only one built in the period before the unification of Egypt. Moreover, the course of the Nile may have been the decisive factor determining its orientation.

EDFU

This pyramid, built of rough pieces of reddish sandstone, is located near the village of Naga el-Goneima on the west bank of the Nile, about five kilometers north of Edfu. Its west side runs parallel to the river.

ELEPHANTINE

The southernmost of these small step pyramids stands on the island of Elephantine, at the first cataract of the Nile near Aswan. It was built of rough pieces of granite bound with clay mortar, on a rock plateau that had been prepared for it. Its west side is angled about seventeen degrees northwest, so that it is approximately parallel to the axis of the west branch of the Nile, which flows around the island.

The pyramid was discovered in 1909 by a French expedition that was looking on Elephantine for the remains of a Jewish settlement from the fifth century B.C.E. The expedition members mistook the ruins for those of a Jewish temple. Near the pyramid, Henri Gauthier found a large, conical object made of granite, on whose base was an inscription with the name of the last ruler of the Third Dynasty, Huni. It has been interpreted as evidence of the foundation of a fortress or even a palace.

In spite of their heterogeneity, the small step pyramids scattered from Seila to Elephantine have a few common traits. Typologically, they can all be placed in the second half of the Third Dynasty, or, more precisely, in the period from Sekhemkhet to Snefru. None of them has any aboveground chambers or underground parts, nor are any other buildings immediately around them. With the exception of the pyramid in Zawiyet el-Meiyitin, all were built on the west bank of the Nile and are oriented with respect to the course of the Nile, not the cardinal directions.

It is not impossible that similar small pyramids were also built in other places. For example, in the nineteenth century one could still be seen near Benha (ancient Athribis) in the central delta.

Opinions regarding these pyramids vary widely. Lauer considers them to be the queens' centotaphs in the provinces where they were born. Maragioglio and Rinaldi thought they were shrines connected with the myth of Horus and Seth. According to Arnold, they embodied the memory of the "high sand" or primeval mound on which life was created. Swelim believes they were sites of the sun cult, and thus in a sense predecessors of the later sun temple. Kaiser and Dreyer offer an interesting interpretation: that they are symbols of palatinates that were established near provincial centers and royal residences, and were intended as reminders of the ruler's presence and authority in places far from the capital.

This last theory was criticized by Edwards, who pointed out that the pyramid in Seila stood within sight of the Meidum Pyramid, and thus so near the capital that a reminder of royal authority would have been superfluous. To this objection we can add another connected with the dating of this small step pyramid in the second half or the final phase of the Third Dynasty. Given its stepped form, this seems at first correct, but the Snefru stela in Seila is so far the only direct chronological evidence for this dating, since the granite conical object from Elephantine has no direct value as proof. Thus we cannot exclude the possibility that all of the step pyramids—both those already known and others that can be hypothesized to have existed in other places in Egypt—were built over a span of time broader than that of the end of the Third Dynasty alone. Clearly, the last word in the debate regarding these structures has not yet been spoken.

Snefru's Bent Pyramid

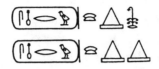

This pyramid, whose form and name seem rather contradictory, was the first to have been planned from the outset to have the shape of a true pyramid. It is sometimes also called the Rhomboidal, False, or Blunt Pyramid. The ancient Egyptians called it "Snefru shines—South (pyramid)." In the text of one of Pepi I's decrees found in Dahshur, two hieroglyphic symbols for "pyramid" appear after Snefru's name—did the ancient Egyptian scribe mean to describe it more precisely as a "double pyramid"? In another part of the decree this series of symbols is used to designate Snefru's pyramid town in Dahshur as "the city of the two pyramids" (i.e., the Bent and Red Pyramids).

The unusual appearance of the pyramid, which rises from an elevated desert plateau about three kilometers west of the village of Dahshur, has attracted European travelers—among them Robert Huntington, Robert Wood, Edward Melton, and Richard Pococke—since the seventeenth century. However, a systematic archaeological investigation of the structure was not made until the nineteenth century, when first Perring, then Lepsius, and later Petrie studied the pyramid. Unfortunately, no documentation from Abdel Salam Hussain's and Alexandre Varille's investigations after 1945 has been preserved. Fundamental results were first provided by research conducted in the Bent Pyramid by the Egyptian archaeologist Ahmad Fakhry in the first half of the 1950s. The later observations and measurements made by Maragioglio and Rinaldi, as well as by Josef Dorner, an Austrian geodesist, are also valuable. The foundation on which the pyramid was built consisted not of rock but rather of a relatively soft layer of slaty clay. The builders apparently did not take this sufficiently into account, and this seriously compromised the stability of the whole structure. The core, made of local limestone, rests directly on the clay, whereas the casing of fine white limestone, which is here better preserved than on any other Egyptian pyramid, stands on an artificially built foundation.

According to the original plan, the walls were to have a relatively steep angle of sixty degrees; during construction, the angle was altered to not quite fifty-five degrees, and this required that the base be enlarged. This change from the first to the second stage of construction can be seen in the ceiling and the side walls of the north access corridor to the pyramid, about twelve meters from the entrance.

When the structure was about forty-five meters high, the angle of inclination was further reduced to only forty-five degrees. This modification, which had the effect of reducing the volume of material required for the upper half of the pyramid, was probably made necessary

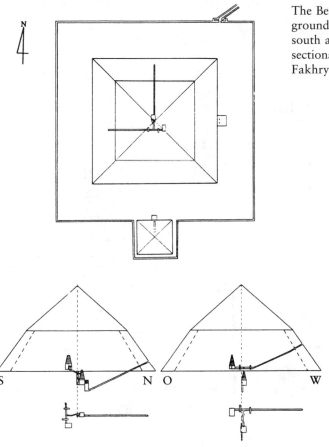

The Bent Pyramid, ground plan, and north-south and east-west sectional views (after Fakhry).

by the danger that some of the internal chambers would be damaged. Thus the pyramid assumed its characteristic form.

In the interests of a complete presentation, we must add that, according to some scholars, the pyramid's unusual shape was not the result of experiments and risks related to static equilibrium, but rather reflects the original structural intention, which was motivated religiously or politically. In one hypothesis, the two angles of the pyramid symbolize the unity of Upper and Lower Egypt; in another, the nine surfaces (including the underside) symbolize the Heliopolitan Great Ennead.

The north entrance, aligned with the pyramid's north-south axis, is located about twelve meters above ground level. A descending corridor behind it opens into the narrow underground chamber whose high ceiling consists of a corbel vault made of large limestone slabs.

Ground plan and north-south sectional view of the substructure of the Bent Pyramid, with entrance from the north (after Fakhry).

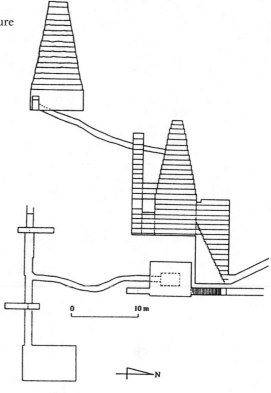

A short passageway in the southwest corner gives access to a vertical shaft, now partly destroyed, which in the course of archaeological investigation became known as the chimney. It is precisely aligned with the vertical axis of the pyramid.

The west entrance is located much higher than the north entrance, some thirty meters above ground level. Behind it opens a descending corridor provided at two points with specially constructed barriers. It ends in the so-called upper chamber, which also has a corbel vault. Fakhry believed that Snefru was buried in this chamber. The blocks composing the vault remained rough. On one of them an inscription is crudely written in script with red pigment and a cartouche bearing Snefru's name—a clear indication that the Bent Pyramid belonged to him. The lower part of the chamber was filled with rough limestone masonry, partly bound with mortar, and partly laid dry. In the openings in the side walls lay the remains of cedar beams, just as in the Meidum Pyramid. In this connection we may recall the information on the Palermo stone, according to which forty ships brought cedar wood from the Lebanese mountains to Egypt during Snefru's reign.

The function of the masonry and the beams in the upper chamber is not entirely clear. Maragioglio and Rinaldi thought they were the remains of a structure that was intended to serve either as a base or as protection for the sarcophagus. Under this hypothesis, the stone masonry into which the wood coffin was set would thus have replaced, in a certain sense, the exterior stone sarcophagus. Stadelmann, however, refuses to exclude the possibility that the masonry as well as the wooden beams might have been used in finishing off the vault or in an effort to prevent the side walls from cracking. In the upper chamber and in the corridor leading into it, cracks were discovered that the builders of the pyramid had tried to cover with gypsum plaster, and this suggests that the appearance of these cracks might have led the architects to modify the angle of the pyramid surface. (It is interesting that very nearby, during the erection of Amenemhet III's brick pyramid almost seven hundred years later, similar stability problems appeared.)

The lower system was accessed from the north and the upper system from the west; they were connected only by a narrow, irregular tunnel roughly hacked through the masonry of the pyramid core. It began in the lower chamber and came out in the western descending corridor, in the space between the two barriers. The post facto and provisional character of this connection is obvious, and from a conceptual point of view raises a series of questions relating to the substructure of the Bent Pyramid. The existence of the two systems may reflect the architects' effort to overcome the contradiction between the traditional north-south orientation of the substructure, including the burial chamber, and the newly introduced east-west orientation of the pyramid complex as a whole. So far as the upper system in the Bent Pyramid is concerned, its orientation and the entrance from the west recall the south tomb in the Djoser complex in Saqqara. Stadelmann sees in the Bent Pyramid the beginnings of the so-called three-chamber module of the substructure, which we encounter here and also in succeeding pyramids.

This structure raises further archaeological questions. Were all the inner chambers of the pyramid really discovered when it was investigated? When on September 20, 1839, Perring began to clean out the northern corridor (the entrance to the western corridor was at that time still blocked by the original stone masonry, which was not removed until the early 1950s as part of Fakhry's investigation), his excavations were hindered by a strong draft blowing through the passageway. In his report, he notes that on October 15 the work nearly had to be interrupted, and two days later he says that because of the draft it was almost impossible to illuminate the passageway. An observation mentioned by Fakhry complements Perring's report: "On some windy days, inside the pyramid, especially in the horizontal part of the west corridor between the two barriers, a sound can be heard that occasionally lasts nearly ten seconds. . . ." It must be emphasized that this happened at a time when the western, walled-in entrance had not yet been opened.

Presumably a small brick structure, the so-called north chapel, was originally attached to the north wall. In it, as we can infer from later chapels, stood a sacrifice table—a large limestone table on whose upper side was chiseled the hieroglyphic sign for *hetep*, "offering" or "offering table."

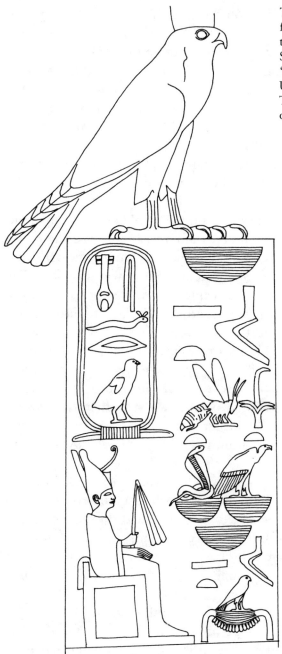

The inscription on a stela
from the offering chapel near
the Bent Pyramid contains
Snefru's name and titles:
"Horus Nebmaat, King of
Upper and Lower Egypt,
Two Ladies Nebmaat, Horus
of Gold" (after Fakhry).

At the foot of the east wall, on the east-west axis of the pyramid, was an open cult chapel. It consisted of an altar in the form of the symbol hetep—this time constructed of three limestone blocks—as well as two nine-meter-high limestone monoliths on its north and south sides. On the latter the ruler's titles and names were represented in bas-relief (the remains of one of the stelae are now on display in the Egyptian Museum, Cairo). Gradually, the cult chapel was surrounded with protective walls made of mudbricks and rebuilt as a small, simple temple. A few structural renovations were made here as late as the Middle Kingdom; these were connected with Snefru's deification and local cult.

Somewhat farther from the south side, but still along the pyramid axis, stands a small cult pyramid. Hussain once thought he had found the name of Snefru's wife, Queen Hetepheres I, among the construction inscriptions and symbols on its blocks, but he was mistaken. The entrance—in Ricke's romantic conception, it was supposed to have been guarded by live cobras—was at ground level. It led into the cult pyramid from the north and turned into a corridor that at first descended and then ascended and came out in a small, corbel-vaulted chamber not quite seven meters high. Many scholars consider this corridor to be the model for the Great Gallery in Khufu's pyramid in Giza. At the foot of the pyramid on the east side, there was also a small offering place with an alabaster altar, at whose sides stood two five-meter-high limestone monoliths bearing the ruler's name and titles.

A huge wall built of yellowish gray limestone surrounded the entire pyramid complex. It enclosed an extensive, square courtyard, in whose northeast corner the causeway paved with limestone blocks that ascended from the valley temple came out. This causeway followed a very irregular course. It also had no roof, and along its sides ran low stone walls that were rounded at the top and slightly inclined on the outside.

The approach causeway led out of the southwest corner of the valley temple, whose remains now lie about a kilometer west of the Nile Valley. The temple is the first one of its kind known and has been relatively well investigated archaeologically. Research on the some-

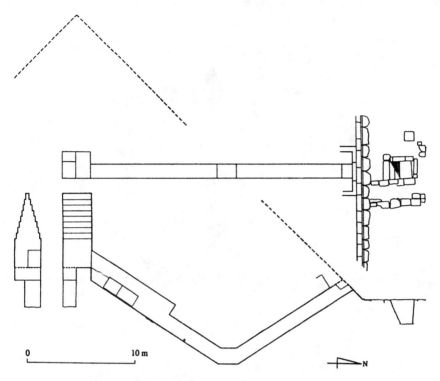

Ground plan and north-south sectional view of the substructure of the cult pyramid near the Bent Pyramid (after Fakhry).

what older valley temple presumed to have existed in Meidum has been hampered by the high water level. It has a rectangular, north-south–oriented ground plan and was built of fine white limestone. The entrance was in the middle of the south facade and was framed by wooden pillars with pennants. During its reconstruction in the Middle Kingdom, a limestone stela taken from the nearby tomb of Snefru's son Netjeraperef was used to frame the door.

The temple is divided into three parts of equal size. In the southernmost part, there are four storerooms, two on each of the entrance corridor's walls. The side walls are decorated with scenes of a procession of personified mortuary estates. On the east wall Upper Egyptian sources and on the west wall Lower Egyptian funerary estates producing supplies for the ruler's temple are represented as female

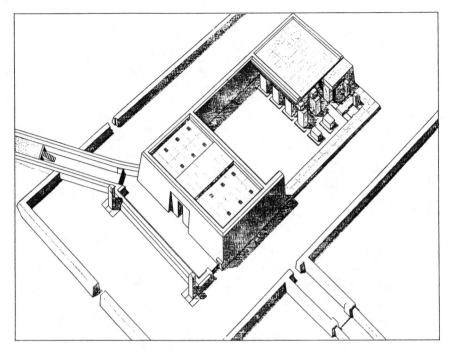

Reconstruction of the valley temple of the Bent Pyramid (after Fakhry).

offering bearers. The reliefs are among the artistic high points of the Fourth Dynasty.

The northern part of the temple consists of a portico with ten lime-stone pillars arranged in two rows. On them were bas-reliefs show-ing the ruler participating in the rituals of the sed festival, while the undecorated walls of the pillars were painted red. Through the por-tico one reached six deep niches, originally provided with wooden doors. Their north walls consisted of large limestone monoliths, on which the figure of the king appeared in half-sculpture. Snefru was represented here at least twice as the ruler of Upper Egypt, and at least once as the ruler of Lower and Upper Egypt.

The whole temple was surrounded by a huge wall made of mudbricks, from which the figure of the king emerges in half-sculpture. In the space between the wall and the temple the priests of Snefru's mortuary cult, which lasted into the Middle Kingdom, gradually took up their residence.

A figure personifying Snefru's mortuary estates brings offerings. Detail from a bas-relief decoration in the valley temple (after Fakhry).

Finally, we should emphasize that the Bent Pyramid complex was not ultimately used for the purpose for which it was built—namely, as a royal tomb. As Stadelmann has shown, the Bent Pyramid became an important part of the cult of the deceased ruler and fulfilled—in relation to Snefru's actual burial site, the Red Pyramid—the function of a south tomb.

Snefru's Red Pyramid

About four kilometers north of the Bent Pyramid, the second of Snefru's pyramids in Dahshur appears. Because today its casing is almost completely gone, it draws its name—the Red Pyramid—from the color of the stone of its core. The local people also call it *el-haram el-watwat,* the "Bat Pyramid." Its original Egyptian name probably meant "Snefru shines." The model of the Bent Pyramid might have led one to expect that the Red Pyramid would be called "Snefru shines—North Pyramid," but this name has not been found in ancient Egyptian texts. Although the name "Snefru shines—Front Pyramid" has been documented, it probably referred to the Bent Pyramid, since south was the most important direction for ancient Egyptians.

European travelers have visited the Red Pyramid since the Middle Ages, as did, for example, the Englishman Edward Melton in 1660 and the Bohemian Franciscan missionary Václav Remedius Prutký in the eighteenth century. In the travel book he wrote in Latin, Prutký described his descent into the interior of the pyramid.

Perring and Lepsius once again stand at the beginning of modern archaeological research on the Red Pyramid; Perring examined it in 1839, and Lepsius in 1843. Petrie and Reisner also studied the Red Pyramid for a short time. After the Second World War Hussain conducted extensive investigations, followed by Fakhry in the early 1950s. However, the first systematic and fundamental archaeological investigation was carried out under Stadelmann's leadership in 1982.

Technical construction problems and the threatened collapse of the west corridor and the upper chamber in the Bent Pyramid seem to have led not only to the decision to build a new pyramid, but also to excessive caution. The angle of the walls was so reduced that the Red Pyramid has the lowest angle of all the Egyptian pyramids. The core consists of blocks of red limestone from the stone quarries a few hundred meters southwest of the pyramid. Here are also preserved the remains of two supply ramps that connected the quarry with the southwest corner of the pyramid. Stadelmann thinks that construction began on the west side and was then continued on all four sides with the help of short ramps. When a height of about twenty-five meters was reached, the ramps were all removed, except for one on each side. After another fifty meters were built those were also finally taken down. In this case, valuable blocks of limestone from the Tura stone quarries were used for the foundation.

The same material was used for the casing. The walls were slightly concave and somewhat irregular, as is also shown by the remains of a limestone pyramidion, the only one of its kind that has been found. However, the pyramidion's angle of inclination differs from that of the Red Pyramid. This difference recently led Corinna Rossia to suggest that the pyramidion did not belong to the Red Pyramid, but was originally intended to top Snefru's Bent Pyramid. However, when the third, final version of this pyramid made it useless, the pyramidion was discarded. The concave form of the walls was intended to increase the stability of the casing.

On both the blocks in the core and the casing were found builders' inscriptions of great historical significance. For example, there is a note concerning the "laying of the west cornerstone in the earth, in the year of the fifteenth cattle census." The dates of other inscriptions on the blocks at varying heights may show that about one-fifth of the pyramid was built over a period of two years.

The entrance into the pyramid is located in the north wall, about four meters east of the north-south axis and about twenty-eight meters above the ground. At the point where it reaches the level of the pyramid base, the descending corridor becomes horizontal and opens out into the so-called antechamber. A short passageway leads to the second antechamber, which is aligned precisely with the pyramid's vertical axis. The antechambers have the same dimensions, and their side walls and corbel-vaulted ceilings are constructed of large, well-dressed blocks of fine white limestone.

The entrance to the burial chamber is in the south wall of the second antechamber, about eight meters above the floor. In contrast to

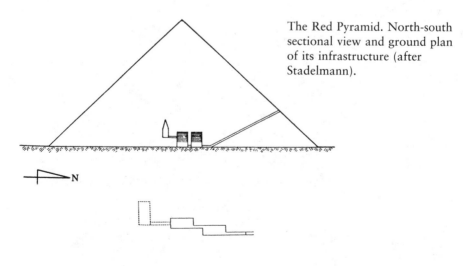

The Red Pyramid. North-south sectional view and ground plan of its infrastructure (after Stadelmann).

the antechamber, which is oriented north-south, the burial chamber is oriented east-west. Whereas the burial chamber in the two preceding Snefru pyramids still followed the Third Dynasty tradition in being oriented north-south, here for the first time the burial chamber was aligned with the orientation of the pyramid complex as a whole. The burial chamber was later damaged, when thieves ripped up some blocks from the floor, and the walls and ceiling have been blackened by the soot from fires and torches.

On the walls of the second antechamber, and especially on the walls of the short, narrow passageway to the burial chamber, visitors—including Perring, Bernardino Drovetti, and other archaeologists—have left behind many graffiti. In the corridor leading into the pyramid, Hussain found a secondary tomb from the Late Period with bones from a young man of small stature.

It is clear that the pyramid was already completed at the time of Snefru's death. However, this is not true for the other buildings that were to compose the ruler's tomb complex. Only a small part of the mortuary temple remains. Its core was composed of a mortuary cult place with a false door of pink granite, of which only a fragment could

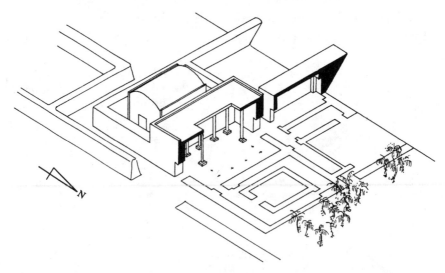

Attempt to reconstruct the Red Pyramid's mortuary temple (after Stadelmann).

be found. Around the cult site were storerooms made of mudbricks. During his excavations in the temple, Stadelmann also found fragments of a limestone relief that represents Snefru in the costume he wore during the sed festival. A large number of copper arrowheads come from the Middle Ages, when the Red Pyramid was used for target practice by Mamluk archers.

Around the pyramid lie the remains of a perimeter wall that was rectangular in shape and oriented east-west. A cult pyramid apparently never existed here. As the remains of an oven show, workshops were located in a relatively large mudbrick structure, traces of which were found southeast of the pyramid.

The causeway was also never completed. All that was found were the remains of supply roads for construction material and paths connecting the mortuary temple with the pyramid town on the edge of the Nile Valley. It was this town that was referred to in the previously mentioned decree, which was partly preserved on a limestone stela dug up in 1904 during construction work in the village of

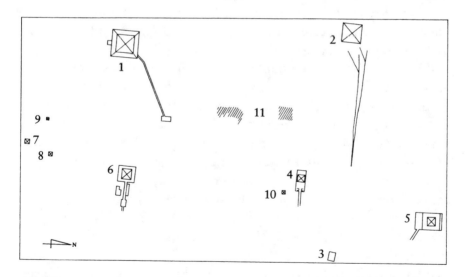

Plan of the necropolis in Dahshur. 1. Bent Pyramid, 2. Red Pyramid, 3. Snefru's pyramid town, 4. Amenemhet II's pyramid, 5. Senusret III's pyramid, 6. Amenemhet III's pyramid, 7. Ameny Kemau's pyramid, 8–10. pyramids from the Thirteenth Dynasty, 11. mastabas from the Old Kingdom.

Dahshur. In addition, the remains of a huge town perimeter wall were uncovered (according to Stadelmann, this wall was part of the Red Pyramid's valley temple). The decree, which granted Snefru's town certain privileges, also mentions the as yet undiscovered pyramid of Menkauhor. The context suggests that it was also in Dahshur. Borchardt identified it with the ruins of a structure northeast of the Red Pyramid that Lepsius had already designated as pyramid L. We shall see later that many experts disagree with his view.

The results of new excavations conducted by German archaeologists in the Red Pyramid, together with the recently acquired knowledge that Snefru was also the builder of the pyramid in Seila, have raised a series of questions—above all, why Snefru constructed not one but several pyramid complexes for himself, in what order these were built, and in which of them he was finally buried.

It is usually assumed that the construction problems and the erroneously calculated static equilibrium forced Snefru first to alter the plan of the Bent Pyramid and ultimately to decide against it as his burial site. However, this view is open to doubt. Why would construction have been continued if the walls of the inner chambers began to burst and any further enlargement of the volume would necessarily increase the risk of collapse?

From the evidence available at this point we can conclude that Snefru first undertook the construction of the pyramid in Meidum. At the end of stage E2, work on that structure was interrupted and the construction of the Bent Pyramid in Dahshur begun. When problems emerged, the builders, undaunted, began constructing the Red Pyramid, but probably the rebuilding of the Meidum Pyramid (E3) was undertaken at the same time. At present, the pyramid in Seila cannot be situated chronologically with greater precision. Nonetheless, given its location and stepped form, it is possible that it was erected during the E1 or E2 stage of the construction of the Meidum Pyramid.

It has already been explained why Snefru decided, during the sixteenth year of his reign, to leave his initial residence and to build a new necropolis in Dahshur. To the reasons given for that decision we can suggest another: might he not also have left Meidum because a step pyramid towered over his royal cemetery? It is possible that just at this time the new religious ideas, and with them a new conception of the royal tomb in the form of a true pyramid, were establishing themselves. In any case, the later decision—on whatever grounds it was made—not to use the Bent Pyramid might have led the ruler to undertake a rapid transformation of the Meidum Pyramid. Before a completely new tomb was finished, there would thus be at least one genuine pyramid available to receive the dead ruler.

In which of his pyramids was Snefru ultimately buried? Neither his bodily remains nor any convincing proof of his interment were found in any of them. Fakhry believed that Snefru was buried in the upper chamber of the Bent Pyramid. Stadelmann considered the Red Pyramid to be Snefru's last resting place, disregarding the fact that certain important parts of that tomb complex were never completed. In his view, the ground plan of the temple and, especially, the fragment of a granite false door and the extensive storerooms testify to the intensity of the cult practiced there.

The Great Pyramid (of Khufu)

*"This drawing is the most astonishing architectural memorial I
have ever seen, and I think it impossible to surpass."*
—Goethe, after he had seen in Rome in 1787 the drawings of the
Great Pyramid made by the French traveler Louis François Cassas.

"Khufu's Horizon," the Great Pyramid, was the first of the ancient Seven Wonders of the World. Surrounded by legends and mysteries, it has always aroused astonishment, admiration, and doubts as to whether it is the product of human hands at all. It has fascinated many generations of scholars and travelers.

It would hardly be possible to list the names of all those who have admired and tried to describe it. According to Diodorus Siculus, Alexander the Great intended to build for his father, the Macedonian king Philip II, a funeral monument as large as the Great Pyramid. It fascinated ancient authors such as Herodotus, Strabo, and Pliny. Many of their accounts, and often their inventions, were handed down over the centuries, and some of them are still repeated today—for example, statements regarding the number of laborers involved or the underground, artificial island on which the pharaoh was supposed to be buried.

Medieval Arab historians such as Masudi, Idrisi, Latif, and Maqrizi also wrote about it. Although they provide absolutely reliable information—concerning, for example, attempts to break into the Great Pyramid or to tear down Menkaure's pyramid—they also cannot help repeating traditional rumors and fantastic notions.

The Great Pyramid was the goal or at least an important stop for European scientific travelers and pilgrims on their way to the Holy Land. For example, it was visited by Christof Harant von Polžice und Bezdružice at the end of the sixteenth century, by Edward Melton in the seventeenth century, and by Carsten Niebuhr, Pococke, and others during the eighteenth century. The English scholar John Greaves's *Pyramidographia, or a Discourse of the Pyramids of Egypt,* which appeared in 1646, is considered the first attempt at an Egyptological study. Greaves climbed the Great Pyramid, measured its blocks, and also made his way inside the pyramid. His sectional drawing of the Great Pyramid is remarkably accurate for its time. Nevertheless, the structure retained its mysterious, hidden meaning for most travelers.

The situation did not essentially change until the turn of the nineteenth century. From then on, archaeological, scientific methods gradually prevailed, though still with many fantastic and amateur characteristics. In the 1760s the English diplomat and traveler Nathaniel Davison discovered a lower relieve chamber as well as a tunnel connecting it with the Great Gallery. The scholars accompanying Napoleon's expedition—Vivant Denon, Joseph Coutelle, Edmé Jomard—measured and described the Great Pyramid again and made exploratory soundings in and around it. Early in the nineteenth century, Giovanni Battista Caviglia cleaned out many spaces inside the pyramid, including the descending corridor, the underground chamber, and the Queen's Chamber. Vyse and Perring investigated the Great Pyramid in 1837. They worked on the relieve chamber system

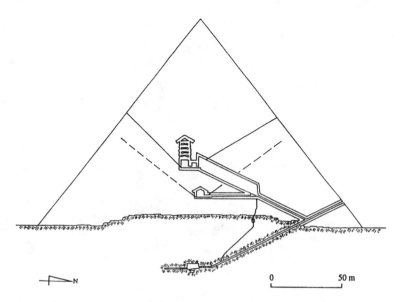

North-south sectional view of the Great Pyramid.

over the royal chamber, the so-called ventilation channels, the masonry, and the three small queen's pyramids in front of the east side of the Great Pyramid. Their books, *Operations Carried Out on the Pyramids of Gizeh in 1837* (3 vols.) and *The Pyramids of Gizeh* (3 vols.), respectively, are still valuable Egyptological sources.

During his Egyptian expedition of 1843–1844, Lepsius focused his attention primarily on the structure of the Great Pyramid and expressed the view that the core consisted of inclined accretion layers of stone masonry. For the birthday of the Prussian King Friedrich Wilhelm IV, the archaeologists honored their prince and patron by scaling the Great Pyramid and flying a flag from its top. This festive moment, which is also preserved in a contemporary picture, was described in these words in Lepsius's correspondence: "At the top of the oldest and largest of all known human works, our flag with the Prussian eagle was unrolled, which we then thrice hailed with 'Long live the king!'" This little episode shows the simultaneously disciplined and enthusiastic spirit that moved the Prussian researchers. It is no accident that his team became by far the most successful in the his-

Karl Richard
Lepsius.

Verlagsanstalt Bruckmann repr.

tory of Egyptology, both as scientists and as collectors. Lepsius and
his colleagues produced what was for a long time the greatest
Egyptological book, *Denkmaeler aus Aegypten und Aethiopien,* and
brought fifteen thousand objects back to Berlin—the greatest collection ever made by a single expedition.

Petrie, who carefully examined the pyramid in 1881–1882, did not
agree with Lepsius's theory. In accord with his disposition and way of
working, he set up his headquarters in one of the nearby rock-cut tombs,
which Waynman Dixon had used before him. A layer of sand served as
his bed, and he used a kerosene stove for cooking. His diet, which did
not vary much, consisted chiefly of herring, unleavened bread, choco-
late, and coffee. He always had a small bag of citric acid in his pocket,
so that he could make himself lemonade whenever he wanted it. His
servant lived in the tomb next door. Petrie went to the pyramid only
after tourists had left, in the early evening. It was so hot in the chambers and corridors that he wore as few clothes as possible. It would

William Matthew
Flinders Petrie.

have been a shocking experience for anyone who happened to come upon the bearded, half-naked scientist scribbling construction details and archaeological notes in his diary by the light of a kerosene lamp. But Petrie founded modern Egyptian archaeology, and his account of his investigations, *The Pyramids and Temples of Gizeh,* remains even today one of the most important studies on the pyramids.

Petrie also wanted to prove that the mystical ideas put forward by the English astronomer Charles Piazzi Smyth in the 1860s were unscientific. Smyth had supporters whose work cannot be regarded as insignificant—for example, that of the Edgar brothers, who at the beginning of the twentieth century collected and published a series of valuable measurements, observations, and photographs.

Borchardt also worked on the famous monument. He first concentrated on explaining the method originally used to measure and orient the ground plan, and on reconstructing the stages in which the pyramid was built.

In 1954, the Egyptian archaeologists Kamal Mallakh and Zaki Iskander and their colleagues discovered on the south side of the Great Pyramid two pits that contained intact buried boats. The easternmost of the two was opened, and the boat was reconstructed in its original form. The other pit remains unopened but was recently investigated using a microcamera.

In the second half of the 1980s the French architects Jean-Patrice Dormion and Gilles Goidin lent fresh impetus to research on the Great Pyramid by making precise geophysical measurements of its inner core. The surprising results of their work, which we will discuss later, won confirmation in later measurements made by a Japanese team.

Another important contribution to research on this famous monument came from the most recent archaeological investigations conducted by the Egyptian archaeologist Zahi Hawass, which focused on the grounds of the presumed valley temple, the causeway, and the mortuary temple. Not long ago, he discovered the cult pyramid as well as its pyramidion.

Khufu presumably abandoned the royal necropolis in Dahshur because it lacked sufficient room for a large pyramid complex and because there was not enough limestone nearby, but he may also have been concerned about the unstable subsoil, which consisted of slaty clay. He decided to build his pyramid on a rocky outcropping in the desert near modern Giza, a location that provided not only a stable subsoil for the pyramid but also an abundant supply of high-quality limestone.

With the exception of a rock jutting up in the middle, which made the pyramid core easier to construct and simultaneously strengthened it, the outcropping was reduced to a horizontal surface. The simple but effective methods used by the ancient Egyptians to make the foundation precisely level have already been described. Because of its greater precision, Borchardt considered the east side to have been the baseline used for the measurements.

The construction material for the core came from the stone quarries southeast of the pyramid. The limestone blocks were transported over a ramp to the construction site. According to Lauer's theory, which we have already outlined, the pyramid was probably erected by means of a whole system of ramps, including the fifty-meter-wide main ramp that led from the quarries to the construction site. It is likely that other, smaller ramps ultimately became part of the pyramid core.

This simple, effective method made it possible to raise, over a surface of about five hectares, blocks weighing from three tons (at the lower levels) to one ton (at the upper levels). Some blocks were even heavier. For the construction of the king's chamber, for example, pink granite blocks weighing forty to sixty tons had to be transported to a height of about seventy meters.

Borchardt agreed with Lepsius's view that the core masonry was arranged in inclined accretion layers. Recently conducted investigations made by French geophysicists have shown, however, that the structure of the core is extremely heterogeneous. It probably also contains compartments filled with sand. This would be not only an economical but also a very sensible method.

The irregular compartments, which may also have been filled with small rubble and other waste material from the construction site, and whose dimensions and arrangement within the pyramid core cannot at this point be precisely determined, diverted the pressure inside the pyramid more effectively than did solid masonry. This must have been helpful during the occasional earthquakes that occur in Egypt.

The outside walls of the core, in contrast, consist of huge blocks laid in horizontal rows. Today, only 203 blocks remain—the upper seven rows seem to have been broken off. The height of the blocks varies between about one and one and a half meters. As in the case of the earlier Red Pyramid, the slightly concave walls were intended to increase the stability of the pyramid's mantle.

The casing was made of large blocks of fine white limestone from the Muqattam range on the east bank of the Nile, and some of it is still in place. Recently, however, has been conjectured that these stones may have come from the closer and more accessible quarries west of Djedefre's pyramid in Abu Rawash, where valuable, high-quality, brilliantly white limestone is also found. Between the core and the mantle, another layer of smaller stones was bound with mortar, which increased the cohesion of the two materials and the two masonry structures. In archaeological terminology, this intermediate layer is known as the "backing stones." The pyramid's apex, the pyramidion, has disappeared, probably forever.

The original entrance, barely a meter high, was located in the north wall, in the nineteenth layer of the blocks in the core. It was located more than seven meters east of the pyramid's axis. When Strabo visited Egypt in 25 B.C.E., he reported that the entrance was blocked by a movable stone barrier.

Today, the pyramid is entered through an entrance that tradition tells us was cut through the masonry in the ninth century by Caliph al-Ma'mun. According to Arab historians' reports, this son of Harun ar-Rashid managed to get in, and at the end of the tunnel found a large key together with some gold coins. The sum exactly corresponded to the cost of the operation. It is more likely that he simply built a connection with the passageway that robbers had already made in antiquity.

The original descending corridor first passes through the core masonry and then through the rock underlying it. More than thirty meters under the base of the pyramid it turns into a horizontal passageway and comes out in a chamber whose purpose is rather unclear. It was not completed, and there is no protective blocking at its entrance. In addition, it never held a stone sarcophagus, which would not have passed through the narrow entrance.

From the south wall an unfinished, dead-end corridor leads south. Many experts consider it to be the original, ultimately unfinished and abandoned, burial chamber intended as a backup in the event that the pharaoh died before the true burial chamber in the upper part of the pyramid was completed. Stadelmann, however, believes that the underground chamber represented the symbolic cavern of the death god Sokar, whose major and perhaps even original place of worship was near modern Giza. In this view, in the grave the dead pharaoh was supposed to merge symbolically with Sokar.

From the descending corridor an ascending passageway branches off that was originally sealed with blocks of pink granite and which Ma'mun's tunnel skirted. There is a seamless transition from this passageway to the Great Gallery—an architectonic masterpiece. The ceiling consists of a corbel vault built of seven layers of enormous lime-stone blocks, each of which projects about seven and a half centimeters.

Low ramps run along both sides of the gallery. On their surfaces twenty-seven large and small square openings alternate at regular intervals, corresponding to the right-angled niches in the side walls. Their significance has long been debated, and it must be admitted that none of the explanations offered so far is wholly satisfactory. The most widely accepted is Borchardt's, according to which a structure of wooden beams and planks was anchored in these openings. But what was this wooden structure's function? Was it used to transport build-ing materials or to support blocks while building the corbel vault? So far, no one has found a reliable answer to this question.

At the lower end of the Great Gallery, just above the floor, is a small opening in the west wall. There begins a narrow passageway known as the service or escape shaft, which leads to a corridor deep under the pyramid, near the entrance to the underground chambers. It was originally sealed and filled with limestone fragments and sand. Petrie's view, that it was conceived as an escape route for the men who were to lower the granite blocks into the ascending corridor when the burial ritual was over, has been challenged on the ground that if that were so, the shaft could not have been filled in from the top. According to other experts, the shaft was supposed to provide fresh air for the workers who were digging the underground chamber out of the rock. According to that view the underground chambers and the shaft were built after the Great Gallery. However, that claim conflicts with the assumption that this was the first stage in the construction of the Great Pyramid's substructure.

The entrance to the so-called Queen's Chamber is through a hori-zontal passageway that also begins at the lower end of the Great Gallery and leads in a southerly direction. It was here that the French team carried out their geophysical investigation. About five meters from the end of the passageway, there is a step, and the passageway slopes downward about sixty centimeters to the floor level of the Queen's Chamber. Why? Some scholars think that the pink granite flooring began there and reached into the Queen's Chamber, before it was hauled away by thieves. Others disagree, arguing that the con-

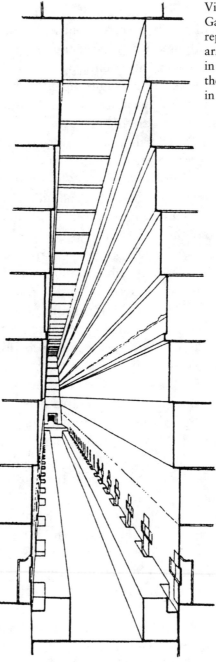

View of the Great
Gallery with a
representation of the
arrangement of niches
in the side walls and
the adjacent openings
in the side ramps.

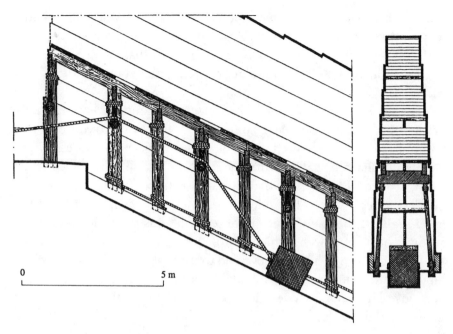

0   5 m

Wooden structure used to maneuver granite blocks into the Great Gallery (after Lauer).

struction plan was changed in order to make an even more sumptuous burial chamber.

The Queen's Chamber lies precisely on the pyramid's east-west axis and consists, including the gabled ceiling, wholly of limestone blocks. In its east wall there is a niche about four and a half meters high, whose ceiling is built as a corbel vault. The significance of this niche is not entirely clear; a statue of the king (or of the king's ka?) might have stood in it.

Equally unclear is the significance of the narrow shafts (averaging about twenty by twenty centimeters) that begin in the north and south walls of the chamber and climb steeply upward. The shafts are not precisely straight (when people talk about the alignment of the shafts, they are referring to an ideal line connecting one end with the other). For example, the north shaft in the Queen's Chamber bends after about seventeen meters (like the north shaft in the King's Chamber). The reasons for this are not clear. Some experts think these are ventilation shafts, while others attribute an astronomical function (the north shaft is aligned with the star Beta Ursae Minoris and the south shaft with Sirius) or a religious function to them. Similar shafts are also found in the King's Chamber.

The openings of the shafts in the Queen's Chamber were originally bricked up and camouflaged, and only in 1872 did Dixon discover and open them. In early 1993, as part of a project sponsored by the German Archaeological Institute, the engineer Rudolf Gantenbrink used a robot called UPUAUT 2, which he had constructed and equipped with a videocamera. The robot made a passage for itself and filmed the inner walls of the south shaft. (Gantenbrink has published a detailed account of his research, which can be viewed on his website: http://www.cheops.org) The films revealed that the shaft ended with a small limestone slab in which two heavily corroded pieces of copper had been inserted. This discovery led to a series of hypotheses as to what might be hidden behind the slab. One theory suggested that behind the entrance there might be a chamber with a statue of the king. It is unlikely, however, that any space would be accessible through so narrow a shaft. Moreover, the end of the shaft is only about six meters from the outer surface of the pyramid.

The discussion was lent further impetus by a "discovery" in the British Museum's depository. Not long ago three objects were found there that Dixon had taken from the north shaft in the Queen's Chamber: a stone sphere, a wooden slat, and a copper object in the form of a swallow's tail.

On the basis of the robot's discoveries and the objects found in the British Museum, Stadelmann concluded that these were not ventilation shafts. In his view, they were model corridors, through which the ruler's soul was to rise up to the "stars that never are extinguished," the circumpolar stars in the northern sky, as well as to the "land of light" in the southern sky. Since the burial chamber lay high above the pyramid's entrance, on its way out the pharaoh's soul would have had first to descend, and so the two shafts were built for the dead king's journey up to heaven.

Certain questions can be raised with regard to this interpretation.

The Great Pyramid was not the only one in which the way out of the tomb led first downward and then upward in the direction of the pyramid's entrance. For example, in the Meidum Pyramid and in the Red Pyramid in Dahshur the ruler's soul had first to descend from the burial chamber in order to reach the ascending corridor that led out of the tomb. The situation was similar in the Bent Pyramid, insofar as the soul would have had to make its way out of the upper chamber by way of the north corridor. In none of those pyramids, however, do narrow shafts lead north or south.

At the same time, the shafts raise doubts regarding the theory that the pyramid was built in accord with a unified plan. But if it was, why was the Queen's Chamber also equipped with shafts? They would have been out of place there.

Where should we seek an explanation? It is not impossible that the Queen's Chamber was intended to serve as a backup burial chamber (perhaps that is why the stone sarcophagus and elaborate blockade are absent) in the event of the pharaoh's sudden death. The builders knew what an enormously complicated and risky project the construction of the Great Gallery and the King's Chamber was to be. Nothing like it had ever before existed, and they could estimate neither the difficulties involved nor exactly how long it would take to complete the job.

Perhaps it was for this reason that the Queen's Chamber was kept ready, and lost its function only after the completion of the saddle ceiling in the highest relieve chamber over the King's Chamber. At that time the shafts in the Queen's Chamber, whatever their significance, were ritually sealed. It is worth noting that the "stopper" the robot revealed in the south shaft of the Queen's Chamber is located at about the level of the vertex of the gabled ceiling of the highest relieve chamber over King's Chamber.

However, this still does not explain the function of the shafts. Of the theories so far proposed, the most probable attributes a ventilating function to them. The architects realized that the circulation of air was made more difficult by the location of the chamber over the level of the pyramid's entrance (both the King's and the Queen's Chambers are above this level), which could have led to serious problems if several people were in the chamber at once—during the burial rites, for example. The fact that the shafts are "astronomically aligned" corresponds to the logic of the structure and to its builders' practical conceptions and religious ideas. The ancient Egyptians were probably well aware that the dominant wind was from the north, as they commonly made use of it in sailing on the Nile. Thus there was nothing unusual about the alignment of the shafts with a given star in the northern and southern skies;* it was thoroughly practical. In addition, these stars played an important role in contemporary ideas about religion and burial. Zeta Orionis was identified with the death god Osiris and Sirius with his divine partner, Isis. After his death, the pharaoh's soul went to the pole star (Alpha Draconis, in the age when the pyramids were built), there to become immortal. For the same reasons, shafts featured in the plans for the King's Chamber. The fact that they exist only in the Great Pyramid is yet another argument for the "ventilation theory"; after all, in other pyramids the burial chamber is not located above the level of the entrance.

In the short passageway between the upper end of the Great Gallery and the Queen's Chamber is located the last plugging block preventing access to the pharaoh's mummy. It consists of three pink granite stones that were originally held vertical by means of ropes and a pulley and then lowered to form a barrier.

The King's Chamber, in which Khufu was probably buried, is another of the ancient Egyptian architects' masterpieces. To resist the enormous pressure, it was built entirely of pink granite. Its flat ceiling is composed of nine huge blocks with a combined weight of more than four hundred tons. The fact that there is only one small crack in the ceiling slabs (which appears only near the south wall) and that the chamber has withstood the tests of more than four and a half millennia, is to be explained not only by the building material used, but especially by the carefully thought out construction of the five relief chambers over its ceiling.

These relieve chambers are low, and their flat upper covering con-

---

* A simulated reconstruction of the sky over Giza in 2,500 B.C.E. shows that the north shaft in the King's Chamber was aimed at Alpha Draconis and the south shaft at Zeta Orionis; in the Queen's Chamber the north shaft was aimed at Beta Ursae Minoris and the south shaft at Sirius (Alpha Canum Majoris).

sists of huge, roughly cut blocks of pink granite. Only the highest of the chambers have saddle ceilings. Their side walls are made of limestone and granite. On the walls many original builders' marks have been preserved along with the graffiti of modern visitors. Among these Petrie claimed to have found the "seventeenth year of the [cattle] census." If so, it would be the latest proven date of Khufu's reign. The present entrance into the chambers is located in the south wall of the Great Gallery, under the ceiling, at the upper end. The lowest of the relieve chambers was visited in the eighteenth century by the English diplomat Nathaniel Davison and bears his name. Others were later named after England's Lord Nelson, Duke Wellington, and Lady Ann Arbuthnot, while the largest was named after the Scottish diplomat and amateur archaeologist Patrick Campbell. The whole astonishing structure, from the floor of the King's Chamber to the apex of the Campbell Chamber, is approximately twenty-one meters high.

Near the west wall of the King's Chamber stands Khufu's pink granite sarcophagus, oriented north-south. Neither the cover nor any of the ruler's bodily remains was found there. In view of the size of the sarcophagus, it is clear that it must have been installed during the construction of the chamber. Its modest simplicity contrasts with the splendid, meticulous construction of the pyramid as a whole. Edwards believed it was a substitute sarcophagus, hastily prepared after the original had been destroyed while being transported from the quarries at Aswan; the boat might have sunk.

According to a legend recounted by Diodorus Siculus, Khufu ultimately was not buried in his pyramid. Medieval Arab historians mention the existence of a mummy-shaped coffin and the ruler's bodily remains but do not say where they lay. This fits in with the Polish architect Koziński's claim that the crack in the ceiling slabs of the King's Chamber had far greater consequences than might at first appear. It suggests that the crack appeared even before the pyramid was finished, accompanied by an ear-splitting noise that must have been audible everywhere around the construction site. This menacing incident may have led to the construction of a new burial chamber.

Despite numerous investigations, many questions remain unanswered, and thus the Great Pyramid continues to keep its secrets. The development of its construction is the subject of a particularly heated debate between those who think the pyramid was built in stages and those who assume that it was built in accord with a single plan.

The first group's view is perhaps best represented by Borchardt. According to him, the pyramid was built in three stages, during which the location of the burial chamber in particular gradually changed. The first phase, in which the burial chamber was underground, ended when the superstructure had reached a height of about thirteen meters. In the second stage, the Queen's Chamber was selected for the ruler's burial. But it also remained unfinished; work on it was stopped before the pavement of red granite. The third stage included the construction of the Great Gallery and the King's Chamber, as well as the service or escape shaft.

Maragioglio and Rinaldi in particular have offered persuasive arguments against Borchardt's theory. In their view, all the spaces in the superstructure form a unified whole and must therefore have been planned at the same time. They believe that the underground chamber was a backup burial site to be used in case the ruler unexpectedly died. Above all, they see the slight narrowing of the lower end of the ascending corridor as indicating that the Great Gallery was already included in the construction plans during this phase, in which the blocks needed to seal the corridor must have been put in place. The Italian researchers reject the interpretation of the Queen's Chamber as a burial site for the king. The niche in the east wall indicates that this space had a special, as yet unexplained, function.

Stadelmann also believes that there was a single, unified construction plan for the Great Pyramid. According to his theory of the three-chamber system in the pyramids,* the significance of the Queen's Chamber corresponded to that of the second antechamber in the Red Pyramid in Dahshur. Gantenbrink's measurements and calculations

---

* According to this theory, the module consisting of three main spaces—the burial chamber, the antechamber, and the storage chamber—was already established at the beginning of the Fourth Dynasty, in Snefru's pyramid in Dahshur. This arrangement continued to be used in the other pyramids of the Old Kingdom, although it was modified in different ways. In the Great Pyramid, however, there are four rooms: the underground chamber, the Queen's Chamber, the Great Gallery, and the King's Chamber (apart from the purely technical relieve chambers).

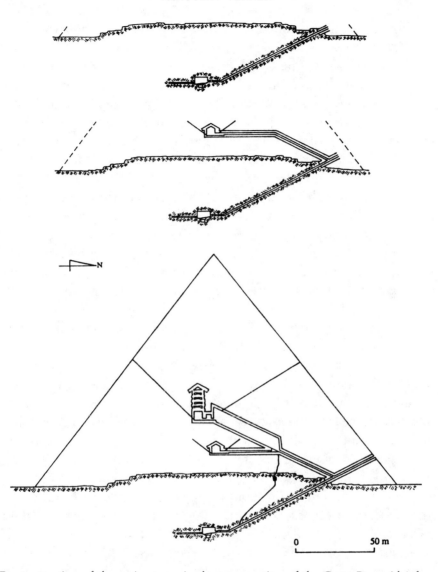

Reconstruction of the main stages in the construction of the Great Pyramid (after Borchardt).

led him to the same conclusion, that the Great Pyramid was constructed in accord with a single plan.

The debate about the Great Pyramid and its complex infrastructure will certainly go on for a long time. In this connection, we may quote a passage from the Westcar papyrus: "His majesty Khufu spent time looking for hidden chambers in the temple of Thoth in order to create something like them for his Horizon" (Khufu's pyramid was named Khufu's Horizon). This suggests that the author of the Middle Kingdom papyrus was aware of the complex plan of Khufu's pyramid and had thought about its origin. The passage quoted above may also justify the efforts of those who are still searching for hidden rooms inside the pyramid.

A huge perimeter wall, about three meters high, completely surrounded the pyramid. It lay only ten meters from the latter, so that the courtyard between them was not very large. Later on, Djedefre probably had the wall extended.

Of the mortuary temple, which originally stood somewhat to the side at the foot of the east wall of the pyramid, no more than a few bits of reliefs and pavement remain. Because its destruction began in the Old Kingdom, it is very difficult to reconstruct its original architecture today. Only a few fragments of ornaments have been found: scenes of the sed festival, of the white hippopotamus festival, and other motifs. Hassan's expedition discovered a few of them. Other fragments were reused in building the step-wall of the medieval tower *bab el-futuh* in Cairo. It is also thought that some blocks used as building material in Amenemhet I's pyramid complex in Lisht were part of the original decoration of Khufu's mortuary temple in Giza. Arnold, who was then leading the archaeological team of New York's Metropolitan Museum working in Lisht, thinks they may even have come from another of Khufu's temples that stood near Lisht and had already fallen into ruins at the beginning of the Middle Kingdom.

The open, pillared courtyard was covered with basalt paving stones, and in its center there was probably an altar. The remains of a drainage system intended to carry off rainwater were discovered in the floor of the courtyard. Moving west, one passed between three tapering rows of pillars to reach the portico of the main cult site. According to

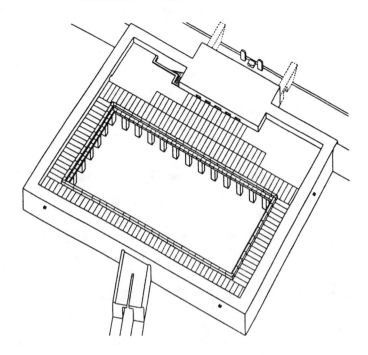

Reconstruction of Khufu's mortuary temple (after Ricke).

Lauer, the cult site contained false doors, while according to Ricke it had five niches with statues of the ruler. In his reconstruction, Lauer located an Upper Egyptian chapel in the southwest corner of the courtyard and a Lower Egyptian chapel in the northeast corner.

The ruins of the valley temple lie northeast of the pyramid, at the edge of the desert, partly just below the village of Nazlet es-Simman. During excavations in this area Hawass recently discovered the remains of a basalt pavement, and at its end, mudbrick walls eight meters thick, suggesting that a pyramid town may have originally existed near the valley temple.

So far, the causeway has been only partly examined. Its total length was originally about 825 meters (according to Hawass), and about 125 meters from the valley temple it turned toward the southwest. Herodotus described the causeway as being a kilometer long and decorated with reliefs, but this account is strongly contested by Egyptologists.

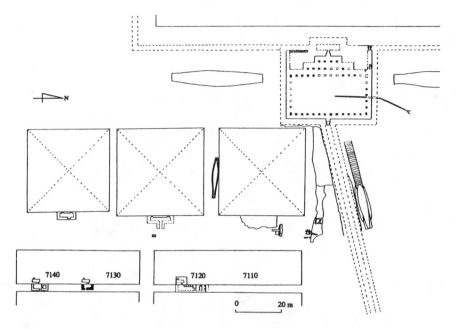

G 1a–c and Khufu's mortuary temple: ground plan (after Reisner). The map of the area reflects the situation in the Fourth Dynasty and therefore does not show the later reconstruction of G 1c's mortuary temple. Khufu's newly discovered cult pyramid is also not shown.

In immediate proximity to the Great Pyramid five boat pits were found. Two of them, on the east side, are now empty. Their walls were probably surfaced with limestone slabs, which reduced their width and simplified construction of a roof over them. The third boat pit is on the upper north edge of the causeway, has a convex floor, and is accessible by way of a staircase. The remaining two pits, in which intact boats were found, are on the south side of the pyramid.

On the walls of the pit in which the boat now displayed in a special museum was found, there were also many builders' marks and inscriptions, among them eighteen cartouches with King Djedefre's name. We can infer from this that some parts of Khufu's tomb complex were not completed until after his death. Dobrev has recently suggested that the two boat pits on the south side of the Great Pyramid were built by Djedefre as a gesture of filial piety connected with the establishment of the local divine cult of his father and the founder of the royal necropolis in Giza, Khufu.

The cedar boat, which was dismantled into 1,224 individual parts in the pit and then reconstructed, is 43.3 meters long. The neighboring pit on the west with the same content remains sealed up with the original covering blocks—the royal boat has not yet been removed. In 1987 the American National Geographic Society, in collaboration with the Egyptian office for historical monuments, examined this pit by boring a hole into it and inserting a microcamera and measuring equipment. Photographs were taken and air measurements made, after which the pit was sealed again.

The discovery of Khufu's royal boat opened the discussion regarding the meaning of boat pits at the Great Pyramid and at royal tombs in general. According to Jaroslav Černý, the four boats buried near the east and south walls of the Great Pyramid were intended for the king's use in traveling into the beyond in all four cardinal directions. The fifth pit near the approach causeway was supposed to contain the boat on which the king's mummy was transported to the burial site. Other experts, in particular Walter Emery and Selim Hassan, considered the boat a sun boat and believed that the pharaoh was supposed to use it to travel over the heavenly ocean following the sun god Re. Finally, the Egyptian archaeologist Abdel Moneim Youssef Abu Bakr maintained that all the boats buried near the Great Pyramid were originally used to carry the pharaoh to Egypt's holy places on pilgrimages and other ceremonial occasions. According to Hawass, however, the boats were never in the water—traces of shavings around the boat pit show that they were built right next to the pyramid—but he also tends to see the boat's meaning as connected with the sun cult.

Only a short time ago Hawass discovered, near the southeast corner of the Great Pyramid, the ruins of a small cult pyramid, including its pyramidion. This discovery put an end both to doubt that such a cult pyramid existed in Khufu's complex and to speculations regarding its identification with the so-called test passageways.

North of the causeway, corridors were cut into the underlying rock, and these imitate on a smaller scale (approximately 1 : 5) part of the Great Pyramid's substructure: the descending and ascending corridors, the lower part of the Great Gallery, and even by implication the horizontal passageway that leads to the Queen's Chamber. It has been suggested that this is a model used by the builders of the Great Pyramid to test their methods of blocking passageways.

Further components of the Khufu complex included three small pyramids that have been given the designation G 1a–c on the archaeological map of the necropolis at Giza. They stand on sloping ground southeast of the Great Pyramid, so that for the lowest of them (G 1c) a special foundation surface had to be constructed. In dimensions, design, and construction method they are very similar to one another.

G 1a, the northernmost, was earlier attributed to Queen Meretites, who was probably one of Khufu's older wives. She is thought to be the mother of Prince Kauab and perhaps made the transition from Snefru's harem to Khufu's. Given her title as King's Mother, one of Khufu's successors must have been her son—perhaps Djedefre. Today, on the basis of Mark Lehner's recently published work, G 1a is considered instead to be the tomb of Queen Hetepheres I, Snefru's wife and probably the mother of Khufu. According to this view, Meretites was buried in pyramid G 1b.

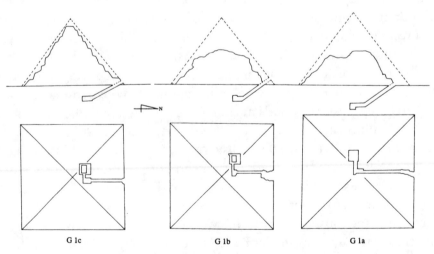

G 1c   G 1b   G 1a

The pyramids G 1a–c: ground plan and north-south sectional view (after Reisner).

The core of G 1a, which originally consisted of three or perhaps even four steps, was built of yellowish gray limestone. As in the case of G 1b and G 1c, only fragments of its casing remain. The entrance in the north wall is located slightly above the base of the pyramid and somewhat east of its north-south axis. Approximately under the midpoint of the pyramid, the descending corridor turns to the right and comes out in a small burial chamber that was cut into the rock and surfaced with limestone blocks. A sarcophagus was not found in it. The fragments of basalt that Vyse found in the burial chamber are thought to be the remains of the pavement.

Only a few ruins remain of the small mortuary temple that originally stood before the east wall of this pyramid. The archaeological reconstruction of this temple is complicated. Its center consists of a north-south–oriented chapel in whose west wall were two false doors and two niches. This particularity has not yet been satisfactorily explained. Reisner suggested that the main cult site was in the south niche, which was usually larger, and behind which the sarcophagus lay in the underground chamber. The north niche would then have been related to the "second" entrance—that is, to the end of the shaft that led into the underground chamber. The Austrian Egyptologist Peter Jánosi, an experienced expert on the queens' pyramids, thinks Reisner's theory is probably valid. He rejects the view that the north niche was reserved for the ruler.

South of G 1a, a pit for a boat burial was dug in the rock, but no traces of the boat have been found. In its plan, including the small mortuary temple and the boat pit, G 1b resembles G 1a. No remains of a buried boat were found in that pyramid, either. Hence it is not clear which queen was buried there—it may have been Meretites.

The southernmost of these pyramids, G 1c, is thought to be that of Queen Henutsen. According to Reisner, its casing remained unfinished. In many respects, its architecture resembles that of the other two pyramids. However, there is no boat burial site on the south side, perhaps because the rock subsoil there slopes considerably to the south. The archaeological development of its mortuary temple, however, differs from that of the pyramids G 1a and G 1b. Reisner thinks it was hastily built from mudbricks during the reign of Shepseskaf. The temple was partly examined in 1858, during Mariette's investigation of the grounds of the surrounding mastabas in the so-called east field; there was found the "King's Daughter's Stela," also known as the "Inventory Stela" (Egyptian Museum, Cairo, JE 2091). After Mariette, Petrie worked there in the early 1880s, and Reisner in the 1920s. These archaeological investigations showed that the small mortuary temple, which already lay in ruins at the end of the Middle Kingdom, was reconstructed and enlarged during the Eighteenth Dynasty. Further reconstruction ensued during the Twenty-First and Twenty-Sixth Dynasties, when the temple served as a religious site for the cult of Isis as goddess of the pyramids; pilgrims went there to worship the goddess and her powers of fertility.

On the stela mentioned above, Henutsen is referred to simply as the "King's daughter." As Jánosi has noted, pyramid G 1c was not part of the original plan of Khufu's complex. Its southern side follows not the model of the Great Pyramid, as one would expect in a unified concept, but that of the south side of the neighboring double mastaba (G 7130–7140). If Stadelmann is correct in thinking that the double mastaba belonged to Prince Khafkhufu I before he became king and was known as Khafre, the latter was probably the builder of pyramid G 1c. If so, he must have had it built before he ascended the throne, since his mother, Henutsen, one of Khufu's wives, had risen to the level of Queen Mother.

During Reisner's investigations in Giza an interesting event occurred that was to lead to a sensational discovery. One day the American team's photographer was on the east side of Khufu's pyramid, north of G 1a, looking for an appropriate place to take good pictures. Suddenly one of the legs of his tripod slipped into an odd crack in the rock. This turned out be the covered-over opening of a shaft that was designated G 7000x on the archaeological map of Giza. Inside it they found objects from Queen Hetepheres I's burial equipment with a few royal cartouches referring to Snefru. This equipment included an empty coffin, gold jewelry, a gilded litter, a baldachin, and a sealed canopic chest, one of the oldest of its kind. There were no bodily remains of the queen, however. This puzzling archaeological find immediately led to intense debate among Egyptologists.

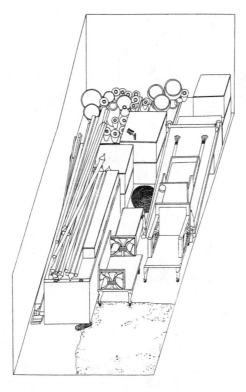

Reconstruction of the original storage place for Queen Hetepheres I's burial equipment in shaft G 7000x (after Reisner and Smith).

The first and most widely accepted explanation was offered by Reisner. In his view, Hetepheres I was originally buried in Dahshur, near her husband, Snefru, but her tomb was robbed and destroyed during Khufu's lifetime. Thereupon Khufu commanded that his mother's remaining burial equipment be reverently buried near his pyramid in Giza.

Nonetheless, there are objections to Reisner's theory. Although there are cases of the plundering of royal tombs and the burning of royal mummies in Egyptian history (we know this, for example, from prosecutions of thieves in the Twentieth Dynasty), it is unlikely that while plundering Hetepheres's tomb, thieves would have destroyed the queen's mummy without taking along the valuable objects from her burial equipment.

Another explanation for the riddle of shaft G 7000x was recently suggested by Mark Lehner. He maintains that the pit cut into the rock

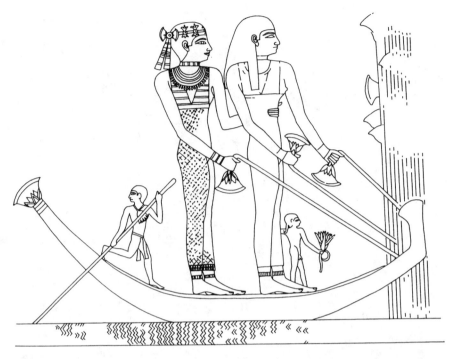

Queen Meresankh III, wearing a richly decorated robe and headdress, accompanies her mother, Queen Hetepheres II, as they travel on a papyrus boat during the papyrus-rustling ritual. Detail from decoration of Queen Meresankh III's tomb in Giza.

subsoil east of G 1a and south of G 7000x is the unfinished entrance to a pyramid—he calls it G 1x—that was never built. Lehner sees both of these as components of Queen Hetepheres I's tomb complex, which remained unfinished because a few meters west of it a new pyramid was erected. While part of the burial equipment was left in G 7000x, the rest were buried in G 1a.

As interesting as Lehner's theory seems at first sight, it is highly questionable on archaeological grounds. Why, for example, should the plan of the substructure of the supposed pyramid complex G 1x and G 7000x differ so fundamentally from that of the other queens' pyramids constructed, not only at this time but during the whole Old Kingdom? Basically, the association of both of these depressions with one and the same tomb complex remains very speculative. Moreover,

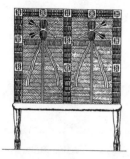

Chair from Queen Hetepheres I's tomb furnishings (after Reisner and Smith).

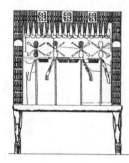

there is no evidence for the existence of a pyramid near G 1x. In addition, at that time it would have been unusual for a queen to be buried near her son rather than her husband. In his important study on the queens' pyramid complexes in the Old and Middle Kingdoms, Jánosi recently offered a series of other serious objections to Lehner's theory. Edwards raised a provocative question in connection with

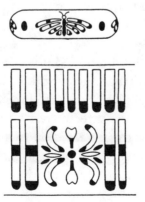

Colorful faience inlays decorating a small chest from Queen Hetepheres I's burial equipment (after Smith).

G 7000x and Queen Hetepheres I: "Is it really necessary to assume that Hetepheres I had a second tomb? Is there any clear evidence for this?" His suggestion that G 7000x was Hetepheres I's only tomb sounds tempting, but it neither solves the riddle of the missing mummy nor meets the objections already made against Reisner's theory.

Thus up to this point, all the proposed solutions to the riddle of G 7000x have weaknesses, and no more satisfactory answers are yet available. A few aspects of this problem are worth more detailed consideration. First of all, these are not the remains of a tomb whose aboveground portion has been wholly destroyed. From an archaeological standpoint, the shaft's form and location suggest that it was built ad hoc, in order to provide a reverent burial place for the queen's burial equipment. Because of its location, it could only have been constructed after Khufu's mortuary temple and G 1a were already in place—and not the other way around. Hence the question is not what happened to the queen's mummy, but rather why part of her tomb furnishings were buried in a special shaft in Giza.

Until the end of the Old Kingdom, Khufu's tomb complex, which ultimately included five pyramids and four mortuary temples, was the site of the worship of the dead ruler and three queens. Because of the analogies with Meidum and Dahshur, it has been suggested that during the First Intermediate Period thieves broke into the pyramid through the original entrance and plundered the burial chamber. At the beginning of the Middle Kingdom, Khufu's death cult might have been revived and the destroyed entrance might even have been repaired.

In the Thirteenth Dynasty, Prince Khaemuase devoted himself to the restoration not only of Djoser's complex, but also of the damaged parts of the Great Pyramid, and it is not impossible that further repairs were made during the Saite period. In addition, we should note Diodorus Siculus's comment that at the apex of the Great Pyramid there was a platform almost three meters wide by three meters long, suggesting not only that the pyramidion (which may have been covered in gold) was already missing, but also that part of the casing was damaged. We will probably never know how many attempts were made to break into the pyramid. In Strabo's time, around 25 B.C.E., it certainly stood open; finally, in the third or fourth century C.E., it was sealed to keep it from being misused.

In any case, the dismantling of the pyramid began before 1250. For example, the historian Abd al-Latif tells us that the small pyramids were torn down during the time of the sultan Saladin (1175–1193). The stones were used for building dams, for instance. Around the middle of the fourteenth century, under Sultan Hassan, stone blocks from the Great Pyramid were used to build his famous mosque. Many others followed his example, but despite all the damage and natural erosion, the Great Pyramid endured.

It is remarkable that in the whole of Khufu's enormous pyramid complex not a single image of the ruler has been found. And so the only picture of the Great Pyramid's builder that can be identified with certainty remains a small ivory statuette nine centimeters high (Egyptian Museum, Cairo, JE 4244), which Petrie found in 1903 under dramatic circumstances. During excavations in the temple of Osiris in Kom es-Sultan, near Abydos, Petrie was brought the headless statuette of a man sitting on a throne. Upon seeing the hieroglyphic inscription and the cartouche with Khufu's name, Petrie ordered his men to sift through all the excavated material that had been thus far piled up. In addition, he offered a reward to the finder of the head, which had apparently been hacked off during the digging. After three weeks of uninterrupted digging and sifting, he finally succeeded in finding the head of the Khufu statuette.

Djedefre's Pyramid

Khufu's son and successor, Djedefre, abandoned the royal cemetery in Giza and chose as the site of his tomb a place about seven kilometers north, on the rocky hills near the modern village of Abu Rawash. He called his pyramid "Djedefre's Starry Sky."

If we set aside the brick masonry ruins that Lepsius took for a pyramid and listed in his register as no. 1, Djedefre's is the northernmost

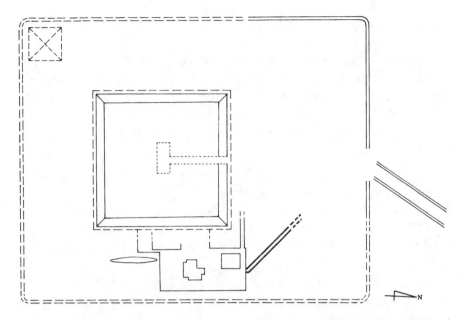

Simplified ground plan of Djedefre's pyramid complex (after Maragioglio and Rinaldi).

of all the pyramids. Perring had briefly examined it before Lepsius, concentrating his attention primarily on the substructure. Petrie approached it in a similar manner in the early 1880s. Only in the first years of the twentieth century were systematic investigations begun by French archaeologists, first Émile Chassinat (1868–1948) and then, about ten years later, Pierre Lacau (1873–1963). Apart from brief reports, however, neither of these researchers published a comprehensive account of the results of their investigations. Despite the later work done by Pierre Montet (1885–1966) and by Maragioglio and Rinaldi, many fundamental questions remain unanswered. Perhaps the archaeological excavations begun in the spring of 1995 by a French-Swiss team led by Michel Valloggia will help us answer them.

The pyramid rises on a rock outcropping about a hundred and fifty meters above the Nile Valley. Its core consists partly of the reshaped rock subsoil and partly of blocks of local limestone. About fifteen horizontally laid layers of the limestone have been preserved, whereas only fragments of the casing exist, a few carefully dressed pink granite blocks that were found in front of the pyramid's east side. Disagreement developed regarding the pyramid's angle of inclination, which could be calculated, on the basis of these blocks, to have been about sixty degrees. Several scholars suggested that it might have been a very steep pyramid that was later totally demolished, an unfinished pyramid, or even a step pyramid. The first discovery made by Michel Valloggia's team showed, however, that the pyramid's walls had a "standard angle of inclination" of about fifty-one degrees. The casing blocks were not laid horizontally, but leaned slightly toward the middle of the pyramid, which caused their sixty-degree angle of inclination to be reduced toward the top (this method was also used in the Step and Bent pyramids, for example). The pyramid was probably never completed. It simply had the bad luck to become a favorite target for later stone thieves.

The underground part of the pyramid was built according to the so-called open-pit method. During its construction, the builders took into account the complicated system of underground and aboveground chambers in the Great Pyramid of Giza, as Stadelmann emphasizes. In the north wall, there is a trench containing the remains of a descending corridor in whose rock foundation Valloggia found a copper ax blade that was buried there during the ceremonies inaugurating the pyramid's construction. The corridor is aligned approximately along the pyramid's north-south axis and leads to the burial chamber. From the relatively large dimensions of the trench, which is now open, we can conclude that there were originally two rooms: the antechamber and the burial chamber. During his investigations inside the pyramid's substructure, Petrie discovered a fragment of pink granite he thought was part of the sarcophagus.

The mortuary temple poses another problem that has not yet been solved. The perimeter wall, some two and half meters thick, surrounds a rectangular, north-south–oriented area around the pyramid. On the north lies a large open space to which the approach causeway leads. Whether remnants of the mortuary temple might still be found there, only future excavations will show. For the time being, a mudbrick structure built east of the pyramid is thought to be what remains of an improvised mortuary temple.

The layout of the latter differs significantly from that of other known Old Kingdom mortuary temples. It contains an open courtyard with part of the original pavement, storehouses, etc. In the middle of one of the spaces in the northeastern part of the structure stood a row of columns. In the courtyard, Chassinat even found a fragment of a column with Djedefre's cartouche, a significant and somewhat strange discovery, because—if we set aside the specific case of the columns and half-columns in the Djoser complex—columns don't appear in pyramid complexes until the beginning of the Fifth Dynasty. In this space fragments of statues of three of Djedefre's sons and two of his daughters were also found, along with a limestone sphinx. If the latter in fact dates from this period, it would be the oldest known monument of its kind, unless Stadelmann is correct in maintaining that the Great Sphinx in Giza was built by Khufu.

A further riddle is posed by the depression in the middle of the east wall of the pyramid core. Given its form and location, Maragioglio and Rinaldi believed that in this place a niche with a stela might have been located and, in front of it, an offering room with an altar. Valloggia disagreed, maintaining that the remains of the mortuary temple could have been located instead on the large and as yet unexamined area north of the pyramid. If his view is confirmed by further excavations, it would have important consequences. Until the end of the Third Dynasty, mortuary temples were erected north of the pyramid, whereas from the beginning of the Fourth Dynasty onward, they were located at the foot of the east side of the pyramid. Wide-ranging religious and political transformations were connected with this change.

To the list of inconsistencies we may add the trench cut in the rock subsoil in front of the east side of the pyramid. In form, it resembles a boat, but no remains of a boat were found there. Instead, it contained many fragments of statues, most of them in reddish quartzite. Altogether, there were at least 120 statues, most of which represented the ruler sitting on his throne. There were also three heads, of which two are now in the Louvre in Paris (E 12626 and E11167) and one in the Egyptian Museum, Cairo (JE 35 35138). Chassinat, who discovered the fragments, believes that the statues were intentionally and thoroughly destroyed in order to extinguish Djedefre's memory, in a sort of *damnatio memoriae*.

The meaning of the structure near the southwest corner of the pyramid is also unclear. Some archaeologists, such as Stadelmann and Jánosi, think it is a cult pyramid, but these normally stood at the southeast corner. Other archaeologists, such as Maragioglio and Rinaldi, believe that it is a pyramid belonging to Djedefre's consort. A statue that was found in Abu Rawash and is currently in the Louvre (N 54) shows that Khentetenka was the consort, apparently along with Hetepheres II. However, in view of the north-south (not east-west) orientation of Djedefre's pyramid complex as a whole, it seems nonetheless to have been a cult pyramid. In this case as well we must wait to see if the planned systematic excavations will shed more light on the subject.

The sparse and incomplete data produced by earlier archaeological investigations led Reisner to develop a theory based on Chassinat's observations and conclusions. According to him, Djedefre was the son of Khufu and a queen of Libyan descent. He murdered his elder half brother Kauab, who, as the son of an Egyptian mother, had a better claim to succeed Khufu. Djedefre himself met a similar end, although not until he had reigned for eight years: he was murdered by his younger half brother Khafre.

Reisner relied chiefly on the previously mentioned discovery of statues of Djedefre that had all been broken into small pieces, on the fact that Djedefre abandoned the royal cemetery in Giza and adopted architectural and conceptual principles different from those that governed Khufu's complex, and finally on the fact that around his pyramid no tombs of family members and high officials were found.

This theory received increasing criticism. In particular, today the myth of Khufu's alleged blond Libyan consort is explained in a different and more plausible way. The broken statues are not necessarily an indication of an act of personal vengeance on the part of Djedefre's successor. Instead, the relative isolation and perhaps also the unfinished state of the pyramid complex might have led the local population to destroy it. The destruction began during the New Kingdom at the latest, and was particularly intense in the Roman and

Early Christian eras, when a Coptic monastery was built in nearby Wadi Karin. It has been proven, moreover, that at the end of the nineteenth century, stone was still being hauled away from the ruins of the pyramid at the rate of three hundred camel loads a day.

The brick structures in front of the east side of Djedefre's pyramid show that a few basic, if hastily built and economical arrangements must have been made for the worship of the dead ruler. The existence of a cult is indicated by not only the significant number of stat-

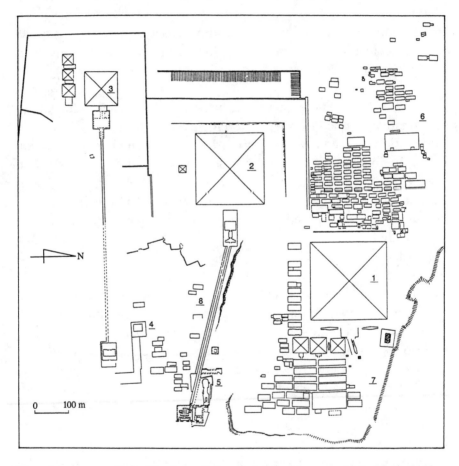

Plan of the necropolis in Giza (after Reisner). 1. Khufu's pyramid, 2. Khafre's pyramid, 3. Menkaure's pyramid, 4. Khentkaues I's step tomb, 5. Great Sphinx, 6. West Cemetery, 7. East Cemetery, 8. Central Cemetery.

ues discovered there, but also a few written documents referring to the existence of priests connected with the worship of Djedefre. Here we must note that the necropolis with private tombs that spread over the hills around the pyramid, and which dates from the First to the Fifth Dynasty, has not yet been carefully investigated. For this reason, before drawing any final conclusions we must await the results of French-Swiss excavations, especially in the pyramid and in the northern part of the pyramid complex. On the basis of the available information, we can already infer that Djedefre's pyramid complex was built in haste and probably remained incomplete in some respects. Ultimately, the length of Djedefre's reign must be reconsidered. If the date of the eleventh cattle count, found on a ceiling block in Khufu's boat pit, really refers to Djedefre, the king must have reigned longer than the eight years attributed to him by the Royal Canon of Turin.

Khafre's Pyramid

From a distance, the middle pyramid at Giza seems to be the highest, although it was originally some three meters lower than Khufu's pyramid. It stands on a more elevated part of the necropolis, the angle of its walls is somewhat steeper, and its apex is in better condition, which makes it look bigger. It is appropriately named "Khafre is Great."

Its possessor was perhaps originally called Khafkhufu, and, according to Stadelmann, he built the large double mastaba (G 7130–40) in the East Cemetery at Giza. The early death of his half brothers Kauab and Djedefre would eventually have brought Khafkhufu to power, whereupon he changed his name to Khafre. He had his tomb built not in Abu Rawash, like his predecessors, but rather in Giza.

The history of modern research on Khafre's pyramid resembles in many respects that on Khufu's monument. In 1817, Giovanni Caviglia had already sought in vain to make his way into the pyramid. Only a year later did Giovanni Belzoni succeed in getting in; he discovered the so-called upper entrance and also investigated the underground

The Great Sphinx and the Great Pyramid, as members of Napoleon's expedition saw them (after Denon).

part of the pyramid. In addition, he excavated a small shrine between the Sphinx's paws, where he found a granite stela with an inscription mentioning Thutmose IV. The first truly painstaking examination of the pyramid was made in 1837, once again by Perring.

In 1853, Mariette directed excavations in the Valley Temple of the Khafre complex, which were actually related to the Great Sphinx as well. A year later, he discovered what was to become one of the most significant items in the Egyptian Museum, Cairo (JE 10062)—the famous diorite statue of Khafre on his throne, his head sheltered from behind by the outstretched wings of the falcon god Horus. Petrie also worked on the complex during his stay in Giza, but the first systematic archaeological investigation was undertaken by the German Ernst von Sieglin expedition in 1909–1910, under the leadership of Uvo Hölscher. However, they did not search for Khafre's famous boats, whose presence in the area around his pyramid no one had expected. Hassan unearthed the boat pits in the early 1930s. Recently, Lehner

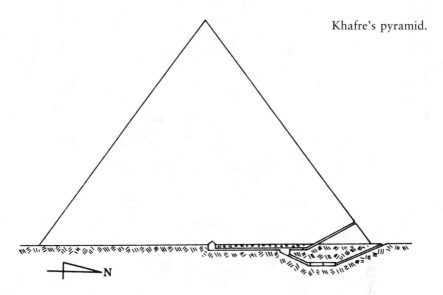

Khafre's pyramid.

N

and Hawass have investigated the tomb complex under the auspices of the American Giza Plateau Mapping Project. Primarily by using modern geodetic measurements, this project was able to advance our knowledge of the archaeology of architecture and to determine the original methods of measurement and construction with relative precision.

As in the case of Khufu's pyramid, a rock outcropping was used to increase the stability of the core, this time to such an extent that the lowest levels of the southwest corner were hacked right out of the rock subsoil. However, by far the largest part of the core consists of horizontally laid layers of large blocks of approximately equal height that were brought from the limestone quarries near the building site. North of the pyramid one can still clearly discern traces that show how the rock was quarried. The core of Khafre's pyramid was less carefully constructed than that of Khufu's Great Pyramid: the layers do not always run exactly horizontally, the joints are sometimes very wide, and mortar is often lacking between the blocks.

The lowest level of the casing is made of pink granite; all the others are of limestone. Only a small portion of the original mantle, just below the apex, has been preserved. This makes it possible to see how the casing blocks were laid and bound to the pyramid core. The

Giovanni Battista
Belzoni.

pyramidion and also part of the pyramid's apex no longer exist. Re-cently, the increasingly clear signs of erosion on the remains of the casing led Italian experts to make a thorough investigation. They dis-covered that the corner edges of the remaining portions of the casing are not completely straight; the individual blocks are slightly turned in various directions. A very simple explanation for this peculiarity was confirmed by a computer simulation and suggests that the cause was seismic activity—not uncommon in either modern or ancient Egypt.

Khafre's pyramid was originally intended to be larger and to stand farther north. However, that plan was quickly abandoned, as the two entrances into the interior of the pyramid show. The older of the two entrances is now located in the ground about thirty meters north of the pyramid. Called the first or lower entrance, it is hacked completely out of the rock subsoil and opens into a corridor that at first descends, then runs horizontally, and finally ascends. Near the middle of the horizontal part of the corridor, a short passageway opens on the west wall and leads to a small room where part of the burial equipment was probably stored. The upper entrance, opening in the pyramid's north wall about twelve meters above ground level, gives access to a passageway lined in blocks of pink granite that at first descends and then runs horizontally after it reaches the base of the pyramid. At the point where it begins to run horizontally, there is a barrier, also of pink granite. Despite all the precautions taken, grave robbers were later able to dig a tunnel that allowed them go around the specially fortified part of the corridor. A few meters farther on, the horizontal part of the passageway continues south to the burial chamber, which lies on the vertical axis of the pyramid.

Except for its ceiling, the burial chamber is cut completely out of the rock, and like earlier structures of its kind, it has a rectangular,

Entrance to Khafre's pyramid (after Denon).

east-west–oriented ground plan. The original intention may have been to cover the walls with pink granite. The gabled ceiling, which is located over the pyramid's base, consists of enormous limestone blocks. The opening of the shafts in the north and south walls of the chamber at first appear similar to those in the Queen's and King's chambers in the Great Pyramid, but in this case, there are only short, horizontal openings that may have been used to reinforce a wooden structure inside the tomb. Near the west wall stands the pink granite sarcophagus, sunk slightly into the floor; originally, it had a sliding top. A small shaft in the burial chamber's floor originally contained the royal canopic vessel. However, no safely identified remains of Khafre's mummy or his tomb furnishings were found. The location and also the relatively simple construction of the access corridor and the burial chamber allow us to conclude that the builders may have tried to avoid the complications that builders had encountered in constructing the technically difficult system of passageways, barriers, and chambers in Khufu's pyramid.

Khafre's pyramid is surrounded on all four sides by an open courtyard barely ten meters wide, which is paved with limestone slabs of irregular form and bounded by a huge stone perimeter wall. Additional walls of rough limestone blocks run farther north, west, and south; despite their apparently unplanned course, they are considered outer perimeter walls of Khafre's complex.

On the south side of the pyramid, on its axis, is a small, almost completely destroyed pyramid (G 2a) that once also had its own perimeter wall. Its substructure is simple, consisting of a descending corridor and an underground chamber with a T-shaped ground plan. In the chamber were found bits of wood, carnelian beads, fragments of animal bones, and covers for vessels. Although there were no signs of a burial, this discovery led Maragioglio and Rinaldi to conclude that one of Khafre's consorts was buried in the pyramid. Stadelmann rightly opposed this view, pointing to the analogous situation in the Bent Pyramid in Dahshur, and proposing instead that it was a cult pyramid. His opinion is supported by the previously mentioned discovery of Khufu's cult pyramid on the southeast corner of the Great Pyramid.

West of Khafre's pyramid, beyond the so-called outside perimeter wall, Petrie discovered in the early 1880s the ruins of a structure that contained long, chiefly east-west–oriented rooms. He assumed that it provided lodging for the workers who were erecting the pyramid. Hölscher agreed, and in his opinion four to five thousand men were lodged there in 111 large rooms. However, Lehner and Hawass's recent investigations suggest another explanation. In their view, this structure was not a settlement, but rather a storehouse and perhaps

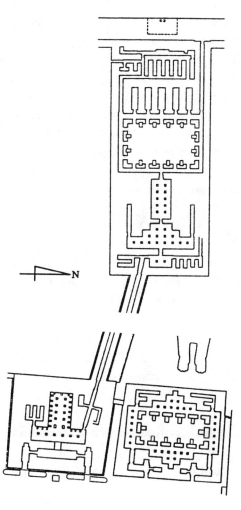

Khafre's mortuary and valley temples, with the temple of the Sphinx (after Ricke).

even held the workshops that supplied the Khafre complex. The great number of mollusk shells found here also indicates that during the Fourth Dynasty the pyramid was surrounded not by an arid desert, as it is today, but rather by a kind of savanna with the corresponding flora and fauna.

The mortuary temple did not border directly on the pyramid, but was separated from its east wall by one wing of its courtyard. It has an east-west–oriented, rectangular ground plan and is built of limestone. In its structure, we already encounter the five basic elements whose composition was ultimately perfected in Sahure's mortuary temple in Abusir: the entrance hall, the open courtyard, five statue chapels, various storehouses, and the offering hall.

The entrance hall running along the longer axis of the temple originally had approximately the form of an inverted letter *T*. It was entered from the east through a small antechamber that contained a pair of monolithic pink granite pillars; twelve similar pairs of pillars followed in the hall itself. Around the entry area lay a few small chambers that are thought to have been storerooms or serdabs. In the plan and execution of this group of rooms, Ricke noted striking similarities to the valley temple, and considered it a kind of repetition. Thus he designated it as the "ante-temple" (*Vortempel*) and the remaining area as the "worship temple" (*Verehrungstempel*).

The large, open courtyard, which lies approximately in the middle of the temple, is oriented north-south. Along its sides runs a covered ambulatory, its flat limestone roof slabs supported by broad pillars of pink granite. The lower part of the ambulatory was formed by a dado in red granite and limestone, with richly colored reliefs over it, of which only fragments have been preserved. According to Ricke, in front of the pillars stood statues, about 3.75 meters high, of Khafre sitting on his throne and looking out over the courtyard. Lehner thinks these were statues of the standing ruler, basing his view on the discovery of a small statuette in the so-called workers' lodging west of the pyramid mentioned above. This statuette shows the ruler standing in front of a kind of pillar with the crown of Upper Egypt on his head.

The ruins of a small drainage canal suggest that an altar stood in the middle of the courtyard, which was paved with slabs of alabaster. A door in the west wing of the ambulatory provided access to five long chapels that originally housed statues of the king. The offering hall in the west part of the temple was entered through a narrower corridor that began in the southwest corner of the courtyard. Through it one reached a narrow, long room oriented north-south (in contrast to later mortuary temples), in whose west wall, precisely on the pyramid's long axis, was a false door.

A group of five storage rooms located in the area between the five cult chapels and the offering hall also belonged to the mortuary temple. In them were kept the cult vessels and offerings used during the ceremonies. Outside the mortuary temple five boat pits were discovered, two of them north of the temple and three south of it. All had been plundered.

The valley and mortuary temples were connected by a causeway that ascended about forty-six meters, and of which only ruins remain. It is thought that it was a covered corridor built of limestone, whose interior was perhaps decorated with reliefs and which was from outside lined with pink granite blocks. The causeway did not run precisely along the east-west axis of the pyramid and the mortuary temple, but rather somewhat to the southeast of it, because the valley temple itself was erected slightly out of line with regard to the Great Sphinx and the mortuary temple.

A corridor cut into the rock separated the causeway from the Sphinx and the mortuary temple. The core wall of the almost square valley temple was built of enormous blocks whose weight reached 150 tons in some cases. Its covering consisted of pink granite slabs. The perimeter wall's slightly inclined outer side and rounded-off top made the structure look like a mastaba. In front of the east facade was an extensive terrace paved with limestone slabs, through which two causeways led from the Nile canal to two entrances in the east facade of the valley temple. In the middle of the terrace traces of what might have been a small, simple, wood-and-matting structure were found. Many experts believe that the statue of the king stood there, while others suggest that the so-called purification tent was erected there; this tent was used during the burial rituals and is known to us only through representations in a few private tombs.

The previous interpretation was made more difficult by an important discovery made in 1995. During restoration work in the area around the Sphinx, additional remnants of the foundation of a group of structures already discovered by Hölscher were found in front of Khafre's valley temple. These structures appear to have been built of lightweight plant material. In addition, there were large brick walls and drainage canals. Particularly noteworthy was the discovery of "tunnels" dug through the rock subsoil under the causeways; these were paved with limestone blocks and led to the two entrances to the valley temple.* The tunnels have a slightly convex profile resembling that of a boat. A definitive interpretation of all these structures will probably not be available until the archaeological investigation is completed; however, they appear to be the remains of quays and structures occasionally used for burial ceremonies. Some Egyptologists hypothesize, perhaps correctly, that east of the Sphinx temple there was a large harbor used by the builders of the pyramids.

Near the south wall of the temple Hölscher discovered the remains of a brick structure from the Fifth or Sixth Dynasty, and in it the bases of two limestone pillars. There a path began that continued upward parallel to the causeway.

The north portal on the east facade of the temple was dedicated to the goddess Bastet, and the southern portal to the goddess Hathor. In the arches of these portals, which were nearly three meters wide and six meters high, great wooden doors originally hung on copper hinges. Each doorway was guarded by a recumbent Sphinx. In the east part of the temple, the approach paths led to a narrow antechamber. Here, in an excavated pit, Mariette discovered in 1860 the famous diorite statue of Khafre.

The pillared hall that fills the central and western part of the temple is another outstanding achievement of ancient Egyptian architecture. Its ground plan has once again the form of an inverted T. Sixteen pink

---

* As we shall see later, in Amenemhet III's pyramid complex in Dahshur a similar tunnel has been shown to run under the temple north of the causeway. It would be more exact to speak of lower corridors that allowed undisturbed movement in inaccessible areas.

granite pillars support architrave blocks in the same material, bound together with copper bands in the form of a swallow's tail. The roof slabs originally rested on these. The floor of the hall was paved with alabaster slabs of irregular form. Along the side walls stood twenty-three statues of Khafre; they were set into the floor and resembled those in the antechamber.* These were made of diorite, slate, and alabaster and were later destroyed *in situ* in the pillared hall.

South of the hall were six narrow, two-storied magazines built of pink granite. On the opposite side was a corridor that led to the northwest corner of the temple and there joined the causeway. Like the pillared hall, it was paved with alabaster. From it a passageway led to a small room (which has sometimes been seen as the guard's lodging, though this is not a very convincing interpretation) and to a staircase by which the roof terrace was reached. The roof terrace extended over the various parts of the temple on six different levels and was provided with a drainage system that directed rainwater into a cistern.

According to some Egyptologists, the valley temple was used for important burial rituals. The Polish scholar Bernhardt Grdseloff, who was already living in Egypt before the Second World War, hypothesized that purification rituals were carried out on the roof terrace, in a tent specially constructed for the purpose, and that afterward the embalming of the dead ruler's body was done in the temple's antechamber. The French Egyptologist Étienne Drioton (1889–1961) proposed a similar view, but he switched the locations of the ceremonies: according to him, the purification took place in the antechamber and the embalming on the roof terrace. Ricke rightly pointed out that the large quantity of water required for these rituals was available only near the canal. The ceremonies performed by the priests in the valley temple could therefore have had only a symbolic character.

The valley temple is not only a masterpiece of ancient Egyptian monumental architecture, but also the best preserved example of its

* The number of statues and their precise function, not only in Khafre's pyramid complex but also in other pyramids, is a subject of debate among Egyptologists. For example, Edwards estimates that there could have been as many as one or two hundred of them in the Khafre complex.

kind in the Old Kingdom. For precisely that reason the area in front of it was cleared of sand, and in 1869 the temple, together with the other monuments of the pyramid necropolis in Giza, represented the background for the ceremonial opening of the Suez Canal, which was witnessed by a hand-picked elite among the entourage of Empress Eugénie.

We do not know when the destruction of the pyramid began. Considering what happened to the other pyramids, we can assume that in the First Intermediate Period thieves had already broken into the burial chamber. The inscriptions on the rock made by the "overseer of temple construction," May, north and west of the pyramid prove that its destruction was already far advanced during the Nineteenth Dynasty. From other written sources we can conclude that May, on Ramesses II's express order, supplied stone for a temple in Heliopolis by removing the casing of Khafre's pyramid.

The Arab historian Ibn Abd as-Salaam notes that the pyramid was opened up in the year 774 after the hegira (1372 C.E.), during the rule of the Great Emir Jalburgh el-Khassaki. The tunnels going around the granite barriers in the entry passage could have been dug at this time as well. Other sources suggest that a large part of the pyramid casing was removed between 1356 and 1362 and used for the construction of Hassan's mosque. It may have been in this way that the entrance to the pyramid and also the earlier thieves' tunnel (which had been closed up again) were first discovered.

The Great Sphinx

The Great Sphinx in Giza is more than simply a symbol of ancient and modern Egypt. It is the very embodiment of antiquity and of mystery itself. Over the centuries it has fired the imaginations of poets and scientists, adventurers and travelers. Although it has often been measured, described, investigated using the most up-to-date technical means, and discussed at special scientific conferences, fundamental questions remain unanswered: Who built it, when, and why?

The Great Sphinx (the local people call it *Abu al-Hawl,* "The Father of Terror") is a colossal statue of a recumbent lion with the head of

Napoleon's savants examining the Great Sphinx in Giza (after Denon).

a ruler. It is over sixty meters long and twenty meters high, and was long considered the largest statue in the world. Thus it is curious that Pliny is the only ancient author who mentions the Great Sphinx. The monument was originally chiseled out of the limestone subsoil and acquired its current appearance through erosion.

The Sphinx, oriented east-west with relative precision, faces east. On its head it wears the royal insignia consisting of the *nemes* crown and the *uraeus*.* Proportionately, the head seems slightly small in relation to the body. This fact is also interpreted as indicating that it was reworked in the past; the body was lengthened in order to increase the strength of the rock, which had been damaged in this section. From the chin once hung a long beard, fragments of which were found by Napoleon's expedition, but they had to be surrendered to the English after the French were defeated in the Battle of the Nile in Abukir bay. The body of the Sphinx was originally painted a reddish ochre color, and remains of the pigment are clearly visible in the head-

---

* The *uraeus* represented the sacred asp (*Naja haje*) and appeared on the headdress of rulers as a symbol of sovereignty.

The Great Sphinx in Giza, "The Father of Terror," after a sketch from Václav Remedius Prutký's description of his travels in Egypt during the eighteenth century (Prague University Library).

dress. According to the latest research, only the front part, which can be seen from a distance, was originally completed.

The statue stands on the site of the quarries from which the materials were taken to build the core of Khufu's pyramid. Work on the Sphinx could thus have begun at that time, but not earlier. Stadelmann dates it in the time of Khufu. Recently Vasil Dobrev has suggested that Djedefre built the Sphinx as a gesture of filial piety connected with the establishment of the local divine cult of Khufu. Discussion of the Sphinx's age has recently been encouraged for commercial reasons, especially by certain American private organizations. However, suggestions that it was created between 7000 and 5000 B.C.E., and possibly even earlier, are so incompatible with the specific archaeological and general historical contexts that they need not be taken seriously. Now as in the past, most Egyptologists believe the Sphinx was Khafre's work and was created during the construction of his pyramid complex. Researchers base their opinion on carefully developed and verified work procedures and methods.

Egyptologists disagree not only regarding the precise date of the Sphinx's creation (that is, in the time of Khafre or Khufu), but also about its meaning. The word *sphinx* derives from a distorted Greek translation of the Egyptian word *shesep-ankh,* "living image." But an image of whom? Of the sun god Re-Atum? Or of King Khafre (or Khufu)? Some experts think it represents the pharaoh presenting a sacrificial offering to the sun god, while others see in it the mythical guardian of the royal tombs in Giza.

As early as the New Kingdom, ancient Egyptians began to interpret the Sphinx as an image of the sun god. During Thutmose IV's reign, sand drifts were removed and a protective brick wall was built around the monument. Between the forepaws, a small religious site was established, where the "Dream Stela"—a pink granite stela with a famous, often quoted inscription—still stands.* It tells how as a young prince, the later pharaoh Thutmose IV, wearied by hunting in the area around the pyramids, fell asleep near the Sphinx. He dreamed that it spoke to him and complained about the sand that weighed on it. The Sphinx promised that if he removed the sand, he would become king. The prince fulfilled the wish and became ruler of both lands, king of Upper and Lower Egypt. From that point on, the cult of the Sphinx—which was called Haremakhet, "Horus in the horizon" (Greek Harmachis)—rapidly grew in significance. There were already a few important buildings in the area, such as the temple of Thutmose's father Amenhotep II and Thutmose I's chapel. Interest in the Sphinx continued, as the comprehensive reconstructions carried out under Seti I and Ramesses II show.

In Roman times, further improvements were made under the emperors Marcus Aurelius (161–180) and Septimius Severus (193–211). In front of the stela, a staircase was built between the forepaws, the pavement was restored, and additional protective walls were erected around the Sphinx. A long period of neglect followed. The last major cleanup of the surrounding area was carried out in the 1920s by the French archaeologist Émile Baraize (1874–1952). Before him,

---

* The stela was made of a single block that came from Khafre's pyramid—certain proof that at this time the temple already lay in ruins.

Caviglia in particular devoted attention to the Sphinx in 1818; he discovered the fragments of the beard, among other things. While looking for underground chambers, Perring bored holes around the Sphinx through which harmful chemicals passed that damaged the monument. Mariette, Maspero, and others have also investigated the Sphinx. In the 1930s, Selim Hassan carried out wide-ranging archaeological research on the Sphinx and summarized his results in the standard work on this monument, *The Great Sphinx and Its Secrets*. On the basis of later discoveries made by Caviglia, Baraize, and others, Lehner recently produced a computerized reconstruction of the Sphinx. In front of its breast and under the beard stood a statue of the striding ruler. The remains of this statue had already been found by some early researchers (Hölscher among them), but they considered it a later addition dating from the New Kingdom. Lehner also thinks that it is an image of Amenhotep II. In addition, he notes a striking resemblance between the Sphinx and the alabaster statue of Khafre in the Museum of Fine Arts in Boston, and attributes the Sphinx to that ruler.

The temple between the Sphinx's forepaws was discovered in 1925 1926 by Baraize. On the basis of the archaeological and structural circumstances, it is assumed that the pink granite Sphinx temple was built (but probably not completed) under Khafre, but after both

An unusual representation of the Sphinx with the pyramids in the background. Detail from the upper part of Mentuher's stela from the New Kingdom, which was discovered in Giza by Selim Hassan (Egyptian Museum, Cairo).

the ruler's valley temple and the Sphinx had already been constructed. There was no direct connection between the two temples. Moreover, there is no direct structural connection between the temple and the Sphinx. For example, the temple's east-west axis is not aligned with that of the Sphinx; it is more than seven meters south of the Sphinx.

The ground plan of the limestone temple, whose inner walls were sheathed in pink granite, is unusual. In the center was an open courtyard, oriented north-south and surrounded on all sides by granite pillars and statues of the king. On the east and west sides, the row of pillars broadened to form a portico in front of a deep niche. Like the nearby valley temple, the structure was reached from the east through two entrances. Its meaning is still debated among Egyptologists, in part because in the heavily damaged temple not a single inscription remains that might give us information about it. Contemporary inscriptions do not even tell us anything about its priests. Ricke's view, that it is a sun temple, is the most widely accepted. It would thus be the predecessor of the Fifth Dynasty sun temples closely associated with the worship of the dead pharaoh.

Lehner's measurements have interesting implications for the meaning and date of the temple. He maintains that during the Fourth Dynasty an observer standing in the temple at the equinoxes would see the sun go down along the temple's axis and behind the tip of Khafre's pyramid. At the summer solstice, the same observer would see the sun set on the western horizon at the precise midpoint between Khufu's and Khafre's pyramids. All this suggests that the temple was built under Khafre and that Ricke's view that it was a sun temple is probably correct.

After much painstaking work carried out under Zahi Hawass's direction, the "entirely restored" Sphinx was formally dedicated on 25 May 1998. In order to avoid repeating earlier mistakes, the most up-to-date methods were used during the restoration. At the beginning of the 1980s cement was used for the restoration, and as a result part of the shoulder broke off and fell to the ground in 1988. One of the goals of this difficult undertaking was to restore the Sphinx to the condition it was in before the Second World War.

Baka's (?) Pyramid

Near Zawiyet el-Aryan, near the so-called Layer Pyramid, lie the remains of a structure assumed to be an unfinished pyramid. A square platform on which the pyramid core was to be erected can be discerned. The slight depression around it is thought to be the foundation for the planned casing.

In the middle of the unfinished structure is an enormous, east-west–oriented trench. On its floor lie large blocks of limestone and granite—the foundation of the burial chamber. In the western part of the trench stands an oval sarcophagus made of pink granite. According to some Egyptologists, it was probably made later, out of one of the foundation blocks.

As Alexandre Barsanti reported, in 1903 a remarkable event occurred that confronted archaeologists with still another riddle about this monument. After a heavy rain had filled the trench to a height of three meters, the water level suddenly sank by one meter. This led to theories regarding the existence of hidden, as yet undiscovered rooms under the trench. Unfortunately, it has not been possible to prove this, since the structure has long been inside a military reservation.

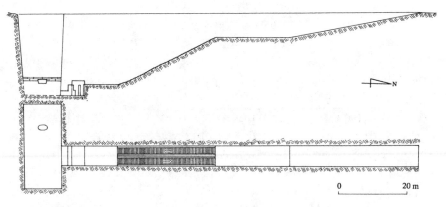

Plan of the substructure of the unfinished pyramid in Zawiyet el-Aryan (after Reisner).

⟳ The Step Pyramid in Saqqara,
view from the south. In the
foreground, a detail of the
decoration of the south tomb—a
frieze representing a series of
erect cobras.

⟳ The Step Pyramid in Saqqara,
view from the east. In the foreground, a detail of the decoration
of the T-temple, a frieze representing a series of *djed* pillars.

The "Famine Stela" on the small island of Sehel at the first cataract of the Nile.

Alabaster sarcophagus in the burial chamber of Sekhemkhet's "Buried Pyramid."

⟳ The perimeter wall around Sekhemkhet's pyramid was constructed in a way similar to that in the Djoser complex.

⟳ Ruins of the step pyramid on Elephantine.

On the way to the pyramid of Seila. The remnants of the pyramid, at the eastern edge of the Fayyum oasis, are not easy to find.

The Meidum Pyramid.

Reconstruction of the limestone pyramidion that a team from the German Archaeological Institute in Cairo found in the 1980s in the rubble at the eastern foot of the Red Pyramid in Dahshur.

⇲ View from the valley temple toward the Bent Pyramid and the causeway.

⇲ The alabaster altar in Niuserre's sun temple in Abu Ghurab. In the background, the pyramids in Abusir.

⟲ The "fourth" pyramid in Giza—
the step tomb of Queen Khentkaues I.

⟲ The Great Sphinx in Giza. In
front of its forepaws is the temple of
the Sphinx.

Neferirkare's pyramid (left) and Niuserre's pyramid in Abusir. In the foreground, a small quartzite basin, into which waste water from Niuserre's mortuary temple flowed.

A pair of palm columns from Sahure's mortuary temple in Abusir. Under favorable conditions, it can offer a unique overview of Giza.

One of the wonders of the world—the Great Pyramid in Giza.

The walls of the burial chamber in Unas's pyramid are decorated with the oldest pyramid texts.

⟳ Amenemhet I's pyramid in Lisht.

⟳ Pepi II's pyramid in South Saqqara was the last large pyramid of the Old Kingdom. In the foreground: ruins of the mortuary temple.

The uncovered brick core of Senusret II's pyramid in el-Lahun.

The limestone casing of Amenemhet III's pyramid in Hawara was removed long ago, and today only its brick core remains.

One of the small, pyramid-shaped chapels that have been reconstructed in the New Kingdom cemetery in Deir el-Medina.

Around the unfinished structure are the remains of a stone perimeter wall whose ground plan is rectangular and, significantly, oriented north-south. This strongly reminds us of Djedefre's complex in Abu Rawash. The grounds around the unfinished pyramid have not been investigated, but large cemeteries seem to extend to the east and especially to the west.

The identity of the possessor of this pyramid is still a subject of debate. Masons' inscriptions with the king's name have been preserved on some of the blocks, but it can be variously interpreted. Some Egyptologists date the pyramid to the Third Dynasty and believe it belonged to Nebka or Neferkare, although since the ruler's name is written in a cartouche, his reign must have followed Huni's.

In addition, Lauer drew attention to some archaeological facts that suggest that this unfinished structure must have been built in the Fourth Dynasty. For example, large blocks were used, whereas in the Third Dynasty smaller blocks were used. The large pink granite blocks in the burial chamber also indicate that the structure was built in the Fourth Dynasty. Ultimately, Lauer dated the pyramid to the period between Snefru's reign and that of Menkaure, and estimated the planned length of its sides to be about four hundred cubits. He hypothesized that Djedefre's son Bikka was the builder.

Maragioglio and Rinaldi basically agreed with Lauer's argument but attributed the structure to either Baufre or Djedefhor (two other sons of Khufu). They considered the brothers, on the basis of an inscription in Wadi Hammamat dating from the Middle Kingdom, to be Khafre's successors, a view that is not shared by many Egyptologists.

Stadelmann also dates the unfinished structure to the Fourth Dynasty, but he reads the possessor's name as Baka (probably Djedefre's eldest son, who reigned only a short time) and identifies him with Manetho. Edwards contributed further interesting details. The way in which the substructure was built suggests that the unfinished pyramid in Zawiyet el-Aryan should be situated typologically between Djedefre's and Khafre's. This dating can be confirmed by the unusual oval shape of the sarcophagus, which Edwards considered the original one, noting that Petrie found fragments of a similar sarcophagus in Abu Rawash.

Menkaure's Pyramid

The smallest pyramid of the "great troika" in Giza stands not far from the Nile and is called "Menkaure is divine." One might almost think that it anticipated, in its dimensions and partly unfinished state, the approaching decline of the Fourth Dynasty. According to Herodotus, some Greeks believed that this pyramid belonged to the Greek hetaera Rhodopis. Manetho thought that the pyramid belonged to Psamtik I's beautiful daughter Nitokris, who had blond hair and a rosy complexion.

Diodorus Siculus described the inscription bearing the name of Mykerinos, and medieval Arab historians witnessed at first hand the destruction of the pyramid. In the late 1630s the English scholar and traveler John Greaves noted that the casing had already been largely removed. The devastation continued into the nineteenth century, when Muhammad Ali Pasha (1805–1848) used pink granite blocks taken from the casing to construct the arsenal in Alexandria. Vyse was the first to enter the pyramid, in 1837. He began an investigation of its substructure, during which he initially followed a tunnel Caviglia had earlier dug in a deep breach in the north wall. The original entrance was not discovered until later. The Lepsius expedition paid little attention to Menkaure's pyramid, and Petrie worked on it for only a brief time in the early 1880s; a thorough archaeological investigation of the whole complex was first begun in 1906 by a team from Harvard University and the Boston Museum of Fine Arts under Reisner's direction, and continued until 1924.

As in the case of Khafre's Pyramid, here too it was necessary to thoroughly prepare the rock subsoil, especially around the northeast corner. The difference in elevation between the base levels of the two pyramids is slight: Menkaure's is only two and one half meters higher. Its core consists of limestone blocks quarried nearby. Up to a height of about fifteen meters, the casing is made of pink granite, while farther up it was probably made of limestone. The surface of the granite casing blocks has not been smoothed, which provides clear evidence that the final touches were not put on the walls until the very end of the construction process, and that the finishing proceeded from the top down. Completely dressed blocks would probably have been damaged during transport and installation, especially on their edges. This procedure also made it possible to achieve great accuracy in evening out the whole surface. The inscription on the granite casing of the north wall dates from the Late Period and may be the one mentioned by Diodorus.

The entrance is on the axis of the north wall, at a height of about four meters above ground level. Only part of the descending corridor that led through the pyramid's masonry consisted of pink granite. It was also originally sealed with blocks of the same stone. Below the level of the pyramid's base a passageway called the lower corridor climbed through the rock and came out in a room whose walls were provided with niches. The significance of the decoration of this room, which is unusual among the underground spaces built in the Old Kingdom, is debated. At its end there is a granite barrier made of three

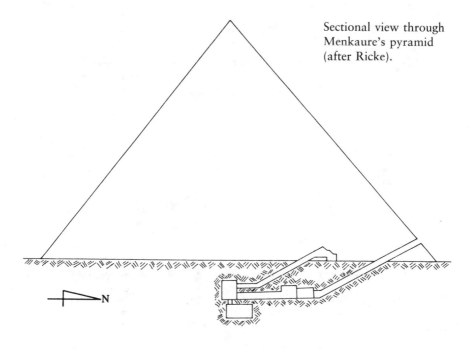

Sectional view through Menkaure's pyramid (after Ricke).

plugging blocks that were lowered after its completion. The corridor then continues at a slight downward angle and comes out in the east-west–oriented upper antechamber, whose walls lack any decoration whatever.

There ends another passageway known as the upper corridor, which runs over the lower corridor and is also oriented north-south. Beginning in the masonry at approximately the level of the pyramid's base, it first climbs, and then becomes a horizontal passageway, finally reaching the upper chamber at the north wall. This doubling of the corridors seems to indicate that the pyramid's original construction

First and second phases in the construction of the substructure of Menkaure's pyramid. Ground plan and sectional view (after Ricke).

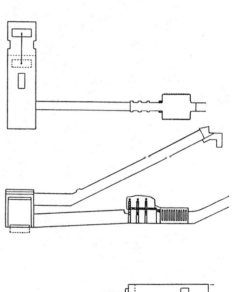

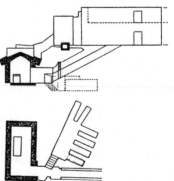

plan was changed. On the basis of his investigation, Petrie formed the opinion that the pyramid was originally only half the size it is today. Stadelmann doubts this claim—perhaps correctly.

In the upper antechamber Vyse discovered the remains of an anthropoid wooden coffin bearing Menkaure's name and containing human bones. Many researchers adopt the view expressed by Kurt Sethe at the end of the nineteenth century, and see in it not Menkaure's original coffin, but rather a substitute from the Saite period. Radiocarbon dating has shown that the bone fragments are probably less than two thousand years old. In the west part of the upper antechamber is a rectangular depression in the floor. It suggests that a sarcophagus may have been intended to stand there.

From the floor of the upper antechamber, a granite corridor leads downward, becoming horizontal shortly before it enters the burial chamber. In its north wall, near the entrance to the burial chamber, there is a short stairway leading to six small, deep niches. Despite a certain similarity to those in Shepseskaf's Mastabat Faraun and in Queen Khentkaues I's stepped tomb, its significance remains unclear. According to Ricke, it was used for the burial of four canopic vessels containing the ruler's entrails (on the east side) and the crowns of Upper and Lower Egypt (on the north side).

The burial chamber has a rectangular ground plan, but in contrast to those in Khufu's and Khafre's pyramids, it is oriented north-south. It consists entirely of pink granite, including the gabled ceiling, which was hollowed out from beneath to make a vault. The construction of this chamber was technically difficult and laborious, because it was carried out after the modification of the plan for the substructure. The chamber lies about 15.5 meters under the level of the pyramid's base; so that the ceiling could be constructed of nine pairs of enormous granite blocks, it was necessary to dig a large descending tunnel in the west part of the upper antechamber. On the burial chamber's west wall Vyse found a beautiful basalt sarcophagus decorated with niches and a lid ornamented with a concave cornice. Ricke saw a certain parallel between these decorations and those of the shrine of the god Anubis, and he interpreted them as an expression of the effort to increase the protection of the tomb by means of that divinity. However, the sarcophagus met with an unfortunate fate. The ship *Beatrice,* which was taking it from Egypt to Great Britain in 1838, shipwrecked and sank between Malta and Spain.

The architectural and archaeological situation previously described indicates that the underground chamber system of Menkaure's pyramid underwent significant changes. Borchardt noticed this at the end of the nineteenth century, and in dating these changes he was obviously influenced by the discovery of wood fragments from the Saite period. Subsequent investigations of Menkaure's pyramid and the tombs of members of the royal family that are closest in time, those of the Mastabat Faraun and Khentkaues I's stepped grave, require us to correct this view. The development of the substructure was completed in three phases, during which the substructure originally planned was enlarged. Only in the third and last phase were the granite burial chamber and the associated sets of niches built—perhaps at the command of Menkaure's successor Shepseskaf. There are good grounds for this view, as discoveries in the valley temple show.

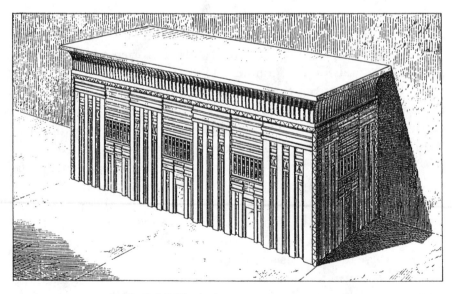

Menkaure's sarcophagus (after Perring).

In contrast to Khufu's and Khafre's pyramids, no boat pits have been found near Menkaure's pyramid, despite intensive investigations made by the Egyptian archaeologist Abdel Aziz Saleh.

As in Khufu's and Khafre's complex, the mortuary temple was not situated adjacent to the pyramid's east wall. It had an almost square ground plan. The original project for the temple obviously remained partially uncompleted, because of the ruler's premature death.

Its appearance can be reconstructed only approximately, as Reisner has sought to do. The long entrance hall made it possible to reach from the east an open courtyard that was originally to have been ornamented by pillars. A portico made of two rows of pillars in the west part of the temple provided access to a long offering hall, in whose west wall stood, according to Reisner, a false door. Maragioglio and Rinaldi rejected this view, however, and suggested that a statue of the ruler stood there (Reisner and others had found fragments of an alabaster statue of Menkaure in the temple), because the temple's back wall was not immediately adjacent to the pyramid. In their opinion, the false door was located on a small, pink granite platform in front of the pyramid's east wall. They supposed that it was at first freely accessible from the east wing of the pyramid's courtyard, before additional rooms were constructed and it was ultimately connected with the pyramid.

In the northwestern part of the mortuary temple were five two-story magazines. There a limestone altar and fragments of a seated statue of Menkaure in pink granite were found. The southwest part of the temple remained uncompleted. Reisner assumed that with the exception of the core wall the whole mortuary temple was originally supposed to be made of pink granite. Ricke rejected this interpretation; in his opinion, only the dado was composed of this material. In any case, the temple was probably completed in large measure by Menkaure's successor, Shepseskaf, chiefly using mudbricks. This can be inferred from the inscription on one of the fragments of a stela Reisner found in Menkaure's valley temple. The inside wall of the large courtyard, which was originally supposed to have a colonnade, was lined with plastered and whitewashed brickwork decorated with niches. Some of the rooms inside the temple as well as its outer walls

Ground plan of Menkaure's mortuary temple (above) at the time of the ruler's death and after Shepseskaf completed it, together with the ground plan of Menkaure's valley temple (below), which was also erected by Shepseskaf (after Ricke).

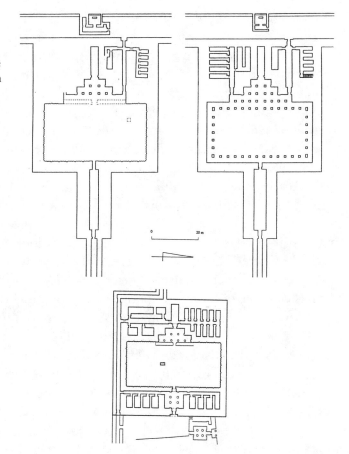

have the same appearance (although they did not have niches). Reisner also dated to Shepseskaf's time the construction of a small shrine in the courtyard, between the pyramid and the mortuary temple.

Especially noteworthy is a small, square room with a single pillar, because it strikingly resembles the so-called antichambre carrée that first appears in the mortuary temples of the Fifth Dynasty. Some works are dated to a still later period, including the stelae of Merenre I and Pepi II, which were discovered in the mortuary temple.

The causeway was probably completed during Shepseskaf's reign as well. The floors were made of limestone blocks and highly compressed clay mixed with limestone fragments, and mudbrick side walls a little more than two meters thick supported the roof. Reisner thought that the roof was made of the wooden beams and mats whose remains he had found at the end of the causeway. Given the width of the side walls and the analogy with the causeway leading to the Mastabat Faraun, Maragioglio and Rinaldi believed the roof consisted of a brick vault. In contrast to other causeways, Menkaure's did not start from the west part of the valley temple but rather ran along its whole south side and part of its west side, and was also accessible from the storerooms in the south part of the temple.

The reconstitution of the stages of construction under Menkaure is more difficult in the case of the valley temple than in that of the mortuary temple. In his time the west part of the limestone-block base and the lower part of the core of the temple's north wall may have been installed. The completion of the temple with clay masonry would in this case be attributed to Shepseskaf.

Immediately behind the entrance to the temple there is a square antechamber with four columns, of which only the alabaster bases, pressed into the clay floor, have been preserved. On each side of the antechamber are four storerooms.

The whole middle part of the valley temple consisted of a large open courtyard, whose inner walls were decorated with niches, as in the mortuary temple. A path paved with limestone slabs ran from the pillared antechamber through the middle of the courtyard to a low stair. The stair led through a portico with two rows of wooden columns to an offering hall, in which an alabaster altar may once have stood. North of the offering hall were twelve storerooms and south of it five storerooms. In this area Reisner found the famous statues of Menkaure, which we shall discuss in a moment. Here he also found, along with fragments of stone vessels, four unfinished statuettes of Menkaure and fragments of other statues. Along the sides of the room with the altar there were also storerooms.

The function of the temple gradually changed. Not long after it was completed, people began living in it, and many grain storehouses and lodgings were built, particularly in the courtyard. Probably during the Fifth Dynasty the temple was severely damaged by water after a heavy rain literally tore away its west side. According to Reisner, it was rebuilt in rough outline during the reign of Pepi II.

Among the most famous discoveries made by Reisner in the valley temple are the previously mentioned triads of Menkaure. The three statues of dark gray slate represent the striding image of the ruler with, on his right, the goddess Hathor and, on his left, divinities symbolizing three Upper Egyptian provinces: Thebes, Abydos, and the jackal-province. They are now on exhibit in the Egyptian Museum in Cairo (JE 40678, JE 40679, and JE 46499). Another triad and a dyad, which depicts Menkaure and probably his consort Khamerernebti II, are in the collection of the Museum of Fine Arts in Boston (nos. 09.200 and 11.738). Reisner found many fragments of other statues of this kind. How many triads were originally in the temple? As many as there were provinces at that time? Or only as many as corresponded to Menkaure's mortuary endowments? That would almost be expected. For the time being, however, it is not possible to determine exactly where these statues stood in the temple and what role they played in the worship of the dead Menkaure. They were often associated with

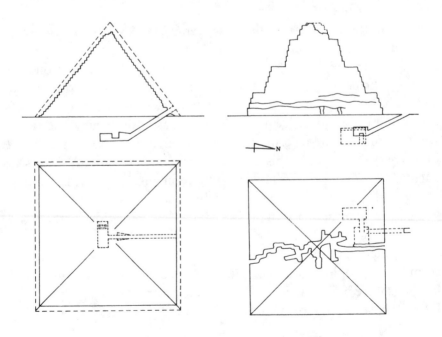

the processions of the personified mortuary estates depicted in the decoration of the valley temple of the Bent Pyramid in Dahshur.

During Selim Hassan's excavations on the grounds of the neighboring tomb complex of the queen mother Khentkaues I, a small brick structure with a platform, low benches, and a small drainage canal together with a basin were discovered at the northeast corner of Menkaure's valley temple. Here were also stored a large number of flint blades and stone vessels. According to some Egyptologists, this structure represented the purification tent and was part of a larger installation in which the mummifying ritual took place.

Another brick structure was built in front of the temple's west wall. It may have been a new, widened entrance, which provided a better connection between the temple and the pyramid town. Ricke hypothesized that for its residents Menkaure was a divinity and that his cult was concentrated in the valley temple, which thus took on an unusual function.

A few other important structures belong to the pyramid complex, above all a group of three smaller pyramids that stand in a row along

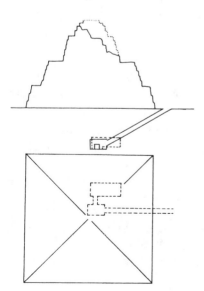

Pyramids G 3a–c. Ground plan and north-south sectional view (after Reisner).

the south wall of the king's pyramid. Archaeologists designate them as G 3a–c and attribute them to the royal consorts. G 3b and G 3c have a four-step core, while G 3a was a true pyramid. The three structures are surrounded by a common perimeter wall.

The entrance to the easternmost and largest of these structures, G 3a, was in the middle of the north wall, not far above ground level. The burial chamber was dug out of the rock under the center of the pyramid's base. In the floor next to its west wall a pink granite sarcophagus was embedded, but it soon fell prey to thieves. In addition, ceramics and charred remains of wood and matting were found in the chamber.

In front of the pyramid's east side stood a small, east-west–oriented mortuary temple. Originally it seems to have been built of limestone, but later on it was hastily finished using mudbricks. It was accessible from the pyramid's courtyard, and its western part consisted of a large, open courtyard, in whose north wall were niches, whereas on its south side a row of wooden columns stood. The way into the offering room, which had a false door in the western part of the temple, led through a small cult chapel. On both sides of the entrance into the offering room the chapel walls were decorated with deep, doubled niches. In the northwest part of the temple were storerooms, and in the southwest a staircase that led to the roof terrace.

On the basis of the location and especially the plan of the substructure, some Egyptologists regard G 3a as the original cult pyramid. The sarcophagus in the underground chamber and the mortuary temple clearly show, however, that the pyramid also served as a real tomb. Reisner hypothesized that it belonged to Menkaure's consort Khamerernebti II. Other Egyptologists maintain that this queen was buried, along with her mother, Khamerernebti I, in the central part of the necropolis at Giza, in the so-called Galarza tomb, named after a count who financially supported research on it. There a statue of Khamerernebti II was discovered (Egyptian Museum, Cairo, JE 48856), the only colossal statue of a queen from the Old Kingdom found so far. The question to whom G 3a belonged thus remains open. It is not impossible, however, that it was originally a cult pyramid, later transformed into a tomb.

G 3b differs from G 3a in certain details, for example, in the place-ment of the descending corridor and the lack of a barrier. In the pink granite sarcophagus, which stood against the west wall of the burial chamber, the bones of a young woman were found. The small brick temple in front of the pyramid's west wall is, in contrast to that of G 3a, oriented north-south.

G 3c never had a complete casing. As in G 3b, its burial chamber was under the northwest part of the pyramid and was not finished. No traces of a burial were found in it, which contrasts with the clear evidence of a cult in the small mortuary temple in front of the east side of the pyramid. The brick temple is oriented in the same way as G 3b's.

Whereas the identity of the possessor of G 3a is disputed, the names of the possessors of pyramids G 3b and G 3c are lost in the obscurity of history. It is certain, however, that they belonged to Menkaure's consorts. There obviously were such consorts, but we know nothing further about them. Indirect evidence of their existence is provided by various princes connected with Menkaure. If pyramids G 3a–c belonged to the queens who could claim the title of queen mother, they might have been at the root of the crisis that occurred at the end of the Fourth Dynasty, to which we will turn in a moment.

Menkaure's complex was surrounded by perimeter walls that cor-respond to differing phases of construction. The so-called inner pe-rimeter wall enclosed a courtyard around the pyramid that was some ten meters across. It was apparently supposed to be made of high-quality white limestone, but ultimately it was hastily completed using less expensive limestone, then plastered and whitewashed. The small queens' pyramids were surrounded by a fence. At a greater distance from the pyramid—to the north, west, and south—the ruins of fur-ther, so-called outer perimeter walls were found; these were also con-structed of stone fragments. Still farther from the west perimeter wall are the remains of a large stone barrier whose significance is not en-tirely clear. Some experts suggest that it contained storerooms and workshops like those found west of Khafre's pyramid.

Southwest of Menkaure's mortuary temple, Saleh found the remains of huge walls made of clay and stone fragments, lodgings, various kinds of ovens, large cisterns, ceramic vessels for everyday use, bits of various raw materials (for example, malachite and ochre), and other things. This was probably a complex of workshops, storerooms, and lodgings for the stonemasons, sculptors, faience makers, and other craftsmen who made objects for the construction of the pyramid complex and later for the worship of the dead ruler.

In contrast to Khufu's and Khafre's pyramids, around Menkaure's pyramid there was no large cemetery for the king's relatives and for high officials. They were buried primarily in the cemeteries west and south of Khufu's pyramid. Only a few of Menkaure's priests had their rock-cut graves and mastabas built southeast of his pyramid.

Shepseskaf's Mastabat Fara'un

The large tomb in South Saqqara, which the local people called the Mastabat Fara'un (Pharaoh's Bench), has certainly not been ignored by archaeologists in recent years. Yet it remains today one of the most enigmatic tombs of the Old Kingdom. It was first described by Perring. Lepsius devoted little time to it, but he did note that the tomb's shape reminded him of a large sarcophagus. In 1858, Mariette began to investigate its underground construction, but his notes were not preserved, except for a few sketches that Maspero later published. This tomb was erroneously ascribed to the last ruler of the Fifth Dynasty, Unas.

In 1924–1925, Gustave Jéquier carried out a systematic investigation in the framework of wide-ranging excavations in South Saqqara. He was the first to determine, if only on indirect evidence, that this tomb belonged to Shepseskaf. In doing that, he was aided by a fragment of a stela bearing a cartouche that contained part of the sign *f* as the last letter of the king's name; by the fact that the name of the tomb, "Shepseskaf is [ritually] purified," concludes with a determinative (an explanatory sign) in the form of a mastaba; and finally by the discovery of another stela from the Middle Kingdom that proved that in that era Shepseskaf was still worshiped on the grounds of the Mastabat Fara'un.

The tomb does not stand on the rock subsoil, but rather on a foundation, and like most mastabas, it has a rectangular, north-south–oriented ground plan. The core is composed of two levels with large, grayish yellow limestone blocks that came from the stone quarries west of the pyramids in Dahshur. Perring, Lepsius, and Jacques de Morgan all found remnants of pathways over which the stone was transported to the construction site. The casing consisted primarily of soft white limestone; only its lowest level was made of pink granite. On some of the casing blocks the remains of Prince Khaemuase's so-called restoration inscription have been found.

The entrance to the substructure resembles that of a pyramid more than that of a mastaba. It lies on the axis of the north wall, about two and one half meters above ground level. Beyond a small vestibule (or perhaps simply a niche), the pink granite descending corridor becomes horizontal. Right at the beginning of this part of the corridor there is a granite barrier consisting of three plugging blocks that were lowered afterward. The substructure, into which the corridor leads, contains an antechamber, a burial chamber, and storerooms. Both chambers, including their ceilings, were built of pink granite. As in Menkaure's pyramid, the slightly vaulted underside of the ceiling was supposed to imitate a barrel vault. Further common points are the basalt sarcophagus (of which only fragments have been preserved) and the arrangement of the five small storerooms.

The mortuary temple differs significantly from previous royal structures of this type. It would be difficult to find a parallel, because Shepseskaf's mortuary temple was not connected with any pyramid. Since the conditions for the worship of the ruler had nonetheless to be provided, they must have been improvised.

The temple stood in front of the east wall of the mastaba and was oriented north-south. Although it was relatively small, at least two phases in its construction can be distinguished on the basis of the materials used (limestone and mudbricks).

The older, stone part had two entrances from the east, one in the middle of the facade and the other near the southeast corner. A third

Sectional view and ground plan of the
substructure of the Mastabat Fara'un
(after Jéquier).

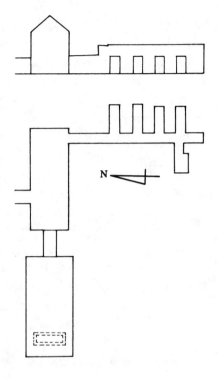

entrance was in the middle of the south facade. The eastern half of
the temple consisted of an open courtyard paved with limestone, in
whose northwest corner an altar originally stood. The offering hall
in the west half of the temple had a ground plan in the form of an
inverted *T*, and in the west wall there was originally a false door. The
northwestern part of the temple contained a group of smaller chambers that may have been storerooms.

During the mudbrick building phase, a large open courtyard was
built to the east, and its inner walls were decorated with niches. This
courtyard was also reached through an entrance in the middle of the
east facade.

The causeway did not lead directly to the entrance of the temple,
but rather to the southeast corner and then along the south wall into
the courtyard surrounding the mastaba. It consisted entirely of plastered and whitewashed mudbricks and resembled a corridor with a

vaulted ceiling. In front of the mastaba, the causeway turned north-east; the valley temple has not yet been discovered. Near the south wall, which is about ten meters from the mastaba, there was an outer perimeter wall, part of which was located about forty-eight meters away.

In the area around the Mastabat Fara'un no tombs of Shepseskaf's family members or officials were found. This leads to still another question about the circumstances under which this tomb was built, which have not yet been entirely explained. Jéquier offered an initial explanation on the basis of his excavations. He was convinced that Shepseskaf had intentionally chosen the unusual form of his royal tomb. As a protest against the increasing influence of the priesthood of the sun god Re, he rejected a tomb in the form of a pyramid, considered a symbol of the sun, and decided to build a mastaba-like structure for himself. According to Jéquier, the break with earlier tradition was emphasized by the fact that Shepseskaf did not have his tomb erected in the old royal cemetery at Giza, but rather in a distant place

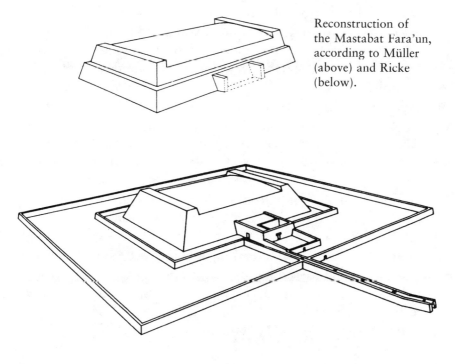

Reconstruction of the Mastabat Fara'un, according to Müller (above) and Ricke (below).

in modern South Saqqara. Jéquier sees further evidence for his theory in the ruler's name, which did not include the component *re*.

Jéquier's theory was attacked from several sides. According to Ricke, the obelisk was considered a symbol of the sun, but the pyramid was not. In his opinion, Shepseskaf's tomb was conceived as a Lower Egyptian, "Buto-type" tomb from the outset. Hans-Wolfgang Müller (1907–1991) held a similar view; he saw the mastaba as an enormous stone version of a hut hung with matting. Stadelmann, drawing on Ricke and Müller, asked what moved Shepseskaf to use niches—archaizing elements from early period architecture used to decorate not only the courtyard of his mortuary temple but also the buildings in Menkaure's pyramid complex that he is supposed to have completed. However, Stadelmann did not answer this question.

Shepseskaf's decision to abandon the necropolis in Giza and to have a mastaba built for himself in Saqqara may not have been determined by religious or political motivations. In Giza there was no appropriate site for the construction of another large royal tomb complex, and Menkaure had already been obliged to situate his pyramid far away from the Nile. In addition, Shepseskaf was responsible for completing his predecessor's extensive, unfinished pyramid complex. This financial and administrative burden, along with the country's weaker overall economic situation, may have led him to substantially reduce the cost of building his own tomb. According to one, not universally accepted, view, the original construction plan for Menkaure's pyramid had already envisioned a structure of relatively modest dimensions. In this context there is a certain analogy with Neferefre's complex in Abusir. Neferefre's tomb was originally planned as a pyramid, but was transformed into a square "mastaba" after his premature death. This also entailed the modification of the construction plan for the mortuary temple, which had not yet been begun when the king died.

In addition, Shepseskaf's choice of the site for his tomb may not have been determined by opposition to his predecessors who were buried in Giza. Many Egyptologists clearly underestimate the fact that although the Mastabat Fara'un was erected in a place that was then remote, it was not far from the pyramids of the founder of the dynasty, Snefru, in Dahshur, whence the stone for its construction came. Thus the selection of this site might also have been, in a certain sense, an expression of Shepseskaf's sense of belonging to this dynastic line.

In any case, Shepseskaf's reign may well have been a time of trouble. Historical sources are few, and the end of the Fourth Dynasty remains very obscure. However, when we look at the final version of Shepseskaf's peculiar, isolated, and improvised tomb complex, another explanation suggests itself. Did the disastrous experiences with Menkaure's complex lead Shepseskaf to exercise greater caution in building his own tomb? It would not have been easy to create, in a short time and in this remote place, the enormous economic, technical, and administrative infrastructure required for the construction of a large pyramid. The infrastructure available in Giza was needed to complete Menkaure's complex. Thus we can ask whether the Mastabat Fara'un might have been provisional, a temporary solution pending later developments. In its plan, the Mastabat Fara'un's substructure corresponds to that of a pyramid; a subsequent transformation would thus have involved only the superstructure and the mortuary temple. However, Menkaure's complex in Giza had to be completed first, and its whole technical, economic, and organizational machinery had to be moved to Shepseskaf's own construction site. Shepseskaf's reign was short, only about four years, and so his provisional tomb may have suddenly become his final one.

Nonetheless, we cannot exclude the possibility that the form chosen for Shepseskaf's tomb was also the expression of a certain crisis of dynastic legitimacy. Shepseskaf might have been the son of one of Menkaure's secondary wives, and therefore not a fully legitimate successor of the glorious Fourth Dynasty pharaohs during whose reign the pyramid had become the symbol of the divine, eternal, and unshakable legitimacy of the pharaohs' rule over Egypt and this world.

Khentkaues I's Step Tomb

The large, two-step tomb structure near Menkaure's valley temple was thought by some early Egyptologists to be the fourth pyramid in Giza. This was, for example, Perring's view, but not that of Lepsius, who listed it among the private tombs and designated it as "100" on his map. Until the 1930s some archaeologists—for instance, Hölscher, and at first Reisner as well—maintained that this structure was an unfinished pyramid built by Menkaure's successor Shepseskaf. Not until 1932 was Selim Hassan able to show that it belonged to the queen mother Khentkaues I.

The superstructure consists of two steps. The lower of the two, which has the form of a low, truncated pyramid, was built by cutting and preparing the rock outcropping. It has an almost square ground plan, oriented north-south. Originally, the surfaces of all four side walls were decorated with niches resembling false doors.

A huge gateway of pink granite, bearing Khentkaues's name and titles, provided access to the tomb from the southeast. In the antechamber there were entrances into rooms on the west and the north.

The first of these rooms originally had three statue niches, and its walls, like those of the antechamber, were lined with fine white limestone and decorated with scenes and inscriptions in bas-relief.

In the west wall of the north room, there was a pair of large false doors made of pink granite. Below one of them opened a shaft that led into the underground part of the tomb. The substructure has an original architecture. In some ways it resembles a private tomb, in others a royal tomb, particularly that of Menkaure, and perhaps that of Shepseskaf as well. It includes six small storerooms (?) near the burial chamber, which has a pair of false doors. Apart from a few fragments of an alabaster sarcophagus, Hassan was not able to find any traces of the queen's burial.

Not long after it was completed, the tomb was substantially altered, probably during the first half of the Fifth Dynasty. Over the west half of the tomb, a limestone structure with a square ground plan that resembled a mastaba was built. It was intentionally not placed over the center of the tomb, since its weight might have ruptured the ceilings of the chambers in the lower part. Thus a two-stepped structure of an unusual form resulted; its side walls were sheathed with blocks of fine white limestone. A perimeter wall of plastered and whitewashed mudbricks ran around the tomb.

In accord with a unified plan, to the east of the tomb a settlement was built of mudbricks and provided with its own perimeter wall. Structurally—and presumably also officially—it connected Khentkaues's tomb and her cult with Menkaure's valley temple and the pyramid town that apparently already existed in close proximity to it. Hassan believed that priests and other people connected with the worship of the dead queen lived in this town until the end of the Sixth Dynasty.

It cannot be precisely determined whether a boat pit and, across from it, a cistern were dug during the construction of the original rock-cut tomb or during the later modification of the tomb. A narrow staircase led into the cistern, and a small drainage canal led out of the space in front of the tomb. Hassan thought it was originally a roofed-over basin used for mummifying rituals.

The transformation of the tomb, which probably took place at the beginning of the Fifth Dynasty, seems to have been intended to ex-

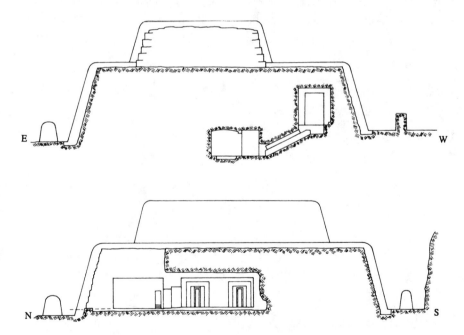

East-west and north-south sectional views through Khentkaues I's tomb (after Maragioglio and Rinaldi).

press a fundamental conceptual change connected with a later elevation of Khentkaues's status and that of her cult. Only concern about the stability of the original rock-cut tomb prevented the construction of a pyramid with two or possibly three steps.

The hieroglyphic inscription Hassan discovered on fragments of the granite gateway must surely have surprised him, for it contained, carved in bas-relief, the queen mother's name and titles. First was listed a previously unknown title that Egyptologists immediately interpreted in different ways. The kind of writing and the peculiarities of the Egyptian script made it possible to discern in the title two different but grammatically correct variants with diametrically opposed meanings. Vladimir Vikentiev (1880–1960) interpreted it as meaning "Mother of two kings of Upper and Lower Egypt," whereas Hermann Junker translated it as "King of Upper and Lower Egypt and Mother of the King of Upper and Lower Egypt." Hassan himself favored Junker's interpretation, and on the basis of these titles and all the archaeological discoveries made in Khentkaues's tomb, he formulated his hypothesis concerning the role of this queen in Egyptian history.

Reworked depiction of Khentkaues I. Detail from the inscription on the granite gateway in the queen's tomb in Giza.

In the agreement of certain stylistic elements he saw the sole connecting link between the Fourth and the Fifth Dynasties, pointing out that the two-stepped form of Khentkaues's tomb resembles that of Shepseskaf's tomb in Saqqara. In his view, its architecture expresses the royal family's spiritual defiance of the growing power of the sun cult's priesthood. He considered Khentkaues I to be Shepseskaf's consort and believed that after Shepseskaf's death she ruled for a short time but was ultimately forced to yield power to the priesthood. The result was her marriage with Userkaf, the high priest of the sun god Re from Heliopolis and the later founder of the Fifth Dynasty. She refused, however, to be buried next to either her first or her second husband, and decided instead to have her own tomb built in Giza, near her royal predecessors.

Borchardt opposed Hassan's account, appealing to Vikentiev's translation of the title. On the basis of an erroneously interpreted discovery from Abusir—where another queen named Khentkaues was buried who bore the same chief title as her like-named predecessor—he elaborated a different explanation of the events that occurred at the end of the Fourth Dynasty. In his view, Shepseskaf was not directly descended from the royal family and was able to mount the throne only because he married Khentkaues I. Shortly afterward, Borchardt

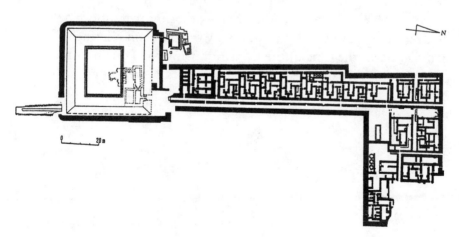

Khentkaues I's tomb complex, including the priests' settlement (after Selim Hassan).

maintained, Shepseskaf died, and before Sahure and Neferirkare, his two underage sons and the actual founders of the Fifth Dynasty, had grown up, Userkaf seized power.

Later on, a few other hypotheses emerged. However, Borchardt's explanation was widely accepted, along with the view that the precise place of the queen mother Khentkaues I was the most complicated genealogical and chronological problem of the Old Kingdom, whose resolution was not possible unless new historical sources were discovered.

Such new sources were found in the late 1970s, when the Czech archaeological team found Khentkaues II's small pyramid complex in Abusir. We shall discuss this complex later. For the moment it will suffice to point out that at least a generation separated the two queens. The discovery of Khentkaues II's pyramid in Abusir also led to a revision of some epigraphic sources. It showed that in describing the text on the fragment of the granite gateway in front of the south side of Khentkaues I's step tomb, Hassan had overlooked certain very important details in the image of the queen included in the text. In that image, the queen was given additional attributes—the vulture diadem, the ritual beard, and the scepter—indicating that she possibly did actually rule. However, her name was not written in a cartouche and does not appear in any of the known king lists. The "Khentkaues problem" thus appeared in an entirely different perspective. The discovery in Abusir and other information from Giza made it possible to tackle in a new way the problem relating to Egyptian history at the time of the transition from the Fourth to the Fifth Dynasty and the role the two queen mothers played in it.

CHAPTER SIX

THE FIFTH DYNASTY—WHEN
THE SUN RULED

The circumstances under which the Fourth Dynasty declined and the Fifth Dynasty arose, as well as the roles played in this by the queens named Khentkaues, fascinated ancient Egyptians for a long time afterward. And ultimately the queen mother Khentkaues probably went down in ancient Egyptian literature as the heroine of the myth of the divine birth of the kings of the Fifth Dynasty. The account given in the Westcar papyrus was written a thousand years after these events, in the era of the Hyksos kings. In it Rudjedjet appears as the consort of a sun-cult priest from the city of Sakhebu and as the mother of the sun kings, whose father was supposed to be the sun god Re himself. Some Egyptologists maintain that the name Rudjedjet is a pseudonym, behind which is hidden none other than Khentkaues. But which Khentkaues?

As exciting as the story in the Westcar papyrus is, it certainly does not explain the origin of Userkaf, the first king of the Fifth Dynasty. His origin remains for the time being obscure, but he may have been, along with Shepseskaf, one of Menkaure's sons. During his reign the sun cult seems to have reached its apogee, since from then on the title "son of Re" became an inseparable part of the royal titulature. On the other hand, it is striking that in both Shepseskaf's and Userkaf's names the name of the sun god Re is lacking. This was the first time since Djedefre that this had occurred.

Some very important acts are connected with Userkaf's name, and these explain to a certain extent his status as the founder of a new dynasty. He undertook a further campaign in Nubia, and during his reign renewed commercial contacts with foreign lands were developed, including contacts with the distant Greek islands, as a stone vessel bearing his name and found on the island Cythera shows. He had temples built and promoted, alongside the cult of Re, the worship of other divinities, as we see in inscriptions from the tomb of the Hathor priest Nikaankh in Tehna, in Middle Egypt.

Userkaf had his own pyramid built at the north end of the Saqqara necropolis, near the Step Pyramid—precisely across from Shepseskaf's tomb. His pyramid is noteworthy chiefly because its mortuary temple stands not at the foot of its east side, as usual, but rather on its south side. However, it was far more important that Userkaf decided to build a sun temple he called Re's Nekhen about three kilometers north of his pyramid complex, near the modern village of Abusir.*

The significance of the sun temples in the Memphite necropolis— after Userkaf, five other Fifth Dynasty rulers built similar temples— remains in dispute. Apparently, however, they composed an important part of the worship of the dead king and were economically and religiously connected with the pyramid complex. A prominent characteristic of the temple was the large obelisk, a symbol of the sun cult; on the altar at its foot meat and vegetables were laid as offerings, before being taken to the altar in the pyramid complex.

Why Userkaf selected Abusir as the site of his sun temple has not yet been satisfactorily explained. However, his decision apparently led to the establishment of a new royal necropolis, in which the rulers of the Fifth Dynasty began to build their tomb complexes. The first of these was Userkaf's successor (who may also have been his son), Sahure. Sahure reigned about fourteen years and followed his predecessor's line in both internal and external politics. For example, inscriptions at a turquoise mine in Wadi Maghara in the Sinai and in

---

* Nekhen (Greek Hierakonpolis) was the center of power for the rulers of Upper Egypt during the period immediately preceding the unification of Egypt at the end of the fourth millennium B.C.E. The inclusion of this name in the designation of Userkaf's sun temple was perhaps intended to evoke an association with the impending unification of the country by means of the sun religion, that is, with the ultimate victory of sun worship. However, Nekhen was also the name of an institution that undertook to provide supplies and labor for the living king and for his worship after his death.

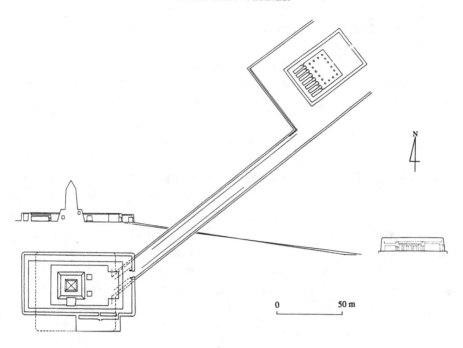

Userkaf's sun temple in Abusir: ground plan and sectional view (after Ricke).

the diorite quarries near Abu Simbel prove that he promoted the exploitation of valuable resources as well as continuing commercial contacts with other countries. An inscription on the Palermo stone indicates that conifer wood was imported from Byblos and even that a trading expedition was sent in the opposite direction, into the mysterious land of Punt on the East African coast, to get spices, ivory, furs, and other commodities.

Sahure had a pyramid complex built for himself near Userkaf's sun temple in Abusir. In size, quality of material, and execution, his pyramid was no match for the pyramids built in Giza by the rulers of the Fourth Dynasty. Sahure's complex is distinguished primarily by its use of many different kinds of stone, its thematically rich and artistically valuable decoration with reliefs, and especially the harmoniously balanced plan of the individual structures and the whole, and for that reason it is considered another milestone in the development of the royal tomb complex. Unfortunately, his sun temple, "Re's sacrifice field," has not yet been found.

Sahure's successor was not his eldest son and the legitimate heir to the throne, Netjerirenre, but rather Neferirkare, whose origin is once again shrouded in mystery. On some reliefs from Sahure's mortuary temple a subsequent reworking can be discerned, whose goal was to provide one of the persons depicted in Sahure's entourage with Neferirkare's name, royal insignia, and titles. Some Egyptologists have concluded from this that Sahure and Neferirkare were brothers. The uncle would thus have usurped the throne at the expense of his nephew, who was apparently still a child. However that may be, the discovery made in Sahure's mortuary temple probably provides further evidence of the dynastic and internal political problems during this time.

Neferirkare reigned for about ten years, and during that time the power of high officials and the priesthood was further strengthened. In the Fifth Dynasty, the highest offices were no longer in the hands

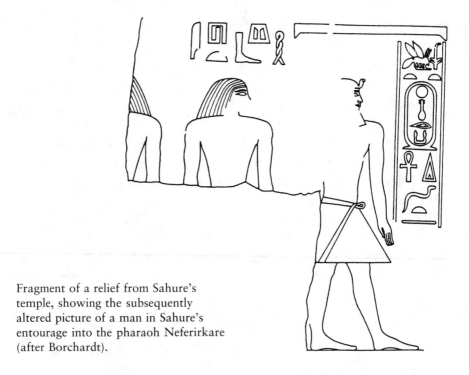

Fragment of a relief from Sahure's temple, showing the subsequently altered picture of a man in Sahure's entourage into the pharaoh Neferirkare (after Borchardt).

of the ruler's close relatives. Royal authority nevertheless continued to be enormous, as is shown, for example, by the inscription on the tomb of Ptahshepses, the high priest of the Memphite god Ptah, in Saqqara: he was granted the special honor of kissing Neferirkare's foot.

Neferirkare was not able to complete his pyramid complex or the small neighboring complex of his consort Khentkaues II during his lifetime. However, he was apparently able to complete the sun temple "Re's favorite place," which—to judge by contemporary documents— was the largest and most significant of them all. The previously mentioned papyrus fragments from Neferirkare's temple archive, which were discovered in the 1890s by grave robbers, made possible an entirely new insight not only into the organization of the worship of dead kings in the pyramid complexes, but also into the complicated economic, political, and religious context of the time.

Neferefre, Neferirkare's eldest son, reigned only a short time. He was barely able to begin work on his pyramid near the tombs of his father and mother in Abusir. His younger brother, Niuserre, hastily completed it, partly at the same time as his own mortuary temple was being constructed. Thanks to important archaeological discoveries, including papyri from the temple archive and statues recently found in this structurally improvised tomb complex, Neferefre, a ruler heretofore almost unknown to Egyptologists, has become one of the best documented figures of the Fifth Dynasty.

During Neferefre's short reign, the career of the important official Ti probably reached its apex. Ti was the overseer of pyramid and sun temple construction for several Fifth Dynasty rulers, including Neferefre, whose sun temple was called "Re's Offering Table." The splendid and relatively well-preserved decoration of his mastaba in North Saqqara is one of the high points of the ancient Egyptian art of the relief.

Neferefre died very young, at about twenty to twenty-three years of age. The reign of his possible successor Shepseskare, whose name is almost all we know about him, was even shorter. On the basis on the so-called Saqqara king list, some Egyptologists think that Shepseskare was a predecessor of Neferefre, although some archaeological discoveries tend to contradict that view. There may have been a struggle for power. After Neferefre's death, disputes within the ruling family, apparently between the members of Sahure's line and that of Neferirkare, probably broke out again.

The internal political situation in the country was not stabilized until Neferefre's brother Niuserre ascended the throne. His rise to power was probably supported by important figures in state administration and the royal court. Among these may have been Ptahshepses, who rose from royal hairdresser to vizier and royal son-in-law. Indirect evidence of Ptahshepses's wealth and power is provided by his splendid tomb, which he had built very close to Niuserre's pyramid complex in Abusir, and for whose construction only first-class materials were used, along with some elements (and apparently also artists and groups of craftsmen) normally reserved for royal edifices.

Niuserre's pyramid is not very large and differs little from the others that were built in Abusir. Its plan was influenced by the lack of space and perhaps also by a shortage of materials; and in addition there was Niuserre's resolution not to abandon the family cemetery.

The inscription on a fragment of an architrave from the pillared courtyard in Ptahshepses's mastaba in Abusir contains part of Ptahshepses's titulature and provides evidence of his high social standing: "Prince, councilor of Nekhen, guardian of Nekhen, priest of Nekhbet—the goddess of the Upper Egyptian shrine—supreme judge, vizier, head of all royal works, beloved of his master, sole friend (of the king), secretary of the morning house, highest lector priest, right hand of the god Duau, Ptahshepses."

Moreover, he had to complete the three pyramid complexes already begun—those of his father, his mother, and his elder brother—and two other small ones for his consorts.

At the end of the nineteenth century, Niuserre's sun temple, "Re's pleasance," was discovered in Abu Ghurab, north of Abusir. Fragments of its unique relief decorations, and particularly the scenes from the Chamber of the Seasons, are now in the collections of the Egyptian Museum in Berlin. The reliefs with scenes of the sed festival are considered by some Egyptologists to constitute indirect evidence that Niuserre reigned for more than three decades.

Less is known about the short reign of Niuserre's successor, Menkauhor, a ruler of somewhat obscure origin. As yet neither his pyramid nor his sun temple, which was called "Re's horizon" and was the last of its kind built during the Old Kingdom, have been

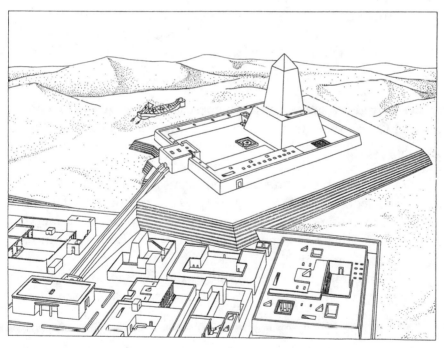

Reconstruction of Niuserre's sun temple in Abu Ghurab (after Borchardt). Over the temple towers a twenty-meter-high obelisk, the symbol of the sun god Re.

found. Among the not very numerous historical documents relating to Menkauhor is a memorial inscription he left on a rock in the Sinai. A small alabaster statue found in Memphis (today in the Egyptian Museum in Cairo) shows the ruler in the ritual cloak worn during the ceremonies of the sed festival. Menkauhor can have celebrated only symbolically the "thirty-year anniversary" of his ascent to the throne, because, according to the extant written documents, his reign lasted only about eight years.

The ancestry of Menkauhor's successor, Djedkare, is also unclear. In contrast to his predecessor, he ruled more than four decades, and many important events are connected with his reign. He has gone down in history primarily as the reformer of the state administration. He founded an administrative office for Upper Egypt in order to strengthen the central power's influence on economic and political events in the southernmost part of the realm. Abydos became the new administrative seat. Further reforms concerned the reorganization of the mortuary cult in the royal necropolis in Abusir; the papyrus archives found there are to some extent related to this reorganization. However, despite these achievements, the central government's control over the country continued to decline.

At this time religious ideas and practices were spreading that had earlier played a role only at the highest level of society. The cult of the god Osiris, the ruler of the realm of the dead and the symbol of the eternal cycle of life and death, moved into the foreground. Shifts in religious ideas or economics or both were the basis for Djedkare's decision not to have a sun temple built. All later rulers followed his example. Djedkare had a pyramid complex erected for himself in South Saqqara and another, smaller one nearby for his consort. The fact that there was no longer any suitable place in Abusir cannot in this case be given as the reason.

Crafts and trade were flourishing in the country, and additional expeditions were sent to Byblos, Nubia, and distant Punt, from whence the expedition's leader, Baurdjed, even brought back a dancing dwarf to entertain the king. The fact that these expeditions did not always involve peaceful trade is shown by a unique scene of conquest preserved on the walls of Inti's tomb in Deshasha in Middle Egypt.

Historically significant scene from the tomb of Inti in Deshasha, showing the conquest of an Asian fortress. Note the ladder used by attackers to scale the fortress's walls.

Writing also flourished. In this period the famous work later known as *The Maxims of Ptahhotep* was probably composed by Djedkare's vizier of the same name. Its goal was to educate young men in absolute accord with the ancient Egyptian worldview and especially with the needs of the state. Ptahhotep's *Maxims* is the oldest testimony to how much the ancient Egyptians prized the beauty and power of the word.

The end of the Fifth Dynasty occurred during the reign of Unas, another king whose ancestry is uncertain. However, so far as we are aware, no dramatic changes were made. The economic and political development of the country advanced basically undisturbed, as it had under Unas's predecessors. In the course of his reign of approximately thirty years, the power of the central government further declined, while the influence of the bureaucracy and the priesthood grew. The ruler devoted special attention to relations with neighbors to the south. Some documents indicate that he may have gone to Elephantine in order to meet with Nubian chieftains. Also attributed to Unas's reign is the so-called Memphite theology, a systematic religious doctrine concerning the creation of the world by the god Ptah, which has been preserved only in a later copy called *The Memphite Theology*.

Unas's pyramid complex in Saqqara represents a new milestone in the development of ancient Egyptian tombs, not because of its size—his pyramid was the smallest built during the Fifth Dynasty—but rather because of the fact that inscriptions appeared for the first time on the walls of its underground chambers: the so-called pyramid texts. They subsequently appeared in the pyramids of all the kings and some of the queens of the late Old Kingdom and contained, as we have already shown, religious ideas about the ruler's life in the beyond.

Userkaf's Pyramid

Userkaf, the founder of the Fifth Dynasty, did not build his pyramid near the mastaba of his predecessor Shepseskaf or the tombs of other Fourth Dynasty rulers. Instead, he selected a site in immediate proximity to Djoser's Step Pyramid. This was probably a calculated move made for political and dynastic reasons. He called his pyramid complex "Pure are the [cult] places of Userkaf." However, its current condition corresponds more to the local description *el-haram el-makherbish*, "ruined pyramid."

Its entrance was discovered by Orazio Marucchi in 1831, but only in 1839 did Perring enter the underground portion, through a tunnel dug by grave robbers. The possessor of the pyramid remained unknown—it was thought to be Djedkare's. Almost a century later it was finally attributed to Userkaf, on the basis of excavations carried out by Firth in 1928. After Firth's death in 1931, the excavations were interrupted for a time. From 1948 to 1955, Lauer pursued further investigations on the site, and in the 1970s Ali el-Kholi worked there for a shorter time.

The ruins of the pyramid as we see them today would hardly suggest to the uninitiated that it originally had a very harmonious form. Its ground plan was designed in such a way that if divided axially it

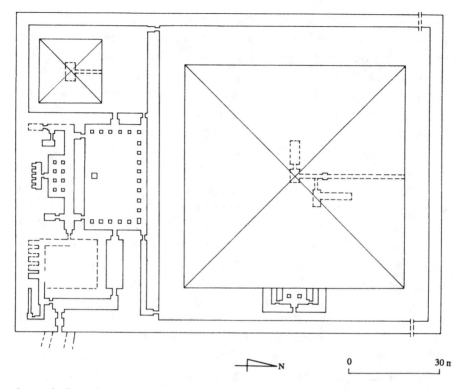

0   30 n

N

Ground plan of Userkaf's pyramid complex without causeway or valley temple (after Margioglio and Rinaldi).

composed two right triangles whose sides were in a ratio of 3 : 4 : 5. The core probably was not built using the accretion layer method, as Leslie Grinsell assumed. Instead, it was probably built, like the immediately following pyramids built by other Fifth Dynasty rulers in Abusir, in horizontal layers. Rough blocks of the usual local limestone were used in its construction, but for the casing fine white limestone from the quarries on the other side of the Nile was used. The remains of a hieroglyphic inscription discovered on fragments of the casing, which probably once again come from Prince Khaemuase, were chiseled during the restoration of the pyramid complex.

In contrast to the preceding pyramids of the Fourth Dynasty, the entrance was located not in the north wall, but rather in the pavement of the courtyard in front of it. A descending corridor that eventually became horizontal led to the underground chambers. Approximately in the middle of its horizontal part, there was a barrier made by a single plugging block of pink granite. Immediately behind it, in the east wall of the corridor, was the entrance to a small chamber whose ground plan resembles the letter *T*. It presumably served as a storeroom for the burial equipment.

About ten meters under the base of the pyramid, the corridor came out in the antechamber, which lies directly on the pyramid's vertical axis. Its walls are sheathed in fine white limestone, and the gabled ceiling consists of enormous blocks of the same material. The burial chamber, which lies west of the antechamber, closely resembles that room in its dimensions and construction but is about twice as long. On its west wall were found the remains of an undecorated basalt sarcophagus that was originally slightly inset into the floor.

We owe this somewhat vague and cursory description of the substructure of Userkaf's pyramid to the only archaeologist who has visited and examined it: Perring, who made his investigation in the 1830s. Since that time the entrance has been blocked by rubble, a situation that an earthquake in October 1991 made even worse.

In contrast to all preceding pyramid complexes, the mortuary temple was located neither on the east side (as was usual in the Fourth Dynasty) nor on the north side (typical of the Third Dynasty) of the pyramid. Its unusual position on the south side of the pyramid has given rise to a number of theories, to which we shall return later. Today it is difficult, and in some details impossible, to reconstruct its architecture, because during the Saite period a large shaft tomb was dug there, and as a result not only the original arrangement but also, because of the theft of stones, the substance of the temple itself was to a great extent destroyed.

The main entrance, which is at the southeast corner and also constitutes the endpoint of the approach causeway, has been particularly badly damaged. The surviving remnants of the masonry indicate that a staircase to the roof terrace was located there, together with a group of five storerooms and an entrance hall in the form of an inverted ell, through which one entered an open pillared courtyard paved in basalt. The pink granite pillars, on which are chiseled hieroglyphic inscriptions with the ruler's name and titles, surrounded the courtyard on only three sides; on the south side there were none. The basalt dado on the limestone walls of the ambulatory was originally decorated with scenes and inscriptions in bas-relief. Their variety and masterful execution are shown by a few fragments found during Firth's archaeological excavations— for example, the famous fragment of a scene of life in a papyrus thicket now on exhibit in the Egyptian Museum in Cairo (JE 56001). In front of the south wall of the courtyard stood a pink granite statue of Userkaf that was originally about five meters high. Next to the Great Sphinx, it constitutes the oldest known colossal statue of an Egyptian ruler. Its head, decorated with the nemes headdress and the uraeus, is also on display in the Egyptian Museum in Cairo (JE 52501).

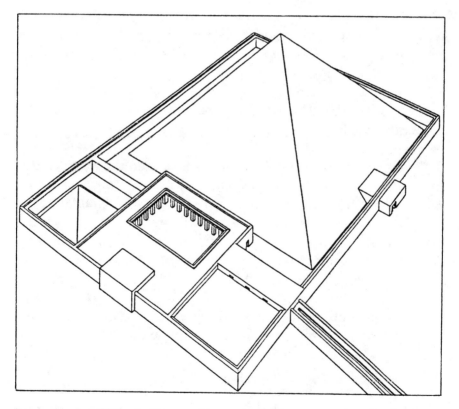

Reconstruction of Userkaf's pyramid complex without causeway or valley temple (after Ricke).

The temple's inner sanctum was reached through two entrances in the south wall of the courtyard. It consisted of a small room with four pairs of pink granite pillars and a chapel with niches (according to Lauer there were five niches; according to Ricke, three), in which cult statues of the ruler stood. At first glance it is surprising that the offering hall indispensable for the worship of the dead was not in this central area of the structure, but rather in a small limestone temple in front of the pyramid's east wall. Lauer attributed this peculiarity to the influence of the sun religion, which reached its apogee during Userkaf's reign. The sacrifice hall's ceiling was supported by two granite pillars, and the wall on the pyramid side was decorated with a large false door made of quartzite. The upper part of the other walls was ornamented with granite dadoes and reliefs depicting scenes of sacrifice.

The cult pyramid stood not in front of the southeast corner of the pyramid, but rather in front of its southwest corner, though only the two lowest levels of its core remain. The underground chamber was accessible from the north.

All the structures mentioned up to this point were surrounded by a large perimeter wall. The remaining components of this complex, the causeway and the valley temple, have not yet been excavated and examined.

The queen's small pyramid complex was structurally separate from the king's complex. It lay to the south and consisted of a small pyramid and a mortuary temple inside their own perimeter wall. It was so severely damaged by stone thieves that all attempts to reconstruct it (especially the mortuary temple) remain hypothetical. Along with Khentkaues I's tomb complex in Giza and that of Djedkare's consort in South Saqqara, this tomb is one of the Old Kingdom's largest pyramid complexes built for a queen.

The pyramid originally had a three-level core, and its mantle consisted of blocks of fine white limestone. Its basic dimensions—the length of its sides, the angle of inclination of its walls, and also its height—are almost identical with those of Queen Khentkaues II's pyramid in Abusir. The underground portion contains an antechamber and a burial chamber. Both of these had almost the same dimensions and the same gabled roof of rough limestone blocks.

The remaining ruins suggest that the mortuary temple in front of the east side of the queen's pyramid included a centrally located, pillared courtyard, an offering hall adjacent to the pyramid wall, three statue niches, storerooms, and perhaps also a staircase leading to the roof terrace. The fragments of a relief decoration found by Firth have not yet been published, but they indicate that the walls of the main areas in the temple (perhaps the sacrifice hall, and the pillared courtyard) were decorated. Unfortunately, it has not been possible to find among the fragments from either the queen's or the king's pyramid complexes any direct proof of the name of Userkaf's consort. On the basis of an indirect clue found in an inscription from the nearby tomb of the priest Persen (now in the Berlin Museum, no. 15004), the name Neferhetepes has been given her.

Let us now return to the unusual location of the royal mortuary temple, which seems to violate all religious norms. Of the theories proposed so far to explain this peculiarity, four are worth notice.

The boldest hypothesis was put forward by Ricke, who sees a direct connection between the location of the temple and the culmination of sun worship. In his view, Userkaf wanted his temple to stand where the sun could shine on it all day long. For Lauer and Edwards, the main reasons for its placement were the topography of the necropolis in Saqqara and the fact that the space east of the pyramid was already occupied by other tombs. Altenmüller suggested that the temple was aligned with the obelisk, which in his opinion stood on the high plateau west of the temple, near the northern perimeter wall of the Djoser complex. Finally, Stadelmann pointed to a possible connection between the location of the temple and the necropolis's administrative center, which at this time was probably at the northeast corner of Djoser's complex.

None of these theories offers a satisfactory solution to the problem. There is, however, another explanation connected with the Great Trench around Djoser's pyramid complex. According to this hypothesis, Userkaf decided to take a very unusual step: he had his pyramid complex built in a narrow strip between the perimeter wall and the Great Trench, on the northeast corner of Djoser's pyramid complex, which already had an exceptional religious significance.

Even though the dimensions of the planned pyramid were modest, the lack of space caused its east side to be built almost on the edge of the trench. In order to build a pyramid complex in this area, it would have been necessary to fill in a large part of the eastern wing of the trench. Even if at this time the trench was already partially filled with sand, filling it in completely would probably have been not only an impious act but a dangerous one. Particularly in the event of an earthquake, the stability of the mortuary temple might be compromised. For that reason Userkaf's mortuary temple was built on the only free, and especially the only solid, ground on the south side of the pyramid. The result was that it was oriented north-south, like Djoser's complex, even if the mortuary temple was situated not to the north but to the south of the pyramid.

As in all areas of research, answering one question here is not equivalent to solving the problem as a whole, but instead raises new questions. One of these is why Userkaf decided to have his pyramid complex built on a site that raised so many structural issues. The great significance of Djoser's tomb, in whose shadow Userkaf wanted to be buried, probably played an important role in his decision. A better understanding of the events at the end of the Fourth and the beginning of the Fifth Dynasty, and especially of Userkaf's ancestry, would be very helpful in arriving at an explanation.

Sahure's Pyramid

Sahure chose for his pyramid complex a site near modern Abusir, not far from Userkaf's sun temple. Why the latter was built in this remote place is not clear. Was there a royal residence or an important sun worship site in the nearby Nile Valley? Or was this, as Werner Kaiser thinks, the southernmost place from which one could see the gilded tip of the obelisk of the temple of Re in Heliopolis? We do not know.

From a conceptual point of view, Sahure's complex, which he called "Sahure's soul shines," continued the tradition of earlier royal tombs.

However, it differed significantly in the choice of construction materials and especially in the kind of relief decoration used. It rightly became, even in antiquity, a source of artistic inspiration and is now considered another milestone in the development of ancient Egyptian royal tomb architecture.

Perhaps because the pyramid resembles a small, weathered mound of rubble, the earliest Egyptologists did not pay much attention to it. Perring was the first to enter the underground chambers of the pyramid, and shortly afterward the Lepsius expedition also investigated the monument, but after that it was neglected for more than half a century. Even de Morgan's reopening of the entry corridor into the inside of the pyramid represented no more than an insignificant archaeological episode. Not until the beginning of the twentieth century was a fundamental investigation of the pyramid complex carried out, under Borchardt's leadership. At a single stroke, his two-volume study, *Das Grabmal des Königs Sahu-re*, a brilliant work for its time that is still frequently cited by Egyptologists, made Sahure's complex a site of first-class archaeological significance.

Ludwig Borchardt.

The excavations Borchardt carried out in Abusir and Abu Ghurab suddenly made him one of the most important figures in Egyptian archaeology. He had come late to the field. He came from a Jewish family in Berlin, studied at the technical college there, and earned a diploma in architecture. Only later on did he begin to attend lectures given by Adolf Erman, who was then the most famous German Egyptologist. Erman considered Borchardt a gifted student and in 1895 helped him take a study trip to Egypt. Borchardt accompanied Henry Lyons (1864–1944) and was entrusted with technical

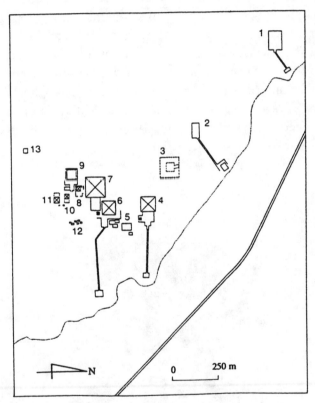

Simplified plan of the pyramid necropolis near Abusir: 1. Niuserre's sun temple; 2. Userkaf's sun temple; 3. Shepseskaf's (?) unfinished pyramid; 4. Sahure's pyramid; 5. Ptahshepses's mastaba; 6. Niuserre's pyramid; 7. Neferirkare's pyramid; 8. Khentkaues II's pyramid; 9. Neferefre's (unfinished) pyramid; 10. pyramid Lepsius no. 24; 11. pyramid Lepsius no. 25; 12. necropolis with mastabas belonging to Khekeretnebti, Hedjetnebu, Mernefu, et al.; 13. Udjahorresnet's shaft tomb.

and documentary tasks on the little island of Philae. Later, on the recommendation of his teacher, Borchardt remained in Egypt. Only an architect, Erman thought, would be truly competent to study an ancient people that had built such great structures. Together with de Morgan, Borchardt helped design the scholarly catalog of the architectural objects in the Egyptian Museum in Cairo. He also showed special talent as a diplomat: in 1899 he was appointed scientific attaché at the German consulate in Cairo. The high point of his work was the foundation of the German Archaeological Institute in Cairo, which he directed from 1909 to 1929. He was also involved in founding the German excavation house in Luxor and the Swiss Institute for Egyptian Architecture and Antiquities in Cairo, in whose garden he was buried under a simple block of pink granite from Aswan, near a group of royal palms on the bank of the Nile.

When Borchardt had finished his investigations of the Sahure complex, they seemed so comprehensive that nothing new, and certainly nothing fundamental, remained to be added. Measurements made by Maragioglio and Rinaldi in the early 1960s produced only a few minor corrections. In 1994, however, there was a surprising turn of events. The Egyptian Supreme Council of Antiquities decided to open the Abusir necropolis to international tourism. To this end a partial reconstruction of selected monuments was undertaken, in particular that of Sahure's complex and Ptahshepses's mastaba. The excavation of the upper part of Sahure's causeway revealed huge blocks decorated with reliefs that are iconographically and artistically unique. For reasons we can only guess at, Borchardt had never investigated the area along the two sides of the upper part of the causeway. The reliefs shed an entirely new light on the character and significance of the pictorial program of the pyramid complex.

Sahure's pyramid stands on a small hill at the edge of the desert, about twenty meters above the Nile Valley. Its subsoil has never been investigated, but to judge by the nearby mastaba of Ptahshepses, it would not have been built on rock, but rather on a platform made of at least two layers of limestone blocks.

The monument's poor condition does not allow us to offer precise information regarding its original appearance, dimensions, and especially the arrangement of rooms in the underground part. The core, which presumably consists of horizontal layers of rough, less valuable limestone blocks, originally had six layers. In contrast, the casing was made of large, carefully dressed blocks of fine white limestone from the quarries near modern Maasara on the opposite bank of the Nile. In measuring the pyramid, the architects made a noteworthy error: the southeast corner is off by about 1.58 meters to the east with respect to the northeast corner, and therefore the ground plan is not entirely square.

The entrance into the substructure is on the north wall, just above ground level. The relatively short descending corridor, made of limestone, comes out in a small vestibule, immediately behind which is a portcullis of pink granite. Then the corridor begins to climb slightly,

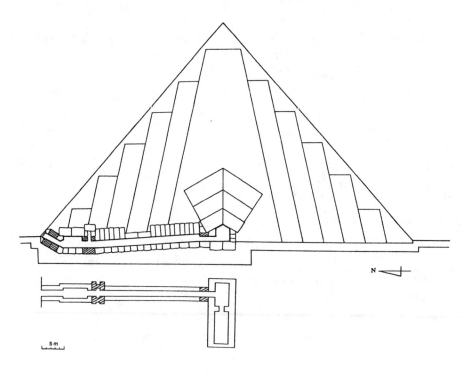

Sahure's pyramid. North-south sectional view and ground plan of the structure (after Borchardt). The representation of the accretion layer–type structure of the core masonry is probably not correct.

until shortly before the entrance into the antechamber it finally becomes horizontal. In three places it is fortified with pink granite.

The antechamber is directly on the pyramid's vertical axis and, like the burial chamber that lies farther to the west, was so destroyed by stone thieves that today the original plan can no longer be reconstructed with precision. The gabled ceiling consisted of three layers of enormous limestone blocks. In the ruins, Perring found stone fragments he took to be the remains of the king's basalt sarcophagus. Around the pyramid no trace was found of the pyramidion, whose transport to the construction site was depicted on the walls of the causeway.

The mortuary temple stands in front of the pyramid's east side, on a level surface made of two layers of rough limestone blocks. Between the foundation blocks of its southern part, Borchardt found a large number of cereal grains, which he connected with ceremonies held at the founding of the temple. However, it seems more likely that the grains fell through cracks in the floor of the temple storerooms, which were located immediately overhead.

Along its east-west axis, the temple is divided into outer and inner parts, which were separated by a transverse corridor. The outer part included the entrance hall and the open, columned courtyard. From a functional point of view, the entrance hall, which in contemporary inscriptions is referred to as the "House of the Great," represented the transition between the causeway and the mortuary temple. In Borchardt's opinion, this was where the procession bearing the deceased ruler's body stopped to pay its last respects. In the ruins of the hall remains of a pink granite dado were found. The side walls of high-quality limestone were decorated with marvelous scenes and inscriptions in bas-relief.

According to Ricke, the open courtyard, which was reached from the entrance hall, had a special, symbolic meaning. It represented the sacred palm grove in Buto, the ancient Egyptians' "national cemetery." Around the courtyard stood sixteen monolithic pink granite columns shaped like the trunk and crown of a palm, the tree that for the ancient Egyptians was the symbol of fertility and eternal life. The columns were ornamented with the names and titles of the king as well

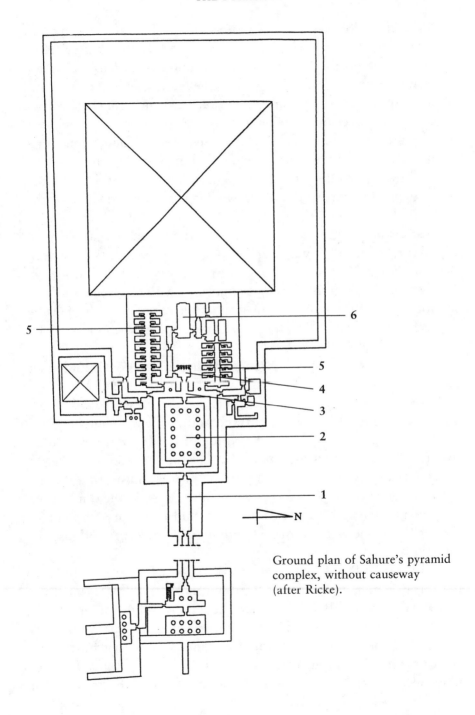

Ground plan of Sahure's pyramid
complex, without causeway
(after Ricke).

as the vulture goddess Nekhbet (in the south half of the courtyard) and the cobra goddess Wadjet (in the north half of the courtyard), the tutelary goddesses of Upper and Lower Egypt. They supported a granite architrave with the royal titulature, on which lay the limestone ceiling slabs decorated with stars. The limestone side walls over the granite dado were decorated with splendid scenes in colored bas-relief. Unfortunately, only fragments of these reliefs have been preserved; they represented, among other things, Sahure's triumph over Asian and Libyan enemies and his magnificent spoils.

In the northwest corner of the open courtyard, which is paved with irregular black basalt slabs, originally stood an alabaster altar decorated with symbols of the unification of Upper and Lower Egypt, a procession of personified mortuary estates carrying offerings to Sahure, and other scenes.

Around the courtyard ran a corridor on whose walls also appeared scenes in colored bas-relief. They represented the ruler catching fish and hunting birds and wild desert animals. This was where the previously mentioned, historically very important reliefs came from. To the figure of one of the members of the royal entourage have been added the insignia of royal power and the brief inscription "Neferirkare King of Upper and Lower Egypt." Kurt Sethe, who worked on the scenes and inscriptions in Sahure's temple and prepared them for publication, developed a theory based on this detail, according to which Neferirkare was the brother of Sahure and gave the order to "correct" the relief in the temple of his elder brother when he himself ascended the throne and had his own pyramid complex erected nearby.

The important local cult of Sekhmet was practiced about a thousand years later (during the Eighteenth Dynasty) on the grounds of the pillared courtyard, probably because of a particularly well-preserved relief sculpture of the lion goddess there. Sekhmet, a "mighty," maternally protective and at the same time warlike goddess, was worshiped along with her consort Ptah in nearby Memphis. The tradition of worship in the columned courtyard survived both Sahure and "his" Sekhmet, since in early Christian times the Copts founded their own shrine on this site.

The transverse corridor was supposed not only to divide the public area of the temple from its intimate area, but also constituted a central intersection that communicated with all parts of the temple, the courtyard around the pyramid, and the cult pyramid. At the northern end was an entrance to a staircase leading to the roof terrace. Like the columned courtyard, the transverse corridor was paved in basalt. The limestone walls over the granite base were sculpted in relief with scenes of sea battles and trading ships returning from Asia, of which only fragments now remain. In the middle of the west wall of the corridor was a low stair leading to an important cult place in the temple—a chapel with five niches. On both sides of the stair rose from deep niches two pillars imitating papyrus bundles of six stalks each, which supported an architrave and the ceiling slabs. A fragment of the architrave was found during excavations in the nearby St. Jeremiah monastery in Saqqara, where it was being used as part of an oil press.

The religious function of the five-niche chapel corresponded to its splendid appearance. The sheathing of the niches in the west wall and the dado were made of pink granite. The walls were sheathed in limestone and here, too, they were decorated with colorful reliefs. The star-studded limestone ceiling was intended to evoke the sky of the underworld. From the alabaster-paved floor a low staircase led to each of the niches. The cult statues that once stood in the niches have not been preserved. From the chapel a path led into the rearmost and, from the point of view of the cult, most important room in the whole temple, the offering hall, which was directly adjacent to the pyramid's east wall. Over the alabaster floor arched a ceiling decorated with stars. Divinities carrying offerings for the dead king decorated the walls of the shadowy hall and represented an intimate environment for the spirit of the dead ruler, who came here to eat. In the builders' conception, the dead ruler came out of the inner part of the pyramid, entered the offering hall through an enormous granite false door set in its west wall, received the offerings that lay ready on a stone altar, and, when he had finished his funerary repast, returned to his grave by the same route. During his excavations, Borchardt was surprised by the very crudely finished surface of the false door, which bore no inscription, and he hypothesized that written signs with the sacrificial formulas and the name and titles of the ruler might have been put on a metal (perhaps copper or even gold?) sheathing that was long ago torn down by thieves and vanished without a trace.

The adjoining rooms were connected functionally with the rituals in the offering hall. Some of these rooms had libation basins, the water from which flowed through copper pipes to a central drainage canal dug into the ground and paved with limestone tiles. The whole system of pipes ran to more than three hundred eighty meters in length! It is also interesting that lead stoppers were used in this carefully designed system.

In the southern and northern parts of the inner half of the mortuary temple, there were large storerooms. In the northern part there were about ten such rooms designated as treasure chambers. This area of almost a hundred square meters probably housed cult objects used in temple rituals. The southern part included sixteen rooms that were used primarily for the temporary storage of sacrificial offerings. The limestone blocks from which the two-storied storerooms were constructed were so large that the steps leading to the second story could be cut directly out of the stone walls.

From the southern end of the transverse corridor one reached the courtyard around the pyramid as well as the cult pyramid. A portico with a pair of columns of pink granite provided access to the necropolis, whose establishment south of the mortuary temple had begun during Sahure's reign. This cemetery has not yet been investigated, but it can be presumed that the ruler's close relatives were also buried there. The tombs of Sahure's consort Nefretkhanebti and her firstborn son, Netjerirenre, are probably also somewhere in this area, as is shown by a block with Netjerirenre's name on it that was found in the nearby mastaba of the vizier Ptahshepses.

The cult pyramid had its own enclosure and a two-stepped core. Into its only chamber, which is oriented east-west and slightly below ground level, leads a bent corridor that initially descends slightly and then climbs again. Inside the pyramid nothing was found; stone thieves had severely damaged it.

Of the causeway, only the base ramp of large, roughly dressed limestone blocks remains. The walls of the originally roofed corridor, which

was illuminated only by small openings in the roof, were richly decorated with scenes in polychrome bas-relief. In the lower part of the
corridor, Borchardt found reliefs that are thought to have an apotropaic
function and represent the king in the form of a sphinx, under whose
paws Egypt's enemies are crushed. When he found no more blocks
decorated with reliefs, Borchardt decided not to investigate the remaining part of the corridor (about three quarters of it). As a result, the
German team failed to find the unique reliefs mentioned above.

Today, Sahure's valley temple lies in ruins at the edge of the desert,
overgrown with reeds and palm trees. Its floor was originally about
five meters above the present ground level, which has been raised by
the silt deposits that have mounted during the annual flooding of the
Nile over the past 4,500 years. In contrast to the mortuary temple,
the valley temple's longer axis was oriented north-south, and it had
two ramps—one on the south and one on the east. In the south portico was a row of four pink granite columns, while the east entrance
had twice as many. Along with the basalt floor and walls decorated
with reliefs, the limestone ceiling was painted with stars meant to
suggest the entrance into the realm of the underworld.

The passages leading from both entrances met in a small room in the
middle of the temple, which had a pair of columns. On the walls of
this nodal point were more scenes in polychrome relief. This room
connected the valley temple's two entrances with the causeway leading
to the mortuary temple; it also had a staircase leading to the roof terrace.

Why Sahure's valley temple had two entrances has not yet been
explained. At first glance, the southern one might seem superfluous.
Why is it there in addition to the main entrance from the east? Perhaps important buildings to the south were connected with the royal
tomb complex. Did boats coming up a special canal from a lake south
of Sahure's temple once anchor at a ramp there? Perhaps the residence
of the kings buried in the pyramids at Abusir stood on its banks, or
perhaps Sahure's pyramid town, Khabasahure, extended in that direction. Sahure's palace, Uetjesneferusahure ("Sahure's splendor soars up
to heaven"), may also have been there. Its existence is proven by inscriptions on ordinary tallow containers recently found in Neferefre's
mortuary temple in Abusir.

MIROSLAV VERNER

Neferirkare's Pyramid

Neferirkare's pyramid, which was originally called "Kakai is a soul," towers over the whole necropolis of Abusir.* It was the largest structure there, and it was also built on the highest site, three hundred thirty meters above the Nile Valley. Today, it looks like a mound of rubble, striking only because of the prominent, stepped structure of its core.

Perring conducted the first archaeological investigation of Neferirkare's pyramid. Lepsius, who examined it shortly afterward, was so fascinated by the uncovered form of the core that he based on it his theory that the Egyptian pyramids were constructed using inclined accretion layers. Borchardt, who thoroughly investigated the pyramid and its mortuary temple from 1904 to 1907, also adopted that theory. "There is perhaps no better place to study the methods used to construct the pyramids," he observed. This turned out to be a rather misleading view, as Maragioglio and Rinaldi discovered while making their measurements in the 1960s, but their conclusions were not entirely precise either.

During its research in Abusir, the Czech archaeological team also began by making a closer examination of Neferirkare's pyramid. This had less to do with the fact that the pyramid's apex (at that time, 44.57 meters above the base) was the highest reference point for taking measurements in the Abusir necropolis, than with the broader archaeological and historical context in which this monument was situated as a result of the excavations in Khentkaues II's and Neferefre's pyramid complexes, which adjoin it.

The pyramid was built in several stages but was never completed. The original plan called for six steps—a very unusual decision, since the era of step pyramids was long past. The lowest level of the core consisted of rough but relatively well-dressed limestone blocks from the local quarries and was twice as high as the other levels. The casing of smaller blocks of fine white limestone was already partially

---

* Kakai is accepted as Neferirkare's birth name.

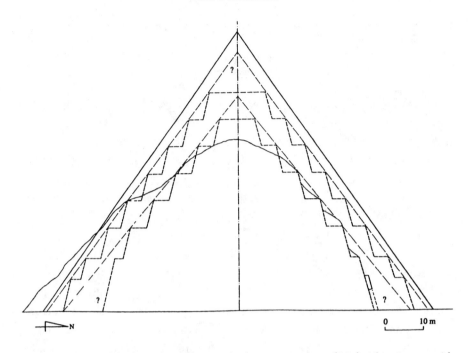

Reconstruction of the hypothetical stages in the construction of Neferirkare's pyramid.

installed but did not extend beyond the first level of the pyramid. Part of it can still be seen in situ on the north side of the site, where Perring had an access tunnel to the pyramid's entrance dug through the rubble.

An interesting episode is connected with Perring's tunnel and the casing, which Howard Vyse reported in his book *Operations Carried Out on the Pyramids of Gizeh in 1837*: "After ten or twelve feet of the corridor had been cleared, the workers were frightened by a loud roar, and they barely escaped as the masonry over the entrance collapsed and revealed the wall built of large blocks." Perring came very close to paying a high price for his haste. The casing was not only unfinished, but also insufficiently attached to the pyramid (the architects of the Third Dynasty step pyramids had used more effective methods of constructing the core and the casing).

When the casing had reached the upper edge of the first level, a decision was apparently made to enlarge the structure and to make it into a true pyramid. From the outset, the then eight-level structure had been planned as a core. This is clearly proven by the less valuable material and the careless methods used in enlarging the structure. The casing of the second stage of construction also remained unfinished. Borchardt was able to find in situ only the lowest row of the pink granite blocks that composed the casing of the east wall. He did not excavate on the other sides, but he did note the complete lack of limestone blocks from the casing in the area around the pyramid and where he had cleared away the rubble.

The corridor leading to the burial chamber, which is approximately in the middle of the north wall, about two meters above ground level, was reinforced at the beginning and the end by a granite casing. The initially descending part of the corridor ended about two and one half meters below the level of the pyramid's base, in a small vestibule behind which the main granite barrier began with a portcullis. The remaining, longer part of the corridor took two turns and headed generally east, finally coming out approximately in the middle of the offset antechamber. The corridor was built of limestone blocks in a rather unusual way. Over the flat roof was an additional gable roof, over which there was also a layer of reeds. This method of construction has not been found in any other Old Kingdom pyramid.

The antechamber and the burial chamber have been so heavily damaged by stone thieves that their original appearance can no longer be reconstructed with precision. Both rooms were oriented east-west, were of the same width, and had gabled ceilings (of the three layers of huge limestone blocks that composed the ceiling, only two remain). The antechamber was somewhat shorter than the burial chamber. Neither Perring nor Borchardt was able to find remains of the king's mummy, the sarcophagus, or the burial equipment.

The mortuary temple was built in stages, and its mode of construction was as complicated as the pyramid's. Its oldest and innermost part consisted of limestone and was built on a small stone platform in front of the middle part of the pyramid's east side. The remaining part, built later, was made of mudbricks, except for a few architectonic elements.

The limestone platform was not situated precisely on the pyramid's east-west axis, but rather slightly to the south of it. As we shall see later, these apparently secondary details play an important role in reconstructing the stages in which the temple was built and their chronology. The limestone construction stage included the offering hall, the small chambers alongside it (two on the south, one on the north), and the five niche chapels.

Only a few fragments of the original relief decoration have been preserved. One of these is a block with the remains of a scene of special historical significance. It shows the king, accompanied by his consort Khentkaues II and his eldest son, Neferre. This block—which was found not during Borchardt's excavations but in the 1930s, by the Egyptian archaeologist Édouard Ghazouli—is one of the key sources in reconstructing genealogical relationships within the royal family at that time.

The temple was gradually enlarged. Because it was important to save time and materials, a solid stone foundation was not placed under the brick part of the structure. The architects dealt with the problem of the uneven terrain, which sloped down toward the east, by using brick chambers filled with sand, shards of pottery, and building waste. The floor consisted of stamped-down clay. While investigating the eastern part of the temple's foundation, Borchardt found the remains of plastered and whitewashed brick walls that were probably part of a structure that must have been removed to make room for Neferirkare's temple. This discovery, which for a long time was not documented archaeologically, is very significant, because it shows that older buildings had stood on the site of the necropolis of the Fifth Dynasty pharaohs. The plan for the enlargement of the mortuary temple was considerably influenced by the decision to build the pyramid complex without a valley temple or causeway. In the southwest part of the temple was a system of storerooms in which grave robbers found, in the early 1890s, the previously mentioned papyrus fragments from Neferirkare's temple archive.

East of the inner part of the temple, but still on its limestone foundation, was a transverse corridor. From its south end a pathway led to the storerooms and the open courtyard around the pyramid. The latter was also accessible from the north end of the corridor through a small room with a row of six wooden columns.

The eastern half of the temple included a columned portico, the columned entrance hall, and the open columned courtyard. A low, stepped ramp led from the courtyard to the higher transverse corridor; the sides of this ramp were originally sheathed in wood.

The rectangular, north-south–oriented courtyard was offset in relation to the complex's main axis. The thirty-seven wooden columns, each shaped to resemble four lotus stems, were not symmetrically aligned: on the south side there were more than on the north side. This asymmetry may have come about subsequently. Ricke, clearly basing his view on Borchardt's documentation of his excavations, hypothesized that one of the columns near the altar was damaged by fire and removed. Paule Posener-Kriéger found confirmation of Ricke's hypothesis in a papyrus fragment from the temple archive that stated that three columns had been damaged, and that one had had to be

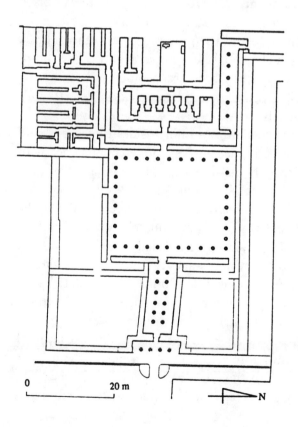

Plan of Neferirkare's mortuary temple (after Ricke).

0   20 m

N

removed entirely, while the other two had been left in place and even repainted.

The peculiar bent shape of the entrance hall was connected with an effort to deal with the shift between the original entrance in the columned courtyard and the one installed in the final phase of construction. The hall was decorated with six pairs of wooden columns, each shaped like four lotus stems. A row of four more (papyrus?) columns stood in the temple's main entrance.

Because of the necessary haste in completing Neferirkare's complex, a cult pyramid was never constructed. In its stead a settlement with simple mudbrick lodgings for priests was built south of the temple, and endured there until the end of the Sixth Dynasty. We owe the discovery of the temple archive to this settlement, because the priests would normally have lived in the pyramid town near the valley temple, where the flooding waters of the Nile would eventually have buried these valuable documents under several meters of silt.

Around the mortuary temple and the pyramid an enormous brick perimeter wall was built, which probably had several gates. The southwestern gate was discovered by the Czech archaeological team during its investigation of the neighboring pyramid complex of Neferirkare's consort, Queen Khentkaues II.

In the courtyard next to the south and north sides of the pyramid large wooden boats were buried. They lay well hidden in pits lined with mudbricks. A mention of the boats in a papyrus fragment from the temple archive finally led Czech archaeologists to look for them. Using geophysical methods, it was possible to determine precisely where the southern boat was and to excavate it. Unfortunately, unlike Khufu's, Neferirkare's funerary boat had already crumbled into dust.

In conclusion, a few remarks are necessary regarding the specific and still not fully understood architectural development of Neferirkare's complex. New discoveries show that the step pyramid was to be transformed into a genuine pyramid during Neferirkare's lifetime. Before he died, the core had already been enlarged and the lowest layer of the casing blocks had presumably also been set in place.

The oldest, limestone part of the temple can probably be ascribed to Neferirkare's successors, Neferefre or Niuserre, and as a compari-

son with Neferefre's mortuary temple shows, it was a simple structure that made it possible to worship the deceased ruler and subsequently to complete the temple in accord with the standard criteria.

Neferefre may also have planned to complete the casing of his
father's pyramid. His premature death and presumably also the resulting disputes over the throne caused the completion of Neferirkare's
complex to be postponed; it was not finished until the reign of Niuserre.
However, the pyramid's casing was not completed, and the valley temple
and causeway were also never built.

The question of the construction stages gone through by Neferirkare's
complex is much more complicated than it may have seemed in previous accounts. The king ruled only about ten years, yet as the example of his immediate predecessors Sahure and Userkaf shows, this
was enough time to complete the standard complex. Then why was
Neferirkare's complex still so unfinished when the king died? Apparently, the problem lay in the change in its conception, from a step
pyramid to a true pyramid.

Why did Neferirkare decide to break with earlier tradition and to
return, after about two centuries, to a tomb in the form of a step pyramid? Were the reasons connected with religion or dynastic and power
politics? In the Nineteenth Dynasty king list on the famous Royal
Canon of Turin, Neferirkare is considered the founder of a new dynasty. Is there some connection between that view and the unusual
character of the original project for Neferirkare's pyramid? To provide an unambiguous answer to this question, new historical sources
would be required. A few such sources were recently tracked down
by the Czech archaeological team in Queen Khentkaues II's pyramid
complex in Abusir.

Khentkaues II's Pyramid

Although he was a talented and experienced archaeologist, during
his fieldwork in Abusir Ludwig Borchardt omitted or overlooked
certain things. This did not, however, reduce the value of his discoveries in any way. Today it is hard to understand, for example, why he

did not examine more closely the ruins of the large structure on the south side of Neferirkare's pyramid in Abusir. Although he made a brief exploration of it, he called off further work because he was convinced that it was a "double mastaba," a kind of structure he viewed as being of secondary importance.

The form of the structure, its location, and especially its clear east-west orientation, make it obvious that it must have been a small pyramid complex, probably belonging to Neferirkare's consort. This view was further supported by a forgotten discovery made by Perring when he was working on the grounds of Neferirkare's pyramid: a block, on which the inscription "King's Wife Khentkaues" was written in red script. The Czech team's excavations in the second half of the 1970s confirmed that the pyramid belonged to Khentkaues II, but at the same time the archaeological situation and especially its historical context became much more complicated than it originally seemed to be.

The pyramid was built in a simple and economical manner of limestone that had been discarded on the site of Neferirkare's neighboring pyramid. The three-level core is composed of small pieces of stone bound with clay mortar. For the casing, easily carried blocks of high-quality white limestone were used. The apex consisted of a pyramidion of dark gray granite, a fragment of which was a very important discovery from an architectural and archaeological point of view. The less valuable material and the rather careless mode of construction no doubt made it easier for stone thieves to tear down the pyramid. Today, its remains are about four meters high.

The underground part of the pyramid is very simple. From the entrance close to ground level in the middle of the north wall, a corridor initially leads downward and then becomes horizontal, turning slightly toward the east. Shortly before it comes out in the burial chamber, there is a simple granite barrier. Both the burial chamber and the corridor were built with small blocks of fine white limestone; only the burial chamber's flat ceiling was made of large blocks of limestone. In the ruins were found a fragment of a pink granite sarcophagus, strips of mummy wrappings, and shards of stone vessels from the queen's burial equipment—unmistakable evidence of Khentkaues's burial there.

A few signs and inscriptions on the pyramid's stone masonry allow us to draw certain important conclusions. They indicate that construction was interrupted, probably at the time of the fifth cattle count, before the tenth year of Neferirkare's reign; at that point, it had reached about the level of the burial chamber ceiling.

This suggests that the premature cessation of work on the pyramid was connected with the king's death. Another inscription indicates that the construction of the pyramid—originally begun for the "King's Wife Khentkaues"—was completed (after a lengthy interruption resulting from Neferirkare's death?) for the "King's Mother Khentkaues." Her son thus finished the work that her consort had begun.

The mortuary temple in front of the east wall of the queen's pyramid was not built until after Neferirkare's pyramid complex was completed. If we set aside a few small additions and transformations, we can say that it was constructed in two main stages distinguished by the materials used—limestone in the first, and mudbricks in the second.

The original small limestone temple was entered from the southeast, through a pillared portico. In addition to the pillared courtyard, it contained a room for the cult statues of the queen,* an offering hall with a false door of pink granite, an altar, and storerooms. A staircase led from the southwest part of the temple to the roof terrace, where certain rituals and astronomical observations were carried out in connection with worship of the dead queen.

The walls of the offering hall and perhaps other rooms were decorated with pictures and inscriptions in bas-relief, such as scenes of a funerary repast, the delivery of offerings, the slaughter of sacrificial animals, a procession of women carrying gifts and representing mortuary estates, and an encounter between the queen and her descendants. The pillars in the courtyard and in the portico were similarly decorated. On one of them the queen is depicted with the uraeus on her forehead—a symbol that at this period was reserved solely for rulers and divinities.

---

* Papyrus fragments from Khentkaues's temple archive indicate that there were at least sixteen cult statues of the queen in the temple.

Khentkaues II's pyramid complex in Abusir. Reconstruction of the ground plan (after Jánosi).

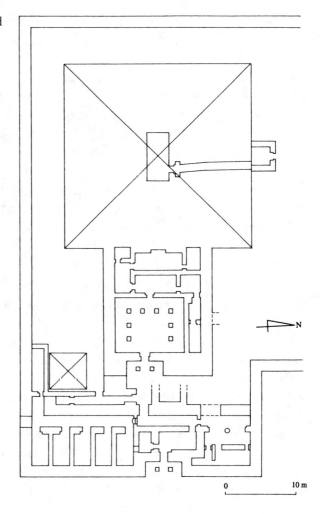

The extension of the temple to the south and west significantly changed its appearance and conception. Near the southeast corner of the pyramid stood, for the first time in the history of the Old Kingdom, queens' tombs and a small cult pyramid. On the east a group of five storerooms, lodging for priests, a new pillared portico, and an entry vestibule were also added.

If the huge but unfinished limestone perimeter wall was supposed to include the original temple and the queen's pyramid within Neferirkare's pyramid complex, that goal was abandoned after the queen's pyramid was enlarged. The new brick wall emphasized the importance and independence of Khentkaues II's pyramid complex.

Inscriptions discovered in the temple confirm the attribution of this complex to Khentkaues II, who bore the same chief title as her famous namesake which some interpret as "Mother of two kings of Upper and Lower Egypt" and others as "King of Upper and Lower Egypt and Mother of the King of Upper and Lower Egypt." As in Giza, in Abusir clear archaeological evidence shows that the queen was not only buried in her tomb complex, but that she was long worshiped there as well.

Thus it cannot have been one and the same person but must have been two different queens separated by one or two generations. Khentkaues I, who was probably Menkaure's daughter, lived at the end of the Fourth and the beginning of the Fifth Dynasty, whereas Khentkaues II, Neferirkare's consort and mother of Neferefre and Niuserre, lived in the middle of the Fifth Dynasty. The two queens may have been related. In any event, the identity of their titles reflects the similar, and no doubt equally unusual, circumstances under which they lived. After the ruler's death, both of them probably had to use their authority to protect the rights of the apparently underage successor to the throne. Who that was in Khentkaues I's case, we do not know, but in the case of Khentkaues II it was very probably Niuserre.

Neferefre's (Unfinished) Pyramid

The lowest level of the core of Neferefre's pyramid, which has been damaged by erosion and half covered with sand, was until recently considered by archaeologists to be the greatest riddle of the necropolis in Abusir. Perring had taken very general notice of it, as had Lepsius, de Morgan, Borchardt, and other archaeologists who worked on the pyramids in Abusir. Some attributed it to the little-known Neferefre, and others to the still less well-known Shepseskare, while many others made no attempt to identify its possessor. However, they all agreed that it was a structure that had been begun and then abandoned, and that had never served its intended function as a tomb for a pharaoh and the site of his worship. Borchardt arrived at this negative conclusion after he had probed the inside of the pyramid.

In the second half of the 1970s, the archaeological team of the Institute of Egyptology at the University of Prague began to make a systematic investigation of this neglected monument. Certain circumstances indicated to whom this tomb, which had long been known as the "Unfinished Pyramid in Abusir," really belonged.

First of all, Neferefre's mortuary temple is explicitly mentioned in a papyrus fragment found in Neferirkare's mortuary temple. The context suggests that it must have been a monument in the necropolis at Abusir.

In addition, the location of the Unfinished Pyramid offers clues for situating it chronologically. The structure lies southwest of Neferirkare's pyramid. As a precise geodetic measurement has confirmed, its northwest corner is on a line that already connected Sahure's and Neferirkare's pyramids and represented the basic axis of the pyramid necropolis in Abusir.*

Neferefre's pyramid was therefore constructed after those of Neferirkare and Sahure. Its greater distance from the Nile Valley also indicates that Neferefre's pyramid was built later than the other two. Its site is the most disadvantageous from the point of view of transporting construction materials.

These conclusions are also confirmed by the already mentioned limestone block found in the village of Abusir by the Egyptian archaeologist Ghazouli before the Second World War. On the stone, which probably came from Neferirkare's mortuary temple, there is an in-

---

* A similar axis existed in the necropolis at Giza. There it consisted of a line that connected the southeast corners of the pyramids of Khufu, Khafre, and Menkaure. Both lines, that of Giza and that of Abusir, are directed toward Heliopolis, where they cross. Their point of intersection was probably in the temple of the sun god Re (at the tip of the obelisk, which may have represented a "fixed point" in the world of the ancient Egyptians in that period).

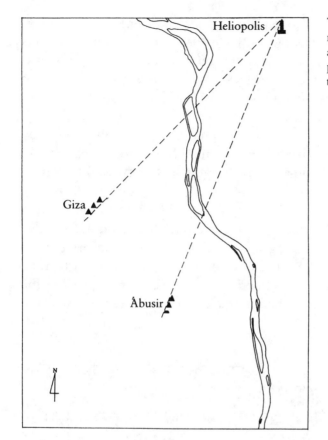

The axes of the necropolises in Giza and Abusir were probably directed toward Heliopolis.

complete scene depicting the ruler with his consort Khentkaues II and his eldest son, Neferre. Therefore, it was more than probable that the Unfinished Pyramid belonged to Neferefre, even though the names differed in a minor way. At the beginning of his reign, he was still called Neferre, "Re is beautiful," and later probably changed his name to Neferefre, "Re is his beauty."

Archaeological excavations have provided further grounds for this assumption. Indeed, they have led to the discovery of a wide-ranging complex of structures around the Unfinished Pyramid and have thrown new light on the previously little-known Fifth Dynasty.

The condition of the Unfinished Pyramid made it possible to carefully investigate its structure and the methods used to construct it, particularly with regard to Lepsius's theory of inclined accretion layers. The pyramid—it was called "Divine is Neferefre's power"—was built not on rock subsoil, but rather on a foundation made of two layers of enormous limestone blocks, which were set in place after the ground was prepared and a pit was dug for the burial chamber and the descending corridor.

Only then did construction of the core begin, using relatively simple methods. It was built in horizontal layers about a meter high. The exterior mantle consisted of large, roughly dressed blocks as much as five meters long, held together with clay mortar. The blocks were especially well bound at the corners. The core's inner mantle around the pit for the burial chamber and the descending corridor was similarly built, but using smaller blocks. The space between the two rows of blocks, the outer and the inner, was filled with stone fragments, sand, fine rubble, and clay. It is very probable that the other pyramids in Abusir, including Neferirkare's, were constructed in the same way.

Schematic horizontal section through the core of Neferefre's Unfinished Pyramid.

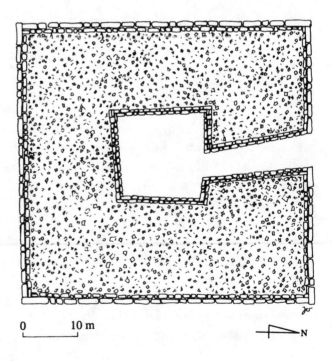

0   10 m

N

In the middle of the pyramid's north side, close to ground level, a descending corridor opens into the ruler's underground funerary apartment. As was generally the rule at that time, it curved slightly to the southeast and came out in the antechamber. At the lower end it was lined with pink granite and sealed with blocks of the same stone. In the middle of the corridor was a massive barrier, also of pink granite, a system of interlocking "jaws" that has been found nowhere else, which the architects presumably thought up because it was relatively easy to break into the descending corridor from the roof terrace.

The antechamber and the burial chamber lying west of it are oriented precisely east-west. Both rooms were provided with a gabled ceiling and were built of fine white limestone. Unfortunately, in antiquity they were severely damaged by extensive quarrying of stone directly inside the pyramid. The form of the Unfinished Pyramid and the convenient access to the roof terrace made stone thieves' work easier. They dug into the pyramid's interior from above and even set up a workshop there in order to break the white limestone into smaller pieces and make it useful for the construction of other tombs in later times. This pyramid and others in Abusir were plundered, probably in the First Intermediate Period, and afterward were repeatedly used as a source of stone—in the later New Kingdom, in the Saite period, and under Persian rule (when the stone was used for the shaft tombs not far away in southwest Abusir), in late Roman times, in Coptic times, and basically from the Arab Middle Ages down into the nineteenth century.

It is hardly surprising that amid such devastation only a few remains of the burial equipment and of the ruler's burial could be found. The archaeological significance of those remains is nonetheless enormous. Among the discoveries were pieces of a pink granite sarcophagus, fragments of four alabaster canopic jars in which the entrails were originally buried, alabaster containers for models of offerings, and—most valuable of all—parts of the ruler's mummy.

A preliminary anatomical investigation of these fragments of the mummy has shown that they probably belonged to a man about twenty to twenty-three years old when he died. The archaeological circumstances and anthropological results allow us to conclude with near certainty that these are the remains of the possessor of the pyramid, Neferefre.

The completed first level of the core, which is about seven meters high, was cased with roughly dressed blocks of fine white limestone; above that level it was covered with a thin layer of clay with gravel stamped into it. The roof terrace perfectly imitated the surrounding desert landscape. The tomb took on the form of a truncated pyramid or large mastaba; however, it was not rectangular and north-south oriented, but instead had a square ground plan. It looked like a hill, and that was what it was originally called (*iat*), as a papyrus fragment discovered in the mortuary temple at the foot of the tomb proves. The symbolism of Neferefre's architecturally modified tomb can be understood only in connection with the myth of the primeval mound.

On the foundation platform in front of the east side, on which the pyramid mantle was originally supposed to rest, a small mortuary temple made of smaller blocks of fine white limestone was built. It was so simple that it would be more appropriate to speak of the core of a temple or of an improvised cult structure.

This original temple was oriented north-south and was reached from the southeast by a low stair-ramp. The open space immediately behind the entrance was used by the priests for ritual purification, as is shown by a small basin set into the floor. The center of the structure consists, as always, of the offering hall. In its west wall there was probably a false door, of which no trace could be found in the almost completely destroyed space. However, in the floor of the hall the impression left by the altar could still be discerned. Under the paving stones, approximately on the east-west axis of the Unfinished Pyramid, intact objects connected with the foundation ceremonies were discovered. These included a bull's head, symbolic miniature vessels of fired clay, a clump of gray clay for sealing the vessels, and other things. It is possible that two wooden funerary boats once lay in the two small chambers alongside the offering hall.

For the time being, we cannot say precisely who had this older part of the mortuary temple built, and therefore became Neferefre's successor. The sealings found not far from there indicate, however, that it may have been Shepseskare, an almost unknown ruler whose reign was perhaps even shorter than Neferefre's.

During Niuserre's reign a significant addition was made along the whole east side of the Unfinished Pyramid. The plan of the new temple was highly original. It was influenced chiefly by the conceptual transformation of the tomb from a true pyramid into a truncated pyramid. Except for a few architectonic elements it was built entirely of mudbricks. The new structure also had a north-south–oriented ground plan, but its entrance, which consisted of a portico with two four-stemmed limestone lotus columns, was now right in the middle of the east facade.

In the central section of the temple there was originally a group of five chambers. These were not used as chapels for statues, however, and instead look more like storerooms. During the later reconstruction a corridor leading from them into the inner part of the temple was made. Another chamber was sealed after the ritual burial of the two cult boats, which were damaged during a fire in the northern part of the temple. All around the boats lay hundreds of small pieces of carnelian beads with holes bored through them; these may originally have been on a string.

In the north part of the temple there was a group of ten two-story magazines. In some of these in the northwest corner a large number of papyri was found—fragments and sometimes whole scrolls from the temple archive, which in its scope and content resembled Neferirkare's archive. Many of the texts have to do with the various structural and functional aspects of the temple and the necropolis as a whole. Thus a unique opportunity was offered to compare the information on the papyri with archaeological discoveries and thus to improve our understanding of the structural evolution and function of Neferefre's pyramid complex and worship, as well as many other mysteries of this structure.

The architectural plan of the southern part of the temple was unique. It consisted of an extensive, east-west–oriented hall with twenty six-stemmed wooden lotus columns. As the remains show, the ceiling of the columned hall had gold stars painted on a blue background, which indicates that it had a special religious function. It may have repre-

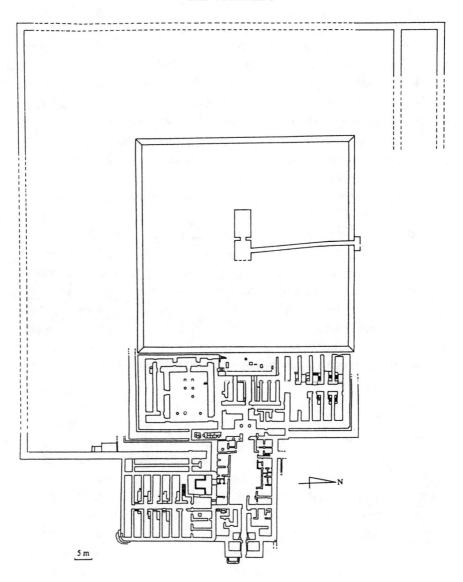

Ground plan of Neferefre's pyramid complex.

sented the royal throne hall in the beyond. In and around the hall fragments of statues of the ruler and many other cult objects were found, including wooden statuettes of captive enemies of Egypt.

The temple and the Unfinished Pyramid were surrounded by a massive brick perimeter wall, whose corners were reinforced with limestone monoliths. However, in contrast to Neferirkare's neighboring complex, these monoliths bore no inscriptions.

The temple was erected during the first stage of the construction of Neferefre's tomb complex, and at the same time the "Sanctuary of the Knife," a slaughter yard that served the needs of the temple cult, was built in front of the southeast wing of the perimeter wall. This is by far the oldest and most unusual example of its kind in Egyptian archaeology.

The Sanctuary of the Knife was built of mudbricks, and its walls had rounded corners. The entrance was on the north. The animals were slaughtered in the open courtyard in the northwest corner, and in the northeast corner the meat was cut up and preserved. A large part of it was dried on the roof terrace. The meat and other supplies were stored in rooms in the central and southern parts of the slaughter yard.

During Niuserre's reign a further large-scale reconstruction of Neferefre's mortuary temple was undertaken that was to give the atypical structure a standard form. The temple was enlarged to the east, and an open, columned courtyard, an entrance hall, and a new, monumental columned entrance were added. The ground plan thus assumed the form of the letter *T*, which was characteristic of mortuary temples from the period.

The new entrance was ornamented by a pair of six-stemmed papyrus columns of limestone. In the courtyard stood twenty-two round wooden columns that may have been meant to imitate palms, as the symbol of live-giving power, fertility, and eternal life.

Because of the unusual circumstances under which the royal tomb complex was finished after Neferefre's premature death, the valley temple and the causeway were not built. Access to the temple from the Nile Valley was either by a detour through Niuserre's and Neferirkare's mortuary temples or from the east, directly across the cemetery where less important members of the royal family and officialdom were buried.

In Djedkare's era, simple brick lodgings for priests stood in the pillared courtyard. Although these priests kept alive the cult of the dead ruler, their constant presence nonetheless resulted in damage to the temple. During the first half of the Sixth Dynasty, the slaughter yard, whose function had already been reduced to the storage of various offerings and materials, was closed. At the end of that dynasty the cult of Neferefre died out, and the temple was abandoned. A revival at the beginning of the Twelfth Dynasty was short-lived.

Shepseskare's (?) Unfinished Pyramid

In the oldest part of Neferefre's mortuary temple, which was not built until after the ruler's death, the previously mentioned seal impressions on clay bearing Shepseskare's Horus name Sekhemkhau were discovered. They indicate that Shepseskare may have been Neferefre's immediate successor—a ruler whose name is attested to only in the king list found in Saqqara. Although in this list he appears as the immediate predecessor of Neferefre, this slight discrepancy can probably be attributed to the disorders of the time and its dynastic disputes. If Shepseskare did reign, then he must have done so very briefly—apparently even more briefly than Neferefre. He may have belonged to the same branch of the royal family as Sahure and Userkaf. If that is the case, the second unfinished pyramid in Abusir, which the Czech archaeological team discovered in the early 1980s, can be attributed to him.

This pyramid lies on the northern edge of the necropolis, halfway between Sahure's pyramid and Userkaf's sun temple. In reality, it consists only of the traces of earthwork halted shortly after it began, which preceded construction of the pyramid itself. In a suitable place, the desert land was leveled out and afterward, in the middle of the square base, the digging of a hole for the burial chamber was begun. The dimensions of the surface allow us to hypothesize that the planned pyramid was to be the largest in Abusir except for that of Neferirkare.

From its location between Sahure's pyramid and Userkaf's sun temple we can infer that the possessor of this unfinished structure was more closely related by his origin to these two rulers than to Neferirkare's family, whose members had had their tombs built in the southern part of the necropolis. Whether Shepseskare had children, and if so, where their tombs are, is not known.

Vivienne Callender has suggested that Shepseskare's consort might have been Queen Nimaathap II, who was buried in the heavily damaged tomb G 4712 in the West Cemetery in Giza. This would not contradict the hypothesis that the ruler had an unfinished pyramid in Abusir; on the contrary, had Shepseskare completed his tomb, his consort would very probably have been buried near it.

Niuserre's Pyramid

In selecting the site for his pyramid complex, Niuserre confronted a difficult task. His predecessor Neferefre had already been forced to move his pyramid deep into the desert in order to respect the basic axis of the necropolis. The cost to Niuserre of constructing his pyramid there would have proven excessive, particularly since he was obliged to complete the unfinished tomb complexes of his closest family members (his father, mother, and elder brother), and to guarantee the maintenance of their regular funerary cult. In addition, he wished to be buried near them.

Niuserre therefore chose the only possible, if also unusual, place, near the north wall of Neferirkare's mortuary temple, which, although it was free, was also hemmed in by existing structures and by the configuration of the area. On the south, it bordered on Neferirkare's mortuary temple; on the north, the ground fell steeply toward Sahure's pyramid; and on the east it fell toward a group of large mastabas that had been built there at the beginning of the Fifth Dynasty. All these topographical and archaeological conditions give Niuserre's pyramid complex, named "The [cult] places of Niuserre are enduring," very specific traits.

Modern archaeological research on Niuserre's pyramid is once again connected with the name of Perring. The Lepsius expedition merely showed the remains of the pyramid complex on its map of the area. A fundamental investigation of the monument was first carried out by Borchardt's expedition at the beginning of the twentieth century. In this connection we should mention an important archaeological discovery that has very little to do with the pyramids in Abusir. In 1902, during the construction of a small road to the pile of excavated material produced during archaeological investigations east of Niuserre's pyramid, the oldest extant Greek literary work was discovered: Timotheus's poem about the battle of Salamis (480 B.C.E.). The Greek papyrus is now in the Egyptian Museum in Berlin.

The pyramid's core consists of seven steps. The stone for its construction probably came from the limestone quarries west of the village of Abusir, about halfway between the Abusir pyramids and the Step Pyramid in Saqqara. The pit for the burial chamber, antechamber, and access corridor was dug out, not through a tunnel, but rather from above. Its location slightly under ground level and under the pyramid's foundation was closely connected with the method of ceiling construction then dominant. The saddle ceiling of the chamber and the antechamber were built of three superimposed layers of huge limestone blocks. In constructing the lowest layer, the blocks were transported overland and set in place from above. Ramps had to be used to lift the blocks for the upper layers to a level of about ten to fifteen meters. Between the layers of ceiling blocks there was a layer of limestone fragments that helped shift the weight, particularly during earthquakes, that bore on the ceiling. This way of using the enormous ceiling blocks was apparently then considered optimal with regard to the labor involved and the static equilibrium of the ceiling. The pyramid's exterior mantle consisted of blocks of fine white limestone. In order to increase its stability, the lowest cornerstones were anchored in the foundation in a special way.

The entrance was at ground level, precisely in the middle of the north side. In front of it no remains of a "north chapel" were found, but it must be pointed out that during his excavations Borchardt obviously did not look for them.

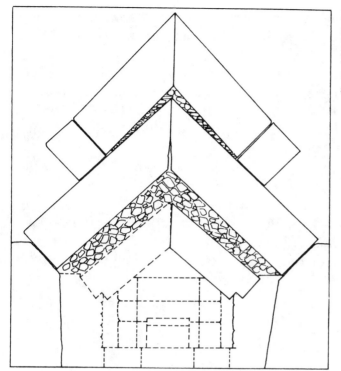

North-south section through the burial chamber of Niuserre's pyramid (after Maragioglio and Rinaldi).

The corridor leading to the burial chamber was lined with fine white limestone and reinforced with pink granite at both ends. About in the middle of the corridor there was a granite barrier with two plugging blocks. The corridor followed an irregular course: first it climbed to the vestibule, and immediately behind the barrier grew larger and turned slightly to the east. At the same time, its slope decreased to about five degrees.

The antechamber and burial chamber lay directly underneath the foundation, on the pyramid's vertical axis. Both were destroyed by stone thieves to the point that it is now almost impossible to reconstruct their architecture. In their ruins Borchardt was unable to find any remains of a burial.

The open, limestone-paved courtyard around the pyramid had an irregular ground plan, the south wing being significantly narrower than the north wing. The cult pyramid, which Borchardt erroneously ascribed to the queen, stood near the southeast corner of the king's pyramid.

Whereas at this time the standard floor plan of a mortuary temple more or less resembled a letter *T*, in the case of Niuserre's mortuary pyramid it resembles instead an inverted letter *L*. This unusual form was determined by the previously mentioned topographical, dynastic, and political circumstances.

The front part of the temple was not oriented east-west, but angled toward the south. Because of the downward-sloping land, a raised foundation surface had to be built for this area. To that end, rough masonry chambers were filled with rubble and sand. Grave robbers damaged this temple even more seriously than Sahure's. Borchardt nonetheless succeeded in reconstructing its ground plan except for certain details.

Ground plan of Niuserre's mortuary and valley temple (after Ricke).

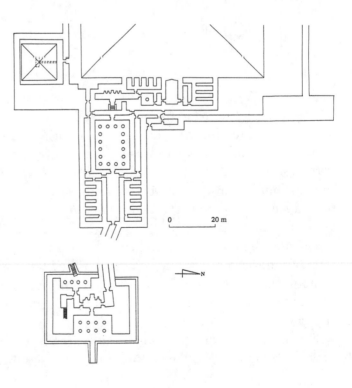

The outer wall of the temple had a slightly inclined face and was topped with a concave cornice. Immediately behind the entrance a staircase led to the roof terrace. The long entrance hall, which was originally vaulted, was paved with basalt, and the dado on the side walls was made of pink granite. Only a few fragments of the limestone walls, which were decorated with reliefs, have been preserved, however. On each side of the hall were five storerooms. The roof of the ambulatory around the open courtyard was supported by sixteen six-stemmed papyrus columns of pink granite. Above the bases, wavy lines in bas-relief on the shafts of the columns produced the illusion of a sheaf of papyrus actually growing in water. The whole hall contributed to the representation of a marshy papyrus grove, which for the ancient Egyptians represented the place where life was constantly renewed. As in Sahure's complex, the middle of the column shafts was decorated with inscriptions containing Niuserre's name and titles as well as symbols representing the north half of the courtyard as under the protection of the cobra goddess Wadjet and the south half as under that of the vulture goddess Nekhbet. The ambulatory's ceiling slabs, which were decorated with stars, produced the illusion of the sky of the underworld. Above all, however, they once protected the rich relief decoration of the side walls, the lower part of which was lined with basalt. In the basalt pavement in the middle of the courtyard there was a small sandstone basin, in which rainwater accumulated. Only fragments of the alabaster altar in the northwest corner were found. The altar was decorated with rows of divinities bringing offerings, scenes of the unification of Upper and Lower Egypt, and other images.

In a deep niche in the northwest corner of the transverse corridor dividing the temple's outer and inner parts, there was, according to Borchardt, a large, pink granite statue of a recumbent lion (fragments of which are now in the Egyptian Museum in Cairo). The statue, which has no peer in the mortuary temples of the Old Kingdom, was supposed to guard the entrance to the inner sanctum. Any reconstruction of the five-niche chapel is very hypothetical because of the extensive damage to this part of the temple.

The transition to the offering hall consists of a small chamber decorated with reliefs; it has an elevated floor, and a column stands in its center. This room, which Lauer named the antichambre carrée because of its square floor plan, here makes its first appearance in the plan of a mortuary temple. It remained a standard component of royal mortuary temples for a long time—until the reign of Senusret I.

The offering hall stood, as was usual for religious reasons, along the east-west axis of the temple, immediately adjoining the pyramid, and had a false door and altar. The vaulted ceiling of the dark hall was decorated with stars in colored bas-relief. On the side walls there were other scenes and inscriptions relating to the ritual sacrifice to the dead. Under the east wall of the hall began a small canal connected with the drainage system east of the temple. North and south of the offering hall were groups of storerooms. The northern group belonged to the hall, the southern group to the five-niche chapel.

In the devastated inner part of the temple a series of relief fragments were found, but in some cases it is difficult to assign them to specific rooms. They came from scenes of the founding of the temple, sacrifices of animals, the delivery of offerings, the ruler fighting with enemies of Egypt, and images of the gods. As in Sahure's temple, there was a secondary entrance. It was near the intersection of the outer and inner parts of the temple and provided direct access from the northeast, that is, from the side where the cemetery with the tombs of Niuserre's family members and officials lay.

In addition to the niche with the lion statue and the antichambre carrée, the architecture of Niuserre's mortuary temple shows two other significant innovations.

One of these is the massive, towerlike structures in the southeast and northeast corners. They are thought to be precursors of the pylons that later became indispensable parts of the monumental entrances into Egyptian temples. The side walls of these corner structures were slightly inclined and topped by a concave cornice. A narrow staircase led to the roof terrace in each.

On the rough limestone blocks from the core of the corner structures were found builders' inscriptions, some of which also contained the name of Sahure's sun temple, "Sahure's sacrifice field." The kings of the Fifth Dynasty erected six sun temples altogether. Userkaf's and Niuserre's have already been discovered. The inscriptions may show

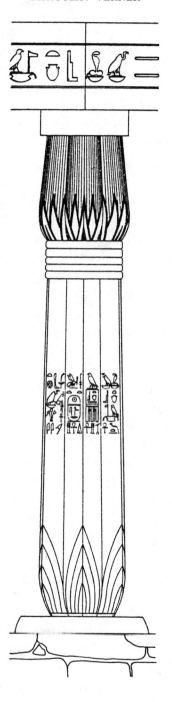

Papyrus column,
Niuserre's mortuary
temple (after
Borchardt).

that the construction material came from Sahure's unfinished (or perhaps already dismantled during Niuserre's reign?) sun temple. This discovery presents archaeology with a further challenge, because it suggests that Sahure's sun temple was not far from the construction site of Niuserre's pyramid. However, these could be blocks that were left over from Sahure's sun temple.

Another innovation that may be closely connected with this discovery is a square platform, about ten meters on a side, adjoining the northeast corner structure. Borchardt could not explain it. In the 1970s, Czech archaeologists working near the southwest corner of Ptahshepses's mastaba, at a point only a few meters from the square surface, found a large, pink granite pyramidion that was originally sheathed in copper and came from an obelisk about ten to fifteen meters high. The platform was probably once its base.

The discovery of blocks with the name of Sahure's sun temple and the large granite obelisk in Niuserre's pyramid complex led to the idea that there might be another, deeper connection between the two structures. The obelisk was the architectonic midpoint of the sun temple, but certainly not that of the mortuary temple. Its appearance in Niuserre's complex is unique. It is entirely possible that the obelisk came from Sahure's sun temple, and that that temple (which may have been unfinished or usurped) became a source of easily accessible building materials for Niuserre's pyramid complex.

During the construction of the causeway and perhaps also of the valley temple, older foundations laid by Neferirkare were used. The lower part of the causeway (about two thirds of it) led toward Neferirkare's pyramid, but the upper part led toward Niuserre's mortuary temple. In its decoration, the causeway originally resembled Sahure's. Borchardt made soundings in only three places here, and therefore it is not impossible that along this causeway, as well as in Sahure's complex, blocks decorated with reliefs still lie undiscovered under the sand.

The causeway had to surmount not only a difference of elevation of slightly more than twenty-eight meters, but also a fairly uneven terrain. It was necessary to build up a relatively high base for the causeway, especially in the upper part. At the beginning of the Twelfth Dynasty, this base was used to build tombs for the priests who served Niuserre's cult. Some tombs were still intact when Borchardt investigated them. The items he found there are now in various German museums, including Herishefhotep's handsome wooden coffin in Leipzig's Egyptian Museum (Inventory no. 3).

The floor of the valley temple was originally more than five meters below the present level of the surrounding land. The foundations for the temple perhaps had already been laid by Neferirkare, next to a canal used for transporting construction materials for the pyramid.

Like Sahure's mortuary temple, Niuserre's had two columned entrances. The west entrance, in front of which was the harbor ramp, was decorated by two colonnades, each of which had four pink granite columns shaped like bundles of six papyrus stems and bearing the name and titles of the ruler, as well as images of the tutelary goddesses Wadjet and Nekhbet. The pavement was made of basalt. On the walls, over the granite dado, there were originally polychrome reliefs. In the west portico, which was reached from outside by a staircase, only four columns stood.

The space in the middle of the valley temple had great religious significance: statues of the ruler may have stood in three niches—one large and two small—in its west wall. Only a few fragments of the reliefs that originally decorated the temple (scenes of the ruler massacring Egypt's enemies and of a goddess suckling the king) have been preserved. The temple contained statues other than those of Niuserre, as is proven by fragments of limestone images of captive enemies of Egypt, an alabaster head of Queen Reputnebu (apparently Niuserre's consort), and a large pink granite statue of a lion also discovered there.

Lepsius Pyramid No. 24

On the southern edge of the pyramid field in Abusir, about fifty meters south of Khentkaues II's pyramid, stand the ruins of two small pyramid complexes. The Lepsius expedition noticed them and gave them the numbers 24 and 25 on its archaeological map. It is truly surprising that some sixty years later another group of German archaeologists led by Borchardt concluded, after a brief examination of the monument identified by Lepsius as "pyramid no. 24," that it was a mastaba, perhaps a double mastaba. The unattractive ruins were ignored until the early 1980s, when the Czech team began to investigate them.

The Czech archaeologists demonstrated that these were the ruins of a small pyramid complex that had been heavily damaged by stone thieves. It consisted of a pyramid, a mortuary temple, and a small cult pyramid. The extensive damage suffered by the pyramid has a positive side: it allows us to examine carefully the pyramid's inner structure in the masonry that has been laid bare both outside and inside. This has been discussed at length above. The name of the vizier Ptahshepses, which appears among countless builders' marks and inscriptions on the masonry, proves that the pyramid was built under his direction—he was the head of all royal works—during the reign of the pharaoh Niuserre.

Ground plan of the pyramid complex known as Lepsius no. 24 (as it appeared in 1995).

N

In the ruins of the burial chamber, amid the remains of the pink granite sarcophagus and bits of rubble from the pyramid core, and near fragments of the burial equipment (miniature symbolic copper objects used for the ritual of the opening of the mouth and alabaster canopic jars), the damaged mummy of a woman about twenty-three years old was found. The mummy bears traces of excerebration, the removal of the brain through the broken nasal septum, and so far as we know, that procedure was not used until the beginning of the Middle Kingdom. The importance of this discovery is still being debated by archaeologists and anthropologists. The archaeological circumstances indicate that it may be the mummy of the pyramid's possessor. However, her name was not found anywhere in the ruins. Since there can be no doubt that the tomb dates from Niuserre's time, she was probably either his consort or his brother Neferefre's.

The plan for the mortuary temple to be built in front of the east wall of the pyramid also confirms that the complex belongs to the queens' tombs. However, during the New Kingdom and the Saite period, the temple was so badly damaged by stone thieves that it is difficult to reconstruct it even theoretically, especially the south part. Since no fragments of reliefs have been discovered, it seems likely that, with the possible exception of the false door, the relief decorations of the temple were not even begun.

The close proximity to another pyramid, Lepsius no. 25, is also puzzling. The latter structure has not yet been investigated, but it also apparently belonged to a queen and was built in the same period. Moreover, even a superficial examination shows that its mortuary temple was almost certainly located not on the east but the west side of the pyramid.

What was the status of these two queens? Was one of them Neferefre's widow, who married his younger brother and successor, Niuserre, after the latter became king? What was the relation of these queens to Niuserre's immediate successors Menkauhor and Djedkare? To these and many other questions fundamental to any explanation of the end of the Fifth Dynasty, we still have no answers. Do they lie in the ruins of the pyramid known as Lepsius no. 25?

Menkauhor's (?) "Headless Pyramid"

Many Egyptian pyramids remain undiscovered. One that written documents prove existed is that of Menkauhor, Niuserre's successor and possibly his son.* Menkauhor was the first Fifth Dynasty ruler to abandon the necropolis in Abusir, even though the extensive desert plateau there was not fully used up, especially in the south. In selecting a new place for the construction of the tomb, named "Divine are the [cult] places of Menkauhor," the issue of the availability of appropriate stone quarries and new workshops for craftsmen obviously played a role.

The completely destroyed pyramid in North Saqqara, which lies on the farthest edge of the desert plateau east of Teti's mortuary temple, is sometimes attributed to Menkauhor. Its lamentable state has led it to be given the unusual, but locally common name, the "Headless Pyramid." No less poetic is the Arabic name for what are thought to be the ruins of its mortuary temple: "Joseph's Prison."

This structure has still not been thoroughly investigated. In 1843, the Lepsius expedition examined it briefly, and gave it the number 30 on its archaeological map. Maspero worked there for a short time in 1881, while he was looking for pyramid texts in the ruins. The first, but unsystematic and very brief, excavations were undertaken in 1930 under Firth's direction. In the rubble of the pit for the burial chamber he found fragments of pink granite and even a sarcophagus lid of bluish gray stone. Although he had no direct proof, he attributed this pyramid to Iti, who was probably one of the ephemeral rulers produced by the Old Kingdom in its final phase.

Lauer and Jean Leclant also expressed opinions regarding the pyramid in connection with their research on Teti's mortuary temple. In their view, during the construction of Teti's complex, the pyramid made it necessary to shift the causeway to the southeast. After investigating

---

* The view that Menkauhor may have been Niuserre's son is based on a few indirect clues taken from the relief decoration of Khentkaues II's mortuary temple.

Clay sealing with the impression of Menkauhor's name, which was found in Neferefre's mortuary temple.

the masonry type and other details, they decided that the pyramid was built in the Fifth Dynasty and may have belonged to Menkauhor.

Maragioglio and Rinaldi arrived at similar conclusions. They noted that the trench for the access corridor leading to the burial chamber did not lie precisely on the north-south axis, but was offset to the east. As we have already mentioned, this was a peculiarity of Fifth Dynasty pyramids in the time between Neferirkare and Djedkare.* This dating could be further supported by the fact that no fragments of pyramid texts were found in the ruins; it is well known that pyramid texts first appeared on the walls of underground chambers in Unas's time.

In the late 1970s Jocelyn Berlandini again tried to determine to whom this pyramid belonged. She evaluated the previous archaeological observations and especially the written sources from the Old and New Kingdoms proving that Menkauhor was worshiped in North Saqqara, and arrived at the opinion that the Headless Pyramid really belonged to this king. However, the text of the previously mentioned decree from Dahshur presents certain difficulties for Berlandini's argument. In it, Menkauhor's pyramid is mentioned in a context suggesting that it was located in Dahshur, and this led Stadelmann to suggest

---

* It is later proven only in Senusret I's pyramid in Lisht.

that the pyramid's remains might be buried in the ruins of the large building northeast of the Red Pyramid, which Lepsius had already thought to be a pyramid—no. 50 in his numbering.

Finally, Jaromír Málek has also worked on the Headless Pyramid. He was led to do so by a fragment of an inscription British archaeologists found on a piece of mortar near the pyramid. Although it cannot be considered direct evidence, Málek completed the text and sees it as proof that the pyramid of the later king Merikare immediately adjoined Teti's. Like Berlandini, he cites a number of indirect grounds for this view, particularly written documents that come from North Saqqara and are connected with the worship of the deceased Merikare. However, his interesting argument does not take into account the structural peculiarity to which Maragioglio and Rinaldi drew attention. The Headless Pyramid is thus destined to remain enigmatic until archaeological investigation can reveal its secret. But wherever Menkauhor's pyramid lies hidden, it is clear that neither he nor the other rulers of the Fifth Dynasty succeeded in founding a new necropolis.

Djedkare's Pyramid

Djedkare, Menkauhor's successor, is thought to have been his son. However, the two rulers may have been brothers (Niuserre's sons) or even cousins (sons of Neferefre and Niuserre).

If this is so, it could be a further sign of the impending end of the Fifth Dynasty. Whatever Djedkare's origin was, his claim to the throne was apparently strongly supported by his royal consort. At least this is how the meaning of the next major queen's pyramid complex to be discussed is interpreted.

Djedkare's pyramid in South Saqqara was originally called "Beautiful is Djedkare," but today the local people call it *Haram el-Shawaf,* the "Sentinel Pyramid." Perring investigated it, and shortly afterward so did the scholars of the Lepsius expedition. In 1880, Maspero made his way into its substructure, in order to look for pyramid texts. A systematic archaeological investigation was not begun until the mid-1940s, and it suffered a series of misfortunes. First Alexandre Varille and Abdel Salam Hussain examined it; but their work was interrupted at the end of the 1940s, and the documentation of the excavation was lost. Much the same happened after Fakhry's investigations at the beginning of the 1950s.

In the mid-1980s the Egyptian archaeologist Mahmud Abdel Razek carried out excavations in the area around the causeway and the mortuary temple. A few fragments of reliefs, which Fakhry had already discovered and put in storage, were published by another Egyptian archaeologist, Muhammad Mursi. The valley temple, whose ruins lie under the first houses of the village of Saqqara at the edge of the Nile Valley, was not archaeologically researched at all. However, it is already clear that the reconstruction of some parts of the pyramid complex from the excavations carried out up to this point would be extremely difficult, because of the damage it has suffered (especially the mortuary temple) and the incomplete state of the documentation.

In comparison to the pyramids in Abusir, under Djedkare and his successors a significant conceptual change occurred. One immediately notices a striking difference in the way the core is constructed. The megalithism characteristic of the Fourth Dynasty, and to a lesser extent of the Fifth Dynasty as well, becomes less prominent from this time on. The core was built using small, irregular pieces of limestone bound with clay mortar to form steps about seven meters high. There were originally six steps; today the upper three steps no longer exist, so that the remainder of the pyramid reaches a height of only about twenty-four meters. Most of the casing of fine white limestone has long since been hauled off by thieves. Nonetheless, on some parts of the pyramid, such as the north side, it has been preserved in remarkably good condition.

The entrance was on the north, but was located not, as had been usual, in the wall of the pyramid, but rather in the pavement of the courtyard in front of it, about two and one-half meters west of the north-south axis. Over it originally stood the north chapel, of which only inconspicuous traces remain. The small ceiling block decorated with stars that now lies near the entrance may have come from this chapel.

Djedkare's pyramid is the last of those whose access corridor was angled slightly to the east. It descends until it comes out in a small vestibule, in which shards of broken vessels were found. Thus it is possible that certain concluding burial rituals (such as the "breaking of red vessels") were performed there. Behind the vestibule the corridor begins to run horizontally, and right at the beginning there is a barrier made of pink granite, consisting of three huge plugging blocks. At the end of the corridor, near the entrance to the antechamber, one finds the last granite barrier.

In contrast to earlier conceptions, the ruler's funerary apartment consisted of three rooms. In addition to the antechamber and burial chamber, there was another room with three niches used for storage. The saddle ceilings of the antechamber and the burial chamber (the storeroom had a flat ceiling) were constructed of three superimposed layers of huge limestone blocks—as in those in the pyramids of Abusir already described. A sarcophagus of dark gray basalt originally stood on the west wall of the burial chamber. It once contained the king's mummy, with its head to the north. In front of the southeast corner of the sarcophagus was a small, square hole in the floor, in which the alabaster canopic jars were buried.

The underground spaces in Djedkare's pyramid were badly damaged by stone thieves, and it is difficult to reconstruct their original plan. Only fragments of the sarcophagus and the canopic vessels were found. The remains of the mummified body of a man about fifty years old were discovered in the pile of rubble in the burial chamber.

In view of the fact that the descending corridor is still partly blocked by the original barrier, because thieves went around it, the mummy must have been Djedkare's, and not one intrusively buried at a later time. A few dates on papyri recently discovered in Neferefre's mortuary temple in Abusir show, however, that Djedkare reigned more than thirty years, which suggests that he lived to an advanced age. Can we assume that Djedkare was very young when he ascended the throne? This supposition is only one of many related to the obscure period between Niuserre's and Djedkare's reigns.

Since the desert in front of the pyramid's east side sloped sharply downward, the ground had to be extensively prepared before the mortuary temple's foundations could be laid. The east facade of the mortuary temple was ornamented by two massive, towerlike structures. They had square ground plans, and, as usual, their walls were slightly inclined. There were probably no rooms inside them, but there may have been an exterior staircase leading to the roof terrace. The function of the towers remains for the time being unclear. They were

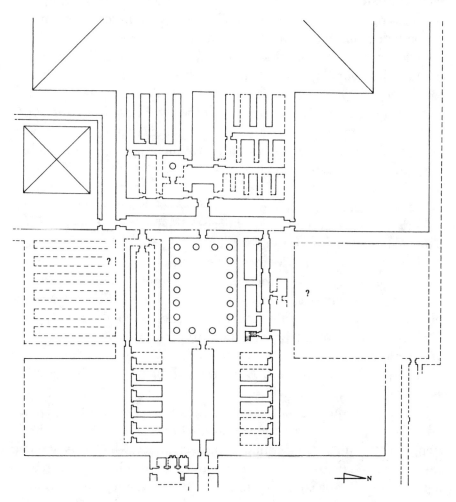

Ground plan of Djedkare's mortuary temple (after Maragioglio and Rinaldi).

probably erected on the model of similar structures in Niuserre's mortuary temple.

To judge by the massive side walls, the temple's entrance hall had a vaulted ceiling. On each side there were six storerooms, and the alabaster pavement continued in the open, columned courtyard. There were, as in Sahure's mortuary temple, sixteen pink granite palm columns bearing the ruler's name and titles. A low staircase in the middle of the west wall of the transverse corridor gave access to the inner part of the temple. From there, a passage led into the offering hall, first passing through the five-niche chapel and the antichambre carrée. The latter's ceiling was supported by palm columns in pink granite bearing Djedkare's name and titles. There was also an image of Nekhbet, because this room lay south of the temple's main axis and was therefore under the protection of the tutelary goddess of Upper Egypt.

The arrangement and decoration of the offering hall do not essentially differ from those of the preceding pyramid complexes of the Fifth Dynasty. However, its western part, in which there was originally a false door, was incorporated directly into the masonry of the pyramid. The inner sanctum was surrounded on both sides by a large number of storerooms.

Little is known about the relief decoration because of the extensive damage done to the temple by stone thieves and the loss of the documentation of the discoveries made there. From the fragments of scenes showing offering bearers, processions of personified mortuary estates, the ruler, and divinities, we can conclude, however, that the pictorial program of Djedkare's pyramid complex reflected contemporary standards in both artistic quality and the workmanship of the reliefs. Some archaeologists think the use of kinds of stone that were more difficult to quarry and transport (for example, basalt and pink granite) shows that the king's treasury was running out of resources.

The cult pyramid in front of the southeast corner of the king's pyramid also did not surpass the standards of the time. It had a three-stepped core, and the single subterranean chamber, which was oriented east-west and lay just under ground level, was reached by a descending corridor that began in the middle of the pyramid's north wall. It was surrounded by a small perimeter wall.

The causeway did not run precisely east-west but rather deviated slightly to the south. South of the causeway, there was a terrace ending at a small building near the facade of the mortuary temple, of which nothing remains but the alabaster pavement. In the 1980s, Razek discovered on the north edge of the upper part of the causeway a necropolis for sacred snakes that presumably dates from the Late Period.

Varille's excavations on the grounds of the valley temple were broken off soon after they began. According to a later report by Leslie Grinsell and Fakhry, remains of walls with reliefs on them were discovered in situ. A few pink granite blocks were also found scattered among the houses in the nearby village.

Up to this point, the area around Djedkare's pyramid has not been thoroughly examined archaeologically, but a brief, superficial examination shows that it contained private tombs and perhaps other structures as well. In this connection we should also mention the cemetery that the Czech team discovered in the mid-1970s south of Niuserre's causeway in Abusir. In it were buried Djedkare's less important relatives, including his daughters, his son, and a few of his officials. Why weren't they buried instead near the king's pyramid in South Saqqara?

This discovery reminds us of how little we know about the reasons or rules determining the choice of a site for a tomb or the establishment of a cemetery. In the case of Djedkare's daughter Khekeretnebti and other princesses, however, this choice may not have been made on mysterious political or social grounds. Djedkare devoted considerable attention to Abusir, the maintenance of his tomb and temple, and the reorganization of the worship of his predecessors. Thus the workshops and construction facilities located at this site may have led him to erect there the tombs just mentioned. This would certainly have made it easier to establish the new technical infrastructure required for the construction of his own pyramid complex in South Saqqara.

The Pyramid of the "Unknown Queen"

At the northeast corner of the wall surrounding Djedkare's pyramid and mortuary temple lies another, smaller pyramid complex. It has neither a valley temple nor a causeway and consists only of a pyramid, a mortuary temple, and its own perimeter wall. Because of its location and especially its structural incorporation into Djedkare's complex, it is highly likely that it belonged to the royal consort. However, her name was not found on the fragments of reliefs discovered at this pyramid complex and at Djedkare's. Callender has asked whether Djedkare's consort might have been Meresankh IV, the mother of Prince Raemka. However, her tomb is in Saqqara (Mariette, D5), north of the Step Pyramid. Did this pyramid belong to another of Djedkare's consorts?

Both Perring and Lepsius briefly investigated and described this monument. The first thorough archaeological examination was begun by Fakhry in 1952, but it was not finished. Thus such basic though incomplete information as we have concerning this structure we owe to Maragioglio and Rinaldi, who worked on it in the 1960s.

The pyramid originally had a three-stepped core, which was erected in a way similar to that of Djedkare's neighboring pyramid. In its ruins, there now yawns a crater, into which a deeper trench leads from the north.

The plan of the mortuary temple has a number of original elements improvised to adapt the standard norms to the local conditions. The temple was entered from the west, and this was determined both by its location and by the desire to connect it with the king's neighboring mortuary temple. To this end the temple was also provided with a special, "northern" columned portico. Between the generally inconspicuous entrance and the open, columned courtyard of the queen's temple there was a hall in whose center five columns of fine white limestone, shaped like six papyrus stems, were aligned in a single row.

The open courtyard, which contained sixteen six-stemmed papyrus columns in limestone, was oriented north-south. Like the temple as a whole, it did not lie on the pyramid's axis. The side walls of the courtyard were originally decorated with reliefs. To the north there was a group of ten storerooms. A transverse corridor divided this area from the inner part of the temple. However, how the spaces were arranged is not at all clear; apparently, the offering hall was located

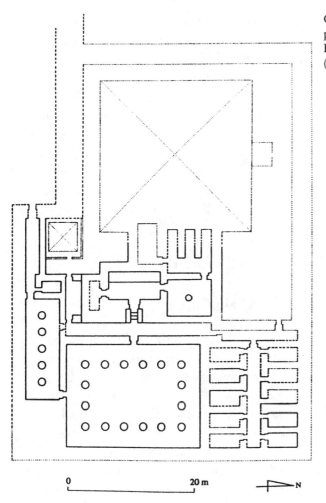

Ground plan of the
pyramid complex of
Djedkare's consort (?)
(after Jánosi).

0   20 m   N

in the middle, and north of it were three niches. The complex also
included a small cult pyramid, which stood at the southeast corner of
the queen's pyramid.

The ground plan of this small pyramid complex was influenced by
Djedkare's neighboring complex, and partly by those of Niuserre and
Neferirkare. As Jánosi has pointed out, it does not correspond to the
ground plans of other contemporary queens' tombs. However, there
can be little doubt that it was basically a tomb for Djedkare's consort. The temple's size, structure, and originality all indicate that it

belonged to someone of high social standing. According to Klaus Baer (1930–1987), the demonstrable improvements and reworkings of some of the reliefs indicate that the queen herself may have ruled for a time after the death of her husband, Djedkare, and the coronation of (her son?) Unas. In Klaus Baer's view, it was Djedkare's marriage to this woman that legitimated his ascent to the throne—something that was not unusual in Egyptian history. In either case, her tomb would have reflected her dynastic significance. However that may be, as another Fifth Dynasty queen's pyramid complex, this tomb indirectly shows the growing role played by queens, and especially by the queen mother, in the turbulent social relationships of the time.

Unas's Pyramid

Unas's pyramid is the smallest built in the Old Kingdom, but in a certain sense it is also the finest. The inscriptions that have come to be known as pyramid texts first appeared on the walls of its subterranean chambers.*

This pyramid, which was once proudly called "Beautiful are the [cult] places of Unas," now looks like a small heap of stones cowering in the shadow of the famous Step Pyramid. However, it did not escape the attention—if only fleeting—of Perring and, shortly thereafter, of Lepsius. The latter gave it the number 35 on his archaeological map of the pyramid fields. The subterranean chambers remained unexamined until 1881, when Maspero, excited by the pyramid texts he had recently found in Pepi I's and Merenre I's pyramids, forced his way into them.

A systematic archaeological investigation of the pyramid and its surroundings was undertaken in 1899 by Alexandre Barsanti, at Maspero's behest, and he continued it until 1901. His work was very

---

* However, these inscriptions were first found in Pepi I's pyramid in South Saqqara.

successful, for he was able to partially excavate the mortuary temple as well as other unexpected but very important structures on its grounds—especially the subterranean galleries of royal tombs from the Second Dynasty and large shaft graves from the Late Period.

Unfortunately, the ultimate investigation of Unas's mortuary temple and pyramid complex was conducted in an unsystematic manner and only with great difficulty. The excavation of the temple, which Barsanti did not finish, was initially continued by Firth, from 1929 until his premature death in 1931, and then from 1936 to 1939 by Lauer. From 1937 to 1949 the Egyptian archaeologists Hassan, Goneim, and Hussain conducted excavations, primarily in the area of Unas's causeway. At the upper edge of the causeway, Hussain found a pair of boat pits lined in limestone. In the 1970s Ahmad Musa continued the work of his Egyptian colleague by excavating the lower half of the causeway and the valley temple.

The relatively small size of Unas's pyramid can hardly be explained by time limitations, since the king might have reigned for at least fifteen years. It is more likely that the resources at his disposal decreased. The core consisted of six layers, built of rough blocks of local limestone that became gradually smaller as they neared the top of the pyramid. The casing was made, as usual, of carefully dressed blocks

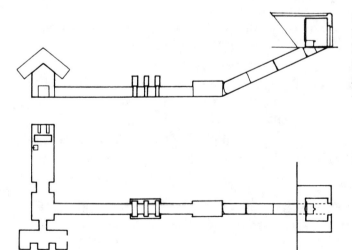

Substructure of Unas's pyramid. North-south sectional view and ground plan (after Lauer).

of fine white limestone. At the lowest levels, the casing has remained partly in place, and it was later rebuilt, especially on the south side. This was done—as in the case of other monuments in Saqqara—during the era of Prince Khamuaset, who had an inscription put on the south side of the pyramid that Lauer was able partially to reconstruct from fragments.

The entrance into the descending corridor originally lay under the north chapel, of which only a few traces remain. It is a single room on whose south wall, the one adjacent to the pyramid, stood a stela and, in front of it, an altar in the shape of the hieroglyphic sign for *hetep* (offering table).

The ground plan of the substructure resembled that of Djedkare's pyramid. As in earlier pyramids of this era, there was a gabled ceiling over the antechamber and burial chamber. On the west wall of the burial chamber, which was sheathed in alabaster and painted to resemble the royal palace facade (five colors were used: white, black, yellow, blue, and red), stood a greywacke sarcophagus.* In both chambers pyramid texts were written on the remaining walls. They were chiseled in bas-relief and colored greenish blue, which symbolized both mourning and belief in rebirth. The ceiling was decorated with yellow stars on a blue background. It is noteworthy that the stars in the burial chamber and the antechamber point toward the zenith, whereas those in the corridor point toward the north.

A canopic chest was originally sunk in the floor at the southeast corner of the sarcophagus. Only a few insignificant remains of the king's burial were found—in the burial chamber a couple of fragments of a mummy (parts of the right arm, the skull, and the shinbone) and in the serdab the wooden handles of two small knives used during the ritual of the opening of the mouth.

Like the substructure, the ground plan of Unas's mortuary temple also resembles that of Djedkare's, with the exception of a pink gran-

* A thorough petrographic analysis recently made by French archaeologists in Saqqara showed that in this case and in that of some of the other Sixth Dynasty pyramids in Saqqara, the material used was not basalt, as had been previously assumed.

ite gateway bearing hieroglyphic inscriptions of the name and titles of Unas's successor, Teti—clear proof that this part of the temple was completed after the ruler's death. Passing through the vaulted, alabaster-paved entrance hall, whose sides were decorated with reliefs depicting the delivery of offerings, one reached an open courtyard. The roof of the ambulatory was supported by eighteen palm columns in pink granite, two more than in Sahure's and Djedkare's complexes. The high artistic quality of these columns is indirectly shown by their afterlife: some of them were reused, presumably many centuries later, in buildings in Tanis in the east delta, the Egyptian capital during the Twenty-First and Twenty-Second Dynasties, while others are now in the Louvre and in the British Museum. The once sumptuous relief decorations had a similar fate, as shown by blocks with relief depictions of Unas found in Amenemhet I's pyramid complex in Lisht.

The storerooms, which were grouped in pairs, were not symmetrically aligned, as in Sahure's complex, but surrounded somewhat irregularly the entrance hall and the open courtyard. There were twice as many in the north section as in the south. In the Late Period, large shaft tombs were built in this area.

A low staircase in the west wall of the transverse corridor—the intersection between the columned courtyard, the cult pyramid, the courtyard surrounding the pyramid, and the inner part of the temple— led into the five-niche chapel, of which nothing now remains. One then passed through the antichambre carrée (also completely destroyed) into the offering hall. Here probably stood another palm column of brownish quartzite, fragments of which were found during excavations in the southwest part of the temple.

Except for the remains of a pink granite false door, little from the offering hall has been preserved. The hieroglyphic inscription on the false door refers to the tutelary divinities protecting the souls of residents of Nekhen (on the south side) and Buto (on the north side). A block from this door is now in the Egyptian Museum in Cairo.

The five-niche chapel and the sacrifice hall were surrounded by more storerooms; again, more of them were on the north side than on the south side. Near the southeast corner of the main pyramid stood a

Ground plan of Unas's
pyramid and mortuary
temple (after Lauer).

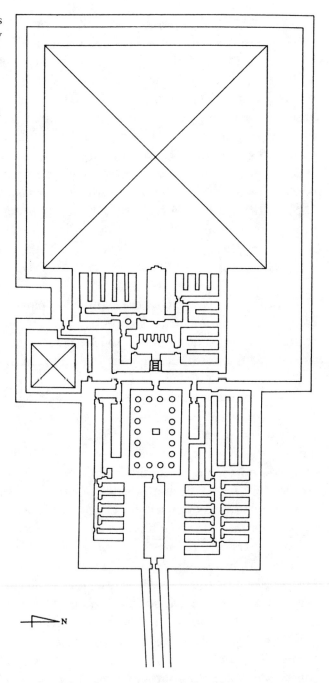

N

small cult pyramid. Around both was a massive stone perimeter wall more than seven meters high.

The causeway was more than 720 meters long. In constructing it, Unas may have appropriated about 250 meters of Djoser's older approach causeway. The causeway was not straight, but made two turns, and this suggests that at the time it had to surmount particularly uneven terrain on which there were already some buildings. A few older structures were torn down and their stone used in the causeway's underlayment. Because of this "ruthlessness," during excavations in the 1970s the Egyptian archaeologist Mousa was able to find blocks that allowed him to reconstruct completely the small but marvelous and historically important "tomb of the two brothers," Niankhkhnum and Khnumhotep, which was richly decorated with relief scenes and inscriptions. The originality of its decoration has made it one of the main tourist attractions in Saqqara.

The causeway's inner walls were decorated with thematically varied scenes in polychrome bas-relief: hunting in the wilderness (for lions, leopards, giraffes), boats transporting granite palm columns and architraves from Aswan to the pyramid construction site, battles with Asian enemies, transport of prisoners, and so on. One of these scenes showed impoverished Bedouins that hunger had reduced to skin and bones. Until recently, this scene was considered unique proof of the decline of the standard of living among oasis dwellers in the Egyptian desert that resulted from the ending of the so-called Neolithic subpluvial period and the beginning of an arid, hot climate in the middle of the third millennium B.C.E. However, a few years ago a similar but older and artistically more valuable scene was discovered on blocks from Sahure's causeway. It seems that the scene in Unas's causeway does not indicate a decline in the standard of living among the Bedouins in his era; they may have even been brought into the pyramid town to demonstrate the dangers and hardships the pyramid builders had to contend with in bringing better qualities of stone from the remote, undeveloped mountain areas.

One of the components of Unas's complex was a structure in the form of a pair of boats forty-five meters long, which was located south of the upper part of the causeway. It was made of white limestone

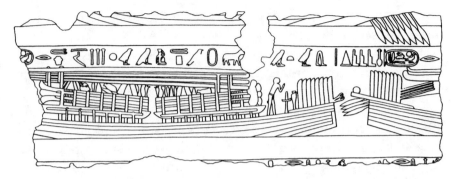

In the causeway leading to Unas's mortuary temple the transportation of granite columns from Aswan to the pyramid building site in Saqqara was depicted. The inscription accompanying the scene reads: "[I brought granite pillars from?] Elephantine for his majesty Unas within seven days. . . . His majesty praised me for this."

blocks and probably contained two slender wooden boats with curved keels symbolizing the day and night vessels of the sun god.

Mousa investigated the valley temple; here, as in the case of the causeway, he was continuing earlier Egyptian excavations begun in the 1940s. On the terrace near the temple, he found a sarcophagus of dark greywacke with a lid ornamented with a concave cornice, which strikingly resembled those of Menkaure and Shepseskaf. In it was the mummy of an elderly man, which had been partly damaged by grave robbers. The inscription on a golden belt (now on exhibit in the Egyptian Museum in Cairo, JE 87078) identified the man as "the king's son Ptahshepses." The British archaeologist Guy Brunton (1878–1948) therefore suggested that Ptahshepses's tomb, as that of Unas's son, was placed near the temple but was robbed by thieves shortly after his burial there. The guardians of the necropolis would then have buried the sarcophagus with the mummy in a safer place in Unas's temple.

Another British archaeologist, Aidon Dodson, recently expressed a different opinion regarding this discovery. He maintains that Ptahshepses was the son of Pepi II and Queen Ankhesenpepi (IV?) and was one of the "new poor," the impoverished aristocracy at the declining royal court in Memphis during the Seventh and Eighth Dynasties. According to Dodson, Ptahshepses appropriated a sarcophagus from the Fourth Dynasty tomb near the Mastabat Fara'un and had himself buried in it in Unas's temple. In doing so, he followed his mother's example, who had had herself buried in the storeroom of Queen Iput II's small pyramid complex in South Saqqara.

Dodson's theory is very daring. Why should Ptahshepses not have had himself buried in South Saqqara, where the Mastabat Fara'un and the tombs of Pepi II and Ankhesenpepi are located? Why would he have undertaken the difficult task of transporting the heavy sarcophagus to Unas's temple, a few kilometers to the north, where at precisely that time Pepi II's complex, as well as the nearby complex of Pepi I, were important centers of the Memphis necropolis? Moreover, no other tombs built during the Fourth Dynasty have been found near the Mastabat Fara'un. Neither Dodson's nor Brunton's theory is ultimately satisfactory. Unfortunately, a better explanation is not yet available.

Unas's consorts Nebet and Khenut were buried not in pyramids, but rather in mastabas northeast of the king's pyramid. One peculiarity of Nebet's mastaba is its chapel with four niches, one of which has a cartouche with Unas's name. A statue of the king may have stood in it, whereas in each of the other three niches there was a statue of the queen.

CHAPTER SEVEN

THE SIXTH DYNASTY—THE END OF AN ERA

The Horus name of Unas's son or son-in-law (?) and successor Teti, the founder of the Sixth Dynasty, meant "He who reconciled both lands." Does this indicate, despite the lack of proof, that at the end of the Fifth Dynasty difficulties in internal or dynastic politics arose that threatened the country's unity?

Artifacts and written sources inform us about contacts with the surrounding world and with traditional trading partners. Further expeditions were sent to the quarries in the Egyptian mountains to get precious stones. Teti had a pyramid complex built for himself in Saqqara. All around the valley temple a large settlement grew up that during the Ninth and Tenth Dynasties became an important administrative center and perhaps also the temporary residence of the so-called Heracleopolitan kings. According to Manetho, Teti was assassinated. Userkare, about whom contemporary sources say little and who apparently ruled for only a short time, may have tried to exploit the situation. However, Teti's son, Pepi I, finally ascended the throne. During his half-century reign, the central state power further declined. The ruler tried to oppose this development by strengthening his family connections with provincial nobles, who had in the meantime gained influence and become highly independent. He married two of the Abydos magnate Khui's daughters, and their brother Djau was made vizier.

The unsuccessful conspiracy mounted against Pepi I within his own harem reflected the unstable political situation in the realm and the increasing rivalry among various interest groups. The judge Uni, who later led a military campaign in Palestine, was assigned to investigate the case and to conduct a hearing with the queen. The increased attention Egypt was obliged to pay to its southern border at this time is also shown by the report of a trip made by Merenre I, Pepi I's eldest son, in order to receive a tribute from the Nubian princes.

Pepi I's pyramid complex in South Saqqara, which included some small pyramid complexes for his queens (four have been found thus far) as well as at least one prince's tomb, was called *Men-nefer-Pepi,* "Pepi's splendor is enduring." A large town grew up all around the valley temple. At the end of the Old Kingdom and the beginning of the Middle Kingdom, the center gradually shifted to the larger agglomeration around the fortress of the White Walls. The Greek name Memphis was based on the abbreviation *Mennefer* and gradually came to be used as the name of the whole capital of Egypt.

Even as a child, Pepi II, the youngest son of Pepi I, probably ruled jointly with his older brother Merenre I. After the latter's premature death, however, the real power was held by Pepi II's mother, Ankhesenmerire II, and her brother Djau, since the successor to the throne was still underage.

The famed expeditions to Nubia, which we know about from the inscriptions in the rock-cut tombs of the Elephantine princes in Qubbet el-Hawa, near Aswan, occurred in Pepi II's time. However, even these internal political measures could no longer do anything to stop the progressive decline of the ancient Egyptian state. On the contrary, during Pepi II's long reign, the provincial nobility became even more autonomous and acted largely independently of the king.

Pepi II's pyramid complex is the last large royal tomb of the Old Kingdom, and it became a source of inspiration for the architects of the Middle Kingdom. It included three small pyramid complexes for his consorts—Neith, Iput II, and Udjebten.

Pepi II reigned longer than any other Egyptian ruler, even though there is still no consensus regarding the interpretation of the dates. Egyptologists' estimates of the length of his reign range between ninety-four and "only" sixty-four years. After his death, the Sixth Dynasty did not immediately end, but events in Egypt took a dramatic course. Another phase of political instability followed that led to the collapse of the country's unity and brought with it serious economic difficulties. It is generally called the First Intermediate Period.

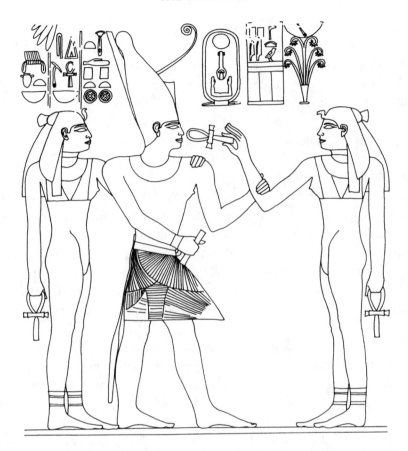

Pepi II receives the symbol of life from the tutelary goddesses of Upper and Lower Egypt, Nekhbet and Wadjet. Detail from a relief decoration in Pepi II's pyramid temple in Saqqara (reconstruction of the scene after Jéquier).

Teti's Pyramid

The northernmost pyramid in Saqqara is now a small, easily acces-sible hill, from the top of which is a panoramic view of the whole necropolis. In looking at the inconspicuous remains of the mortuary temple, one may be overcome by the feeling of skepticism and irony sometimes produced by history, for this pyramid complex was once called "Teti's [cult] places are enduring."

It is generally assumed that Teti's predecessor, Unas, was also his father. However, Altenmüller suggests that his father was Shepesipuptah, a man of noble but not royal origin. Teti's mother is supposed to be Queen Sesheshet.

The history of modern research on the monument follows the familiar pattern: Perring investigated it in 1839, and Lepsius in 1842–1843. Maspero, driven by his desire to find pyramid texts, made his way inside it in 1882. Copies of the inscriptions inside the pyramid were made by the German Émile Brugsch (1842–1930), by the Frenchman Urbain Bouriant (1849–1903), and partly by the American Charles Wilbour. More systematic investigation, though interrupted for long periods, began in the early twentieth century. In 1905 Quibell made a thorough examination of the pyramid and continued his work there until 1908, before shifting his excavations to the Coptic monastery of St. Jeremiah, south of Unas's causeway. From 1920 to 1924, Firth uncovered a major part of the mortuary temple. Since the early 1950s Sainte Fare Garnot, Lauer, and Leclant have continued these excavations.

The pyramid's core had five levels, and the underground part looked very much like those of Djedkare's and Unas's pyramids. The entrance into the subterranean part of the pyramid was under the north chapel, in the pavement of the courtyard at the foot of the pyramid's north wall. Both ends of the corridor were sheathed with pink granite, whereas the main barrier consisted of three granite plugging blocks in the middle of its horizontal part.

The antechamber and the burial chamber adjoining it on the west also had gabled ceilings made of three layers of huge limestone blocks. The apex of the lowest layer was slightly above the base of the pyramid. On the west wall of the burial chamber stood the sarcophagus, which was long ago plundered along with the tomb furnishings. It was originally decorated with gilded inscriptions, but its lower part was not entirely finished. In the rubble in the burial chamber, only the blackened remains of an arm and shoulder that might have come from the king's mummy were found, together with a fragment of a small alabaster tablet bearing the names of the so-called seven sacred oils. A small hole in the floor near the southeast corner of the sarcophagus once held a canopic chest. The walls behind the sarcophagus and part of its north and south sides were painted to resemble the royal palace facade. In contrast to Unas's burial chamber, however, the wall thus decorated was not of alabaster but of limestone. In this and similar cases it would be more appropriate to speak of a stylized representation of the original fortified facade—a representation that was closely connected with the religious and magical conception of protection and security. The walls of the antechamber and burial chamber are ornamented with pyramid texts, and the ceiling once again imitates a starry sky, though here the stars are all oriented toward the east. The serdab, which is located east of the antechamber, as it is in Unas's pyramid, has three deep niches and is undecorated.

The open courtyard around the pyramid is surrounded by a limestone perimeter wall. In the northwest part of the courtyard, Firth discovered a square shaft about forty meters deep, which may have served as a well during the construction of the pyramid.

Neither the temple nor the causeway (originally about three hundred meters long) from Teti's pyramid have been archaeologically investigated. They too were located not to the east but to the southwest of the pyramid, as is clearly shown by the orientation of the upper causeway uncovered along with the mortuary temple. Apparently, this anomaly resulted from respect for the large structures already standing east of the pyramid, in particular the Headless Pyramid, and perhaps also from the intention to orient the causeway in the direction of the royal palace in the valley, as Audran Labrousse assumes.

In the arrangement of its spaces, the mortuary temple follows the line of development marked out by Djedkare's and Unas's temples. The basic parts and their position were not changed, but the overall number of storerooms increased, and a symmetrical order prevails throughout the temple area.

A peculiarity of Teti's mortuary temple connected with the causeway's bend to the southeast is a small courtyard along the south part of the east facade. The entrance hall began in the middle of this courtyard and had a heavy, single-panel, wooden door with a quartzite

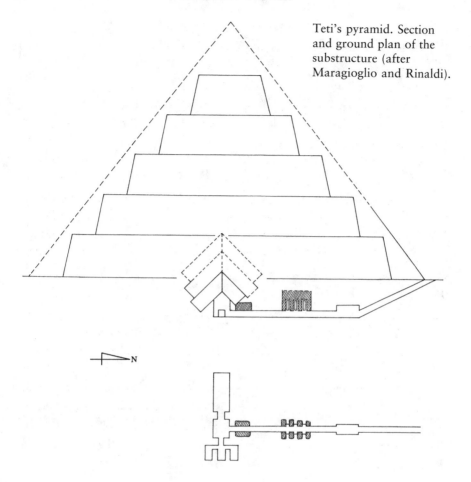

Teti's pyramid. Section and ground plan of the substructure (after Maragioglio and Rinaldi).

doorstep. In its shape and pictorial program, the hall follows the preceding pattern of development, since once again it is a long, narrow room about five and one half meters high with a vaulted ceiling decorated with stars, illuminated only by a small opening in the east wall. Very little remains of the reliefs that once decorated the side walls. The paving was of alabaster.

The open courtyard was surrounded by eighteen pink granite pillars; all but the corner pillars were square. On the courtyard side, they bore the king's name and titles in deep relief. The walls of the ambulatory were originally decorated with scenes and inscriptions in polychrome

Ground plan of Teti's pyramid
and mortuary temple (after
Lauer and Leclant).

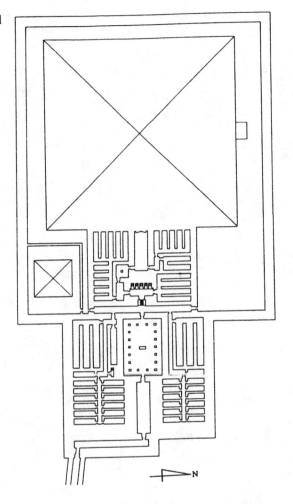

bas-relief, and in the middle of the courtyard stood a low stone altar.
The entrance hall and the courtyard were surrounded by symmetrically arranged storerooms. The walls of the transverse corridor were
originally ornamented with reliefs showing the ruler and the gods,
the sed festival, and the defeat of Egypt's enemies. A low staircase
in the middle of the west wall gave access to the five-niche chapel, to
the antichambre carrée (its ceiling was once supported by a quartzite
pillar), and, through the latter, to the offering hall. Of the false door
in the west wall of the offering hall, only the huge, monolithic, quartz-

ite base remains. Themes of sacrifice dominated the original relief decorations; of these, too, only fragments have been preserved. The religious sites in the inner part of the temple—the five-niche chapel, the antichambre carrée, and the offering hall—were surrounded on both sides by storerooms.

The cult pyramid, enclosed by its own perimeter wall, stands near the southeast corner of the pyramid, as was usual at this time. In the pavement of the surrounding courtyard, there were quartzite basins for libations. The valley temple has not yet been excavated.

All around the pyramid a large necropolis grew up. In it are the small pyramid complexes of Teti's consorts Khuit and Iput I, as well as the tombs of the famous viziers Mereruka and Kagemni, in which marvelous reliefs have been preserved.

Lauer has recounted an absurd episode from Firth's everyday research on this pyramid complex. Firth was lending the talented English philologist Battiscomb Gunn a hand, especially in preparing and publishing written documents. The families of the two archaeologists were living in Saqqara, in houses built on the excavation site. The Firths had two small dogs, Penny and Guinea, and the Gunns had one. One day Mrs. Firth went for a walk with her dogs and visited

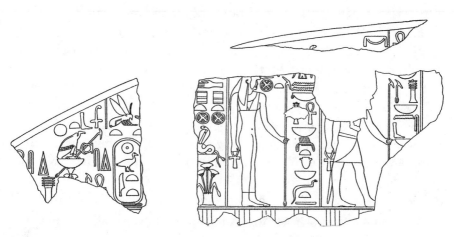

Fragment of a relief from the tympanum on the west wall of the entrance hall in Teti's mortuary temple. The various divinities represented on it guarantee Teti—as the inscription says—life, strength, and health for all eternity (after Lauer and Leclant).

her neighbor. Suddenly the Gunns' aggressive little pug ran out, and the dogs all started to fight. When Mrs. Gunn tried to separate them, one of the Firths' dogs bit her hand. This enraged Gunn; he said that the dog might have rabies and might have infected his pregnant wife. He insisted that the dog had to be taken to Cairo, killed, and examined in the laboratory. Firth refused, assuring him that the dog was friendly and healthy and maintaining that the Gunns' dog was to blame for everything. As time went on, the conflict became increasingly acute. Gunn feared that his wife would have a miscarriage. The episode eventually indirectly affected the whole Egyptological world in the pyramid fields and even in Cairo. Some sided with Gunn, others with Firth, and still others tried to calm the parties to the feud—without success. Only when Gunn received a job offer in America did the conflict come to an end. He took the post and, taking his wife with him, left the scene of the row. So ended the collaboration between two important British archaeologists during the excavations on Teti's pyramid—much to the disadvantage of Egyptology.

Khuit's Pyramid

Teti's consort Khuit was buried north of his pyramid, and next to the pyramid complex of Iput I, another of the king's consorts. For a long time, no one was sure whether this site had actually been a pyramid. The French Egyptologist Victor Loret, who discovered Khuit's tomb in 1898, thought it had not. Its investigation has not yet been completed.

The archaeological-structural analysis of the ruins of part of the monument undertaken by Maragioglio and Rinaldi in the 1960s led to rather contradictory results. The remains of the masonry, which some Egyptologists think are the ruins of a small mortuary temple, are interpreted by others as a mastaba's cult site. Excavations conducted by Hawass in 1995 have shed light on the whole question and confirm that the structure was a pyramid. The solidly constructed underground funerary apartment, as well as the pink granite sarcophagus, led Hawass to make the justified assumption that Queen Khuit, like Iput I, had a significant status. The pyramid's substructure consists of a burial chamber situated on the vertical axis of the monument. East of the burial chamber is a storage room. The substructure was entered through a descending corridor beginning in the floor of the courtyard, in front of the middle of the north side of the pyramid.

The mortuary temple is in front of the pyramid's east wall. The previously unearthed part of the temple includes an offering room with a false door and an altar. The walls of the room are decorated with low reliefs showing offering bearers.

These new excavations on the grounds of Khuit's pyramid might lead to further discoveries regarding the older mastaba that originally lay south of this pyramid, whose remains were later incorporated into the tomb of the vizier Khentika. Jánosi, like Callender, for example, thought this queen was the mother of King Userkare.

Iput I's Pyramid

Iput was the mother of Pepi I, and probably Unas's daughter. Her small pyramid complex, which Loret discovered at the turn of the twentieth century, was further investigated in the early 1920s by Firth, with Gunn's assistance. Hawass is currently completing the investigation.

The pyramid had a three-stepped core. In front of its north side stood a small north chapel; however, it was not located, as was usual, over the entrance to the underground chambers. Instead of a corridor descending into the underground part of the pyramid, as was customary, a vertical shaft began at the level of the second layer of the core. From this we can conclude that the tomb was probably originally conceived as a mastaba and was transformed into a pyramid only after Pepi I became king. In view of this subsequent reconstruction, the question arises of whether the queen's son, Pepi I, was originally considered the successor to the throne.

In the burial chamber were found a limestone sarcophagus, fragments of a cedar coffin, and the remains of the bones of a middle-aged woman. A few precious objects that were part of the queen's burial equipment have survived, among them five limestone canopic vessels, an alabaster headrest, a small alabaster tablet with the names

Queen Iput I's pyramid complex, north-south sectional view through the pyramid and ground plan (after Maragioglio and Rinaldi). The ground plan was drawn before the excavations led by Hawass since 1992. For example, it is already known that there were two rows of pillars in the courtyard.

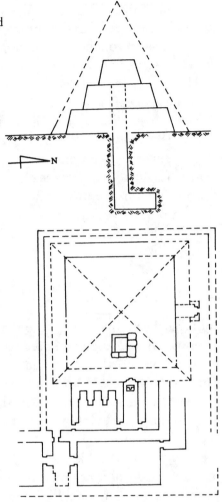

of the seven sacred oils, a gold bracelet, fragments of a necklace, models of alabaster vessels and copper utensils, and other items.

The mortuary temple on the east side of the pyramid has a somewhat atypical ground plan. Its entrance was on the south and came from Teti's pyramid. The entrance hall was decorated with four limestone pillars, the antechamber with two. The offering hall was in the inner part of temple; south of it were three deep niches for statues of the queen, and north of it was still another storeroom. In the west wall of the offering hall, which was somewhat north of the pyramid's east-west axis, there was originally a limestone false door. Before it stood a pink granite altar, with an inscription qualifying Iput I as "Queen mother [of the pyramid] 'Pepi's splendor is enduring.'" This is the oldest proof of the connection of a queen with the cult of a king's pyramid.

From the entrance hall one could reach not only the inner part of the temple but also the open, pillared courtyard and thence the storerooms and the open court surrounding the pyramid. The whole complex was surrounded by a limestone perimeter wall.

In the temple, Hawass found a unique limestone doorjamb. It was broken into two pieces and probably came from Djoser's pyramid complex. However, both the original emplacement and the meaning of the doorjamb, which is decorated with images of snakes and recumbent jackals and lions, remain rather obscure.

Further proof of Iput I's elevated standing is provided by the posthumous mortuary temple erected for her in remote Coptos in southern Egypt, an important intersection of the trading routes and a cult center for the fertility god Min.

Pepi I's Pyramid

Today one can hardly believe that the unprepossessing ruins about twelve meters high belonged to a structure that in its heyday dazzled contemporaries and of all the Egyptian pyramids may be the one that has most deeply put its stamp on history. It belonged to Pepi I—some Egyptologists say his name would be more precisely spelled "Pipi"— who called it *Men-nefer-Pepi,* "Pepi's splendor is enduring," as mentioned previously.

Modern archaeological research on the pyramid began in the 1830s with Perring, and in 1881 Maspero made his way into the underground part of the pyramid and there first discovered pyramid texts. Since 1950, the French archaeological mission in Saqqara has been pursu-

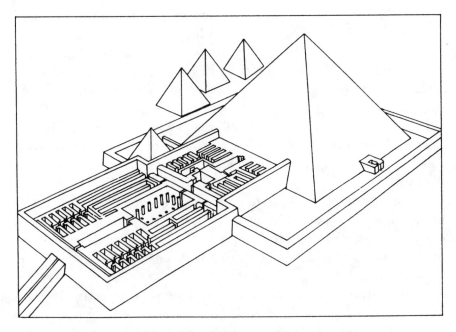

Schematic computer reconstruction of Pepi I's pyramid complex (after Labrousse and Cornon). This reconstruction reflects the state of research in 1985; in the meantime, other queens' pyramids have been discovered.

ing a systematic investigation of the pyramid. This was begun by Lauer and Sainte Fare Garnot, and since 1963 it has been led by Leclant and Labrousse. Their investigations have produced, especially in recent years, important results, such as the discovery of the small pyramid complexes of Pepi's consorts. The ambitious project of documenting and editing the pyramid texts found in this and other pyramids in Saqqara is currently being carried out.

The six-stepped pyramid core was constructed in the same way as others since Djedkare's pyramid, by using small pieces of limestone bound with clay mortar. Many builders' marks and inscriptions were found on the limestone masonry of the core. Blocks with the name of Queen Sesheshet, Teti's mother, were also reused in building the core. It appears that the relief blocks were deliberately damaged (perhaps by Userkare, one of Pepi I's rivals). Were they

Gaston Maspero.

taken from a destroyed building and reused in Pepi I's pyramid? Or are they evidence that Pepi built a cult site for his grandmother Sesheshet in his mortuary temple? Thus far, we have no explanation, and this discovery remains a riddle not only of Pepi I's pyramid, but of this era as a whole.

The casing of fine white limestone is intact only at the lowest levels. Fragments of Khamuaset's so-called restoration text, which the French team discovered during excavations in 1993, show that the pyramid was still in a relatively good condition during the Nineteenth Dynasty and that only a few small improvements were made to it.

Next to the pyramid's north wall, over the entrance to the corridor leading to the burial chamber, almost certainly stood a north chapel, though nothing of it remains. The ground plan of the underground rooms does not essentially differ from that of earlier pyramids of the end of the Fifth and the beginning of the Sixth Dynasty. The limestone corridor had a descending and a horizontal part, and at the transition point between the two parts there was a vestibule. There, too, pink granite was used to reinforce the corridor at three places and to make the main barrier of three portcullis slabs located approximately in the middle of the horizontal part of the corridor.

In general, the ground plan of the three other underground rooms also corresponded to that of its predecessors. The antechamber was located on the pyramid's vertical axis; east of it was the serdab with three niches, and west of it the burial chamber. The antechamber and burial chamber had gabled ceilings made of enormous limestone monoliths. The ceiling consists of three layers of blocks, and each layer again has sixteen blocks. Their total weight is about five thousand tons. As in the earlier pyramids, the ceiling is painted with white stars, but in this case they are oriented toward the west and painted on a black background. The sarcophagus stood on the west wall of the burial chamber. It resembled those in the pyramids of Teti and Unas. However, thorough examination shows that it was probably a substitute sarcophagus, as Labrousse maintains. According to him, either the original was damaged during transport into the burial chamber or hidden flaws appeared in the stone that was used for it. The origin of a fragment of a mummy found in the pyramid's substructure is uncertain, but it could easily have been from Pepi I. The same goes for the remains of fine linen wrappings.

Other components of the burial equipment were canopic vessels of yellowish alabaster, of which fourteen shards were found, together with a left sandal of reddish (sycamore?) wood, a piece of linen bearing the inscription "Linen for the king of Upper and Lower Egypt, may he live forever," a piece of pleated linen, and a small flint knife.

The pyramid texts were not only on the walls of the burial chamber and antechamber, but even in the access corridor. Some of them have remained in their original place, and some are on fragments that number about three thousand. The French team has been working for several years to solve the very complicated practical and theoretical problems connected with their reconstruction, and has made extensive use of modern computer technology. This has led to unexpected discoveries. For example, it can be shown that in the antechamber and burial chamber, about two thirds of the inscriptions have been altered from a large type of sign to a smaller type. No less interesting was the discovery that the king's older royal throne name Nefersahor was changed to Merire. The reasons for these important changes have not yet been explained.

In the case of the mortuary temple, we can almost speak of a standard plan, on which Teti's complex was already based. Later on, the temple was seriously damaged by stone thieves, who even set up a lime-roasting oven. Nonetheless, a series of archaeologically important discoveries were made there, such as limestone statues of kneeling enemies of Egypt with their hands tied behind their backs. Originally, they decorated the open, pillared courtyard and perhaps also the entrance hall. In the conception of the temple's decoration, they had an apotropaic function: they symbolized evil conquered and were supposed to frighten away anyone attempting to damage the king's tomb and thus the world order.

The location and ground plan of the small cult pyramid followed the model of its immediate predecessors. Even though it was also ravaged by stone thieves, parts of its casing, including the pyramidion, have been found.

The French team had expected to find a queen's pyramid on the south side of the king's pyramid but probably never dreamed that they would discover six of them—and they may discover still more as time goes on. This is an unusually large number; near Khufu's, Menkaure's, and Pepi II's pyramids there are only three queens' pyramids each.

The queens played an important, and sometimes fateful role, as we learn from the previously mentioned contemporary inscription. This inscription describes the preparation of a lawsuit against a queen after an unsuccessful conspiracy against the king that may have been planned right in his harem. Further details are lacking, but it would surely not be wrong to assume that competing queens stood in the background, plotting to promote their own sons' claims to the throne. The conspiracy took place at the time of the "twenty-first [cattle] census," but the queen's name is not mentioned; was this intentional? Was its omission connected with the damnatio memoriae, the eternal erasure of all memory of the queen? Callender thinks that it was not one of Pepi's consorts who was involved, but rather the mother of his opponent Userkare.

Nebuunet's Pyramid

Nebuunet's complex is the easternmost of the queen's tombs found up to this point (it is thought, however, that another complex may be located east of it). It was reached from an open courtyard around the king's pyramid. The complex, which included a pyramid and a small mortuary temple, is now largely destroyed, but its ground plan can be roughly reconstructed.

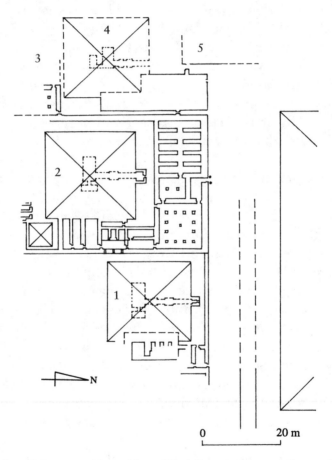

Ground plan of the pyramid complex of Pepi I's consort, according to the state of research in 1995: 1. Nebuunet, 2. Inenek-Inti, 3. Meretites, 4. "Southwestern pyramid," 5. Prince Hernetjerikhet (after Leclant and Labrousse).

The pyramid was built of limestone. The entrance to the corridor leading into the burial chamber was in the pavement of the court-yard in front of the north side of the pyramid, under the north chapel. The chapel was built of mudbricks, and in its unprepossessing ruins a fragment of a limestone altar was found. The corridor had a descending and a horizontal part, and at the point of transition it became slightly broader, constituting the so-called vestibule. In front of the entrance to the burial chamber, which was located south of the pyramid's vertical axis, there was a simple barrier of pink granite.

The burial chamber's ground plan was oriented east-west, and it had a flat ceiling. Only fragments of the pink granite sarcophagus have been found. The meaning of the fragments of an alabaster slab with the remains of a hieroglyphic inscription in bas-relief is not entirely clear. Neither a mummy nor pyramid texts were found in the burial chamber. In the serdab, the small room east of the burial chamber, archaeologists discovered fragments of the burial equipment: a cylindrical wooden weight used in weaving, wooden objects in the form of ostrich feathers (symbols of the goddess Maat?), and other items.

The mortuary temple in front of the pyramid's east wall was small and simple in shape; its entrance was on the north and was located in an antechamber from which a path led to a small open courtyard around the pyramid. The sacrifice hall had a false door and was located somewhat south of the pyramid's east-west axis; it served as a cult center. Between it and the antechamber there were three niches for statues of the queen. Unfortunately, only insignificant fragments of the original relief decoration of the temple have been found—for example, a piece of one of the ceiling slabs with stars and part of the king's (?) title.

Inenek-Inti's Pyramid

West of Nebuunet's complex lies the complex of Queen Inenek-Inti. It has its own perimeter wall, and both the pyramid and the mortuary temple are larger than Nebuunet's. Inside the pyramid's substructure, only the location of the burial chamber on the pyramid's vertical axis represents a basic difference from the arrangement of Nebuunet's pyramid.

Because its rooms were crowded close together, the mortuary temple actually wound around the east, north, and south sides of the pyramid. The offering hall and a room with three niches were on the east side, while a group of storerooms was on the north and south sides. Near the northeast corner of the pyramid there was an open, pillared courtyard. Around the north, west, and south sides of the pyramid, however, there was a smaller open courtyard in whose pavement a large number of offering tables were inset. There was a small cult pyramid at the southeast corner.

The "Southwestern Pyramid"

The ruins of the third pyramid are about three meters high. Its original dimensions did not differ from those of Nebuunet's pyramid, but the ground plan of its substructure differed substantially from hers. In this case the serdab was located not east but south of the burial chamber, which lay on the pyramid's vertical axis. In it were found two rolls of fine linen, a gilded wooden sandal, and copper utensils—obviously the remains of the burial equipment.

In the burial chamber were discovered fragments of a pink granite sarcophagus and objects similar to those found in Nebuunet's burial chamber, although in greater numbers: wooden weights used in weaving, wooden symbols of Maat shaped like ostrich feathers, and also copper fishhooks and large vessels made of fired clay.

The mortuary temple was built in haste. Next to the offering hall was a room with not three but only two niches for statues. Among the relief fragments found there were scenes of processions of courtiers and personified mortuary estates, part of a cartouche with Pepi I's name (the temple decoration was not completed until his reign), and other items.

MIROSLAV VERNER

The Pyramids of Meretites, Ankhesenpepi II, and Ankhesenpepi III

Two neighboring structures are currently being investigated. To the south lies the small pyramid complex of another queen named Meretites, and to the north the tomb of prince Hernetjerikhet. It is worth noting that the pyramids discovered so far do not include that of Ankhesenmerire I, the elder of the two sisters of the same name whose father was the influential vizier Djau, from Abydos. However, a pink granite block bearing the name of the queen Ankhesenpepi, found in 1997 near the southwest corner of the king's pyramid, clearly showed that it cannot be long before the French team finds the pyramids of one or both of the two queens bearing this name (it might be either Ankhesenmerire or Ankhesenpepi, depending on whether the ruler's throne name or birth name was added). Ankhesenmerire I was Pepi I's consort and the mother of his immediate successor Merenre I. Following Khentkaues I and Khentkaues II, as queen mother Ankhesenmerire I had an exceptionally important social and religious status. An inscription from the pyramid complex of Neith, Pepi II's consort and probably Ankhesenmerire I's daughter, shows that the place where the queen was worshiped had the rank of a "shrine" and its priests that of "the god's servants." This was normally a privilege reserved for pharaohs.

Quite recently, Ankhesenpepi III's pyramid was found near the southwest corner of the king's pyramid. In the badly damaged burial chamber, the chest of the queen's sarcophagus cut from a huge sandstone block is embedded in the floor The sarcophagus's lid is formed by an enormous, roughly dressed pink granite monolith.

Moreover, south of Ankhesenpepi III's pyramid still another pyramid was discovered. Surprisingly, it belonged to Ankhesenpepi II, who was another of Pepi I's consorts and also Pepi II's mother. This queen later ruled for her son, who succeeded to the throne at the age of six, according to Manetho. The relationship between the queen mother and the child pharaoh is vividly depicted by the famous small alabaster statue of Ankhesenmerire II with Pepi II sitting on her lap, which is now in the Brooklyn Museum (B 13.119). A carving on the rock at Wadi Maghara in the Sinai, which undoubtedly dates from the queen's reign, depicts the queen wearing the tight-fitting cap and uraeus on her head—a very unusual bit of evidence from the Old Kingdom (a still older one is the previously mentioned representation of Khentkaues II wearing the uraeus, which was discovered in Abusir).

In the burial chamber of Ankhesenpepi II lies an enormous, carefully dressed basalt sarcophagus. But the most exciting discovery was the pyramid texts inscribed on the walls of the chamber.

However, it looks as though the riddles regarding the queens who were buried near the pyramid will not soon be solved. Recently, fragments of a relief with inscriptions were discovered there that contain the name of another, previously unknown queen. It sounds very exotic: Nedjeftet—"Who belongs to the pomegranate tree." This tree was the symbol of two provinces in Upper Egypt, the thirteenth and fourteenth. Can we thus assume that Nedjeftet came from one of those areas? That she is further proof of Pepi I's "diplomatic" marriages, which were made in an effort to strengthen his control over the areas in which the power of the province's princes was growing?

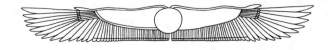

Merenre I's Pyramid

It is not easy for a modern visitor to the burial sites in Saqqara to find the pyramid complex that was once grandiosely called "Merenre's beauty shines." Its ruins, drifted with sand, lie relatively deep in the desert, right at the southwest edge of the necropolis, where the visitor's eyes are more likely to be drawn to the nearby Mastabat Fara'un and Pepi II's pyramid. However, that is not why Egyptologists know so little about this pyramid. Up to now, they have relied primarily on the biographical inscription made by the high official Uni (mentioned earlier in connection with the harem conspiracy against Pepi I), who provided valuable material for the construction of the pyramid—pink granite from Aswan, alabaster from Hatnub, and dark greywacke from the quarries in Ibhat. This stone was used to make the pyramidion and the sarcophagus, on which a few traces of gilding remain.

When he investigated the monument in the 1830s, Perring noted the presence in the pyramid's casing of blocks of fine white limestone that are no longer visible in the rubble. He also observed the remains of a perimeter wall built of mudbricks and a causeway about two hundred fifty meters long. The causeway went around Djedkare's pyramid complex, which lay closer to the edge of the desert. In the early 1880s Maspero, looking for pyramid texts, entered the underground part of the pyramid. He made a simple ground plan of the subterranean chambers, which do not essentially differ from those in Pepi I's pyramid. The west wall of the burial chamber, on which the sarcophagus stood, was decorated by a beautiful polychrome relief with the royal palace facade motif. White stars oriented westward, on a black ceiling background, symbolized the night sky of the underworld. Only a few insignificant remains of the burial equipment are extant, among them two alabaster shells and a small wooden knob or handle for a chest.

Inside Merenre's pyramid, Maspero found the mummy of a young man whose hair was combed into a side curl such as those worn by children in ancient Egypt. At first, the type of mummy wrappings led scholars to conclude that this burial took place later. For example, Elliot Smith (1871–1937), an expert on Egyptian mummies, assigned it to the Eighteenth Dynasty. Later on, a few Egyptologists suggested that it was Merenre's mummy after all. However that may be, the king's reign was apparently short, and he died very young. His consort was Ankhesenpepi II. The golden pectoral bearing the names of Merenre I and his father, Pepi I, is considered proof of their joint rule, the first of its kind.

Decades passed before the investigation of the pyramid was continued by the French archaeology team under Leclant's direction. However, so far it has yielded only a little information, because of the extent of the pyramid's devastation. The many fragments with remains of pyramid texts found around the crater left by stone robbers indicate how complicated the reconstruction of the underground chambers will be.

Pepi II's Pyramid

Pepi II's pyramid complex was called "Pepi's life is enduring," and in fact Pepi II was the pharaoh who lived and reigned longest of all. However, the complex's special role in the architectural history of Egypt is based on the fact that it was the last pyramid built in accord with the best traditions of the Old Kingdom. This circumstance and also its location at the southern edge of the Saqqara necropolis made it a source of inspiration for the builders of the pyramid complexes of the Middle Kingdom.

It was once again Maspero who followed Perring's lead and entered the pyramid in 1881. However, a systematic investigation was first begun by Jéquier from 1926 to 1932. Next to the main pyramid he discovered the immediately adjoining pyramid complex of Pepi II's consorts Neith, Iput II, and Udjebten. Near the causeway he also found the small pyramid of an unimportant ruler of the Eighth Dynasty, Ibi, as well as a cemetery for important figures of the end of the Sixth Dynasty.

Like its predecessors, the pyramid core was built of small pieces of limestone bound with clay mortar. For the casing, however, valuable white limestone was used. A peculiarity of the pyramid that has not yet been satisfactorily explained is its subsequent enlargement.

After work on the casing and the north chapel was completed, a band of brick about seven meters wide was installed around the pyramid at the level of the third layer of core blocks. The north chapel disappeared, and the perimeter wall also had to be torn down and then rebuilt a little farther from the pyramid. However, the band of brickwork did not reach above the top of the perimeter wall around the pyramid. Religious and aesthetic considerations, such as an intention to produce the illusion of an elevated platform on which the pyramid rose, can therefore hardly have played an important role. Edwards expressed the opinion that the band might have been an effort to deal with damage caused by an earthquake. However, it was not strong enough to increase significantly the pyramid's static equilibrium. Perhaps the goal was instead to strengthen the lowest level of the casing—as if the builders did not fully trust the solidity of their foundations and the quality of the bond with the core.

The pyramid's substructure has the basic characteristics that were established in Djedkare's era. In the vestibule, at the point of transition between the descending and horizontal parts of the corridor, many fragments of alabaster and diorite vessels were found, along with the golden blade of a small, rounded knife. Immediately behind the vestibule was a granite barrier with three massive portcullis slabs, and on the walls of the horizontal part of the corridor there were pyramid texts.

The serdab had no niches and consisted of a single room. Stars shone from the gabled ceiling of the antechamber and burial chamber, and their side walls were covered with pyramid texts. Only the west wall behind the sarcophagus was decorated with motifs of a stylized palace facade. About halfway up the side of the black granite sarcophagus was a hieroglyphic inscription with the ruler's name and titles. Up to the moment when the ruler's mummy was placed in the sarcophagus, its cover rested on two low walls between the sarcophagus

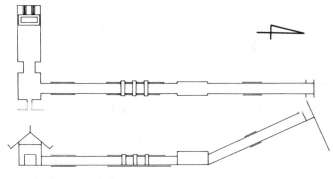

Substructure of Pepi II's pyramid. Ground plan and sectional view (after Jéquier).

and the west wall. Of the granite canopic chest that was sunk into the floor at the southeast corner of the sarcophagus, only the square cover remains. The ruler's mummy has never been found.

The builders of the mortuary temple may have taken their inspiration not only from the temples of the last phases of the Fifth and Sixth Dynasties, but also from Sahure's mortuary temple. However, here we also encounter some new elements. Thus, for example, between the end of the causeway and the entrance hall three north-south–oriented rooms were discovered, which, according to Ricke, symbolized important religious centers of the land: Heliopolis (the central chapel), Buto (the north chapel), and Sais (the south chapel). From the rooms at the north and south ends, staircases led to the temple's roof terrace.

The open courtyard, paved with limestone, was surrounded by eighteen pillars of reddish quartzite. One of them, at the northwest corner of the courtyard, remains in situ. It is ornamented with an image of the ruler embracing the god Re-Harakhty. North and south of the entrance corridor and the courtyard lies the complex of temple storerooms.

In the transverse corridor, at the entry to the inner part of the temple, noteworthy remains of the original relief decoration have been preserved: on the west wall, a stylized model of a niche, and on the east wall scenes of the sed festival, the festival of the god Min, and the triumphal execution of the Libyan chieftain, accompanied by his consort and his son. The last scene in particular, which is already known from Sahure's mortuary temple, is seen as proof that the decoration was copied from older models. It thus had a purely mythical significance and is not evidence of an actual military victory by Pepi II over the Libyans.

The inner part of the temple was about a meter higher than the outer part. The five pink granite niches in the cult chapel were provided with narrow double doors. From the five-niche chapel one passed into the antichambre carrée, whose ceiling, decorated with stars, was originally supported by an octagonal pillar of reddish quartzite. The extant remains of the relief decoration on the walls contribute to our understanding of the significance of this still rather enigmatic room. On the lower part of the east and west walls, courtiers bringing tribute are represented, and over them—separated by a row of stars—is the ruler, who is meeting with the gods. On the north wall, over the entrance into the offering hall, the ruler was depicted embracing the tutelary goddess Nekhbet and the jackal god Anubis.

Remains of the original relief decoration have been preserved in the offering hall as well. There no divinities are pictured, however, only

Ground plan of Pepi II's pyramid complex, along with the pyramid complex of his consorts (from top to bottom) Iput II, Neith, and Udjebten (after Jéquier).

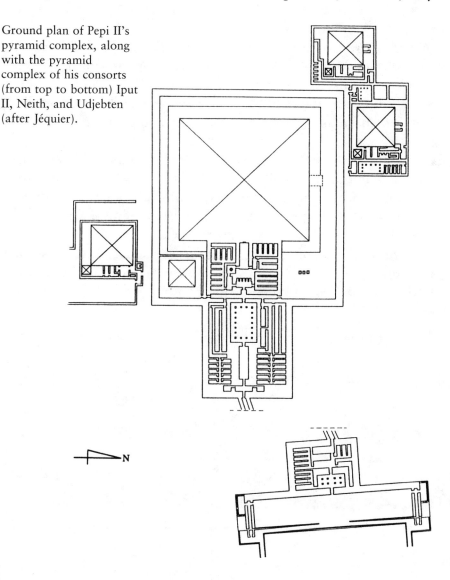

the ruler sitting at the offering table, along with a list of sacrifices, sacrifice bearers, and men slaughtering sacrificial animals. There are extensive storeroom complexes in the inner part of the temple as well.

The small cult pyramid was at the southeast corner of the main pyramid, and in its original form did not essentially differ from earlier structures of the same kind in the complexes of the Fifth and Sixth Dynasties. The causeway connecting the valley temple with the mortuary temple takes two turns and angles to the northeast. At the upper turning, there is a small room for the temple guard. The remaining fragments of the causeway's original decoration show the ruler in the form of a sphinx and a griffin massacring prisoners and enemies of Egypt brought by the gods, processions of servants bringing offerings from the mortuary estates, and divinities approaching the ruler on his throne.

In contrast to the mortuary temple's ground plan, the valley temple's ground plan does not follow Sahure's. In front of it lay a large rectangular terrace, open on the east side, which is oriented northwest-southeast, following the course of the canal along the edge of the valley. At the northern and southern ends it could be reached by a harbor ramp. According to Ricke, the procession of mourners accompanying the coffin, the canopic chests, the statue, and the funerary boat passed over both ramps to the terrace.

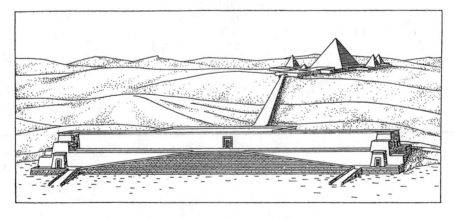

Reconstruction of Pepi II's pyramid complex (after Jéquier).

The entrance to the valley temple was located in the middle of the terrace's west wall. Like the terrace, the valley temple had a rectangular ground plan. Its front portion consisted of a hall supported by eight pillars; fragments of its relief decoration have been preserved that show the ruler being received by the gods, the victory of Egypt's enemies, and a hunt in a papyrus thicket. From the vestibule behind the pillared hall a passage led to the staircase to the temple's roof terrace, into the temple storeroom, and into the ascending corridor to the mortuary temple. Among the fragments of the vestibule's relief decoration, the scenes of hunting a hippopotamus and the transportation of a captive hippopotamus on a wooden sled are especially noteworthy.

Neith's Pyramid

At the northwest corner of the king's pyramid stood the oldest of the three queens' pyramid complexes, that of Merenre's sister Neith. It included a small pyramid and a mortuary temple, both of which were surrounded by a perimeter wall.

The pyramid's core consisted of three steps, which were built of the same materials and in the same way as the king's pyramid. Its entrance opened in the pavement of the courtyard, in front of the middle of the pyramid's north wall. Behind the barrier of pink granite at the end of the descending corridor was an entrance barrier in front of the burial chamber, which was located on the pyramid's vertical axis and had a rectangular, east-west–oriented ground plan. Its flat ceiling was decorated with stars, and there were pyramid texts on three of its side walls. On the fourth wall, west of the sarcophagus, there was a stylized palace facade. In the room many fragments of alabaster and diorite vessels from the queen's burial equipment were found, but not her mummy. East of the chamber was a small serdab.

The entrance into the mortuary temple, which was framed by a pair of small limestone obelisks bearing hieroglyphic inscriptions with the queen's name and titles, was at the southeast corner of the perimeter wall. The vestibule immediately behind the entrance was

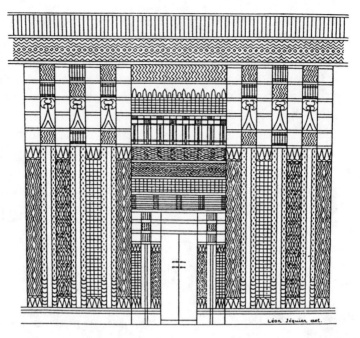

The decoration on the west wall of Queen Neith's burial chamber resembled the facade of the royal palace (after Jéquier).

named the lion room after the relief fragments found there, which show lions carrying ornamental sashes. The open, pillared courtyard and five storerooms complete the outer part of the temple. The offering hall with a false door constituted the center of the inner part of the temple and began in the middle of the east wall of the pyramid. In front of the false door a stepped altar still stands in its original place. North of the hall is a room with three niches for statues of the queen.

In the area between the small cult pyramid and the southeast corner of the queen's pyramid, Jéquier discovered sixteen wooden models of ships lying in a shallow pit. Their number, the variety, and the state of preservation make them a unique discovery. As components of the burial equipment, the boats were closely connected with the worship of the dead as well as with conceptions of the deceased's travel by boat into the beyond.

Iput II's Pyramid

Iput II's pyramid, now almost completely destroyed, hardly differs from Neith's. The only striking differences are its smaller dimensions and the poorer quality of the tomb furnishings. The sarcophagus was presumably made of pink granite.

The mortuary temple had the form of the letter *L*. It was entered from the south through a pink granite gateway framed by two obelisks; the gateway bore the queen's name and titles. Interestingly, the name of the ruler's pyramid complex became an inseparable part of the queen's titulature. Among the titles of Iput II that of queen mother is lacking—after the Fifth Dynasty pyramids were also built for queens whose sons did not become pharaoh. On the east side of the pyramid stood the offering hall, which had a reddish quartzite false door that has been largely preserved.

In the westernmost storeroom Jéquier discovered the granite sarcophagus of Queen Ankhesenpepi IV (?), one of Pepi II's consorts and

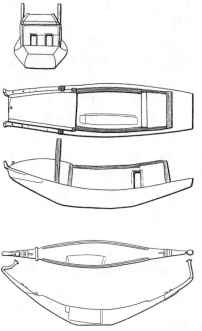

Models of Queen Neith's funerary boats (after Jéquier).

the mother of an unimportant ruler of the Eighth Dynasty, Neferkare Nebi. The tomb clearly illustrates the material and social decline of the royal family after Pepi II's death. Ankhesenpepi probably survived her husband and married again: if she is the "royal consort" of the same name mentioned in the stela inscription from Abydos, she became the wife of Prince Iuu.

On the sarcophagus's basalt cover Jéquier found the remains of an inscription that seemed to him uninterpretable and unreadable. His discovery was subsequently put in the Egyptian Museum in Cairo (JE 65908) and forgotten. However, the French Egyptologists Michel Baud and Vasil Dobrev have recently examined it anew. Using modern photographic techniques, they were able to reconstruct and read part of the inscription. The result was sensational.

It turned out that the basalt tablet, which resembles the famous Palermo stone, contains part of the royal annals of the Sixth Dynasty, with much new and interesting information. It is still debated whether the sarcophagus was buried in the storeroom of Iput II's pyramid temple during the turbulent events at the beginning of the First Intermediate Period, or only after them. Although explicit proof is lacking in the text, the context provided by the extant parts of the inscription seems to indicate that at the beginning of the Sixth Dynasty Userkare did in fact rule (for about four years?). During Pepi I's reign Userkare was condemned to damnatio memoriae, and this may have had to do with the rumor reported by Manetho that King Teti had been murdered by his own guard. Among other things, the inscription suggests that the discovery of blocks from the destroyed building of Queen Sesheshet, Teti's mother, should be seen in the context of the highly conflictual climate of that time. The debate launched by the discovery of this inscription has just begun and will no doubt lead to many new insights into Egyptian history.

Udjebten's Pyramid

The small pyramid complex of Pepi II's third consort lies at the southeast corner of the king's pyramid. It also includes only a pyramid, a small mortuary temple, and a small cult pyramid, but it is surrounded by two perimeter walls (the second encloses the larger area around the complex, especially on the east side).

The pyramid was discovered by Jéquier in such a devastated condition that even the core structure was barely discernible. He was able to find only a small casing block on which the pyramidion rested. But by a conjunction of several strokes of luck, he discovered in the mortuary temple a fragment of an inscription that proved that this pyramidion, which has not yet been found, was originally plated with the finest gold.

The substructure's ground plan does not greatly differ from that of the two earlier pyramids of Pepi II's consorts. At most, an enormous basalt block that was originally part of the barrier in the corridor that led to the burial chamber is worthy of notice. The walls of the burial chamber and perhaps also of the corridor were covered with pyramid texts, of which eighty-four fragments—about a tenth of the original total—have been preserved. Furthermore, there is no serdab in the underground part of the pyramid. At the southeast corner of the pyramid stood a small cult pyramid.

The entrance to the very simply decorated temple was on the north side, and from there the passage led into the offering hall via a small vestibule, an open courtyard without pillars, and a room with only two niches. The modern visitor is reminded of the place where the

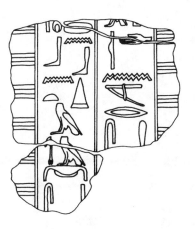

Fragment of an inscription showing that the apex of Queen Udjebten's pyramid was sheathed in gold (after Jéquier).

temple once stood only by an offering table of alabaster, which bears an inscription with a funerary formula and the queen's name.

Even if Udjebten was not a queen mother, the place where she was worshiped nonetheless had a high rank: during his excavations Jéquier discovered the fragment of an inscription with a decree protecting the queen's cult.

CHAPTER EIGHT

THE FIRST INTERMEDIATE PERIOD
(SEVENTH DYNASTY TO THE BEGINNING OF THE ELEVENTH)

At the end of a long, gradually deepening economic and social crisis during the Sixth Dynasty, new battles over the succession to the throne probably broke out, but this has not been proven by any direct historical evidence. Pepi II's extraordinarily long reign might have meant that the legitimate heir to the throne either predeceased him or became king at an excessively advanced age; in either case, the result would have been an increase in the number of pretenders to the throne. The supposed succession of a woman (Nitokris) to the throne would have reflected a lack of legitimacy or ability to rule among the current pretenders. The rapid change of kings—probably insignificant usurpers—in the period after the collapse of the Sixth Dynasty shows that the succession was unclear at this time. The Ptolemaic historian Manetho appropriately described the Seventh Dynasty as anarchic.

For Egyptians of that time, this certainly meant an unimaginable loss of the basic certainties and principles on which their worldview had previously been based, the fall of the "eternal" order given men by the gods at the creation of the cosmos and guaranteed by the pharaoh. The disintegration of the state, which manifested itself in the collapse of the central government, was the result of several causes. One of these was no doubt the excessive exploitation of material resources and manpower in building the monumental tombs, maintaining their operations, and supporting the cult of the dead. At the same time, the system of redistribution that originally concentrated power and possessions in the hands of the pharaoh was showing increasing signs of paralysis and dissolution. Although the king functioned both ideologically and legally as the sole, "divine" possessor of all the country's resources, including manpower, he had to provide "from his own pocket" increasingly large sums not only for the development and operation of the economy (construction of irrigation canals, draining of marshes, etc.) and for the improvement of communications and security, but also for the erection of royal and private tombs and support of the worship of the dead. The state budget was also burdened by other factors—for example, the awarding of so-called decrees of immunity to temples (privileges that guaranteed them economic advantages) and declining income from foreign trade.

Also contributing to the gradual collapse of the system were the drastic changes in the structure of the administrative apparatus. The inflationary growth of new offices and titles among the bureaucracy did not reflect the actual economic and political status of this stratum of society. The slow decline of the official's position in the central government was accompanied by a contrary process in the provinces, where legal, economic, and military power was increasingly concentrated in the hands of the local rulers, the provincial princes. The latter in particular became a delicate problem. During the Old Kingdom, Egypt had no standing army, and the pharaoh evidently did not personally lead military campaigns, which were generally entrusted—as the biographical inscription of the Sixth Dynasty official Uni shows—to provincial administrators. No doubt the latter used these opportunities to consolidate their personal power at the expense of the central state power.

The general worsening of the natural conditions related to the end of a long period of frequent rainfall in Northeast Africa (the so-called Neolithic subpluvial phase) and the rapid development of a hot, arid climate may also have contributed to the decline of the ancient Egyptian state at this time. As a result, pasturelands grew smaller, men and animals moved to the water sources, and the fields at the edge of the desert became increasingly sandy.

The decline of the state at the end of the Old Kingdom found a remarkable echo in ancient Egyptian literature. This consisted not of a direct, contemporary description of the collapse, but rather of literary works about a past era when the land was destroyed. Ipuwer's famous admonition offers a multifaceted, dramatic description of the period as a time when "the land was turned as if on a potter's wheel, plundered and overworked, the ruler was overthrown by force of arms, men died of hunger, and Egypt fell into the hands of Asians." The "Instruction for Merikare," Neferti's *Prophecy,* and other works also inform us about this turbulent period of decline. The deep crisis in values is reflected in the "Dialogue of a World-Weary Man"—a conversation of a man with his soul (ba) that puts in question not only the afterlife but even belief in the gods.

Valuable information about the unsettled period after the fall of the Old Kingdom is also provided by inscriptions on some private tombs. For example, in his tomb in Moalla in Upper Egypt, the provincial prince Ankhtify described people's suffering, their poverty and hunger, and his own efforts to improve their living conditions. Ankhtify also took part in the war that overwhelmed the whole country. He and his army probably fought on the side of the northern kingdom, which had been formed after the fall of the last Memphite, that is, the Eighth Dynasty. The northern kingdom's center was Heracleopolis (Egyptian Nennisut). Its opponents were concentrated in Thebes (Egyptian Waset) in Upper Egypt.*

Thus Egypt was broken into two rival parts, a northern and a southern. At first, the northern kingdom, whose power extended as far as the thirteenth province in Upper Egypt, was more successful. However, the Theban kings were eventually able to unify the whole area from Elephantine to Coptos under their rule. During the reign of the Theban king Antef II, the victory of the southern kingdom became clear. The north's efforts to form an alliance with the princes of Lower Nubia, whom the collapse of the central power and the weakening of Egypt had benefited and who had made themselves independent, proved fruitless.

The disintegration of the central government and the emergence of ephemeral local rulers, together with their mutual rivalry and the general economic and social difficulties of the country did not consti-

---

* The rulers in Heracleopolis, who often took the name of Khety, represented the Ninth and Tenth Dynasties, whereas the Theban kings, who were also descended from the local princes, are counted as the Eleventh Dynasty, even though they ruled concurrently.

tute favorable conditions for the construction of monumental pyramid complexes. This is shown by the already very modest dimensions and poor architectonic quality of the last known pyramid of the Old Kingdom, that of King Ibi.

The tombs of the rulers of the First Intermediate Period have not yet been found. The relatively meager written sources allow us to conclude that some of those rulers might have been buried in pyramids. One such source, which was already mentioned in connection with the Headless Pyramid in North Saqqara, mentions the name of the tomb of Merikare, one of the rulers of the Heracleopolitan kingdom. It was called "Green [i.e., blooming] are the [cult] places of Merikare," and in writing this name the hieroglyphic sign for *pyramid* was used as a determinative. His tomb has not yet been found, although according to one theory it is the Headless Pyramid.

Merikare's pyramid raises other questions of a general kind. In "Instruction for Merikare," a famous programmatic-political work dealing with Egypt's wretched internal political and social situation, explicit reference is made to royal tombs that were plundered and destroyed. If this is accurate, it may explain why they have been im-

Tomb stela in the form of a house, which was found near Pepi II's pyramid complex in Saqqara. This type of stela is characteristic of the tombs built during the final phase of the Old Kingdom and at the beginning of the First Intermediate Period (after Jéquier).

possible to find. As the pyramid of Ibi at the end of the Old Kingdom shows, the royal tombs of the First Intermediate Period were not particularly large or built in such a way that they could be quickly and totally destroyed, whether as a result of social unrest or through natural erosion.

A few Egyptologists, basing their view on rather indirect and fragmentary written sources, have suggested that the royal necropolis of this period was located in North Saqqara, perhaps near Teti's pyramid complex. One might object, however, that the capital in the Ninth and Tenth Dynasties was located in Nennisut in Middle Egypt. Moreover, the Spanish archaeological expedition, which has carried out extensive excavations in this area over the past few years, has so far not discovered any royal tombs, not to mention pyramids.

The Eighth Dynasty—Ibi's Pyramid

The tombs of the last rulers of the Sixth Dynasty, and particularly those of Merenre II and Queen Nitokris (whose existence is still debated), have not yet been found. Either it was no longer possible to erect them because the rulers' reigns were too short and insufficient financial means were available, or archaeologists have thus far had poor luck in finding them. If the construction of these tombs was at least begun, their ruins must lie in South Saqqara near Pepi II's pyramid. Despite Jéquier's already extensive efforts, it will still be a while before the whole necropolis has been investigated.

During his excavations in South Saqqara Jéquier focused his attention on the small ruins (they are only three meters high) that the Lepsius expedition had given the number 40 on its archaeological map. His investigation confirmed that Lepsius was correct in believing that this was pyramid—a belief that was questioned by his contemporaries because the monument, which was not quite oriented in accord with the cardinal directions, was near the causeway leading to Pepi II's complex and looked like a mastaba. Jéquier's excavations have also shown that older tombs from the Sixth Dynasty are located in this place.

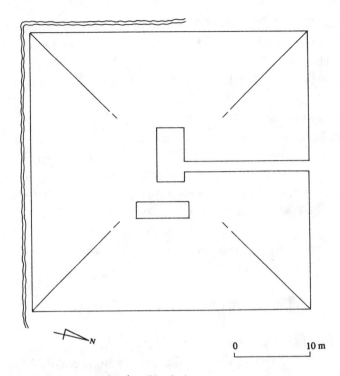

Ground plan of Ibi's pyramid (after Jéquier).

The pyramid was almost completely destroyed by stone thieves. On the limestone blocks of its core Jéquier found a large number of inscriptions crudely written in red color with the title "Prince of Libya," for which he was not able to offer a satisfactory explanation.

The underground part of the pyramid consisted of a descending corridor, a burial chamber, and a serdab. The walls of the burial chamber were originally covered with pyramid texts, with whose help it was possible to determine that the pyramid belonged to the almost unknown ruler Qakare Ibi, who ruled for only a short time in the Eighth Dynasty, and thus it dated from the First Intermediate Period. Despite their fragmentary state, their limited scope, and the simplicity of their execution, the inscriptions have an important place in the history of Egypt: they are the most recent pyramid texts that have thus far been found.

The Ninth and Tenth Dynasties—The Monumental Tomb in Dara

The ruins of a large structure near Dara, in Middle Egypt, show how little we know about the royal tombs of the First Intermediate Period. It is not clear whether this structure is a pyramid or a stepped mastaba. It was investigated in the late 1940s and early 1950s by the French Egyptologist Raymond Weill, but much remains to be done.

The north-south–oriented structure has an almost square ground plan, and its substructure somewhat resembles that of a large brick mastaba from the Third Dynasty in Beit Khallaf. The underground part of the structure is reached from the north by a long passageway that is at first horizontal and open and then becomes a descending, vaulted tunnel leading to the burial chamber. The burial chamber's

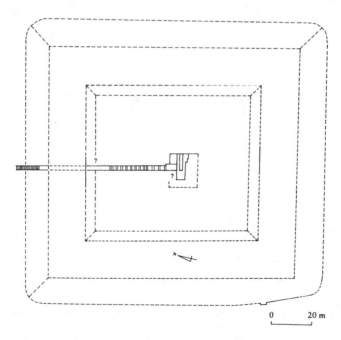

0   20 m

Monumental tomb in Dara (after Weill). The plan shows the inclined layers of brick masonry. The middle part of the structure was evidently filled with sand and rubble.

walls were sheathed with roughly dressed limestone blocks. It was pillaged and destroyed, and no remains of a burial were found there.

So little remains of the superstructure with rounded corners that it is questionable whether it was later extensively destroyed or never finished in the first place. The outer part of the masonry, whose structure is unclear, consists of a massive, strong mantle about thirty-five meters in length and built of mudbricks; the inside was probably filled with sand.

In the tomb itself nothing was discovered that might have helped identify to whom it belonged. However, a cartouche with the name of Khui—an otherwise unknown, probably merely local ruler from the First Intermediate Period—was found in one of the nearby tombs.

CHAPTER NINE

THE MIDDLE KINGDOM
(ELEVENTH TO TWELFTH DYNASTY?)

After the victory over the princes of Asyut, who were allies of the Heracleopolitan rulers, the way toward reuniting the country lay open. Around 1968 B.C.E., reunification was achieved by Mentuhotep II, the son of Antef III. In accord with his successes, he changed his Horus name several times in the course of his almost half-century reign. At first he was called Sankhibtawy, then Netjerihedjet, and finally Sematawy, "[he] who unified both countries." This name expresses his absolute dominance over both parts of Egypt. Upon ascending the throne, he also took the throne name Nebhepetre.

Mentuhotep II's residence was in the Upper Egyptian city of Thebes. A number of high officials and artists followed him there from the north, especially from Memphis. After the reunification of the country, art soon flourished anew, as the state administration was reorganized to deprive the regional rulers of power and increase the power of the central government. The exhausted country urgently needed reforms, as a famine clearly showed. The economic and social conditions that then prevailed in Egypt are described in the letters that Hekanakht, a mortuary priest serving the vizier Ipi in the time of Mentuhotep II, wrote to his family in a provincial town in Upper Egypt. The documents are now in the Metropolitan Museum in New York and offer eloquent testimony.

Mentuhotep II also took the initiative in foreign policy. He invaded Nubia, which had grown independent during the period of crisis, and battled enemy tribes on the northern border of Egypt. In addition, after a long interruption he started sending trading expeditions to Punt in the south and to Lebanon in the north, to procure cedar wood and other goods.

In contrast to his predecessors, who were buried in the Theban necropolis of Tarif on the west bank of the Nile, Mentuhotep II decided to build a unique, monumental tomb in the form of a terracelike complex of pillared colonnades.

Mentuhotep III, who was Mentuhotep II's successor and probably his son, further strengthened the country's unity, but in doing so encountered considerable resistance. Construction greatly increased at this time, as is shown by a large expedition the ruler sent to the stone quarries in Wadi Hammamat, in the middle of the Eastern desert. It was during Mentuhotep III's reign that the high official Meketre lived; in his tomb in West Thebes a large collection of wooden models of various workshops, storerooms, and goods was found that gives a vivid idea of life in ancient Egypt at the beginning of the Twelfth Dynasty. Meketre's models are now on exhibit in the Egyptian Museum in Cairo and in New York's Metropolitan Museum.

At this time of unrest in which conflicts probably threatened the country's unity, the figure of the vizier Amenemhet steps into the limelight. The following passage from Neferti's *Prophecy*—a famous ancient Egyptian literary work that describes the oppressive situation in an Egypt ruined and tormented by inner divisions, hunger, and attacks by hostile tribes—probably refers to him (under the abbreviated name of Ameny): "And see now, a king will come out of the south, with name of Ameny . . . a son of a woman from Taseti, a child of Upper Egypt.

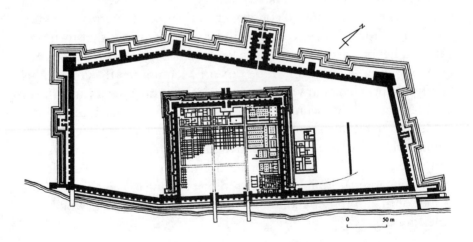

0   50 m

He will seize the White Crown and put on the Red Crown, he will unite the two powers (the crowns of Upper and Lower Egypt). . . ."

The vizier Ameny came from the southernmost tip of Egypt, and his mother was probably of Nubian descent. His name, "Amon is in front," expressed not only the growing authority of the god Amon, the lord of Thebes and "king of the gods," but also Thebes' increasing dominance over all Egypt. However, Amenemhet I (Greek Ammenemes) prudently moved his residence and the Egyptian administration to the north. At the place where the Nile delta approaches the Fayyum oasis, probably near modern Lisht, he founded a new capital. It was given the name *Amenemhet-itj-towy,* abbreviated as *Itj-towy,* "[Amenemhet is] he who takes possession of the two lands." No trace of this capital has yet been found.

The fortress in Buhen (left) and reconstruction of the tower (opposite) (after Emery). The fortress protected the passage over the Nile at the second cataract.

The new residence was closer to the northeast border, allowing quick and energetic action against the advancing Asians, and Amenemhet I had a system of border fortifications built. He defied the threat on his southern border and provided security for his military actions by building mighty fortresses near the second cataract of the Nile.

During Amenemhet I's reign (1991–1962 B.C.E.) of almost thirty years, significant efforts were made to reorganize state administration and to stabilize the economy; agricultural development played a key role in those efforts, which were also associated with the project to cultivate the marshy Fayyum oasis near the new residential city. Written documents suggest that during the last ten years of his reign, Amenemhet I ruled jointly with his son and future successor, Senusret I. This unusual arrangement probably reflected the still somewhat delicate power situation. From that time on, co-regency became an important though not regularly used way of ensuring the continuity of the central power and the unity of the country. Amenemhet's assassination during a palace revolt plotted within his harem shows the necessity of such security measures. At the time Amenemhet was assassinated, his son Senusret was not in the residential city, but on a campaign against Libya, from which he at once returned and quickly brought the situation under control. The events that occurred at the end of Amenemhet I's reign are also referred to in the scribe Akhty's "King Amenemhet's Instructions for his Son Senusret" as well as in "The Story of Sinuhe," both famous literary works.

Senusret I (reigned 1971–1928 B.C.E.) went down in Egyptian history as a successful and powerful ruler. During his forty-four-year reign, he devoted himself primarily to an offensive foreign policy and the securing of Egypt's borders. Lower Nubia was definitively conquered and colonized as far as the second cataract of the Nile, and Egypt's sphere of influence now reached as far as the third cataract. There, Egypt began to build fortresses and temples for the Egyptian gods; but above all it began to exploit on a grand scale the local deposits of gold, copper, and precious stones. In addition, Senusret seems to have taken further military action against the savage Bedouin tribes on the northern border.

In spite of all that, peaceful trading expeditions were also sent out. They went south toward Punt to get spices, incense, and valuable products from East Africa, and north toward Palestine to get cedar wood. Archaeological evidence indicates that there were also trading contacts with remote islands in the Aegean Sea. In connection with his building activities, Senusret I also sent expeditions to Wadi Hammamat in the eastern desert, to the amethyst mines in Wadi el-Hudi in Nubia, and to the alabaster quarries in Hatnub in Middle Egypt.

The important administrative measures taken by Senusret I, which were to lead to a strengthening of the management of the country, are manifested in particular by the erection of stelae that marked out clear provincial boundaries. The power of the individual regional princes was still respected, but it was more fully subordinated to royal authority. For this reason the country flourished under Senusret I's rule. Egyptians saw their ruler, as they had earlier seen Snefru, as a good and just king, and they worshiped him for a long time.

His son Amenemhet II (reigned 1929–1895 B.C.E.) did not enjoy similar expressions of respect, although he also ruled the country for many years, bringing peace and relative prosperity. At the same time, the regional princes were able to further consolidate their power in their own areas. Both Amenemhet II and his successor, Senusret II, had to deal with powerful regional princes such as Sirenput II on Elephantine, Djehutihotep in Bersha, and Khnumhotep II in Beni Hassan.

Economic development was accompanied by active foreign trade. Thus, in the twenty-first year of Amenemhet II's reign, a large expedition returned to Egypt with precious goods from Punt. In addition, silver and lapis lazuli from the mountains east of Mesopotamia, along with other valuable objects, were found in the storehouses of the temple of the god Mont in Tod, in southern Egypt. This treasure (now on display in the Egyptian Museum in Cairo and in the Louvre) is proof of significant trading contacts with more remote areas as well. The mastery achieved by Egyptian artists and craftsmen of this time is shown by the wonderful jewelry found in the princesses' tombs in Dahshur, near the ruler's pyramid.

Senusret II (reigned 1897–1877 B.C.E.) was Amenemhet II's son and perhaps also his co-regent. Under him, the attention the kings of the Twelfth Dynasty had gradually begun to pay to the Fayyum oasis produced concrete changes. A large part of the oasis was originally filled by an enormous lake (its name derived from the Egyptian word *paiom,* "the sea"), a remnant of which is Lake Qarun, now forty-five meters below sea level. At the time the pyramids were built, it was connected with the Nile by the Great Canal. From its Egyptian name *mer uer,* "Great Canal," was derived the bastardized Greek name Moeris Lake; today, Arabs call the canal *Bahr el-Youssef,* "Joseph's River." This canal, together with the Bahr el-Libeini canal that connects with it north of Fayyum, was evidently used by the Old Kingdom pyramid builders to transport stone.

Fish were caught in the lake, but its marshy, reed-choked banks could not be used for farming. Senusret II directed energetic measures designed to make the oasis arable. First he had the Great Canal dammed near the point where it enters the lake. The water level began to sink, and the banks, which were covered with fertile silt, began to dry out. Along this area Senusret II had a large dam built. The flow of the waters of the Nile was finally regulated in such a way that the lake water could be distributed through a network of canals to irrigate the newly developed agricultural land.

The great increase in Fayyum's economic and political importance had other consequences as well. The local divinity, the crocodile Sebek, began to enjoy unprecedented reverence. Senusret II ultimately decided to have his tomb built, not near his royal predecessors in Dahshur or Lisht, but rather in Fayyum, near modern el-Lahun.

Senusret III (reigned 1878–1843 B.C.E.), in contrast to his two immediate predecessors, seems to have been a very warlike ruler. His reign represented another high point of the Twelfth Dynasty. Once again military action had to be taken against the Bedouin tribes in the northeast, because they were threatening the trade routes to the Sinai and were also gradually advancing into the fertile parts of the east delta. The constant threat they posed is shown by the so-called incantation texts dating from the end of the Old Kingdom and the beginning of the New Kingdom. These texts bore the names of enemy princes and were inscribed on clay vessels and statues that were then ritually destroyed.

Senusret III's military efforts consisted chiefly of repeated campaigns against Nubia, as is shown by stone stelae near Semna and Uronarti at the second cataract of the Nile. These campaigns were followed by a period of peace and economic cooperation with Egypt's southern neighbor, the kingdom of Kush.

Senusret III proceeded within Egypt just as energetically as he did outside it. With the help of certain administrative measures, such as the combination of several provinces into larger administrative units, he tried to reduce significantly the power of the regional princes. These steps not only made the country's management more efficient and increased the strength of the central government, but also led to a flourishing of craftwork and trade that promoted urban development and, in turn, the rise of a relatively large middle class that also began to assert its interests and exercise its social influence.

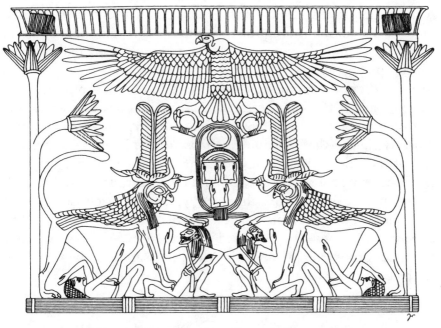

Obverse of a golden pectoral enameled in color, which belonged to Princess Merit from Dahshur (Egyptian Museum in Cairo). The pectoral has the form of a portico ornamented with two lotus pillars and a concave cornice. In the middle of the pectoral there is a cartouche with the throne names of the princess's father, Senusret III, over which the goddess Nekhbet hovers. The ruler, in the form of a griffin, crushes Egypt's enemies under his paws.

Amenemhet III, Senusret III's son, was the last great pharaoh of the Twelfth Dynasty. During his reign (1808–1797 B.C.E.), Egypt enjoyed relative peace and economic growth. As rock inscriptions over the level of the Nile floods at the second cataract show, favorable climatic conditions prevailed. As agriculture flourished, so did trade, particularly with Syria and Palestine. The expeditions to Nubia served as both punitive actions and ways of gaining important resources. According to the inscription on a stela from the thirty-third year of Amenemhet III's reign, in which structural improvements to the fortress in Semna are mentioned, it was possible to maintain the border at the second cataract.

Large construction projects—the pyramid complexes in Dahshur and Hawara, the temple in Medinet Maadi, and others—contributed to the development of the arts. Sculpture reached a high point. Particularly noteworthy are the statues that represent the ruler not in a more or less idealized form full of youth and strength, but as an old, tired man. Naturally, science and literature also benefited from the general prosperity.

In addition, the fading of the provincial nobility's importance is striking, as are the king's efforts to use strict rules to regulate the status and work of the bureaucracy. Some Egyptologists see in this an early sign of the impending collapse of the Egyptian state. The end of the Middle Kingdom is unclear in many respects. With the death of Amenemhet IV, the son and co-regent of Amenemhet III, the main male line ended. Subsequently, his sister Nefrusebek ruled for a short time. The tombs of these last two members of the Twelfth Dynasty have not yet been located with certainty. Although we have no direct proof, the pyramids in Mazghuna are usually attributed to them.

The Eleventh Dynasty—Mentuhotep II's Terraced Tomb

The ruler who unified Egypt at the end of the First Intermediate Period, (about 2000 B.C.E.), Nebhepetre Mentuhotep II came from

Waset (Thebes) and had his tomb erected there rather than near the old capital in Memphis. He selected a site on a rocky hillside at modern Deir el-Bahari on the west bank of the Nile, near the rock-cut tombs of his predecessors—called "saff tombs" (from Arabic *saff*, "row") because of the rows of pillars on their facades—in the present-day village of Tarif. Mentuhotep II broke with this tradition, not only in the dimensions, but also in the conception of his tomb. Egyptologists do not agree regarding the original appearance of Mentuhotep's tomb, which the ruler named "Mentuhotep's [cult] sites shine blissfully." However, they are in accord on one point: its ground plan combined elements of the saff tomb and the pyramid complex.

Henri Édouard Naville and Henry Hall (1873–1930) investigated Mentuhotep's tomb complex from 1903 to 1907 with the support of the Egypt Exploration Fund. The Metropolitan Museum of New York's archaeologists, under the direction of Herbert Winlock, continued this investigation from 1911 to 1931. However, they too were unable to complete their excavations. Their excavations were completed only from 1968 to 1971, by a team from the German Archaeological Institute in Cairo, under Dieter Arnold's direction.

The construction of the tomb complex—which went through three (Winlock) or four (Arnold) phases—consists of a valley temple, whose ruins now lie under the fields and gardens at the edge of the Nile Valley; a long causeway; the stepped, terraced mortuary temple, whose western part is cut into the rock; and an underground burial chamber. The longer axis of the whole complex initially runs in an east-west direction and then bends slightly to the north.

In contrast to most similar structures from the Old Kingdom, the causeway was open. Statues of the king, who was identified with the god Osiris, ruler over the realm of the dead, stood at regular intervals along its sides. The causeway ended in a large courtyard surrounded by a limestone wall.

In the west part of the courtyard, against the background of a craggy rock wall, stood the massive, terracelike structure of the mortuary temple, which was reached via a broad ramp of limestone blocks. On both sides of the ramp a grove of sycamores and tamarisks had been planted, through which there were avenues. The east facade of the

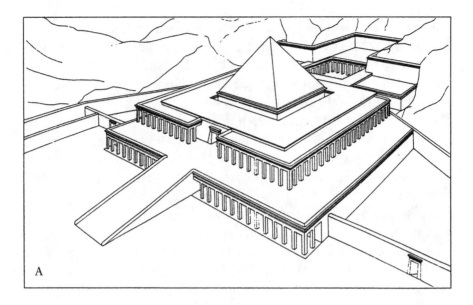

A

lowest level with the lower pillared hall consisted of a portico built of limestone blocks. The portico was divided in half by a ramp and had two rows of pillars. On its walls there were originally reliefs with scenes of battle.

The middle terrace had three parts. Its core was a symbolic version of the primeval mound, made of hard clay that had been shaped into a roughly cubic form. It was surrounded on all four sides by a pillared ambulatory and at a somewhat greater distance on the east, north, and south sides by a pillared portico, known as the upper pillared hall.

The latter consisted, like its lower counterpart, of two rows of limestone pillars. The front side of the pillars was decorated with pictures of the ruler and the gods, as well as with inscriptions in low relief. Behind them was a wall, also built of limestone. Its slight inclination suggests that it once composed the outer facade of the pillared ambulatory, and thus that the upper pillared hall was built later.

The entrance into the limestone ambulatory was on the east wing of the pillared hall and was located on the main axis of the structure as a whole. In the ambulatory stood 140 octagonal pillars arranged

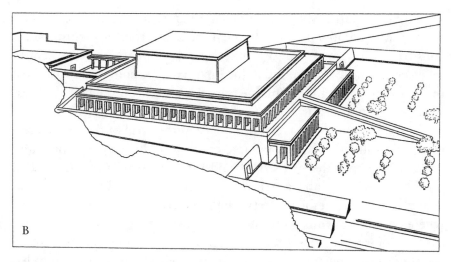

Reconstruction of Mentuhotep's tomb complex, according to Naville (A) and Arnold (B).

in two rows on the west side and three rows on the other sides. The ambulatory was dimly illuminated by shafts in the massive exterior wall near the portico.

On the west side of the middle terrace there was originally a row of six shaft tombs cut into the rock subsoil. Their underground part consisted of chapels built of limestone blocks, with false doors and cult statues. Queens and princesses were buried there, evidently members of Mentuhotep's family. All the women died very young, the eldest at about twenty-two, the youngest at five years of age. They may have all died at the same time, and the general hypothesis is that they fell victim to an accident or an epidemic. The actual relationship between these women and the ruler is unclear, for only four of them bore the title "royal consort." Arnold placed them in the special category of priestesses of Hathor, the tutelary goddess of the Theban necropolis. Callender assumes that they were connected with Mentuhotep through diplomatic marriages contracted in connection with the king's effort to subordinate rebellious magnates, to stabilize the social situation, and to unify the country. Alongside these women are buried consorts of Mentuhotep.

Among the latter was Aashait, a Nubian whose rank is shown by her decorated wooden coffin. In the tomb of another of Mentuhotep's consorts, Kauit, was found a limestone sarcophagus with splendid reliefs; it can now be admired in the Egyptian Museum in Cairo. When the decision was made to enlarge the ruler's tomb complex, the tombs were integrated into it.

The expansion to the west took place at the level of the middle terrace and included the open, pillared courtyard, the hypostyle hall, and a rock-cut temple, the Speos. The sandstone courtyard was surrounded on the south, east, and north by octagonal pillars. There were also eighty-two pillars in the hypostyle hall. Its pavement was of limestone, whereas the side walls were built of sandstone.

On the far west side of the complex was the Speos, a long, vaulted room built of limestone with a sandstone pavement. A low ramp led to the limestone altar in its west part. In this room there were originally a false door and a larger-than-life-size cult statue of the ruler. In addition to other cult objects there was a sitting statue of the god Amon. The shrine functioned simultaneously as a cult site for important gods such as Amon, Mont, Osiris, and Hathor.

On the axis of the pillared courtyard, a vaulted descending corridor begins in the pavement and leads into the royal burial chamber. Naville opened the corridor in 1906, but it had already been plundered by grave robbers in antiquity. Arnold reexamined it in 1971. In the niches of its side walls were six hundred wooden figurines that were once part of the models of workshops, bakeries, and boats that made up the royal tomb furnishings. The passageway, about a dozen meters long, ends in a granite burial chamber with a saddle ceiling. A large part of the room is taken up by an alabaster chapel, entered through a wooden double door. A sarcophagus was not found there, leading Naville to conclude that it was a symbolic burial chamber for the king's ka. Arnold, however, defended—probably correctly—a different thesis based on another strange discovery in the history of Egyptian archaeology.

One evening in 1899, Howard Carter, who was later to become famous as the discoverer of Tutankhamen's tomb, was riding over the front part of the courtyard before Mentuhotep's terraced tomb complex; he was at that time conducting archaeological work nearby. Suddenly, his horse stumbled. Carter dismounted to see if his horse had been injured, and himself stumbled onto a discovery—the entrance to the underground part of the tomb. The Arab excavation workers therefore named it Bab el-Hussan, "horse door."

The entrance was initially an open trench, and then became a vaulted corridor built of mudbricks. At a depth of about seventeen meters, Carter discovered a door sealed by a brick wall about four meters thick. Behind it, the corridor at first continued westward, and then turned north. At the turning point, Carter discovered a shaft in the floor, barely two meters deep; in it were the remains of a wooden chest that bore Mentuhotep's name. At its end, the long corridor became a further shaft, on whose floor was the access to the burial chamber. In the burial chamber (located under the temple's step-structure) were found—together with the remains of an empty, uninscribed wooden coffin, ceramics, and the bones of sacrificial animals—the most valuable object: a polychrome statue of the sitting king, wrapped in fine linen. It represents Mentuhotep II with the crown of Lower Egypt on his head, and is now one of the famous exhibits in the Egyptian Museum in Cairo (JE 36.195). According to Arnold, the tomb in Bab el-Hussan is symbolic, and Mentuhotep may have built it in connection with the sed festivities.

The structure on the upper terrace was almost completely destroyed, and its architecture is still a subject of debate. Naville, who was the first archaeologist to investigate Mentuhotep's tomb complex, reconstructed the original monument as a pyramid, which was built on the previously mentioned rock subsoil.

Arnold rejected this interpretation, primarily because no evidence— for example, part of an inclined pyramid wall—was found to support it. He suggested that it was a structure with a more or less rectangular ground plan and a flat roof terrace, and saw it as a stylized representation of the primeval mound.

The third, most recent, view was offered by Stadelmann. It is essentially a variant of Arnold's reconstruction, with the addition of a sand hill planted with trees—a version, according to the German Egyptologist, in which ideas about the primeval mound and the tomb of the god Osiris are combined.

However the upper part of the structure may have looked, uncertainties about its reconstruction have to do not only with a lack of archaeological sources but also with another interesting issue. Almost a thousand years after Mentuhotep's tomb complex was built, investigators were sent to look into the plundering that was going on there. Written reports relating to that investigation and the prosecution of grave robbers have come down to us. In the Abbott papyrus we find the following remark: "On the eighteenth day of the third month of flood season in the sixteenth year of the reign of the ruler of Upper and Lower Egypt, of the Lord of both lands, Neferkare Setepenre—long may he live, be healthy, and flourish!—, son of Re, Lord of the revelation in the splendor of Ramesses Miamun. . . . On this day inspectors were sent to the great and sublime tomb sites, the vizier's scribe and the scribe of the pharaoh's treasury, in order to examine the tombs of the old kings. . . . Pyramids, tombs, and graves that were examined by the inspectors on this day . . ."

In this report from the time of Ramesses IX, Mentuhotep's tomb complex is explicitly designated as a pyramid. However, a persuasive contemporary note with a description of the tomb has unfortunately not been preserved. Nonetheless, during his excavations Arnold came across two fragments of inscriptions that may contain the tomb's name, which ends with a determinative qualifying it as a pyramid. A similar name also appears in other written documents, especially one from the "Tomb of Slain Soldiers" dating from Mentuhotep II's reign. This is a symbol the famous American Egyptologist L. Bull saw as representing "a truncated obelisk or pyramid, projecting above another structure. Over the obelisk appears to be a sun-disk from which . . . usually extend two rays of light on each side." According to Bull, who worked in West Thebes for a long time, the symbol is a stylized image of Mentuhotep II's funeral monument. In the inscription on the Twelfth Dynasty Tutu stela, the tomb's name is qualified by the hieroglyphic sign for a pyramid. However, in the New Kingdom graffiti found nearby, the determinative used in references to Mentuhotep's tomb looks more like a terrace with an obelisk culminating in a pyramidion than like a pyramid.

Despite these written documents, most Egyptologists remain skeptical regarding the interpretation of the structure as a pyramid. In the text on the Abbott papyrus, other tombs are designated as pyramids that were demonstrably not pyramids, such as the nearby tombs of Eleventh Dynasty rulers from Tarif and Dra Abu el-Naga. Egyptologists now presume either that the form of the ruins of the tomb looked somewhat like a funeral mound or a pyramid, or that the traditional idea of a monumental royal tomb was so strongly associated with the pyramid that in this case the hieroglyphic of a pyramid represented the qualifying determinative in the designation of the tomb. Evidence for this view is provided, for example, by contemporary variations in the way the name of Neferefre's Fifth Dynasty tomb complex was written. Although the tomb did not end up as a true, but only a low, truncated, pyramid, the scribes used the pyramid sign as a determinative.

Nevertheless, we must again emphasize that the question of the true appearance of the upper level of Mentuhotep's tomb complex remains open. While the large amount of time separating the note on the Abbott papyrus from the original erection of the monument may explain a certain misunderstanding, the almost contemporary written sources, such as the signs from the tombs of slain soldiers or from Tutu's stela, are not so easily explained. Any massive upper structure arouses general doubts of an architectonic or aesthetic nature, because the underlying structure is not very impressive, consisting of the pillared hall in the facade.

The nature of the structure and its ruins allow other interpretations based on ancient Egyptian religious ideas and on their ability to bring the structure into harmony with its environment (the amphitheater of cleft rock in the background). In any case, this very original monument inspired later masters, as is shown by Queen Hatshepsut's terraced temple, built nearby almost six hundred years later, during the Eighteenth Dynasty. Debate among Egyptologists concerning the original form of Mentuhotep's tomb in Deir el-Bahari is far from over.

The Twelfth Dynasty—From Stone to Mudbricks

AMENEMHET I'S PYRAMID

Amenemhet, who was first vizier and then the founding ruler of the Twelfth Dynasty, abandoned Waset as his residential city and also left unfinished his tomb there. He moved the center of state administration north to the new capital, Itj-towy, near Memphis, where it was easier to consolidate power over both parts of Egypt. Some Egyptologists, basing their view on contemporary documents, locate Itj-towy on the east bank of the Nile, but it was more probably near Lisht, for it was there that the ruler had his pyramid complex built, which evidently lay close to the new capital. He named the pyramid "Cult places of Amenemhet's appearance." Here we should mention that by so doing, Amenemhet I founded a new tradition. While the names of pyramids previously included all the associated structures, including the pyramid town, from Amenemhet's time on the major components of the complex had their own names.

In 1882, Maspero became the first archaeologist to descend into the interior of this pyramid. In 1894 and 1895, his work was continued by the French archaeological expedition under the direction of Gautier and Jéquier. From 1902 to 1934, a team from the Metropolitan Museum in New York, led by Albert Lythgoe (1868–1934) and Arthur Mace (1874–1928), pursued the investigations further.

Of the pyramid, only ruins about twenty meters high remain. This lamentable situation was caused not only by grave robbers but also by the way the pyramid was built. The quality of the construction methods and materials used in building pyramids had already declined during the Old Kingdom, although stone continued to be used. At the beginning of the Twelfth Dynasty, another construction material, mudbricks, became dominant. This development may have been related not only to efforts to reduce costs and labor, but also to the rich clay deposits nearby, in Middle Egypt and in the Fayyum oasis, where the pyramids were built. Moreover, from the age of Senusret I onward, a masonry framework of stone blocks was constructed, and mudbricks were laid over the diagonals as well as perpendicular to the future pyramid walls. That framework was filled with mudbricks and, if necessary, pieces of less valuable stone and other waste construction materials. High-quality limestone casing blocks were laid over the core constructed in this manner.

The entrance into the underground part of Amenemhet's pyramid was located, as was the general rule in earlier pyramids, in the middle of the north wall, at ground level. It is important to note that in many respects the builders of the tomb complex took their inspiration from the Old Kingdom pyramids in Dahshur and South Saqqara, but also from some elements typical of the immediately preceding royal tombs in Tarif and Deir el-Bahari. Over the entrance stood the north chapel, and in it opened, behind a granite false door, a corridor that gradually descended to the burial chamber. The corridor was lined with pink granite and sealed with blocks of the same material.

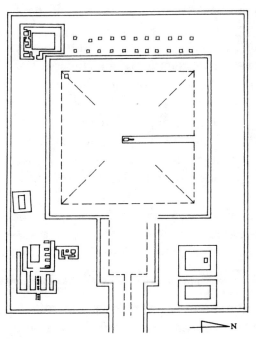

Ground plan of Amenemhet I's pyramid complex, without causeway or valley temple (after Mace). Behind the pyramid was a row of shaft tombs for the princesses and courtiers.

The corridor came out in a square chamber that lay on the pyramid's vertical axis. In its floor opened a vertical shaft that led to the burial chamber. Access to the latter is now hindered by the groundwater that collects there in such quantity that all efforts to pump it out have failed.

The mortuary temple on the east side of the pyramid had its own, different name: "High [rises up] Amenemhet's beauty." In contrast to similar edifices of the Old Kingdom, it had very modest dimensions and lay below the level of the pyramid's base (this peculiarity might be a distant echo of the conception of Mentuhotep's terraced temple in Deir el-Bahari). Of the temple, which was oriented east-west, almost nothing remains, so that reconstructing its original plan is difficult. A few inscriptions and relief fragments found in the temple suggest that it was probably rebuilt during the rule of Senusret I. Among the few things remaining are a limestone false door and a granite altar that was once in the offering hall.

Only the upper end of the courtyard (which was originally open and decorated with reliefs, and may have been modeled on its predecessor in Mentuhotep II's complex in Deir el-Bahari) has been investigated. The valley temple has not been thoroughly examined, either; on its site the local Muslim cemetery is now spreading.

The pyramid and the mortuary temple were surrounded by two perimeter walls. In the area between them, the tombs of members of the royal family and courtiers were discovered. Alongside the pyramid's west wall was a double row of shaft tombs. The tomb of the vizier Antefiker, an important official during the reign of Amenemhet I, was also found near the southwest corner of the pyramid. He had had an earlier edifice built in Waset. A stela from his Nubian campaign was found in the early 1960s by a Czech team of Egyptologists led by Zbyněk Žába (1917–1971).

On his first visit to the pyramid, Maspero noted that stone blocks from older royal tomb complexes had been used in its construction—a discovery that later investigations have fully confirmed. In various parts of the complex stones were found that bore the names of the rulers Khufu, Khafre, Unas, and Pepi (II?), suggesting that the valley temples of those rulers in Giza and Saqqara already lay in ruins in Amenemhet I's time, and that he did not hesitate to make them into his personal quarry. This is the view of Hans Goedicke, who has thoroughly examined the blocks and cataloged them, and it is shared by most Egyptologists. However, Arnold does not exclude the possibility that the blocks came also from other edifices—for example, from the temples those rulers erected in Middle Egypt, near Lisht.

SENUSRET I'S PYRAMID

Archaeological investigations of Senusret I's pyramid complex have followed almost the same course of historical development as those of his father Amenemhet I's complex. Gautier and Jéquier worked there in 1894–1895, followed by a team from the Metropolitan Museum of New York led by Lythgoe, Mace, and Ambrose Lansing (1891–1959). Arnold built on their work and the documentation they collected when he pursued his excavations there from 1984 to 1987.

Senusret I also had his pyramid erected in Lisht, about one and one-half kilometers south of Amenemhet I's. It was called "Senusret looks down on both lands" and was somewhat larger than his father's pyramid, though they did not basically differ.

Limestone from the nearby quarries was the chief material used. A stone masonry framework supported the core, which rested on a foundation platform of stone blocks. The empty space inside the framework was filled with fragments of limestone, sand, and waste material from the construction site. The casing of blocks of fine white limestone was firmly anchored in a flat trench dug around the pyramid's base.

This was the method typically used by the pyramid builders of the Middle Kingdom, and it lent not only the casing but the whole pyramid increased stability, which was urgently needed since the core was composed of lower-quality material. Under the corners of the pyramid, items buried during the foundation ceremonies were found, and others lay outside. Interestingly, no stones from older pyramid complexes were found in this one.

The entrance to the underground part of the pyramid was in the pavement of the courtyard, in front of the middle of the pyramid's north side. Over it stood, as was usual in the pyramids of the Old Kingdom, the north chapel.* An alabaster stela was inset into the wall closest to the pyramid, in front of which a granite altar stood. The other walls were decorated with scenes in colored bas-relief and—so far as we can tell from the poorly preserved fragments that remain—depicted sacrifice rituals, processions of divinities, and so on. A gargoyle in the form of a recumbent lion carried rainwater away from the roof terrace.

A descending corridor that began under the pavement of the north chapel did not continue, like that in Amenemhet I's pyramid, along the axis, but instead turned, as in some Fifth Dynasty pyramids, toward the southeast. At the entrance, the corridor was sheathed in granite, and the barrier of enormous blocks of the same stone, weighing as much as twenty tons, is still there. As in Amenemhet I's pyramid, the underground portion is filled with water. Arnold estimates that the burial chamber lay about twenty-four meters under ground level.

Beneath the descending corridor, a longer and somewhat flatter descending tunnel was discovered. It began in the courtyard in front of the pyramid's north side and was used to transport material for the substructure. After the royal burial site under the pyramid was completed, the tunnel was blocked.

The pyramid was surrounded by an inner perimeter wall that delimited the grounds of the royal tomb proper and the area where the dead king was worshiped (it also included the west half of the mortuary temple and the small cult pyramid). Somewhat farther away was the outer perimeter wall, which surrounded the tombs of the members of the royal family as well.

The inner perimeter wall, built of limestone blocks, was absolutely unique. On its inner side, at intervals of five meters, there were narrow panels decorated with images in bas-relief. In the lower part,

---

* In a later period of the Twelfth Dynasty, this standard placement was abandoned; it had lost its function because of a change in the substructure's ground plan and because the entrance was moved to different places.

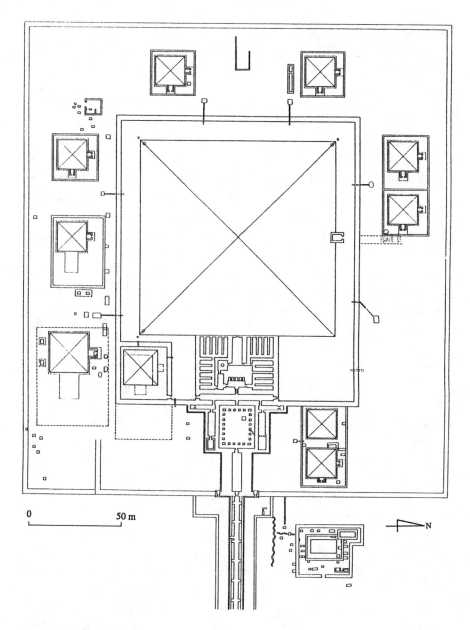

Ground plan of Senusret I's pyramid complex, including the pyramids of the queens and princesses, but without causeway or valley temple (after Arnold).

fertility gods brought gifts, and above them appeared the serekh with the ruler's name. On it was always his Horus name, Ankhmesut, and then either his throne name, Kheperkare, or his birth name, Senusret.

The small cult pyramid—the last of its kind to be erected in a royal tomb complex—stood, as was usual in the earlier royal complexes of the Old Kingdom, at the southeast corner of the pyramid. In contrast to its Old Kingdom predecessors, however, it had two chapels: a sacrifice chapel at the base of the pyramid on the east, and on the north a so-called entrance chapel or north chapel. The cult pyramid was plundered in antiquity and destroyed by stone thieves. In Arnold's view, the statue of the king's ka might have been buried in one of its underground chambers and the canopic chest in the other.

The mortuary temple, which was called "United are the [cult] places [of Senusret]," was also almost completely destroyed by stone thieves. Fortunately, however, some fairly large parts of the pavement remain and make it possible to reconstruct the original ground plan. The ground plan strikingly resembles those of late Fifth Dynasty and Sixth Dynasty mortuary temples, except that the number of storehouses, particularly in the western part, was significantly smaller. The reconstruction of the decoration is difficult, even though about six hundred relief fragments have been found.

The long, vaulted entrance hall provides a natural transition between the upper end of the approach causeway and the open, pillared courtyard. Together with the courtyard and the long string of storage rooms along its sides, it constitutes the east half of the temple. Twenty-four limestone monolithic pillars support the ceiling. In the northwest corner of the courtyard, which is paved with limestone, Gautier discovered an altar in the form of a square block of granite decorated with inscriptions and reliefs. The courtyard also had a drainage system, used particularly for rainwater.

A transverse corridor divided the eastern from the western, inner part of the temple, and simultaneously allowed communication in a north-south direction with the open courtyard around the pyramid and with the small cult pyramid. A small staircase in the west wall of the corridor led to a five-niche chapel. Like the rest of the temple, it

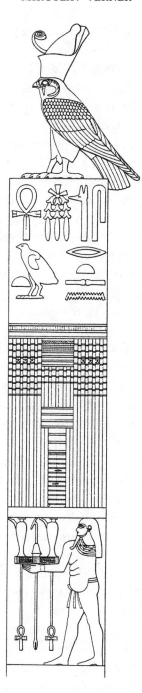

Panel decoration from the perimeter wall of Senusret I's pyramid (after Arnold).

was completely destroyed, but the American team was nonetheless able to find in the rubble fragments of the base and part of the feet of a limestone standing statue of the king. The inscription indicates that this was a statue of Senusret I, and the remains of the feet allow us to estimate its original height at about 2.7 meters, without the crown. This important discovery shed some light on the original appearance of chapels in mortuary temples as well as on the cult statues that stood in their five niches.

Although it was almost completely destroyed, the antichambre carrée also represents an important discovery: in its pavement the foundation block of pink granite and its impression of a column that once supported the ceiling have been preserved. This suggests that it was a twleve-stemmed papyrus column, which is surprising, since in the older mortuary temples octagonal or cylindrical columns were generally preferred.

The offering hall, with its vaulted ceiling, had a false door on the west wall, which was adjacent to the pyramid. In front of it was a granite altar. Arnold thinks it possible that a greater-than-life-size granite statue of the king once stood there, a fragment of which was found east of the temple. The decoration of the hall consists primarily of scenes of sacrifice, as was generally the rule. The remaining part of the west half of the temple, that is, the area north and south of the five-niche chapel and the offering hall, was filled with storerooms. The temple's side walls were slightly inclined and had a concave cornice at the top. On them rested a roof terrace, eight meters above ground level at its highest point.

In the relatively extensive open space between the inner and the outer perimeter walls, nine small pyramid complexes were discovered, three on the south side and two each on the west, north, and east sides of the pyramid. Ambrose Lansing earlier thought they were simple cenotaphs. The pyramids and mortuary temples each had their own perimeter walls. Sometimes inside, sometimes outside these complexes were other tomb shafts, reserved for members of the royal family. So far, the pyramid complexes of Nofret I and Itakaiet have been identified. The former was Amenemhet I's daughter and the consort of Senusret I. For the first time in Egyptian history her name was also

written in a cartouche, a privilege previously reserved for the pharaoh alone. Some Egyptologists assume that this queen had her father
murdered by agreement with her husband, and they can base their
view to a certain extent on the famous ancient Egyptian literary work
The Story of Sinuhe. Many experts believe Itakaiet was Senusret I's
daughter, while others believe she was his consort.

The valley temple now lies under massive deposits of sand between
the desert and the Nile Valley and has not yet been precisely located.
As usual, it was connected with the mortuary temple by a causeway.
Its builders were inspired more by Mentuhotep II's tomb complex in
far-off Thebes than by nearby pyramid complexes in the necropolis
at Memphis. It was rebuilt and reconceived, and at regular intervals
in the inner walls there were deep niches in which stood larger-than-
life-size statues of the king. These corresponded to the Osiris type (in
mummy form, with the arms crossed over the breast) and bore alter-
nately the crowns of Upper and Lower Egypt. These statues are now
in the Egyptian Museum in Cairo and the Metropolitan Museum in
New York.

Around Senusret I's pyramid complex were tombs of important
figures of his reign. The most prominent of these is the tomb of
Senusretankh, which lies northeast of the outer perimeter wall of
the king's complex. It is distinguished by the well-preserved decoration of its burial chamber and the beautifully ornamented sarcophagus. It is worth noting that the walls of the chamber are covered
with mortuary texts that are familiar from the royal tombs of the
Old Kingdom.

The description of Senusret I's funerary monument would not be
complete without at least some mention of the important discovery
Gautier made there on 21 December 1884. In a hiding place north of
the mortuary temple, under the pavement of the pyramid courtyard,
he found ten sitting statues of Senusret I, in limestone and larger than
life size. Today they are among the most famous exhibits in the Egyptian Museum in Cairo. They were originally painted to resemble granite. Some of them were obviously left unfinished. The prevailing opinion
among Egyptologists has been that these statues first stood in the
temple's open, pillared courtyard, from which priests quickly removed

them at the beginning of the Hyksos period, concealing them in the fear that they would be desecrated by Egypt's Asian conquerors.

Arnold does not share this view. He maintains that the statues might have been intended as decoration for the approach corridor, but after the plan was changed they were replaced by the previously mentioned Osiris statues and reverently "buried" under the pavement in the pyramid's courtyard.

AMENEMHET II'S PYRAMID

Amenemhet II chose to build his tomb in the old royal cemetery in Dahshur, which dates from the beginning of the Fourth Dynasty, east of the Red Pyramid and on the edge of the desert. The pyramid, which he probably called "Amenemhet is well cared for," now resembles an unprepossessing, gray pile of mudbricks, grossly contradicting its local name, "White Pyramid." That name may be connected with the framework of its core, which once rose out of the ruins and was made of white limestone blocks, or with the countless small fragments of white limestone that now cover the pyramid's ruins.

In 1894–1895, Jacques de Morgan made an archaeological investigation of the ruins, but unfortunately it was hasty and therefore superficial. Fascinated by the wonderful jewelry found in the princesses' tombs, he did not make a careful examination of the mortuary temple, the causeway, or the valley temple.

The entrance into the underground chambers was in the middle of the pyramid's north side and hidden by the north chapel. Through it one reached a descending corridor built of limestone blocks whose construction resembled that of Neferirkare's pyramid in Abusir. Over the flat ceiling there was another gabled ceiling made of limestone slabs leaned one against the other, in order to divert the pressure bearing on the corridor from above. At its lower end, the corridor became horizontal and came out in the burial chamber, which was located on the pyramid's vertical axis. Not far in front of it was a

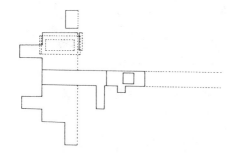

Ground plan and north-south sectional view through the burial chamber in Amenemhet II's pyramid (after de Morgan).

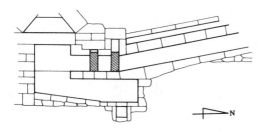

barrier made of two vertical granite slabs. The burial chamber itself (whose ceiling was built in the same way as the corridor in order to reduce the pressure from above) is remarkable because of its somewhat irregular ground plan: while its main part was oriented east-west, one segment came up under the part of the corridor with the barrier. A quartzite sarcophagus stood on the west wall.

The mortuary temple, which may have been called "Lighted is the place of Amenemhet's pleasure," was almost completely destroyed. As yet, its ruins in front of the pyramid's east wall have not been thoroughly investigated. How much might be learned from doing so is indicated not only by the many fragments of architectural elements and relief decorations de Morgan found on its grounds, but also by the massive, towerlike structures resembling pylons in the temple's east facade, already encountered in Djedkare's pyramid complex. It seems clear that the plan of Amenemhet II's mortuary temple had a certain originality. The causeway and the valley temple have not been investigated at all.

Plan of Amenemhet II's
pyramid complex, with-
out causeway and valley
temple (after de Morgan).

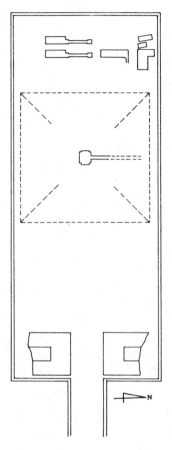

The mortuary temple and the pyramid were surrounded by a large
perimeter wall. In the area between its west wing and the west wall
of the pyramid, de Morgan discovered tombs in which members of
the royal family were buried: Prince Amenemhetankh as well as the
princesses Ita, Khnemet, Itiueret, and Sithathormeret. In the princesses' tombs he found the remains of the tomb furnishings, including wooden coffins, canopic chests, and alabaster vessels for fragrant
balms. However, the most valuable discovery was the wonderful
jewelry from the tombs of Ita and Khnemet, which can now be admired in the Treasure Chamber of the Egyptian Museum in Cairo.

SENUSRET II'S PYRAMID

Senusret II devoted special attention to the Fayyum oasis, and thus it is not surprising that he chose it as his last resting place. The improvements he made to the marshy land there and the subsequent colonization contributed significantly to the increase in the country's agricultural production. So that he could also take pleasure in his work in the beyond, the ruler had his pyramid built near el-Lahun at the entrance from the Nile Valley and named it "Senusret shines."

The first archaeological inquiries into this monument were made in the 1840s by the Lepsius expedition, but a genuine investigation was first undertaken fifty years later, by Petrie. His first attempt to make his way into the underground part of the pyramid was unsuccessful, because he was looking for the entrance in the middle of the north side, where it was normally located during the Old Kingdom and at the beginning of the Middle Kingdom. The clever builders of

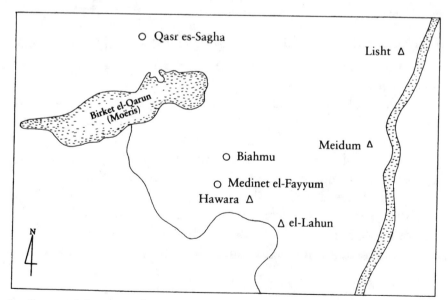

Small map of the pyramids in the Fayyum oasis.

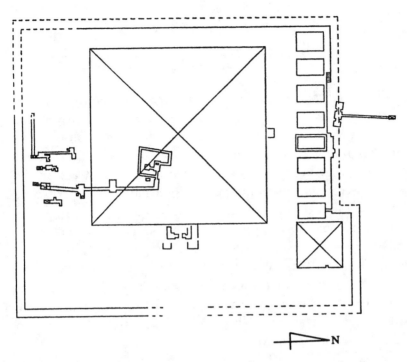

Plan of Senusret II's pyramid complex, without causeway and valley temple (after Petrie).

the pyramid had also erected there the small chapel that usually concealed the entrance. Petrie had no idea that Senusret II had decided—not only for religious reasons but also on the basis of his experience with grave robbers—to alter the basic plan of the pyramid's substructure. After many attempts and a long, difficult search, Petrie found the entrance to the pyramid in a place where hardly anyone would have expected it to be—under the tomb (no. 10) of a princess, about a dozen yards away from the south side of the pyramid.

As in the case of Amenemhet II's pyramid, the core was built of mudbricks, with a framework of stone masonry. The builders used a rock outcropping to anchor the core and to make construction quicker and cheaper. Petrie learned from an inscription that the pyramid's white limestone casing was removed during the Nineteenth Dynasty and used for a structure built by Ramesses II. Only a few fragments of the black granite pyramidion have been found.

The builders made another highly interesting innovation. They dug a trench in the rock subsoil around the pyramid and filled it with sand. In this way they prevented the pyramid as well as the structures immediately around it from being flooded from below, for even after a heavy rainfall the water that flowed off the walls disappeared into the sand. Around the trench ran a low, stone perimeter wall, decorated with niches and partly cut into the rock subsoil.

But now let us return to the change in the substructure. The entrance's orientation to the north had been from the outset—that is, since Djoser's pyramid in Saqqara—one of the fundamental axioms of pyramid construction, because the dead pharaoh, as a god, strove to leave his tomb toward the north, where he was himself to become one of the circumpolar stars. Since the end of the Old Kingdom, however, the earlier conceptions of the astral and stellar religions had taken a back seat to those of the cult of the god of the dead, Osiris. Here the circle closed: in its conception, Senusret II's tomb was supposed to resemble Osiris's tomb. Trees were also planted around the pyramid as a reference to the Osiris cult.

We have already mentioned that the entrance into the substructure was finally discovered in the floor of a princess's tomb near the pyramid. However, the original entrance was a larger shaft of relatively complicated construction in which there was also a room with deep niches. Given its dimensions and ground plan, it was doubtless initially used for transporting construction material into the pyramid's substructure and was later reworked in such a way as to simulate a burial chamber in order to deceive possible grave robbers.

From the floor of this large shaft a horizontal, vaulted corridor led north to a vaulted room. There ended still another relatively narrow vertical shaft, which was probably used to transport the king's mummy after the main entrance through the princess's tomb had been covered over. The corridor, no longer horizontal but slightly ascending, continued north to the antechamber. In the west part of the vaulted room, however, there was another shaft (now flooded and therefore unexplored). Its significance remains unclear, yet it is not impossible that the builders of the substructure used it to monitor the level of the groundwater.

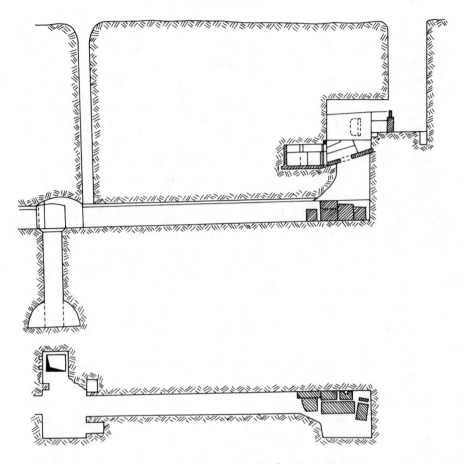

Plan of the entrance into Senusret II's pyramid (after Petrie).

From the antechamber a direct passageway led into the burial chamber, which lay to the west of it. At the same time, the entrance to another passageway opened in the south wall of the antechamber, made a right-angle turn, and went around the burial chamber, eventually entering it from the north.

The substructure of Senusret II's pyramid, with the whole system of shafts, chambers, and passageways surrounding the burial chamber, thus reminds one of a labyrinth. In contrast to earlier pyramids, the burial chamber was located not on the vertical axis but shifted considerably to the southeast—as was the whole substructure. The burial chamber, which was oriented east-west, consisted of the vaulted ceiling of granite blocks and the masterfully worked sarcophagus, which stood on the west wall. Since the sarcophagus is larger than the entrance from the antechamber, it must have been set in place during construction of the burial chamber.

Despite the carefully thought out plan of the substructure and the disguising of the entrance, ancient grave robbers succeeded in finding and plundering the king's burial place. Of the once rich tomb furnishings, Petrie was able to find in the underground part of the pyramid only a golden uraeus, which probably came from a statue of the king.

The relatively small mortuary temple stood before the east side of the pyramid and was almost completely destroyed.

Near the northeast corner of the pyramid a small pyramid (belonging to the queen?) was discovered. Behind it lay eight large mastabas in a row along the north side of the pyramid. Their superstructures were cut into the rock subsoil and walled in with mudbricks. Smaller, genuine princess's tombs were found to the southeast. West of the hidden entrance shaft was the tomb of Princess Sithathoriunet, in which Petrie found the famous Treasure of el-Lahun—marvelous jewelry and other items from the princess's burial equipment, including a gold headband, a gold necklace of small leopard's heads, a gold pectoral ornamented with precious stones and bearing Senusret II's name, another with Amenemhet III's name, bracelets, rings, and alabaster and obsidian vessels, decorated with gold, for fragrant balms. These objects are now on exhibit in the Treasure Chamber in the Egyptian Museum in Cairo.

The pyramid, the mortuary temple, and the tombs of members of the royal family were surrounded by a perimeter wall along which trees were planted. North of it, Petrie discovered the ruins of another heavily damaged structure with an extensive courtyard, thought to have been a sed festival chapel.

The valley temple was located relatively far from the pyramid, with which it was probably not, according to Arnold, directly connected. Northeast of the temple the workers and officials associated with the construction and later with the worship of the ruler once lived. Their settlement was called "Senusret is contented" and is known in Egyptology under the modern name of the place, Kahun.

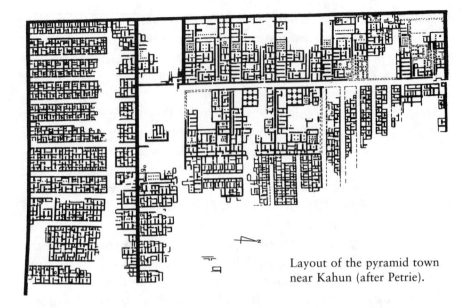

Layout of the pyramid town near Kahun (after Petrie).

As was then usual, the town's buildings were built of mudbrick, sometimes combined with light plant material. The settlement was built in accord with a unified plan. A brick wall three meters thick surrounded it on the outside, whereas a similar wall inside the settlement divided it into a smaller part and a larger part. Open canals carrying off rainwater ran down the middle of the streets; in the western part of the settlement the streets intersected and could be supervised at night by a small number of guards. The house types (Petrie distinguished eight of them) ranged from small and simple to a palace-like edifice with an extensive courtyard and highly structured architecture. The part of the settlement discovered by Petrie included 2,145 houses, on the basis of which the population has been estimated at five to eight thousand people.

Papyri are among the most valuable archaeological discoveries Petrie made in the settlement. Most come from the temple archive and date from the reigns of Senusret III and his immediate successors. They include administrative, business, literary, medical, astronomical, veterinary, and religious documents. Today they are in the Egyptian Museum in Cairo, the Egyptian Museum in Berlin, and the collection of the University College in London.

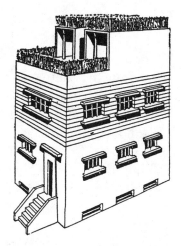

Limestone models of a house from the New Kingdom (Louvre E. 5357). On the right, a reconstruction of one of the common residential dwellings of the same time (after Desroches).

Egyptian villa with garden (after Chipiez).

SENUSRET III'S PYRAMID

When Herodotus visited Egypt in the fifth century B.C.E., Senusret III, despite his relatively short reign, was considered the most important ruler of the Middle Kingdom, and many legends were told about him. His pyramid complex, which was built northeast of the Red Pyramid in Dahshur, far surpassed the tombs of his predecessors from the early Twelfth Dynasty, and not only in size. In both its plan and its underlying religious conception, it differed in many respects from earlier royal tombs and represented another developmental milestone.

The plan of the pyramid complex of Senusret III (after Arnold).

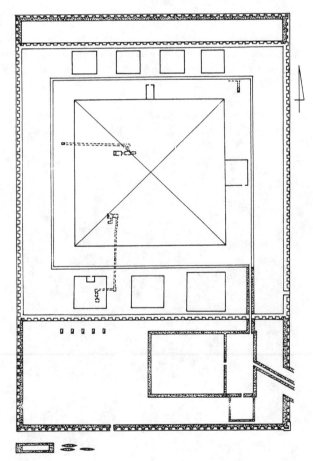

The pyramid—its name is not yet known—was investigated in 1894–1895 by de Morgan. Its superstructure differed from those of earlier pyramids: the core was made of mudbricks, but it no longer had a stone masonry framework. On the other hand, the casing of white limestone followed the earlier mode of construction. Like Petrie in exploring Senusret II's pyramid in el-Lahun, de Morgan had great difficulty finding the entrance to the pyramid, because the north chapel was once again conceived in a way intended to confuse potential grave robbers. This time, the entrance was hidden in the courtyard pavement west of the pyramid. Moreover, it was shifted to the northwest corner. The king's funerary apartment was reached by way of a vertical shaft and a descending corridor leading to the east.

The burial chamber, which like the false-vaulted ceiling was sheathed with granite blocks, did not lie on the pyramid's vertical axis, but northwest of it. Oddly, in this case the walls of the granite chamber were finished with a thin layer of white stucco, whereas the cheaper white limestone walls, ceiling, false door, etc., were painted with red and black dots in an effort to imitate the expensive and more durable pink granite. On the west wall of the chamber stood a marvelous granite sarcophagus, whose fifteen niches probably represented stylized gateways. This decorative motif and the number of doors are no accident. So far as we know, both appeared for the first time on the perimeter wall in Djoser's pyramid complex in Saqqara. They are usually seen as a royal and apotropaic motif connected with the sed festival, in which the number fifteen is supposed to refer to the middle of the lunar month as the time of the ceremonies.

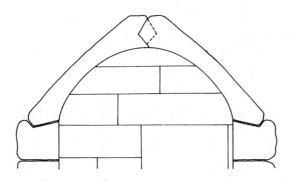

Vaulted construction in Senusret III's pyramid (after de Morgan).

Portraits sketched by grave robbers on
the walls of Senusret III's antechamber
(after de Morgan).

In this case as well the ancient builders' carefully considered plan
did not succeed in preventing theft. During the Hyksos period in the
Second Intermediate Period, presumably, grave robbers cleaned out
this royal tomb, and even brazenly left behind their portraits on the
white limestone walls of the antechamber.

However, the fact that the tomb was empty may not be attribut-
able to grave robbers. Joe Wegner expressed the view (as did Lehner
and others) that Senusret III was not necessarily buried in the pyramid in Dahshur at all, but could have been buried in his large and
complicated funerary complex in Abydos (named "Enduring are the
places of Khakaure, true of voice, in Abydos"). The complex has until
now been thought to be a royal cenotaph. Wegner's is a daring but
still unproven hypothesis. Why should Senusret III, unlike his predecessors and successors, have abandoned the traditional royal tomb in
the form of a pyramid? What serious political or religious grounds
could there have been for such a fundamental decision? The question
Arnold asks (in a personal communication) about the very simple
burial chamber, which is located in an unusual place under the pyramid, seems more justified: Wasn't this the burial chamber of a queen
instead of a king? A king should lie under the middle of the pyramid
or in immediate proximity to it.

North of the pyramid de Morgan discovered princesses' tombs arranged in two galleries of unequal height. According to Arnold, four
tombs in the upper gallery had an aboveground portion in the form

of a pyramid. In two hiding places in the lower gallery de Morgan found splendid jewelry as well as other items from the burial equipment. One treasure belonged to Princess Sithathor, one of Senusret II's daughters, and the other to Merit, one of Senusret III's daughters. Sithathor's treasure contained, for instance, a gold pectoral studded with precious stones and bearing the name of her father, while

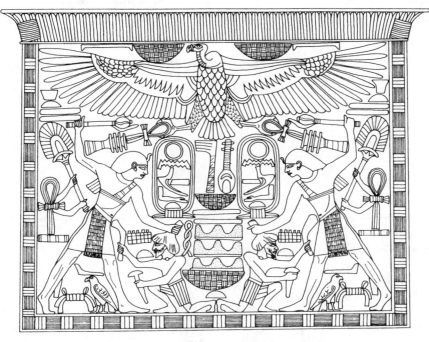

Obverse of a gold pectoral enameled in color belonging to Princess Merit, from Dahshur (Egyptian Museum in Cairo). The upper edge is decorated with a concave cornice. In the middle are an inscription and two cartouches with Amenemhet III's throne name, Nimaatre. The inscription is connected with the cartouches and reads as follows: "Nimaatre, good god, lord of both lands [i.e., of Upper and Lower Egypt] and all foreign lands." In each case, the ruler is represented alongside the inscription, as he uses a mace to strike down Egypt's enemies, identified in the short inscription as Asian Mentju-Bedouins. The figure of the ruler is surrounded by divine "life symbols." Over the triumphal scene hovers the vulture goddess Nekhbet, who is described in one inscription as the mistress of heaven and ruler of both lands. She holds the symbols of "life" and "permanence" in her claws.

Gilded rudder decorated with a
lotus-blossom motif and the
sacred *wadjet* eye. It comes
from the treasure found in the
princesses' tombs near Senusret
III's pyramid (after de Morgan).

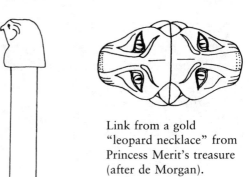

Link from a gold
"leopard necklace" from
Princess Merit's treasure
(after de Morgan).

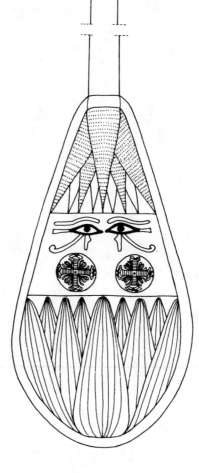

Merit's contained gold pectorals studded with precious stones and bearing the names of Senusret III and Amenemhet III, gold bracelets, and other precious things. The jewelry is now in the Treasure Chamber in the Egyptian Museum in Cairo. Three other small pyramids stood along the south wall of the king's pyramid.

The king's pyramid and the row of small pyramids along its north and south walls were surrounded by a perimeter wall whose exterior facade was decorated with niches. The north-south orientation of Senusret III's pyramid complex as a whole, as well as the apparent modeling of certain aspects of its plan on Djoser's complex in Saqqara, was further emphasized by the construction of another brick wall decorated with niches. This greatly extended the complex, particularly toward the south. More than two hundred visitors' graffiti testify to its splendor, which still aroused admiration in the time of Ramesses II (who reigned 1304–1237 B.C.E.). Two hundred years later, however, the complex already lay in ruins. The causeway, which led to the pyramid complex from the southeast, has not yet been investigated. Near the southwest corner of the complex six wooden funerary boats were found buried in the sand.

AMENEMHET III'S PYRAMID IN DAHSHUR

As the last powerful ruler of the Twelfth Dynasty, Amenemhet III could not have had any idea, when he began building a pyramid in Dahshur in the first year of his reign, what a turbulent fate his tomb was to have. History repeated itself—even though his builders might have learned something from Snefru's nearby Bent Pyramid.

Only an unprepossessing dark gray ruin remains of the pyramid that the ruler named "Amenemhet is mighty," and its local name now seems more appropriate: Black Pyramid. Modern research on it began in 1839, when Perring briefly described it during his visit to Dahshur. He had neither the time nor the desire to examine it more carefully, because his camp was attacked by Bedouins. The Lepsius expedition gave it even less attention in 1843. Thus almost half a century went by before the first archaeological excavations around the pyramid began. They were directed by de Morgan, assisted by Georges Legrain (1865–1917) and Jéquier. Despite extensive excavations carried out by a large number of workers and despite the somewhat "crude" research methods—common enough in the nineteenth century—the investigation was not completed, and many questions remained unanswered. Afterward, almost three quarters of a century elapsed before a team from the German Archaeological Institute in Cairo, led by Arnold, returned to Amenemhet III's pyramid. Between 1976 and 1983, it completed the groundwork.

The core was made of mudbricks, but in contrast to the pyramids built at the beginning of the Twelfth Dynasty, it lacked the stabilizing stone framework. In an effort to increase the stability of the five-meter-thick limestone mantle, the brick core was built in stepped form. The individual mantle blocks were held together by wooden dovetail joining pegs. Near the apex, the pyramid wall's angle of inclination decreased.

The apex of the pyramid was crowned by a beautiful dark gray granite pyramidion that was originally about 1.3 meters high. In-

In Amenemhet III's pyramid, wooden dovetail joining pegs were used to connect the limestone casing blocks (after de Morgan).

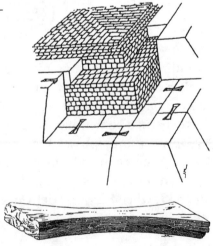

scriptions and religious symbols appeared on each of its sides. The pyramidion was discovered in 1900, in the rubble on the east side of the pyramid, when the Egyptian Antiquities Service ordered an inspection of the pyramid field in Dahshur after thefts and an attack on the guards there. After the not very wide-ranging excavations connected with the inspection were concluded, the pyramidion was taken to a government office in Saqqara and ultimately to the Egyptian Museum in Cairo (JE 35133). The almost intact pyramidion and the erased name of the god Amon in its inscription have raised questions that have still not been satisfactorily answered. Could the pyramidion have fallen from the pyramid's apex without being damaged? Amon's name must have been erased under Akhenaton, and that means that the pyramidion already lay on the ground during his reign. Was it ever placed on the pyramid's apex at all? Was it merely a votive pyramidion, which stood on the ground in front of the pyramid?

The pyramid's substructure is articulated in a relatively complicated way and differs significantly from that of early Twelfth Dynasty pyramids. It consists of two parts, of which one belonged to the ruler and the other to his two consorts. The two parts were connected by a corridor.

Detail from the decoration on Amenemhet III's pyramidion, now in the Egyptian Museum in Cairo.

The entrance into the ruler's tomb was on the east, at the level of the lowest foundation layer, near the southeast corner of the pyramid. A stairway led to the entrance corridor and then into a whole system of passageways, shafts, barriers, and chambers that were sheathed in limestone and were located at varying levels. About twenty meters from the entrance, it turned to the north toward the royal burial chamber. At the turning point, another corridor coming from the queens' burial chambers entered from the west. The center of the whole system was the ruler's burial chamber, which was near the pyramid's vertical axis. (It was probably intended to lie precisely on the axis, but the builders were not able to determine its location in the underground labyrinth with sufficient accuracy.) It was oriented east-west and sheathed with blocks of fine white limestone. On the west wall stood a pink granite sarcophagus with a vaulted top and niches whose arrangement imitated that of the perimeter wall of Djoser's complex in Saqqara. The ruler was never buried there, however.

Whereas the system of chambers and passageways of the ruler's tomb lay under the east half of the pyramid, the somewhat simpler system associated with the queens' burial chambers lay under its southwest part. The two entrances are virtually mirror images of each other. The entrance corridor also had a descending stairway. Coming from the west, one first entered the burial chamber of Queen Aat, and then that of a queen who has not been precisely identified (Neferuptah?). Near the west wall of Aat's burial chamber stood a sarcophagus whose material and decoration resemble that of the king. The queen was about thirty-five when she died. The sarcophagus of the as yet unnamed queen was similar, except that it lacked the niches imitating the perimeter wall.

Another branch of the underground labyrinth was the so-called south tomb, a system of passageways and chapels. It begins in the entrance corridor to the king's system and is located under the south side of the pyramid. As its archaeological designation suggests, it is in some ways analogous to the south tomb in Djoser's complex in Saqqara.

The mortuary temple in front of the east side of the pyramid was small and relatively simple. Its western part was dominated by a long sacrifice hall, while the eastern part consisted of an open courtyard with eighteen granite columns shaped like eight stems of papyrus.

Around the pyramid and the mortuary temple ran two plastered and whitewashed perimeter walls made of mudbricks. The inner one, which bounded the area of the ruler's tomb itself, also included the

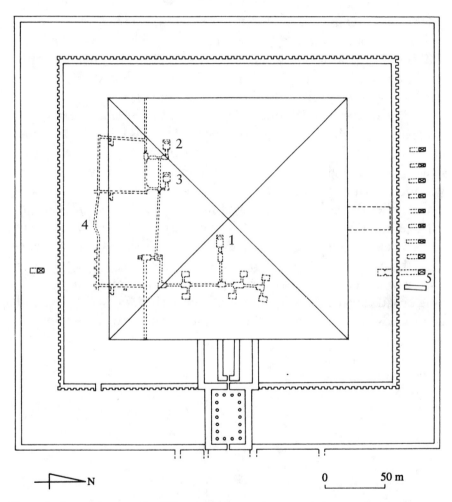

Ground plan of Amenemhet III's pyramid complex in Dahshur, without approach corridor or valley temple (after Arnold). The easternmost row of shaft tombs is along the north side; the first tomb from the east belonged to King Auibre Hor. 1. king's chamber, 2. Aat's chamber, 3. anonymous queen's chamber, 4. south tomb, 5. Auibre Hor's tomb.

west half of the temple and was decorated with niches. The outer wall, which also enclosed the east half of the temple and the open, columned courtyard, had no niches.

North of the pyramid, in the courtyard between the inner and outer perimeter walls, is a row of ten shaft tombs that belonged to members of the royal family. In the second tomb from the east, one of the ruler's daughters, Princess Nubheteptikhered, was buried.

The first tomb from the east was later usurped by one of the insignificant rulers of the Thirteenth Dynasty, Auibre Hor, made famous by the wooden standing statue of his ka. It was found in the tomb and is now among the most valuable exhibits in the Egyptian Museum in Cairo (CG 259 and CG 70035). However, another rather enigmatic and still not entirely explained object was found in the tomb: along with the ruler's mummy, which was buried in a wooden coffin, and objects belonging to his burial equipment, a wooden canopic chest was found that bore on its seal the throne name Nimaatre. But this was Amenemhet III's name! Some Egyptologists used to assume that Hor ruled jointly with Amenemhet III. Today the prevailing view is that the name Nimaatre refers to Khendjer, one of Hor's successors who later took the name Userkare—or else was used out of reverence or as an amulet when Hor was buried in Amenemhet's pyramid complex.

A broad, open causeway, bordered on both sides by a brick wall, connected the mortuary temple with the valley temple. North of the

Wooden ka statue of King Auibre Hor, now in the Egyptian Museum in Cairo (after de Morgan).

causeway was the priests' settlement, which was also built of mudbricks. One of the most interesting objects found in the badly damaged valley temple was the limestone model of the underground passageways and chambers in a Thirteenth Dynasty pyramid that has not yet been discovered.

Despite the carefully thought out plan and the careful construction of the underground rooms, Amenemhet was ultimately not buried in his pyramid in Dahshur. In a certain sense, as we have already suggested, the story of the Bent Pyramid repeated itself. Amenemhet III's pyramid was also built on an unstable subsoil. This time it was not compacted gravel, as in the case of the Bent Pyramid, but rather hard clay. In it was built the delicate and complicated web of the underground labyrinth. However, because groundwater from the nearby Nile Valley seeped into it, the substructure proved to be incapable of bearing the weight. Immediately after construction ended, the enormous pressure of the superstructure began to cause menacing cracks to appear in some of the underground spaces. The pyramid in Dahshur was completed in about the fifteenth year of the ruler's reign and was probably abandoned soon thereafter. It was decided to build a new pyramid in a more promising place and to take advantage of the experience acquired in Dahshur. The site chosen for the new pyramid was in Hawara, in the Fayyum oasis.

AMENEMHET III'S PYRAMID IN HAWARA

Amenemhet III's economic and religious policies gave more attention to the Fayyum oasis than had those of his predecessor. Thus he had a temple built to the oasis's chief divinity, the crocodile Sobek, in Shedet (Greek Krokodilopolis). Not far away, near the modern village of Biahmu, two colossal, twelve-meter-high quartzite statues were erected on enormous bases; they represent the ruler looking out over the lake, which was then still quite large. Logically enough, in view of the catastrophe that threatened to occur immediately after construction in Dahshur had ended, he decided to abandon the royal necropolis near Memphis and build himself a new tomb in the Fayyum oasis. He chose

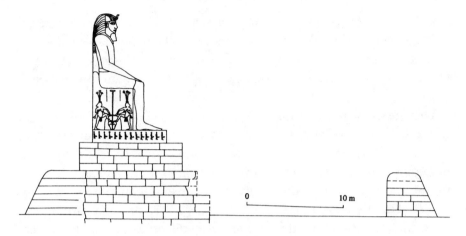

Colossal statue of Amenemhet III, from Biahmu (reconstruction after Petrie).

a site near the modern village of Hawara el-Makta, not far from Senusret II's pyramid at el-Lahun.

In 1843, Lepsius attempted to enter the pyramid, and forty years later Luigi Vassalli tried again, but Petrie was the first to enter it, in 1889. Collaborating with Wainwright and MacKay, Petrie investigated, in several stages, not only the pyramid but also the huge temple complex at its foot, whose extent and splendid construction had already so fascinated the travelers and writers of antiquity that they called it the labyrinth.

The pyramid—its name remains unknown—was built in the traditional Twelfth Dynasty way, that is, with a mudbrick core and a casing of fine white limestone. The entrance into the substructure was placed directly in the casing, on the south side of the pyramid, very close to the southeast corner. There a descending corridor with a stairway led north. It was sheathed with limestone and provided with barriers, and underground it turned several times around the pyramid's axis before finally reaching the burial chamber.

After the disastrous experience with the pyramid in Dahshur, the builders took several precautions to increase the strength of the burial chamber. They dug a rectangular hole in the rock subsoil, lined it with limestone blocks, and thus formed the side walls of the burial chamber. Then they lowered into the hole a quartzite monolith weighing more than a hundred tons, which completely filled the chamber. A rectangular hole was chiseled into the monolith to receive the quartzite sarcophagus decorated with niches. On the quartzite monolith rested three massive blocks of the same material, laid next to one another, as in the ceiling of a chamber.

The builders of the pyramid did not consider even this mode of construction sufficiently strong and secure. To reinforce it, they took two more safety precautions above the chamber. Over the flat ceiling composed of limestone monoliths rose a saddle vault of enormous limestone monoliths weighing more than fifty tons, and over them, another massive brick vault about seven meters high. In this way they created a masterful structure that withstood the enormous pressure of the pyramid's mass—but not the efforts of robbers, who were ultimately able to penetrate the burial chamber, despite a clever additional precaution that camouflaged the entrance into the chamber in the pavement of the neighboring, more elevated antechamber. Undaunted, the robbers plundered the burial chamber and then burned the ruler's inner wooden coffin.

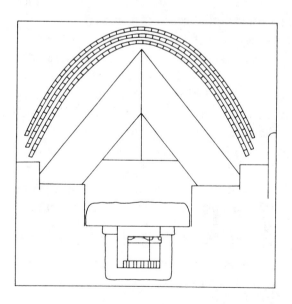

Sectional view through the burial chamber in Amenemhet III's pyramid in Hawara (after Petrie).

The archaeological situation in the burial chamber is not as easy to interpret as the preceding description may make it seem. In it, Petrie discovered the remains of a second wooden coffin, as well as an alabaster sacrifice table bearing the name of Princess Neferuptah, one of Amenemhet III's daughters. It was initially thought that Neferuptah had been buried with her father, which was not as unusual in the Twelfth Dynasty as it had been in the Old Kingdom. In the mid-1950s, however, Naguib Farag unearthed, about two kilometers southeast of the king's pyramid, the remains of an almost completely destroyed pyramid that the famed Egyptian archaeologist Labib Habashi had already located in 1936. The inscription on the pink granite sarcophagus found in the burial chamber bore, to the great surprise of archaeologists, the name of Princess Neferuptah. Her name was also on other objects from her burial equipment discovered in the burial chamber. The body itself was not found there; only a few scraps of the mummy's binding were discovered, on which microscopic remains of skin were found. If someone was buried there, was it Neferuptah? Then how can we explain the fragments of a second coffin and the tomb furnishings? Was a tomb in her father's pyramid initially prepared for her that could no longer be used after her father's death and the subsequent blockage of the access to the burial chamber, so that the small pyramid nearby had to be built? These and other questions relating to the tombs of Amenemhet III and his daughter Neferuptah have not yet been satisfactorily answered.

In front of the south side of Amenemhet III's pyramid Petrie excavated the remains of an extensive and highly structured temple complex, probably the Labyrinth mentioned by ancient travelers. Herodotus, Diodorus Siculus, Strabo, and Pliny all refer to it. According to Diodorus, Daedalus was so impressed by this monument during his journey through Egypt that he decided to build a labyrinth for Minos in Crete on the same model.

Because of the early destruction of the complex, the original plan of the Labyrinth cannot be precisely reconstructed. Probably the inner part with the sacrifice hall was in the back part of the temple, and thus near the south side of the pyramid. In front of it was the complex of columned halls, columned courtyards, porticos, colonnades, chambers, and passageways. To the south lay another extensive open courtyard. The

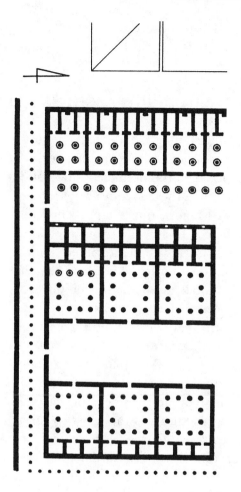

Reconstruction of part of the Labyrinth in front of the southwest corner of Amenemhet III's pyramid in Hawara (after Petrie).

fact that the Labyrinth was not just another building is shown by its unusual size: it covered an area of about 28,000 square meters.

According to Strabo, there were as many halls as there were provinces in Egypt—that is, forty-two. In the halls were supposed to have been honored the divinities of these provinces. Petrie found here the remains of the limestone statues of two gods, Sobek and Hathor. A limestone statue of the ruler found not far away during the excavation of the irrigation canal apparently also belonged to the temple.

The whole temple complex as well as the pyramid and a small north chapel were surrounded by a rectangular, north-south–oriented perimeter wall. Near its southwest corner, an open causeway entered it; like the valley temple, it has for the most part not yet been investigated.

THE NORTH AND SOUTH PYRAMIDS IN MAZGHUNA

After Amenemhet III's death, the ruling family's star sank. The royal tombs built during this period bear eloquent witness to this decline. During his reign, Amenemhet IV managed to complete a few building projects that his father had begun in the Fayyum oasis (for example, the small temple in Medinet Maadi), but he apparently did not have a tomb built for himself there. The so-called South Pyramid in Mazghuna, between Dahshur and Lisht, is often attributed to him, though the correctness of such attribution is far from certain. The ruins of this pyramid, which was heavily damaged long ago, were investigated by the British archaeologist Ernest MacKay in 1910.

Whereas the mudbrick core can still be discerned, no trace of the limestone casing has been found. The inclination of the wall and the height of the pyramid thus remain unknown. Presumably, it basically resembled the pyramid in Hawara, though not in its dimensions. This view as well as the attribution of the pyramid to Amenemhet IV are based on the ground plan of the substructure and the way the burial chamber was built, which appear to resemble those of Amenemhet III's pyramid to Hawara. However, some Egyptologists date the pyramid to the Thirteenth Dynasty.

The entrance to the underground part of the pyramid was in the middle of the south side. A descending corridor led down a staircase and was blocked at three points; it eventually came out in the burial chamber, which was located on the pyramid's vertical axis. This was once again filled with an enormous quartzite monolith with a hole for the coffin. The structure of the ceiling was probably reinforced by a saddle vault of limestone blocks.

A distinguishing feature is the undulating mudbrick perimeter wall that surrounds the pyramid on all four sides. Apparently, the mortuary temple did not immediately adjoin the pyramid but corresponded to the brick structure in the middle of the east wing of the perimeter

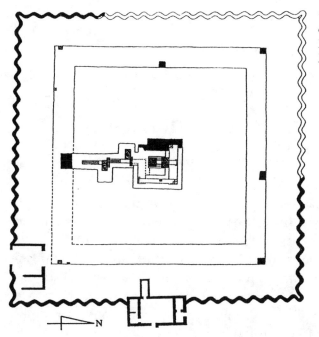

Ground plan of the so-called South Pyramid in Mazghuna (after MacKay).

N

wall, at whose southeast corner the entrance to the pyramid was once again located.

As in the case of the South Pyramid in Mazghuna, the North Pyramid is attributed solely on the grounds of a few bits of structural and archaeological evidence to Queen Nefrusebek. She reigned not quite four years, and her relationship to the preceding rulers has not been determined with certainty. It is assumed that she was Amenemhet III's daughter and thus the full or half sister—and possibly a consort—of Amenemhet IV. It is also possible that she ruled jointly with Amenemhet IV.

The North Pyramid in Mazghuna was larger than the South Pyramid, and the plan of its substructure is more advanced from a typological point of view. The access corridor, with a descending stairway, made several turns and was blocked at two places. The sarcophagus was once again a huge quartzite monolith. Although the pyramid's substructure was completed, no one was buried in it. Moreover, neither the pyramid's superstructure nor the complex as a whole was ever finished.

CHAPTER TEN

THE SECOND INTERMEDIATE PERIOD
(THIRTEENTH TO SEVENTEENTH DYNASTY)

The Thirteenth Dynasty remains the least investigated period in ancient Egyptian history. In this turbulent period, which lasted a century and a half, some sixty rulers reigned. They came not from a single family but from various families belonging to the military and officialdom and competing with each other for power. In some cases they were even foreigners. Often we cannot determine either their order or the length of their reigns. We know just as little about their tombs. Many of these monarchs probably had small pyramids built in the Memphis necropolis, especially in the area between South Saqqara and Mazghuna.

One of the favored royal names was Sebekhotep, along with Amenemhet, Senusret, Mentuhotep, and Antef. However, despite waning royal authority, the government apparently functioned relatively normally until it collapsed in the seventeenth century B.C.E. At that point, the gradual penetration of Semitic residents from Palestine and the surrounding area turned into open aggression, to which all of northern Egypt ultimately succumbed. Thus the country came under the control of the Hyksos.

According to Manetho, the Fourteenth Dynasty had seventy-four rulers, but that figure is doubtful. It may express the fragmentation of the country into small, independently existing kingdoms. Only one ruler from this time has been identified with certainty, Nehesi, but the domain over which he ruled is less clear. Manfred Bietak believes that the center of Nehesi's kingdom was in the east delta, near the later capital of the Hyksos conquerors, Hatuaret. Bietak dates Nehesi's reign to the transition between the eighteenth and the seventeenth

Representation of Asian nomads on a scarab from the Hyksos period (Egyptian Museum in Berlin, no. 9517).

centuries B.C.E. Nehesi's tomb has not yet been found, and the idea that it might have had the form of a pyramid is pure speculation.

The name of Egypt's conquerors, who had already infiltrated the northern part of the country in the course of the Thirteenth Dynasty, is derived from the Egyptian *heka khasut,* "ruler of foreign lands" (literally, "the mountainous desert lands"). In addition to what we can learn about the Hyksos from Manetho and the so-called Hyksos scarabs, valuable information regarding them has been provided by the long-standing Austrian archaeological excavations in the east delta. In particular, the precise date of their conquest of northern Egypt is debated. An important role is played in this debate by the so-called Four-hundred-year stela from Ramesses II's reign, which was found in Tanis. The inscription on the stela has been seen as proof that the reign of the Hyksos began four hundred years before the stela was made, that is, around 1720 B.C.E. However, the meaning of the inscription remains somewhat obscure.

The Fifteenth Dynasty was the age of the great Hyksos kings. Although a later tradition also ascribes an Asian origin to the rulers of the Sixteenth Dynasty, it is extremely difficult to determine their order. In the famous Royal Canon of Turin, the rulers of the Fifteenth Dynasty are the only ones not given the title of king of Upper and Lower Egypt, and this is considered proof that they were later classified as non-Egyptians and intruders. As their residential city, they chose Hatuaret (Greek Avaris, probably modern-day Tell ed-Dab'a) in the east delta, and as their main divinity they chose Seth, the Egyptian god of war and evil.

Hyksos Abisha. Detail from a wall
painting in the tomb of Khnumhotep
in Beni Hassan.

We know very little about the tombs of the Hyksos rulers. We can
only speculate as to whether some of them adopted Egyptian burial
customs and might have built a pyramid.

In connection with the rulers of the later Thirteenth to Fifteenth
Dynasties, we should mention a few archaeological discoveries in the
delta that are related to the pyramids. At Faqus and near Tell ed-Dab'a,
for example, two pyramidions were found. Were they brought there
from other parts of Egypt? And to whom belonged the already mentioned brick pyramid at Athribis (modern Benha) in the middle delta,
which could still be seen in the early nineteenth century and has now
vanished without a trace?

Only the southern part of Egypt managed to resist the Hyksos on-
slaught and to maintain a certain degree of independence. Thebes in
Upper Egypt gradually became a center of resistance against the intruders. In the van were the local rulers, who reigned alongside the
Hyksos in the south and were considered to constitute the Seventeenth
Dynasty. During the rule of the last of them (first half of the sixteenth
century B.C.E.), the efforts to drive out the Hyksos reached their peak.
The deep wound in the skull of the Egyptian ruler Seqenenre, caused
by a Hyksos battle-ax, testifies to the violence of the fighting. His elder
son and successor, Kamose, won other important battles before his

younger brother brought the campaign for liberation to a successful end. The capital Avaris fell, and the besieged Hyksos were driven out of Egypt. With Ahmose I began not only the Eighteenth Dynasty but also a great new era in Egyptian history: that of the New Kingdom. However, its kings no longer built pyramids.

The Thirteenth Dynasty—The Twilight of the Pyramids

Among the pyramids of the Thirteenth Dynasty, which have been little investigated, only two have thus far been identified with certainty: Khendjer's pyramid in South Saqqara and Ameny Kemau's pyramid in South Dahshur. The others, in which no inscriptions giving us direct evidence are extant, have been assigned to this period on the basis of the arrangement of their substructures. This is not a very precise method, however, since the conclusions are based on insufficiently representative materials. Recently, Aidon Dodson dealt with the question of the Thirteenth Dynasty pyramids known so far and suggested the following chronology:

1. Ameny Kemau's pyramid in South Dahshur
2. The North Pyramid in Mazghuna (nameless)
3. The South Pyramid in Mazghuna (nameless)
4. Khendjer's pyramid in South Saqqara
5. The pyramid that lies south of Khendjer's (nameless)

Dodson's chronological order is not definitive and will certainly give rise to much discussion among experts, as even a very superficial examination of the substructures of these monuments indicates.

AMENY KEMAU'S PYRAMID

In 1957, the American expedition in Dahshur discovered a small, heavily damaged pyramid that is attributed to a little-known ruler of the Thirteenth Dynasty, Ameny Kemau. Maragioglio and Rinaldi investigated it further in 1968.

The superstructure has been almost completely destroyed, so that one can only estimate that the length of its sides was about fifty meters. Its substructure is much better known. The entrance into the underground part of the pyramid was in front of the east side, slightly north of its axis. Before arriving at the burial chamber, the corridor turned three times and had a staircase and a barrier. The burial chamber lay almost exactly on the pyramid's vertical axis and once again consisted of an enormous quartzite monolith in which the workers had cut a mold for the coffin and, next to it, another hole for the canopic chest. So long as the coffin with the king's mummy had not yet been buried there, the mighty lid remained on the floor of the antechamber, which was at the same level as the upper end of the monolith. After the coffin was buried and the lid put on it, a barrier in the form of another huge quartzite monolith in front of the north wall of the chamber and the coffin was let down from a niche on the west. Nonetheless, even this painstaking attempt did not foil grave robbers, who plundered the tomb and left only fragments of the canopic chest with the ruler's name on them.

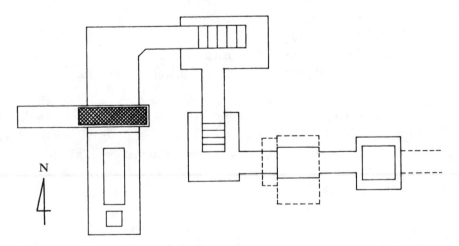

Ground plan of the substructure of Ameny Kemau's pyramid (after Maragioglio and Rinaldi).

KHENDJER'S PYRAMID AND THE ANONYMOUS PYRAMID
IN SOUTH SAQQARA

Just how profoundly times changed in the course of the Thirteenth Dynasty is shown by a pharaoh with the somewhat unusual name of Khendjer ("Boar"). The bearer of this name was probably not a native Egyptian; he may have been a leader of foreign mercenaries serving in Egypt. His pyramid was discovered by Jéquier in 1929, during his excavations in South Saqqara, southeast of the Mastabat Fara'un.

The mudbrick core was covered with an outer mantle of limestone blocks. A pyramidion bearing inscriptions has been reconstructed from many fragments. In this case, the substructure was entered at the foot of the west wall, near the pyramid's southwest corner. The access corridor was a descending ramp, in the middle of which was a stairway. Underground, it changed in level four times and wound around under the middle of the pyramid before coming out in the burial chamber.

The builders of Khendjer's burial chamber essentially followed the plan first used in Amenemhet III's pyramid in Hawara, but they introduced a very carefully considered innovation. The burial chamber

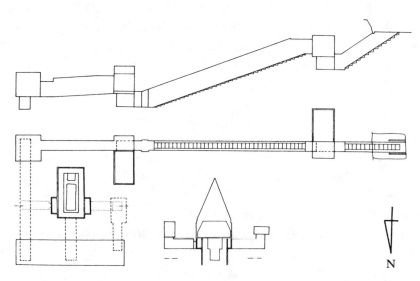

Ground plan of Khendjer's pyramid (after Jéquier).

was made of a huge quartzite monolith lowered into a hole in the rock subsoil. The burial chamber's ceiling consisted of two additional quartzite blocks. One of these was set in place during the construction of the chamber, while the other was left about half a meter above the top of the lower monolith, in which the coffin with the king's mummy was to be buried. The ceiling blocks were held in this position by two granite posts resting on sand in narrow shafts along the sides of the lower monolith. After the king's burial, the sand was drained out of the side shafts, allowing the granite posts to sink, and along with them the second ceiling block. In order to reduce the pressure of the superstructure, over the quartzite burial chamber a saddle ceiling of massive limestone blocks was built and, above it, an additional brick vault.

The mortuary temple, which was later almost completely destroyed, stood before the pyramid's east side. In the ruins Jéquier found bits of reliefs and columns, and with them fragments of a black granite pyramidion bearing hieroglyphs. The inner perimeter wall was made of limestone blocks, and its outside was decorated with niches. The outer perimeter wall was made of mudbricks.

Between the north side of the pyramid and the inner perimeter wall, a north chapel stood on an elevated platform reached by two stairways. It is noteworthy that the chapel's false door was in its north wall rather than the south wall, which was closer to the pyramid. In the northeast corner of the outer perimeter wall was a small pyramid. Its mode of construction corresponded to that of the king's pyramid. In its substructure, into which a stairway led from the west, were the burial chambers of two of Khendjer's consorts.

Southwest of Khendjer's pyramid, Jéquier has discovered still another pyramid built at about the same time, but whose possessor is unknown. The mudbrick core of its superstructure was not completed. Thus it is all the more surprising that the substructure itself was not only completed, but is one of the finest of the whole Middle Kingdom. Regular rows of black-painted stripes decorate the white limestone walls of almost every room in the substructure.

Around the pyramid ran an undulating perimeter wall built of mudbricks. The entrance to the pyramid was on its axis, at the foot of the east wall. A descending staircase led to a long horizontal corridor with three plugging blocks, which turned three times before coming out in the antechamber in front of two burial chambers. The king's chamber, the larger of the two, was west of the antechamber, the queen's chamber north of it.

The king's burial chamber consisted of a huge quartzite monolith with a hole for a coffin, the canopic vessel, and objects buried with the body. Of the three quartzite blocks composing the cover, two were found in situ, while the third still rested on two short walls, which means that the king's body was never buried there.

Two pyramidions also discovered in this pyramid complex have given rise to much debate. Both are made of black granite, and both were unfinished. One of them has the form of a truncated pyramid. Why were there two pyramidions? Was the truncated pyramidion supposed to be covered with gold leaf and placed on the pyramid's apex? Was the second pyramidion intended to remain on the ground as a votive pyramidion?

POSTSCRIPT

The royal tombs of the Seventeenth Dynasty were located on the west bank of the Nile in Thebes and in Dra Abu el-Naga, north of the causeway leading to Mentuhotep I's terraced tomb complex. They were mentioned in the report on tomb plundering given in the Abbott papyrus, but again it has not been possible to confirm archaeologically that they were really pyramids. The ancient commission charged with investigating tomb robberies (see below, p. 394) inspected ten royal tombs from the beginning of the Middle Kingdom, the end of the Second Intermediate Period, and the beginning of the New Kingdom. The Leopold II papyrus and the complementary Amherst VII papyrus contain a similar report of the statements made by robbers who plundered and destroyed the tomb of a Seventeenth Dynasty king, Sebekemsaf III—one of the tombs that had already been mentioned in the Abbott papyrus.* In all these reports the royal tombs concerned are called pyramids.

A revisionary archaeological investigation could shed light on the whole situation. What such an investigation might discover is shown by a pyramidion of a Seventeenth Dynasty ruler, Antef VI, that is now in the British Museum (BM 478). It has relatively steeply angled sides, and if it belonged to a real pyramid, that pyramid could not have been very high. It may not have resembled its predecessors from the Old and Middle Kingdoms. Perhaps it is a decorative pyramid that was

---

* The English collector William Amherst (1835–1909) financed Petrie's excavations. The upper part of the Amherst VII papyrus corresponds to the papyrus named after the Belgian king Leopold II.

part of a mortuary temple, like those found in some private New Kingdom tombs.

On the grounds of the Seventeenth Dynasty's royal necropolis, the ruins of a complex of mudbrick buildings were discovered by Herbert Winlock in the 1930s. It was reached from the east and included a small pyramid with a small mortuary temple on its east side, together with a perimeter wall. The casing has long been missing, but on the basis of the lowest part of the core, which has been preserved, the angle of inclination has been estimated to be about sixty degrees. The underground part of the pyramid has not yet been investigated, so we have no indication of whom it belonged to. On the basis of indirect evidence of a written document found nearby, it is sometimes attributed to the first ruler of the Eighteenth Dynasty, Ahmose I, and sometimes to his brother and predecessor Kamose. In the former case, Ahmose would have been the last Egyptian ruler to have his tomb built in the form of a pyramid. An American-German team, led by Daniel Polz, recently began excavations in an effort to find and investigate the Seventeenth Dynasty royal tombs in this area.

Another edifice in the form of a pyramid, not in Thebes but in Abydos, is connected with Ahmose I. South of Senusret III's temple and cenotaph, Ahmose had his own temple and cenotaph erected. He

The anonymous pyramid in South Saqqara.

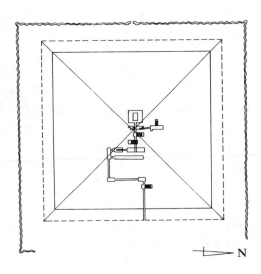

also built a chapel there for his grandmother, Queen Tetisheri, which contained a stela depicting sacrificial offerings being brought to her. The inscription on the stela indicates that Ahmose also had a pyramid built for Tetisheri, near which were supposed to be a garden and an artificial lake. The ruins of this pyramid have been discovered east of the chapel. Although they are now inconspicuous, they nonetheless show that in its time the pyramid was fairly large. Its sides were a hundred ells (100 cubits) long, and with an angle of inclination of almost sixty degrees it reached a respectable height. An archaeological investigation currently being pursued will produce—as its results thus far show—interesting new knowledge regarding not only this last of the large Egyptian royal pyramids, but also the historical events that accompanied the driving of the Hyksos out of Egypt and the founding of the Eighteenth Dynasty.

However, the idea of the pyramid lived on in another form, and even spread. In a certain sense it became popular, and its meaning

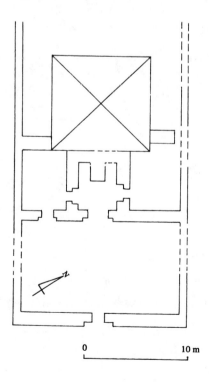

Ground plan of pyramid complex near Dra Abu el-Naga, attributed to Ahmose I (after Winlock).

0   10 m

moved to a different level. From the Eighteenth Dynasty on, it symbolized the primeval mound, as well as the sun god who rose on the eastern horizon and the memory of the royal tomb. It became an important decorative element in private tombs in the cemeteries on the west bank of the Nile, in Thebes, and in the Memphis necropolis as well.

As an example of the new conception of the pyramid we can take the rock-cut tomb of the vizier Useramon from the Eighteenth Dynasty, built during the reigns of Hatshepsut and Thutmose III. It included a mudbrick pyramid whose lower part was surrounded by a vertical wall that was twenty meters long and decorated with niches. Over this rose the pyramid, to a height of about thirteen meters. The angle of inclination of its side walls was fifty-five degrees. On the east side of the pyramid was a small cult niche, in which a tomb

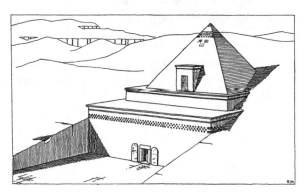

Private tombs from Deir el-Medina, with chapels in the form of a pyramid (after Borchardt).

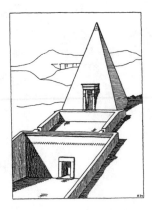

stela presumably earlier stood. In front of the pyramid was a small open courtyard.

In the Theban necropolises of the New Kingdom there were many such edifices. Pyramid-shaped chapels were also once typical of the rock-cut tombs on the steep overhangs above Deir el-Medina. In them artists and craftsmen were buried who had created and decorated the famous royal tombs in the "Valley of the Kings" not far away.

These are also connected in an unusual way with the idea of the pyramid as a royal tomb. They were cut into the rock cliffs of the branching valley, over which a mountain towered whose form strikingly resembled a pyramid and was called by the local folk *el-Qurn*,

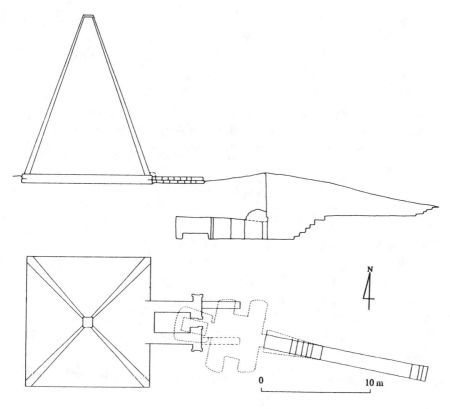

Pyramid of an unknown king (perhaps Akinkad) from Meroe. Ground plan and sectional view (after Dunham).

"the Horn." On its peak lived the revered mistress of the rocks and the protectress of the pharaohs' eternal peace, the serpent goddess Meresger, "Who loves silence."

While the artists from Deir el-Medina were embellishing the first rock-cut tombs in the Valley of the Kings, the Egyptians were founding a new city far to the south, at the foot of Gebel Barkal at the fourth cataract of the Nile, in modern Sudan. This city quickly became an important military outpost and a center for trade with regions deep in the African hinterland. It also developed into an important religious center of the cult of Amon, which was taken over from Thebes. After the fall of the New Kingdom in the second half of the eleventh century B.C.E., this region gradually became independent, and the kingdom established there took the name of the new city: Napata. For a time, the local rulers even succeeded in gaining control of all of Egypt, where they were counted as the Twenty-Fifth Dynasty. They also adopted the full range of Egyptian customs, from coronation to burial ceremonies.

In their necropolis in Kurru, north of Napata, Piye (fl. eighth century B.C.E.), who had conquered all Egypt, had a tomb in the form of a pyramid erected and thus founded a tradition followed by his successors. He may have been inspired by the monuments he had seen during his campaign in the north. However, the pyramid in Kurru was much smaller than the Egyptian pyramids and also differently conceived from an architectonic point of view. During the rule of Taharqa, one of Piye's successors, the royal necropolis in Nuri was established, where the tombs continued to have the form of pyramids.

In the seventh century B.C.E., the capital was moved to Meroe, between the fifth and the sixth cataracts of the Nile. Later on, in the third century B.C.E., a royal cemetery was established in Meroe as well, where the tradition of tombs in the form of a sharply pointed pyramid was continued. With the fall of the Meroe kingdom around 350 B.C.E. the African epilogue of the Egyptian pyramids ended.

EPILOGUE: THE SECRET OF THE PYRAMIDS

The Egyptian pyramids, which are astonishing in size and pleasing in their simple, perfectly harmonious form, were already considered by the ancients as one of the wonders of the world. They still challenge us to explain why and how they were built. And in many respects they remain a great secret of the past.

The deciphering of hieroglyphics and the first great archaeological discoveries initially made Egypt seem even more enigmatic—Europeans were fascinated by this newly revealed world. This quickly grew into a conviction that the original source of European civilization was on the Nile. The romantic western European spirit of the nineteenth century was particularly open to the message of the ancient Egyptian monuments and the legends and myths that surrounded them. This spirit also affected science, which was supposed to seek objective knowledge. Even scientific researchers tried to ascertain the "true meaning" of monuments that were so marvelous and perfect that they could not have been created by prehistoric savages. The goal was to solve the riddles and to discover "the secret of the pyramids." Science merged with mysticism, the rational with the irrational.

This was only slightly altered by the revolutionary archaeological discoveries of the twentieth century and the scope and depth of modern Egyptological research. The belief in the secret of the pyramids is unshakable. It has evolved into a kind of religion—pyramidology. In a certain sense it is older than Egyptology itself. Depending on their individual propensities, its adherents support different theories that claim to explain the secret of the pyramids.

And there are many such theories, some proposed by astronomers, mathematicians, and practitioners of other professions. It is impossible to present them all and to discuss their assumptions and results. Moreover, it would be pointless to do so.

Characteristically, pyramidology concentrates chiefly on the Great Pyramid. In the view of many pyramidologists, it constitutes the "original." But, as Mariette once pointedly remarked, why in principle should it be any different than the others? Only because it is the largest and has the most complicated infrastructure?

Egyptologists regard pyramidology as outlandish and generally ignore or ridicule it. There are exceptions, however. Jean-Philippe Lauer, for instance, has discussed some of the main pyramidological theories of the nineteenth and twentieth centuries. In his books *Le problème des pyramides d'Égypte ancienne* (Paris, 1952) and *Le mystère des pyramides* (new, expanded edition, 1988), he concentrated in particular on the theosophical, biblical, astronomical, and mathematical theories and their basic ideas.

Adherents to theosophical theories are convinced that the Great Pyramid was closely connected with Egyptian mysteries. It was there, they believe, that the elect were ordained. According to one such theory, a descending passageway led into mystical darkness and doubt, while another, ascending passageway, together with the Great Gallery, led the spirit to light and truth. The true "hall of mysteries" was supposed to be the burial chamber.

According to another theory of elect ordination, a group of priests led the chosen individual into the pyramid, where he lay down in the sarcophagus in the King's Chamber and fell into a deep slumber that lasted three days and three nights, during which his self descended into the underworld where it could meet the gods and spirits of his ancestors and accomplish good deeds. There he was allowed to understand the secret of Osiris and the wisdom of Thoth in all their profundity. At the end of the last night the sleeper was carried outside the pyramid, where he was awakened at the break of day by the first rays of the sun. Then he was ordained.

The beginning of astronomical theories is usually associated with a member of the commission of learned men accompanying Napoleon's

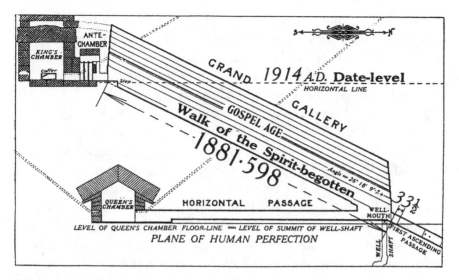

Religious-symbolic meaning of places in the Great Pyramid (after Edgar).

expedition, Edmé Jomard (1777–1862). Jomard was an engineer and geographer who also took part in the production of the *Description de l'Égypte* and himself published a few works dealing with measurements and descriptions of his travels. In the Great Pyramid, he saw a metrical monument and a star observatory, in whose dimensions were encoded information concerning its geographical location and all the astronomical and geodetic knowledge required to determine it. From the outset, his theory was based on imprecise data. Jomard assumed that the length of each side was 230.92 meters (in fact, it is 230.38 meters), the wall's angle of inclination 51°19'4" (in fact, it is 51°50'34"), and the height 144.19 meters (in fact, it is 146.5 meters). In accord with these assumptions, he erroneously calculated the "pyramid cubit" as a basic unit of .462 meters). In all the edifices from ancient Egypt, and thus also in the pyramids, the ancient Egyptian cubit has been shown, both in fact and also often in documents, to have been .5235 meters.

The biblical theory was founded in the middle of the nineteenth century by John Taylor. In his book *The Great Pyramid: Why Was It Built and Who Built It?* (1859), he starts out from the assumption that primitive people such as lived in Egypt at the time the pyramids were built could not have had the astronomical, mathematical, geodetic, and other kinds of knowledge required to build such gigantic edifices. Therefore, the builders must have been directly inspired by God and thus have belonged to a chosen people.

Taylor's opinion was adopted and further developed by writers such as Morton Edgar (*The Great Pyramid: Its Scientific Features,* Glasgow, 1924). In Edgar's view, each wall and each projection in the Great Pyramid has a deep biblical and symbolic meaning. Man's past and future are encoded in it: past and future wars, catastrophes and successes, the beginning and the end of the world. If pyramidologists want to interpret the Great Pyramid in accord with the Bible, they should keep in mind that Moses gained his knowledge and wisdom in Egypt.

Taylor's theory also influenced the British astronomer Piazzi Smyth. To demonstrate its truth, Smyth spent a long time in Egypt, where he himself observed and measured the pyramids. He summarized the results in his three-volume work, *Life and Work at the Great Pyramid* (1867). Together with his other study, *Our Inheritance in the Great Pyramid* (1864), this work quickly became the basic handbook for pyramidologists. All of Smyth's calculations and theoretical constructions are based on a specific unit of measurement, the "pyramid inch." The pyramid inch was supposed to be 1/25 of the sacred cubit, which itself was supposed to correspond to 25.025 inches (0.6356 meters); one pyramid inch was thus equivalent to 1.001 inches. However, this does not correspond to the historical standard measurement. What credibility can calculations have that do not respect reality and were simply invented to support a theory of some kind?

A few scholars have concentrated on another set of problems. In the 1880s Richard Proctor suggested that the Great Pyramid was built at the time when the star Alpha Draconis could be seen on the horizon in the north through the ascending corridor, which was still under construction, and in the south the star Alpha Centauri could be seen through the still unfinished, open Great Gallery. In his opinion, this occurred in 3400 B.C.E.

According to other theories, at the point where the descending corridor begins to ascend, there was a pool of water that reflected Sirius

Kneeling priest, surrounded by stars. The table contains notes on the observation of the stars at regular intervals in time.

and was used to orient the structure in relation to that star. This is supposed to have occurred between 5600 and 5100 B.C.E. Even if we disregard the large discrepancy between these two dates, making such a measurement at that stage in the construction of the pyramid, when the volume of the masonry was already one and one-half million cubic meters, would be simply pointless.

Other astronomical-pyramidological theories maintain that the Great Pyramid is a gigantic sundial. But why would the Egyptians have had to produce such a monumental instrument when they could determine time in a relatively easy way by using wooden sundials or water clocks?

A major argument advanced by many pyramidologists has to do with the location of the pyramid very close to the intersection of the thirtieth parallel with the thirtieth meridian. However, the builders of the pyramid could hardly have known that sometime in the future Great Britain would exist and that Greenwich would be chosen as the site of the prime meridian. The grounds on which this site, where the Nile Valley broadened out into the delta, was chosen for the capital were of a purely practical nature. And the large pyramid necropolis was located west of the capital, on the edge of the desert, primarily for religious reasons. Moreover, the Nile flows along the thirtieth meridian for a hundred kilometers before reaching the delta. Should that be considered another supernatural sign?

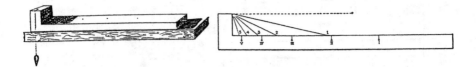

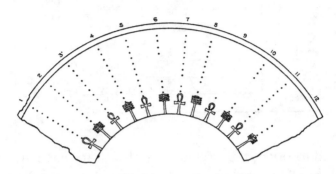

Ancient Egyptian sundials and water clocks. In the sundial, the length of the shadow that the vertical bar throws on the horizontal scale shows the time. In the water clock, time is measured on a scale on the side of a small, barrel-shaped vessel provided with a system of small openings on the side, through which the water in the vessel flows out.

The various mathematical theories on the Great Pyramid were subjected to a persuasive critique by the great pyramid expert Ludwig Borchardt in his book *Gegen die Zahlenmystik an der Großen Pyramide bei Gise* (Berlin, 1922). No one disputes that the ancient Egyptians had a deep knowledge of mathematics and geometry. According to Diodorus Siculus, Pythagoras learned the art of calculation and the principles of geometry from the Egyptians, from whom he is also supposed to have adopted the doctrine of the transmigration of souls. Today, Egyptologists rightly ask whether Archimedes, to whom the discovery of *pi* is attributed, might have become acquainted with that principle during his stay in Egypt.

Almost four decades passed between the publication of Lauer's book *Le problème des pyramides d'Égypte ancienne* and his discussion of the same subject in his 1988 book, *Le mystère des pyramides*. In the interim, a genuine revolution had taken place in science and technology. The beliefs of the pyramidologists remain untouched by that revolution. To the already colorful catalog of their theories, new ones have been added that connect the pyramids in Giza with UFOs and see the pyramids as reference points or landing ramps for spaceships from other worlds. They are also said to be gigantic energy transformers, created by higher "crystal races" from outer space. There is no telling what roles they may play in future human fantasies.

It has also become fashionable to see the pyramid form itself as affecting the preservation of organic materials in extraordinary ways and as intensifying the effects of mummification. For that purpose, a position on the vertical axis of the pyramid, between the upper and the middle third, is held to be optimal. It only remains to be determined whether the ancient Egyptians discovered this effect themselves or learned about it from someone else—perhaps extraterrestrials, as some pyramidologists suggest. However, these ideas and speculations ignore the fact that with few exceptions, from the beginning of the Third Dynasty to the beginning of the Eighteenth Dynasty, the burial chamber for the king's mummy was located under or level with the pyramid's base. And in the exceptions to that rule—the Bent Pyramid and the Red Pyramid in Dahshur and the Great Pyramid in Giza—we can determine not only the circumstances that led builders to experiment with placing the burial chamber directly in the substance of the pyramid and above the level of the base, but also the reasons that the ancient Egyptian architects were forced to abandon these technically complicated and risky solutions.

In the hope of making a commercial sensation, some opportunists resort to arguments that are made of whole cloth and often run counter to the enthusiastic motives of the pyramidologists, whose views are often based on deep knowledge. A few years ago Zecharia Sitchin set out to reveal the true secret of the Great Pyramid (*The Stairway to Heaven*, 1980), and purely incidentally, he "unmasked" a fraud supposedly committed by Vyse and Perring. As proof, he pointed to a cursive inscription accompanying a Khufu cartouche that the two scientists, in their search for fame, were supposed to have forged on the wall of a relieve chamber over the King's Chamber. According to Sitchin, a sign in Khufu's name was written incorrectly, in a way that corresponded remarkably to erroneous conceptions of Egyptian writing at the beginning of the nineteenth century. In addition, Vyse and Perring were the first to enter the four sealed upper relieve chambers, into which they had blasted their way with dynamite. Finally and ultimately, the inscription is supposed to have been as well preserved as if it had been "freshly" made. These arguments and conclusions, which Erich von Däniken adopted without reservation (*Die Augen der Sphinx,* Munich, 1980), are all nonsense. First of all, not only a cursive inscription but a whole series of so-called builders' marks and inscriptions were found along with the Khufu cartouche in the relieve chambers. Among these are also some inscriptions with the Khufu cartouche and the names of the work teams that were responsible for transporting the huge blocks to the pyramid construction site. From a paleographic, grammatical, and historical point of view, there is not the slightest doubt as to their authenticity. Vyse and Perring therefore did not forge any inscription with the Khufu cartouche. Moreover, the evaluation of the archaeological sources found in the Giza necropolis does not allow Egyptologists to question in any way that the Great Pyramid belonged to Khufu.

Among the most recent sensational "discoveries" is Robert Bauval and Adrian Gilbert's revelation of the so-called secret of Orion (*The Orion Mystery: Unlocking the Secrets of the Pyramids,* London, 1994) and G. Hancock and Bauval's discovery of the enigmatic message of the Great Sphinx in Giza (*The Message of the Sphinx: A Quest for the Hidden Legacy of Mankind,* New York, 1996).

These authors maintain, in short, that the spatial arrangement of the three royal pyramids in the Giza necropolis corresponds to the positions of the three stars in the belt of Orion around 10,500 B.C.E.

Khufu's cartouche from a builders' graffito found in the relieve chamber over the King's Chamber in the Great Pyramid (after Lepsius).

According to this view, the south shaft of the King's Chamber in the Great Pyramid was aimed at one of these stars and was built, not around 2,500 B.C.E., as Egyptologists think, but around 10,500 B.C.E. These authors propose the same date for the construction of the Great Pyramid, because at that time the Sphinx was opposite the precise point where its heavenly counterpart—the constellation Leo—rose on the eastern horizon.

We could mention here many other sensational discoveries of covert or overt allusions to the ancient secret civilization that erected these monuments and the message it sought to communicate. That message, pyramidologists maintain, is vital to understanding both the past and the future of humankind, and its wider dissemination is prevented only by ignorance—and perhaps a conspiracy among Egyptologists.

Is there any point in arguing against such claims? They amount to deliberate manipulations of various facts and dates that are often taken out of context, partly true and partly false, sometimes consistent with each other and sometimes not. What can we say about the methods employed by authors who can tell us the original height of the Great Pyramid down to a ten-thousandth of a foot—481.3949 feet—and in the same breath say that the length of the pyramid's sides was *about* 755 feet? (The four sides deviate only slightly in length and from the ideal of 440 ancient Egyptian cubits, or 230.38 meters. The height of the Great Pyramid can be extrapolated from the length of its sides and its angle of inclination. The height of the Great Pyramid can thus be calculated only approximately.)

No Egyptologist would deny that the ancient Egyptians made use of their basic knowledge of astronomy in building their temples, pyramids, and other structures. However, Egyptologists also maintain that the royal pyramids in Giza not only are very precisely oriented astronomically, but also were built in such a way that the line connecting their southeast corners was aimed at Heliopolis. Similarly, the pyramids in the Abusir necropolis were built so that the line connecting their northwest corners is aimed at Heliopolis. Seen from Heliopolis, the pyramids in Giza as well as those in Abusir thus appear to stand one behind the other. The religious and political consequences resulting from this arrangement of the pyramids are very significant, but this is not the place to develop them further. If the pyramids in Abusir and the pyramids in Giza, including the Great Pyramid, all point toward Heliopolis, then the pyramidologists' logic would require us to conclude that Heliopolis and its temple of the sun god Re were also built by members of the ancient "higher" civilization. Thus we may wonder which heavenly constellation the pyramids in Abusir are supposed to reflect and what secret message is concealed in their position in the necropolis . . .

Unfortunately, in these "new discoveries" we encounter the same old pyramidological claims: (1) an older, "higher" civilization preceded the ancient Egyptian civilization; (2) the Great Pyramid is not only (or not at all) Khufu's tomb, but (like the Great Sphinx) a monument left by the "higher" civilization, and in which a secret message is encoded; (3) Vyse forged the inscriptions in the relieve chambers over the King's Chamber in the Great Pyramid, covertly and, as it were, overnight.

Egyptology and pyramidology both deal with ancient Egypt, but the methods they use are fundamentally different. Petrie, who went to Egypt with the intention of contributing to archaeological research on the pyramids, in part by making extremely precise measurements, remarked with resignation about pyramidological theories: "It is pointless to establish the true state of affairs, for it has no effect on this [pyramidological] form of hallucination. They [the adherents of these theories] can surely be counted among those who believe that the earth is flat, and those who prefer theory to reality."

What else can we say? Will any pyramidologist ever be convinced that it can now be unequivocally proven, on the basis of a huge amount of scientific knowledge gained from archaeological excavations, that the pyramids were royal tombs? That we can follow the development of the pyramids step by step, in their basic plan and in the individual parts of the edifice? That in Djoser's pyramid in Saqqara we can analyze the groping attempts of its builders as well as reconstruct the individual phases of construction on the way to the stepped pyramid form? That on the basis of Snefru's pyramid in Meidum we can prove the transition from the step pyramid to the true pyramid? That we can locate in earlier structures some of the important elements in the construction plan for the Great Pyramid—for example, the combination, first tested in the cult pyramid in the Bent Pyramid complex in Dahshur, of the descending with an ascending corridor opening out into a great gallery? Here we must add that precisely that structural element plays a key role in pyramidologists' astronomical theories.

Will pyramidology ever acknowledge that on the basis of contemporary masons' marks and inscriptions on stone blocks we can reconstruct the way work was conducted on the pyramid construction sites? And from the quarrying of stone to the delivery of the pyramidion how work was directed, who took part in it, when it occurred, and who was responsible for it? That these signs and inscriptions also include concrete and very detailed building instructions that the architects gave the workers: the prescribed height of rooms, the width of the walls, the construction of stairways, including the number and size of the steps, lines that marked the axes of the individual rooms and whole structures, written instructions indicating that paving stones should be laid a certain number of cubits from a marked point?

It would probably be fruitless to assemble further archaeological arguments. People are always going to dream, and therefore there will always be some who want to delve into secret mysteries and others who throw themselves into the adventure of scientific inquiry. They will always be moving along the path, but they will never meet each other.

However, Egyptologists struggle in their own way with the "secret of the pyramids." Many questions remain open—for example, how many pyramids were built in Egypt? The answer to that question may never be known, since some of them have disappeared without a trace, destroyed by stone thieves or buried under desert sands. Moreover, we do not know to whom some of the pyramids that have been discovered belonged, or conversely, where some of the pyramids are that are mentioned in contemporary documents.

Egyptologists themselves are not entirely certain as to the origin of the word *pyramid*. Some of them derive it from the special mathematical or geometrical term *per-em-us*, which appears in the mathematical Rhind papyri I and II and expresses the height of the pyramid.

The hieroglyphic sign *mer,* "pyramid," from Ptahhotep's mastaba in Saqqara. The speckled area (in the original, reddish with black dots) indicates that the lower portion of the pyramid was cased with red granite.

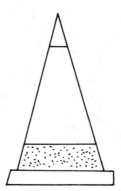

Others see its origin in the Greek word *pyr,* "fire," or even in the Greek *pyramis,* a "wheat cake." In the interest of completeness, we should also mention that the ancient Egyptians themselves used the term *mer* to designate the pyramid, and in the polychrome hieroglyphic inscriptions it is almost always represented as a white (i.e., limestone) pyramid standing on a small black line (i.e., the earth).

The question that most occupies Egyptologists today, however, is the future fate of the pyramids. The worldwide environmental catastrophe has not spared the pyramids. Only professionals realize what enormous efforts and financial means Egypt will have to provide in order to maintain this wonder of antiquity. There is no lack of pessimistic estimates that at the rate of erosion during the previous several decades, the pyramids will be permanently damaged, if not physically destroyed, in one to two hundred years, unless large-scale, fundamental steps are taken to preserve them. They were built by human hands, in order to ensure their creators' eternal life, and as a result of human activities they are now beginning to be threatened by time.

APPENDIX I

BASIC DIMENSIONS OF THE PYRAMIDS

The data presented here (following the chronological order of the building of the pyramids) represent only the most indispensable minimum, in an effort not to overburden this book with technical information that is normally the object of professional debate or of further, more precise measurements. Sometimes the concrete data regarding the size, angle, etc., vary according to the author. A more detailed presentation of this subject can be found by consulting at the selected bibliography.

Djoser's (Netjerikhet's) Pyramid
Length of sides of base of stage M1:
  71.5 × 71.5 meters
Height: 8.4 m
Length of sides of base of stage P2:
  109 m × 121 m
Height: 62.5 m
Perimeter wall: 544.9 m × 277.6 m
Height: 10.5 m

Sekhemkhet's Pyramid
Perimeter wall: 262 m × 185 m
After enlargement: c. 500 m × 185 m

Khaba's Pyramid
Length of sides of base: 84 m
Angle of inclination of core's shell: 68°

Snefru's Pyramid in Meidum
Length of sides of base of stage E3:
  144 m
Angle of inclination of walls: 51° 53'
Height: 92 m

The Pyramid in Seila
Length of sides of core's base: c. 25 m
Angle of inclination of core's shell: 76°

The Pyramid in Zawiyet el-Meiyitin
Length of sides of core's base:
  c. 22.4 m
Angle of inclination of core's shell: 80°

The Pyramid in Sinki
Length of sides of core's base:
  c. 18.2 m
Angle of inclination of core's shell: c. 80°

The Pyramid in Ombos
Length of sides of core's base:
  c. 18.2 m
Angle of inclination of core's shell:
  c. 80°

The Pyramid in Kula
Length of sides of core's base:
  c. 18.2 m
Angle of inclination of core's shell:
  c. 77°

The Pyramid in Edfu
Length of sides of core's base:
  c. 18.2 m
Angle of inclination of core's shell:
  c. 77°

The Pyramid on Elephantine
Length of sides of core's base:
    c. 23.4 m
Angles of inclination of core's shell:
    82° 30' and 77°

Snefru's Bent Pyramid in Dahshur
Length of sides of base: 189.43 m
Length of sides at bend: 123.58 m
Height of pyramid: 104.71 m
Height of lower part: 47.04 m
Height of upper part: 57.67 m
Angle of inclination of lower part's
    walls: 55°
Angle of inclination of upper part's
    walls: 43°
Length of causeway: 704 m

Snefru's Red Pyramid in Dahshur
Length of sides of base: 220 m
Height: 104 m
Angle of inclination of walls: 45°

Khufu's Pyramid
Length of sides: 230.38 m
Height: 146.5 m
Angle of inclination of walls: 51° 50'
    35"

Great Gallery
Length: 47.85 m
Height: 8.48 to 8.74 m (according to
    Maragioglio and Rinaldi)
Angle of inclination: 26° 16' 40"

Queen's Chamber
Length: 5.76 m
Width: 5.23 m
Height: 6.26 m

King's Chamber
Length: 10.49 m
Width: 5.42 m
Height: 5.84 m
Length of causeway: 825 m

*Boat Pits on Northeast and Southeast
Corners of Pyramid*
Length: 52 m
Width: 7.5 m
Depth: 8 m

Pyramid G 1a
Base of pyramid: 45.5 m × 47.4 m ×
    46.5 m × 45.7 m
Height: c. 29 m
Angle of inclination of walls:
    c. 51° 50'

Pyramid G 1b
Base of pyramid: 47.8 m × 49.4 m ×
    48.2 m × 47.1 m
Angle of inclination of walls: c. 51° 50'
Angle of inclination of descending
    corridor: 33° 10'

Burial Chamber
Length: 3.95 m
Width: 3.15 m
Height: 2.95 m

Pyramid G 1c
Base of pyramid: 45.5 m × 46.7 m ×
    46.8 m × 45.2 m
Angle of inclination of walls: 52° 40'
Angle of inclination of descending
    corridor: 27° 30'

Burial Chamber
Length: 3.72 m
Width: 2.95 m
Height: 2.7 m

Djedefre's Pyramid
Length of sides of base: 106 m
Present height: 11.4 m
Angle of inclination of walls: 51°
Length of sides of cult pyramid: 60 m
Length of causeway: 1,500 m

Baka's (?) Pyramid
Length of sides of base of core: c. 180 m
    (This suggests that the side of the

base of the future pyramid was originally projected to be 400 ells, slightly more than 200 m.)

Perimeter wall (north-south orientation!): c. 465 m × 420 m

Khafre's Pyramid

Length of sides of base: 215.25 m
Height: 143.5 m
Angle of inclination of walls: 53° 10'
Length of sides of base of cult pyramid: 20.9 m
Angle of inclination of walls of cult pyramid: 53° to 54°
Length of causeway: 494.6 m

Menkaure's Pyramid

Length of sides of base: 104.6 m (according to Maragioglio and Rinaldi)
Height: 66.45 m
Angle of inclination of walls: 51° 20' (according to Maragioglio and Rinaldi)
Length of causeway: 608 m

Pyramid G 3a

Length of sides of base: c. 44 m
Height: c. 28.4 m
Angle of inclination of walls: 52° 15'

Pyramid G 3b

Length of sides of base: 31.24 m

Pyramid G 3c

Length of sides of base: 31.24 m

Shepseskaf's Mastaba

Base of mastaba: 99.6 m × 74.4 m
Height: 18.7 m
Angle of inclination of casing: 61° (north and south walls) to 65° (east and west walls) (after Maragioglio and Rinaldi)
Length of causeway: c. 760 m

Khentkaues I's Step Tomb

Base of first step: 45.8 m × 45.5 m
Height: c. 10 m
Angle of inclination of walls of first step: 74°
Base of second step: 28.5 m × 21 m
Height: c. 7 m

Userkaf's Pyramid

Length of sides of base: 73.3 m
Height: 49 m
Angle of inclination of walls: 53°
Length of sides of base of cult pyramid: 20.2 m
Angle of inclination of walls: 53°
Height: c. 15 m
Length of sides of base of queen's pyramid: 26.15 m
Height: 17 m
Angle of inclination of walls: 52°

Sahure's Pyramid

Length of sides of base: 78.5 m
Angle of inclination of walls: 50° 30'
Height: c. 48 m
Length of sides of base of cult pyramid: 15.7 m
Angle of inclination of walls: 56°
Height: 11.6 m

Neferirkare's Pyramid

First phase
Length of sides of base: c. 72 m
Angle of inclination of step walls: 76°
Height: c. 52 m

Second phase
Length of sides of base: c. 104 m
Angle of inclination of walls: 54° 30'
Height: c. 72 m

Khentkaues II's Pyramid

Length of sides of base: c. 25 m
Angle of inclination of walls: 52°
Height: c. 72 m

Neferefre's unfinished pyramid
Length of sides of base of originally
planned pyramid: 150 cubits
(c. 78 m)
Sides of base (of core rebuilt as a
"mastaba"): 65.5 m
Angle of inclination of walls: 64° 30'
Height: 7 m

Nieuserre's Pyramid
Length of sides of base: c. 78.5 m
Angle of inclination of walls: 51° 50'
35"
Height: c. 50 m
Length of sides of cult pyramid:
c. 15.5 m
Height: c. 10.5 m
Length of causeway: 368 m

The "Headless Pyramid"
Length of sides of base: c. 65 m × 68 m
(according to Maragioglio and
Rinaldi)

Djedkare's Pyramid
Length of sides of base: 78.5 m
Angle of inclination of walls: 52°
Height: c. 52 m
Length of sides of base of cult pyra-
mid: c. 15.5 m
Angle of inclination of walls: 65°
Height: c. 16 m
Length of causeway: c. 220 m

Pyramid of Unknown Queen
(Djedkare's consort?)
Length of sides of base: c. 41 m
Angle of inclination of walls: 62°
Height: c. 21 m
Length of sides of base of cult pyra-
mid: c. 4 m

Unas's Pyramid
Length of sides of base: 57.75 m

Angle of inclination of walls: 56°
Height: 43 m

Teti's Pyramid
Length of sides of base: 78.5 m
Angle of inclination of walls: 53° 13'
Height: 52.5 m
Length of sides of base of cult pyra-
mid: 15.7 m
Angle of inclination of walls: 63°
Height: 15.7 m

Khuit's Pyramid
Precise dimensions not available

Iput I's Pyramid
Length of sides of base: c. 21 m
Angle of inclination of walls: 63°
Height: c. 21 m

Pepi I's Pyramid
Length of sides of base: c. 78 m
Angle of inclination of walls: 53° 13'
Height: c. 52 m

Nebuunet's Pyramid
Length of sides of base: 20.96 m
Height: c. 21 m

Southwestern Pyramid
Length of sides of base: 20.96 m
Height: c. 21 m

Pepi II's Pyramid
Length of sides of base: 78.75 m
Angle of inclination of walls: 53° 13'
Height: 52.5 m
Length of sides of base of cult pyramid:
15.75 m
Angle of inclination of walls: 63°
Length of causeway: c. 400 m

Neith's Pyramid
Length of sides of base: c. 23.5 m

Angle of inclination of walls: 61°
Height: c. 21.5 m

Iput II's Pyramid
Angle of inclination of walls: 55°

Udjebten's Pyramid
Length of sides of base: c. 23.5 m
Angle of inclination of walls: 63° 30'

Ibi's Pyramid
Length of sides of base: 31.5 m

Mentuhotep II's Terraced Tomb
Length of sides of middle terrace:
   60.18 m × 43 m
Length of approach causeway: 1,200 m

Amenemhet I's Pyramid
Length of sides of base: 84 m
Angle of inclination of the walls: 54° 27'
Height: c. 59 m

Senusret I's Pyramid
Length of sides of base: 105.2 m
Angle of inclination of walls: 49° 24'
Height: 48.65 m

Amenemhet II's Pyramid
Precise measurements unavailable

Senusret II's Pyramid
Length of sides of base: 107 m
Angle of inclination of walls: 42° 35'
Height: 48.65 m

Senusret III's Pyramid
Length of sides of base: 105 m
Angle of inclination of walls: c. 56°
Height: 61.25 m

Amenemhet III's Pyramid in Dahshur
Length of sides of base: 105 m
Angle of inclination of walls: 54° 30'
   to 56°
Height: 75 m

Amenemhet III's Pyramid in Hawara
Length of sides of base: c. 102 m
Angle of inclination of walls: 48° to
   52°
Height: 58 m

The South Pyramid in Mazghuna
Length of sides of base: 52.5 m

Khendjer's Pyramid
Length of sides of base: 52.5 m
Angle of inclination of walls: 55°
Height: 37.35 m

APPENDIX 2

EGYPTOLOGISTS AND PYRAMID SCHOLARS

In this brief overview I mention the Egyptologists who have made major contributions to research on the Egyptian pyramids. Experts cited in the text but not specifically identified are all Egyptologists; further information can be found in W. R. Dawson, E. C. Uphill, and M. L. Bierbrier, *Who Was Who in Egyptology*, 3rd edition, London 1995 (deceased Egyptologists), and in J. S. Karig, *International Directory of Egyptology*, 2nd edition, Berlin, 1990 (contemporary Egyptologists). In the following list and throughout this text, dates are not given for living Egyptologists.

Arnold, Dieter
Contemporary German Egyptologist and architect who carried out excavations in Tarif, Deir el-Bahari, and Dahshur for the German Archaeological Institute in Cairo. His research focuses on the pyramids of the Middle Kingdom and on pyramid construction. Today he is directing the excavations in Lisht and Dahshur being carried out by the American archaeological expedition from New York's Metropolitan Museum.

Belzoni, Giovanni Battista (1778–1823)
Italian traveler, adventurer, and archaeologist who worked for the Egyptian vice regent Muhammad Ali. He directed excavations—often using crude methods—and documented and collected antiquities. During later excavations, such as the opening of the entrance to Khafre's

pyramid, he nonetheless showed more respect for the monuments than did Vyse, for instance.

Borchardt, Ludwig (1863–1938)
German Egyptologist and architect who became famous for his excavations in Abusir, Abu Ghurab, and Amarna (where he discovered the celebrated bust of Queen Nefertiti). He made an outstanding contribution to the understanding of the architecture of the pyramid complex and founded the German Archaeological Institute in Cairo as well as the Swiss Institute for Egyptian Archaeology and Architecture in Cairo.

Carter, Howard (1874–1939)
British Egyptologist, draftsman, and archaeologist who did documentation work and excavations at various places in Egypt, especially in the Valley of the

Kings, where in November 1922 he discovered the rock-cut tomb of Tutankhamen that made him famous.

Černý, Jaroslav (1898–1970)
Czech Egyptologist, who lived in Great Britain after the Second World War. Before the war, he took part in the French excavations in Deir el-Medina. Outstanding expert on Egyptian (especially New Egyptian), the hieratic script, and the history of Egypt in the era of the New Kingdom.

Champollion, Jean-François (1790–1832)
French Egyptologist who succeeded in deciphering the Egyptian hieroglyphics and founded the science of Egyptology. He published a series of scholarly works on Egyptian history, religion, language, and monuments and also visited Egypt, where he studied the monuments and collected a wide range of documentation.

Edwards, Iorwerth Eiddon Stephen (1909–1996)
British Egyptologist who for many years worked at the British Museum and was an important authority on the Egyptian pyramids. His book *The Pyramids of Egypt,* which is one of the standard works on the subject, went through a number of editions and was translated into other languages.

Emery, Walter Brian (1903–1971)
British Egyptologist and archaeologist who made a name for himself by his excavations and discoveries in Nubia as well as in the Early Dynastic period necropolis in Saqqara.

Erman, Adolf (1854–1937)
German Egyptologist and linguist, founder of the so-called Berlin school of Egyptology. He made an important contribution to our knowledge of the Egyptian language, focusing in particular on the relationship between Egyptian and Semitic languages. He produced a grammar of classical Egyptian and New Egyptian, helped bring out a dictionary of Egyptian, and also worked on Egyptian history.

Fakhry, Ahmad (1905–1973)
Egyptian archaeologist who played an important role in archaeological investigations, particularly in the oases of the Western desert and in the necropolis in Dahshur.

Firth, Cecil Mallaby (1878–1931)
British Egyptologist who played a major role in archaeological research in Nubia and later in the Early Dynastic period necropolis in Saqqara and in the Djoser complex.

Goneim, Muhammad Zakaria (1905–1959)
Egyptian archaeologist whose name is associated especially with the discovery of Sekhemkhet's unfinished step pyramid in Saqqara.

Hassan, Selim (1886–1961)
Egyptian Egyptologist and archaeologist who played an important role in the development of the discipline of Egyptology at the University of Cairo. His work focused on archaeological excavations in the necropolis at Giza; he published the results of his work in a ten-volume study.

Hawass, Zahi
Contemporary Egyptian archaeologist who has carried out archaeological excavations in Giza, especially around the

Great Pyramid and in the cemetery for craftsmen and artists—the creators of the pyramids—that he discovered.

Vyse, Richard William Howard (1784–1853)

English military officer and researcher who, working in collaboration with Perring, made an important contribution to research on the pyramids in Giza.

Jéquier, Gustave (1868–1946)

Swiss Egyptologist who worked on ancient Egyptian art and architecture and participated in archaeological research at various Egyptian localities. The most important were his excavations in South Saqqara.

Junker, Hermann (1877–1962)

German Egyptologist who worked at the University of Vienna and was later director of the German Archaeological Institute in Cairo. He conducted archaeological research at various locations in Egypt, the most important of which was the necropolis in Giza. His twelve-volume work on the results of those excavations is one of the most important contributions to the history of Egypt in the time of the Old Kingdom.

Lauer, Jean-Philippe (1902–2001)

French architect and archaeologist who was already working in Egypt in the 1920s. His activity was almost exclusively connected with the pyramid complexes in Saqqara, especially Djoser's. He undertook ambitious theoretical reconstructions of the original edifices in that complex. He is considered the most important expert on ancient Egyptian construction methods in the period when the pyramids were built.

Leclant, Jean

Important contemporary French Egyptologist and professor at the Sorbonne in Paris, who concentrates on history, philology, and archaeology. He is concerned with the cultural legacy of ancient and Greco-Roman Egypt and is involved in excavations in Sudan and in research on the pyramids, especially in connection with the documentation and editing of the pyramid texts.

Lehner, Mark

Contemporary American Egyptologist who directed the Sphinx and Isis Temple Project from 1979 to 1983 and since 1984 has directed the Giza Plateau Mapping Project. He has done important work on the G 1a pyramid in Khufu's pyramid complex and has also provided computerized reconstructions of the Sphinx and the Giza plateau.

Lepsius, Karl Richard (1810–1884)

German Egyptologist, considered after Champollion the most important figure in the history of the discipline of Egyptology. As the founder of the study of Egyptology at the University of Berlin, he was also heavily involved in the development of the Egyptian Museum in Berlin. From 1842 to 1845 he led the famous Prussian expedition to Egypt and Nubia. The results of his work, published in the twelve-volume *Denkmäler aus Aegypten und Aethiopien*, constitute what is probably the greatest Egyptological study published thus far.

Mariette, François Auguste Ferdinand Pasha (1821–1881)

French Egyptologist, the celebrated founder of modern archaeological excavations and the preservation of Egyptian monuments. With phenomenal endurance, he led excavations in several dozen archaeological locations throughout Egypt and Nubia and prepared the way for the founding of the French Institute for Oriental Archaeology in Cairo. He also participated in writing the libretto for Verdi's opera *Aida*.

Maspero, Gaston Camille Charles (1846–1916)

French Egyptologist who directed the French archaeological mission in Egypt, which was later transformed into the French Institute for Oriental Archaeology in Cairo. He was also director of the first museum of Egyptian antiquities in Bulaq (a quarter in Cairo) and longtime director of the Egyptian Antiquities Service. He edited a series of standard works on Egyptology, including the four-volume, comprehensive catalog of the Egyptian Museum in Cairo.

Morgan, Jacques Jean Marie de (1857–1924)

French archaeologist and geologist who was among the founders of archaeological study of prehistoric Egypt and prepared an archaeological map of the necropolis in Saqqara. He conducted excavations in Dahshur and Saqqara.

Naville, Henri Édouard (1844–1926)

Swiss Egyptologist and Bible scholar, a student of Lepsius, and one of the leading figures in Egyptology around the turn of the century. He conducted archaeological excavations in the east delta, in Abydos, and especially in Deir el-Bahari.

Perring, John Shae (1813–1869)

English engineer and archaeologist who gained fame chiefly for his investigations of the Egyptian pyramids.

Petrie, William Matthew Flinders (1853–1942)

English Egyptologist, founder of modern Egyptian archaeology. He had no academic training and was essentially self-taught in the areas in which he worked. It was perhaps precisely this, along with his extraordinary toughness and diligence, that allowed him to devote himself, so intensively and in such an unconventional manner for his time, to the organization and methodology of archaeological investigations at dozens of sites in Egypt. In particular, his investigation of the pyramids in Giza set the trend for later research.

Posener-Kriéger, Paule (1925–1996)

French Egyptologist who made a name for herself chiefly by editing the oldest Egyptian documents in hieratic script. By publishing the papyrus archives from Neferirkare's mortuary temple, she made a fundamental contribution to our understanding of the organization of the cult of the deceased kings in the pyramid complexes of the Old Kingdom.

Reisner, George Andrew (1867–1942)

American Egyptologist and archaeologist who worked at Harvard University and led American excavations in Egypt and Sudan. He became known for his excavations at various sites, especially the pyramid necropolises in Sudan and the royal necropolis in Giza.

Stadelmann, Rainer

Contemporary German Egyptologist, former director of the German Archaeological Institute in Cairo. He has conducted archaeological excavations at various sites in Egypt (especially in the pyramid necropolis in Dahshur) and is considered one of the most important contemporary experts on the Egyptian pyramids.

Winlock, Herbert Eustis (1884–1950) American Egyptologist who conducted archaeological excavations at various sites in Egypt. He led the Egyptian expedition sponsored by New York's Metropolitan Museum.

APPENDIX 3

CHRONOLOGICAL LIST OF RULERS
AND DYNASTIES

A complete chronological table can be found in D. B. Redford, *The Oxford Encyclopedia of Ancient Egypt,* vols. 1–3 (Cairo, 2001).

End of Predynastic Period
   (c. 3150–3050 B.C.E.)

Zero Dynasty (c. 3150–3050 B.C.E.)
(About fifteen rulers in all)
Skorpion
Ka
Narmer

First Dynasty (c. 3050–2850 B.C.E.)
Aha (Menes?)
Iti
Djer
Wadj (Djet)
Den
Adjib
Semerkhet
Kaa

Second Dynasty (c. 2850–2680 B.C.E.)
Hetepsekhemwy
Raneb (Nebre)
Ninetjer
Peribsen
Khasekhemwy

Old Kingdom (c. 2680 to 2190 B.C.E.)

Third Dynasty (c. 2680–2640 B.C.E.)
Netjerikhet (Djoser)
Sekhemkhet
Sanakhte

Khaba
Huni

Fourth Dynasty (c. 2640–2510 B.C.E.)
Snefru
Khufu
Djedefre (Rajedef)
Khafre
Baka
Menkaure
Shepscskaf

Fifth Dynasty (c. 2510–2370 B.C.E.)
Userkaf
Sahure
Neferirkare
Neferefre
Shepseskare
Niuserre
Menkauhor
Djedkare
Unas

Sixth Dynasty (c. 2370–2190 B.C.E.)
Teti
Userkare
Pepi I
Merenre I (Antiemsaf I)
Pepi II
Merenre II (Antiemsaf II)
Nitokris (uncertain)

First Intermediate Period (c. 2190 to 2061 B.C.E.)

Seventh and Eighth Dynasties (c. 2190–2165 B.C.E.)
(Numerous ephemeral kings who reigned only a short time)
Ibi
Neferkare Nebi

Ninth and Tenth Dynasties (Heracleopolitan) (c. 2165–2040 B.C.E.)
(About eighteen less important kings, some of whom bore the name Khety)
Merikare

Eleventh Dynasty (Theban) (c. 2134–2061 B.C.E.)
(Mentuhotep I)
Antef I
Antef II
Antef III

Middle Kingdom (2061 to c. 1664 B.C.E.)

Late Eleventh Dynasty (2061–1991 B.C.E.)
Mentuhotep II
Mentuhotep III
Mentuhotep IV

Twelfth Dynasty (1991–1786 B.C.E.)
Amenemhet I
Senusret I
Amenemhet II
Senusret II
Senusret III
Amenemhet III
Amenemhet IV
Nefrusebek

Second Intermediate Period (c. 1786 to c. 1569 B.C.E.)

Thirteenth Dynasty
(Several dozen less important kings, some of whom bore the name Sebekhotep)
Khendjer
Ameny Kemau
Auibre Hor

Fourteenth Dynasty
Nehesi

Fifteenth Dynasty (Hyksos) (c. 1664–1555 B.C.E.)
(Seven kings altogether)
Khayan
Apophis

Early Sixteenth Dynasty (Hyksos)

Late Seventeenth Dynasty (Theban) (c. 1600–1569 B.C.E.)

New Kingdom (c. 1569 to 1081 B.C.E.)

Eighteenth Dynasty (c. 1569–1315 B.C.E.)
Ahmose I
Amenhotep I
Thutmose I
Thutmose II
Hatshepsut
Thutmose III
Amenhotep II
Thutmose IV
Amenhotep III
Amenhotep IV / Akhenaton
Smenkhkare
Tutankhamen
Ay
Horemheb

Nineteenth Dynasty (1315–1201 B.C.E.)
Ramesses I
Seti I
Ramesses II
Merneptah
Seti II
Amenmesses
Siptah
Tausert

Twentieth Dynasty (c. 1200–1081 B.C.E.)
Setnakht
Ramesses III
Ramesses IV
Ramesses V
Ramesses VI

Ramesses VII
Ramesses VIII
Ramesses IX
Ramesses X
Ramesses XI

Third Intermediate Period (c. 1081 to 711 B.C.E.)

Twenty-First Dynasty (Tanite) (1081–931 B.C.E.)
Smendes
Psuennes I
Amenemisu
Amenemhet
Osochor
Siamun
Psusennes II

Twenty-Second Dynasty (Bubasite Libyan) (931–725 B.C.E.)
Sheshonk I
Osorkon I
Sheshonk II
Takelot I
Osorkon II
Takelot II
Sheshonk III
Pemu
Sheshonk V
Osorkon IV

Twenty-Third Dynasty (Tanite Libyan) (813–711 B.C.E.)
Petubastis I
Osorkon III
Takelot III
Osorkon

Twenty-Fourth Dynasty (724–711 B.C.E.)
Tefnakht
Bakenrenef

Late Period (c. 711 to 333 B.C.E.)

Twenty-Fifth Dynasty (Kushite) (early 8th cent. B.C.E.–656 B.C.E.)
Kashta
Piye

Shabaqa
Shabataqa
Taharqa
Tanutamon

Twenty-Sixth Dynasty (Saite) (664–525 B.C.E.)
(Necho I)
Psammetik I
Necho II
Psammetik II
Apries
Ahmose II (Amasis)
Psammetik III

Twenty-Seventh Dynasty (1st Persian period) (525–405 B.C.E.)
Cambyses
Darius I
Xerxes I
Artaxerxes I
Darius II

Twenty-Eighth Dynasty (405–399 B.C.E.)
Amyrtaeos

Twenty-Ninth Dynasty (399–393 B.C.E.)
Nepherites I
Psammuthis
Hakoris

Thirtieth Dynasty (380–343 B.C.E.)
Nektanebo I
Tachos
Nektanebo II

Thirty-First Dynasty (2nd Persian period) (343–333 B.C.E.)
Artaxerxes III
Arses
Darius III
Khababash

Ptolemaic Period (332 to 30 B.C.E.)

Roman Period (30 B.C.E. to 337 C.E.)

Byzantine Period (337 to 642)

Arab Conquest of Egypt (642)

APPENDIX 4

GLOSSARY

Abbott papyrus—Named after Henry William Charles Abbott (1807–1859), British physician and collector of Egyptian antiquities.

Amherst papyrus—Named after Baron William Amhurst Thyssen-Amherst (1835–1909), an important British collector of Egyptian antiquities, including papyruses. He also sponsored archaeological excavations in Egypt as well as publications of ancient Egyptian documents.

Anastasi papyrus—Named after Giovanni Anastasi (1780–1860), a Greek businessman and collector of antiquities who lived in Alexandria.

Antichambre carrée—"Square antechamber," French designation for a room with a column that appears in pyramid temples from the Fifth Dynasty onward and through which the way to the offering hall led; the precise significance of this room remains a subject of debate among professionals in the field.

Apotropaia—Magical means of protection that is supposed to ward off the effects of evil and enemy powers.

Architrave—Latin term for the horizontal beam laid on top of pillars or columns.

Book of the Dead—A collection of religious ideas about the beyond, which are to some extent continuations of the older pyramid and coffin texts; in the New Kingdom and the late period, the texts were generally written on a papyrus roll and accompanied the deceased on his journey into the beyond.

Breaking of red vessels—At the end of the burial ritual, ceramic vessels were broken; this was probably done to ensure that the cult vessels were not reused.

Canopic vessel—A container in which the entrails were deposited during the mummification of the corpse; the name comes from the Greek description of the city of Canopos in Lower Egypt, where the god Osiris was worshiped in the form of an egg-shaped vessel.

Cattle census—Until the end of the Old Kingdom, this took place irregularly and constituted the basis for official dating. This makes reconstructing the chronology of the Old Kingdom very complicated.

Cenotaph—A tomb or monument erected in honor of a person buried elsewhere; also, a monument and cult site for that person.

Coffin texts—A collection of religious conceptions of the beyond that were inspired in part by the pyramid texts and written on the coffins of private individuals during the First Intermediate Period and the Middle Kingdom.

Copts—The word derives from a deformation of the Greek description for an

Egyptian, which Christianity adopted and used to designate the original inhabitants of the land before the Arab invasion.

Co-regency—Joint rule; an institution that developed especially at the beginning of the Middle Kingdom, whose purpose was to forestall struggles over the succession to the throne and thereby to strengthen the king's power.

Dado—Sheathing that decorated and protected the lower part of a wall; in the pyramid temples it was usually made of harder kinds of stone such as granite or basalt.

Damnatio memoriae—"Condemnation of memory," a ban on any mention of a person or thing.

En chican—French term that in archaeology refers to an entrance whose structure deliberately makes it difficult to use, for example, one that narrows or zigzags.

Ennead—Also the "the divine Ennead"; the foundation of the Heliopolitan doctrine of the creation of the world in the form of a divine family tree including the creator god Atum and four pairs of divinities (Shu and Tefnut, Geb and Nut, Osiris and Isis, and Seth and Nephthys).

Famine inscription—A rock inscription on the island of Seh at the first cataract of the Nile near Aswan. It recounts the seven-year period of low flooding and the resulting famine that did not end until the priests prayed to the god Khnum, who was lord of the sources of the Nile; for propaganda purposes, the priests deliberately predated this event in the age of Djoser.

Great White—The white baboon worshiped in Abydos; it was considered one of the kings' ancestors and identified with the god of wisdom, Thoth.

Hyksos—Derived from the Egyptian *hekakhasut,* "ruler of the desert regions"; designation of the Asiatic conquerors of Egypt at the end of the Middle Kingdom.

Infrastructure—In archaeology, the spaces inside an edifice, regardless of whether they are in its upper or lower parts.

In situ—At the original location.

Journey to Abydos—Abydos, an important religious center in Upper Egypt, a cult site of the god Osiris, and the last resting place of the oldest Egyptian kings, was a much visited pilgrimage site from the earliest times of the Egyptian state. Egyptians wanted to be buried there or at least to have a tomb stela there; the symbolic "journey to Abydos" became a component of the burial ritual.

Libation basins—Containers for libations in temples or tombs, and sometimes near them. The libation was an important component of worship and was used for purification before the water sacrifice (natron was added to the water); however, it also symbolized the recovery of the life force, etc.

Mastaba—Arabic "bench"; in archaeology, the term for a rectangular tomb that has the form of a bench.

Memphite theology—Doctrine of the creation of the world by the Memphite god Ptah.

Palermo stone—An important written document on a black basalt tablet; it has been preserved only in fragments and contains the royal annals. The largest fragment is in the archaeological museum in Palermo, which gave the monument its name. Other fragments are in the Egyptian Museum in Cairo and in the University College in London. The text on the tablet, which is presented as a list, begins with the earliest rulers of Egypt and continues to the Fifth Dynasty, including the most important events in each reign—for example, the building of important edifices, the creation of statues, military expeditions, festivals—as well as information about the height of the Nile floods. Precise information regarding the earliest times is lacking, and the earliest rulers have a mythological character. The information concerning the following periods is fuller and more detailed. The origin, reconstruction, and interpretation of the Palermo stone and the meaning of this discovery for Egyptian history are still being debated among Egyptologists.

Palm grove in Buto—A sacred grove in the Early Dynastic Period religious center of Lower Egypt, which was considered the "national cemetery" of ancient Egypt.

Pharaoh—Derived from the Egyptian *per-aa*, "the large house"; designation for the royal palace and, in a figurative sense, for the ruler himself.

Primeval mound—A sand hill that rose out of the waters at the creation of the world and on which life was created; a symbol of life and resurrection.

Pyramid texts—A collection of religious conceptions of the beyond that were written on the walls of burial chambers between the end of the Fifth Dynasty and the Eighth Dynasty and describe chiefly the king's path into the beyond.

Radiocarbon dating—A method of dating widely used in archaeology that makes use of radioactive carbon isotopes.

Rhind papyrus—Named after Alexander Henry Rhind (1833–1863), a British jurist and collector of antiquities who lived on excavation sites in Egypt

from 1855 to 1857. He was the first owner of the mathematical papyri I and II (now in the British Museum in London, EA 10057–8).

Ritual of the opening of the mouth—A ritual in which the priest touched the eyes, mouth, and other parts of the mummy with certain utensils; the goal was to revive the senses and limbs of the deceased in the beyond.

Rosetta stone—The fragment of a stone stela with the text of a decree from the time of Ptolemy V Epiphanes (196 B.C.E.), written in hieroglyphic, demotic, and Greek scripts. The stela, which was found in a fortress in the town of Rosetta during Napoleon's campaign in Egypt, played a central role in the deciphering of the Egyptian hieroglyphics.

Saff—Arabic "row"; an archaeological term designating rock-cut tombs whose facades are decorated with a row of pillars.

Sed **festival**—An important festival, originally celebrated on the occasion of the thirtieth anniversary of the pharaoh's ascension to the throne; its purpose was the renewal and strengthening of his power and authority as ruler.

Serapeum—The subterranean cemetery of Apis, a bull deity, in Saqqara; it was founded in the Eighteenth Dynasty and lasted into the Ptolemaic period.

Serdab—Arabic "cellar"; archaeological term for a sealed burial chamber in which the statue of the deceased was kept.

Serekh—Stylized representation of the facade of the royal palace, in the form of a vertically oriented rectangle in which the pharaoh's Horus name was written.

Shadoof—Horizontal pole used to lift water, first used at the beginning of the New Kingdom.

Simulacrum—A semblance or imitation (for example, an imitation of a tomb).

Sons of Horus—The four sons of Horus (Amset, Hapi, Kebehsenuf, and Duamutef) were the tutelary spirits of the four canopic vessels in which the deceased's entrails were preserved.

Speos—A rock-cut temple (*Hemispeos* = a temple of which half is cut into a rock wall and the other half is built in front of it).

Stela—A stone or wooden tablet, on which there was usually an inscription or image (tomb stela, border stela, etc.).

Subpluvial—A brief phase of rainfall following a longer rainy phase; phases of heavy rainfall—pluvial phases—occurred during the Pleistocene in warm southern regions and corresponded to colder periods in northern regions.

Substructure—Underground part of an edifice.

Superstructure—Aboveground part of an edifice.

Tafla—Arabic "clay"; often hardened and resembling soft rock.

Torus—In Egyptology, a stylized architectural element that was originally a broader portion of a wall that imitated a pole-shaped sill made of mats woven from plant material; the point where the mats rested was held together with ropes or straps.

Westcar papyrus—Named after Henry Westcar (1798–1868), British traveler and collector of antiquities.

Wisdom literature—A generic term for ancient Egyptian literary works that included instructions for living a righteous life and that were especially intended for the education of loyal state officials.

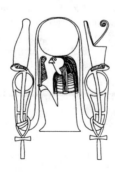

SELECTED BIBLIOGRAPHY

Arnold, D., *Building Ancient Egypt.* Pharaonic Stone Masonry. New York/ Oxford 1991.

Arnold, D., *The Temple of Mentuhotep at Deir el-Bahari.* New York 1979.

Arnold, D., *Der Pyramid enbezirk des Königs Amenemhet III in Dahschur. I. Die Pyramide.* Mainz 1987.

Arnold, D., Rituale und Pyramiden-tempel, in: *MDAIK* 33, 1977, 1–14.

Arnold, D., Überlegungen zum Problem des Pyramidenbaues, in: *MDAIK* 37 (1981), 15–28.

Arnold, D., *Lexikon der ägyptischen Baukunst.* Zürich 1994.

Arnold, D., *The South Cemeteries of Lisht. I. The Pyramid of Senwosret I.* New York 1988.

Aufrere, S., Golvin, J.-C., *L'Égypte restituée.* Vol. 3. Paris 1997.

Ayrton, E. R., Currelly, C. T., Weigall, A. E. P., *Abydos III.* London 1904.

Badawy, A., *Le dessin architectural chez les anciennes Égyptiens.* Le Caire 1948.

Bárta, M., Krejčí, J. (eds.), *Abusir and Saqqara in the Year 2000,* Praha 2000.

Berlandini, J., La pyramide «ruinée», in: *BSFÉ* 83, Oct. 1978, 24–34.

Borchardt, L., *Das Re-Heiligtum des Königs Ne-woser-re. I. Der Bau.* Berlin 1905.

Borchardt, L., Die *Entsthung der Pyramide an der Baugeschichte der Pyramide bei Mejdum nachgewiesen.* Berlin 1928.

Borchardt, L., *Das Grabmal des Königs Ne-user-re.* Leipzig 1907.

Borchardt, L., *Das Grabmal des Königs Nefer-ir-ke–re.* Leipzig 1909.

Borchardt, L., *Das Grabmal des Königs Sa-ḫu-re, I.–II.* Leipzig 1910 bis 1913.

Callender, V. G., *The Wives of the Egyptian Kings. Dyn. I–XVII.* 3 vols. (Ph. D. dissertation, Macquaire University, Sydney 1992).

Clarke, S., Engelbach, R., *Ancient Egyptian Masonry.* Oxford 1930.

Dodson, A., The Tombs of the Kings of the Thirteenth Dynasty in the Memphite Necropolis, in: *ZÄS* 114 (1987), 36–45.

Dodson, A., The Tombs of the Kings of the Early Eighteenth Dynasty, in: *ZÄS* 115 (1988), 110-123.

Dodson, A., From Dahshur to Dra Abu el-Naga. The Decline and Fall of the Royal Pyramid, in: *KMT* 5, no. 3/ 1994, 25–39.

Dreyer G., Kaiser, W., Zu den kleinen Stufenpyramiden Ober- und Mittel-ägyptens, in: *MDAIK* 36 (1980), 43–59.

Dreyer G., Swelim, N., Die kleine Stufenpyramide von Abydos-Süd (Sinki), in: *MDAIK* 38 (1982), 83–91.

Dunham, D., *The Royal Cemeteries of Kush. I.–IV.* Boston 1950–1957.

Edwards, I. E. S., *The Pyramids of Egypt.* Harmondsworth 1993 (rev. ed.).

Emery, W. B., *Archaic Egypt.* Harmondsworth 1962.

Fakhry, A., *The Monuments of Sneferu at Dahshur. I. The Bent Pyramid.* Cairo 1959.

Fakhry, A., *The Pyramids.* Chicago 1961.

Faulkner, R. O., *The Ancient Egyptian Pyramid Texts.* Oxford 1969.

Firth, C. M., Gunn, B., *Teti Pyramid Cemeteries. I–II.* Le Caire 1926.

Germer, R., *Mumien. Zeugen des Pharaonenreiches.* München 1991.

Goedicke, H., *Re-used Blocks from the Pyramid of Amenemhet I at Lisht.* New York 1971.

Goneim, M. Z., *Horus Sekhem-Khet. The Unfinished Step Pyramid at Saqqara. I.* Cairo 1957.

Goyon, G., *Les secrets des bâtisseurs des grandes pyramides. «Khéops».* Paris 1977.

Hassan, S., *Excavations at Giza. IV.* Cairo 1943.

Hassan, S., *The Sphinx: Its History in the Light of Recent Excavations.* Cairo 1949.

Hawass, Z., Lehner, M., The Sphinx. Who Built It and Why?, in: *Archaeology* 47, no. 5 (1994), 30–47.

Helck, W., Eberhard, O., *Lexikon der Ägyptologie.* 7 vols. Wiesbaden 1972–1992.

Jánosi, P., *Die Pyramidenanlagen der Königinnen.* Wien 1995.

Jéquier, G., *Deux pyramides du Moyen Empire.* Cairo 1938.

Jéquier, G., *Douze ans de fouilles dans la nécropole memphite 1924–1936.* Neuchâtel 1940.

Jéquier, G., *Le Mastabat Faraoun.* Le Caire 1928.

Jéquier, G., *La pyramide d'Oudjebten.* Le Caire 1928.

Jéquier, G., *Les pyramides des reines Neit et Apouit.* Le Caire 1933.

Jéquier, G., *Le monument funéraire de Pepi II. I–III.* Le Caire 1936–1940.

Kees, H., *Totenglauben und Jenseitsvorstellungen der alten Ägypter.* 2. Auflage, Berlin 1956.

Klemm, R. und D., *Steinbrüche im Alten Ägypten.* Berlin 1993.

Labrousse, A., *L'architecture des pyramides à textes.* 2 Bde. Le Caire 1996.

Labrousse, A., *L'architecture des pyramides à texts.* I–III, Le Caire 1996.

Labrousse, A., Lauer, J.-Ph., Leclant, J., *Le temple haut du complex funéraire du roi Ounas.* Cairo 1977.

Labrousse, A., *Les pyramides des reines, une nouvelle nécropole à Saqqara.* Paris 1999.

Lauer, J.-Ph., *La Pyramide à degrés. I.* Le Caire 1936.

Lauer, J.-Pb., Le temple haut de la pyramide du roi Ouserkaf à Saqqara, in: *ASAE* 53 (1955), 119–133.

Lauer, J.-Ph., *Saqqara. The Royal Cemetery of Memphis.* London 1976.

Lauer, J.-Ph., *Le mystère des pyramides.* Paris 1988.

Lauer, J.-Ph., Le problème de la construction de la Grande pyramide, in: *RdE* 40 (1989), 91–111.

Lauer, J.-Ph., Leclant, J., *Le temple haut du complex funéraire du roi Teti.* (BdE 51). Le Caire 1972.

Leclant, J., A la quête des pyramides des reines de Pépi Ier, in: *BSFE* 113, Oct. 1988, 20–31.

Lehner, M., *The Pyramid Tomb of Queen Hetepheres and the Satellite Pyramid of Khufu.* Mainz 1985.

Lehner, M., *The Complete Pyramids*. London/Cairo 1997.

Lepre, J. P., *The Egyptian Pyramids*. Jefferson (NC)/London 1990.

Lepsius, K. R., *Denkmaeler aus Aegypten und Aethiopien*. 12 vols. Berlin 1849–1859.

Lloyd, A. B., The Egyptian Labyrinth, in: *JEA* 56 (1970), 81–100.

Málek, J., King Merykare and his Pyramid, in: *Hommages à J. Leclant IV*, Le Caire 1994, 203 bis 214.

Maragioglio, V., Rinaldi, C., *L'architettura delle piramidi menfite. II–VII.* Rapallo/Torino 1963–1977.

Maragioglio, V., Rinaldi, C., Note sulla piramide di Ameny «Aamu», in: *Orientalia* 37(1968), 325–338.

Maragioglio, V., Rinaldi, C., *Notizie sulle piramidi di Zedefra, Zedkara Isesi, Teti.* Torino 1962.

Perring, J. S., *The Pyramids of Gizeh. I–III.* London 1839–1842.

Petrie, W. M. F., *Hawara, Biahmu and Arsinoe.* London 1889.

Petrie, W. M. F., *Illahun, Kahun and Gurob.* London 1890.

Petrie, W. M. F., *Kahun, Gurob and Hawara.* London 1890.

Petrie, W. M. F., *The Pyramids and Temples of Gizeh.* London 1883 (new edition with an update by Hawass, Z. London 1990).

Petrie, W. M. F., Brunton, G., Murray, M. A., *Lahun II.* London 1923.

Petrie, W. M. F., Wainwright, G. A., Mackay, E., *The Labyrinth, Gerzeh and Mazghuneh.* London 1912.

Porter, B., Moss, R. L. B., Málek, J., *Topographical Bibliography of Ancient Egyptian Hieroglyphic Texts, Reliefs and Paintings III* (2nd ed.). Oxford 1974.

Posener-Kriéger, P., *Les archives du temple funéraire de Néferirkare-Kakai.*

Les papyrus d'Abousir. Traduction et commentaire. Le Caire 1976.

Redford, D. B. (ed.), *The Oxford Encyclopedia of Ancient Egypt.* 1-3, Cairo 2001.

Reisner, G. A., *A History of the Giza Necropolis. I.* London 1942.

Reisner, G. A., *Mycerinus. The Temples of the Third Pyramid at Giza.* Cambridge 1931.

Reisner, G. A., Smith, W. S., *A History of the Giza Necropolis. II. The Tomb of Hetepheres, the Mother of Cheops.* Cambridge 1955.

Ricke, H., *Bemerkungen zur ägyptischen Baukunst des Alten Reiches. I* (Beiträge Bf 4, Zürich 1944), *II* (Beiträge Bf 5, Cairo 1950).

Schneider, T., *Lexikon der Pharaonen.* Zürich 1994.

Schott, S., *Bemerkungen zum ägyptischen Pyramidenkult.* (Beiträge Bf 5, Cairo 1950).

Sethe, K., *Übersetzung und Kommentar zu den altägyptischen Pyramidentexten. I–IV.* Glückstadt 1935–1962.

Sethe, K., *Urkunden des Alten Reiches. I.* Leipzig 1933.

Stadelmann, R., Das Dreikammersystem der Königsgräber der Frühzeit und des Alten Reiches in: *MDAIK* 47 (1991), 373–387.

Stadelmann, R., *Die grossen Pyramiden von Giza.* Graz 1990.

Stadelmann, R., *Die ägyptischen Pyramiden. Vom Ziegelbau zum Weltwunder.* Mainz 1985 (2. Aufl. 1991).

Swelim, N., *Some Problems on the History of the Third Dynasty.* Alexandria 1983.

Vandier, J., *Manuel d'archéologie égyptienne.* Band I., II. Paris 1952–1955.

Verner, M., *Baugraffiti der Ptahschepses-Mastaba.* Praha 1992.

Verner, M., *Forgotten Pharaohs, Lost Pyramids. Abusir.* Praha 1994.

Vyse, H., *Operations Carried Out on the Pyramids of Gizeh. I–II.* London 1840–1842.

Winlock, H. E., The Tombs of the Kings of the Seventeenth Dynasty at Thebes, in: *JEA* 10 (1924) 217–277.

Žába, Z., *L'orientation astronomique dans l'ancienne Égypte, et la précession de l'axe du monde.* Prague 1953.

Journals

Archaeology—Archaeology. A Magazine Dealing with the Antiquity of the World. New York.

ASAE—Annales du Service des Antiquités. Le Caire.

Beiträge Bf—Beiträge zur ägyptischen Bauforschung und Altertumskunde. Zürich/Kairo/Wiesbaden.

BIÉ—Bulletin de l'Institut d'Égypte, Cairo.

BSFÉ—Bulletin de la Société française d'égyptologie. Paris.

JEA—Journal of Egyptian Archaeology, London.

KMT—KMT, A Modern Journal of Ancient Egypt. San Francisco.

MDAIK—Mitteilungen des Deutschen Archäologischen Instituts, Abteilung Kairo. Berlin/Mainz.

Orientalia—Orientalia, Nova Series. Roma.

RdÉ—Revue d'égyptologie, Le Caire/Paris.

ZÄS—Zeitschrift für ägyptische Sprache und Altertumskunde. Leipzig.

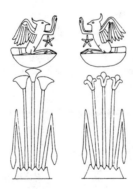

NAME INDEX

PLACES INDEX

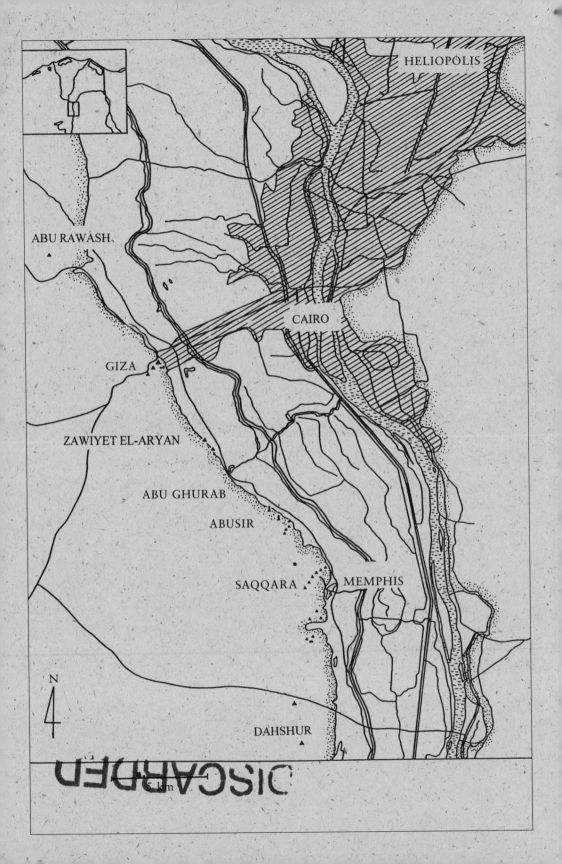

HELIOPOLIS

ABU RAWASH

CAIRO

GIZA

ZAWIYET EL-ARYAN

ABU GHURAB

ABUSIR

SAQQARA   MEMPHIS

N

DAHSHUR

5 km